Walt Disney World & Orlando For Dummies® 2002

FOR DUMMIES
BESTSELLING BOOK SERIES

Cheat Sheet

Orlando & Walt Disney World

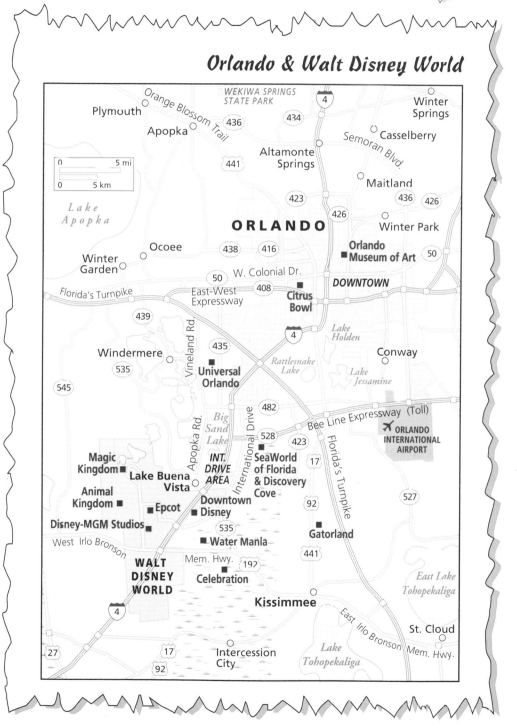

Plymouth
Orange Blossom Trail
WEKIWA SPRINGS STATE PARK
4
Winter Springs
436
434
Apopka
Semoran Blvd.
Casselberry
441
Altamonte Springs
0 — 5 mi
0 — 5 km
423
Maitland
436 426
Lake Apopka
426
ORLANDO
Winter Park
Ocoee
438 416
Orlando ■ Museum of Art
50
Winter Garden
50 W. Colonial Dr.
DOWNTOWN
Florida's Turnpike
East-West Expressway
408
Citrus Bowl
439
Lake Holden
Windermere
435
Rattlesnake Lake
Conway
535
Universal Orlando
Lake Jessamine
545
482
Vineland Rd.
Big Sand Lake
528 423
Bee Line Expressway (Toll)
✈ ORLANDO INTERNATIONAL AIRPORT
Magic Kingdom ■
Lake Buena Vista
Apopka Rd.
INT. DRIVE AREA
SeaWorld of Florida & Discovery Cove
17
Florida's Turnpike
Animal Kingdom ■
■ Epcot
International Drive
Downtown ■ Disney
92
527
Disney-MGM Studios ■
535
Gatorland
West Irlo Bronson
■ Water Manla
441
WALT DISNEY WORLD
Mem. Hwy. 192
Celebration
East Lake Tohopekaliga
4
Kissimmee
East Irlo Bronson Mem. Hwy.
St. Cloud
27
17
92
Intercession City
Lake Tohopekaliga

For Dummies: Bestselling Book Series for Beginners

Walt Disney World & Orlando For Dummies® 2002

Cheat Sheet

Downtown Disney

Buena Vista Dr.

To International Drive

MARKETPLACE

PLEASURE ISLAND

WEST SIDE

To Typhoon Lagoon

To Epcot

Adventurers Club **12**
AMC Theater Complex **7**
BET Soundstage **11**
Bongo's Cuban Café **8**
Cirque du Soleil **1**
Comedy Warehouse **13**
DisneyQuest **2**
8Trax **14**
Fulton's Crab House **20**

Ghirardelli Soda Fountain
& Chocolate Shop **23**
Guitar Gallery **5**
House of Blues **3**
Lego Imagination Center **22**
Mannequins Dance Palace **15**
McDonald's Fun House **21**
Planet Hollywood **9**
PI Jazz Company **16**

Portobello Yacht Club **19**
Rainforest Café **24**
Rock 'n' Roll Beach Club **17**
Virgin Megastore **4**
West End Plaza **10**
Wildhorse Saloon **18**
Wolfgang Puck Café **6**

Hungry Minds™

For Dummies: Bestselling Book Series for Beginners

Walt Disney World & Orlando

FOR

DUMMIES®

2002

by Jim and Cynthia Tunstall

Hungry Minds™

Best-Selling Books • Digital Downloads • e-Books • Answer Networks
e-Newsletters • Branded Web Sites • e-Learning

New York, NY ◆ Cleveland, OH ◆ Indianapolis, IN

Walt Disney World & Orlando for Dummies® 2002

Published by:
Hungry Minds, Inc.
909 Third Avenue
New York, NY 10022
www.hungryminds.com
www.dummies.com

Library of Congress Control Number: 2001092745

ISBN: 0-7645-5388-7

ISSN: 1528-2112

Printed in the United States of America

10 9 8 7 6 5 4 3 2 1

1B/RQ/QZ/QR/IN

Distributed in the United States by Hungry Minds, Inc.

Distributed by CDG Books Canada Inc. for Canada; by Transworld Publishers Limited in the United Kingdom; by IDG Norge Books for Norway; by IDG Sweden Books for Sweden; by IDG Books Australia Publishing Corporation Pty. Ltd. for Australia and New Zealand; by TransQuest Publishers Pte Ltd. for Singapore, Malaysia, Thailand, Indonesia, and Hong Kong; by Gotop Information Inc. for Taiwan; by ICG Muse, Inc. for Japan; by Intersoft for South Africa; by Eyrolles for France; by International Thomson Publishing for Germany, Austria and Switzerland; by Distribuidora Cuspide for Argentina; by LR International for Brazil; by Galileo Libros for Chile; by Ediciones ZETA S.C.R. Ltda. for Peru; by WS Computer Publishing Corporation, Inc., for the Philippines; by Contemporanea de Ediciones for Venezuela; by Express Computer Distributors for the Caribbean and West Indies; by Micronesia Media Distributor, Inc. for Micronesia; by Chips Computadoras S.A. de C.V. for Mexico; by Editorial Norma de Panama S.A. for Panama; by American Bookshops for Finland.

For general information on Hungry Minds' products and services please contact our Customer Care department; within the U.S. at 800-762-2974, outside the U.S. at 317-572-3993 or fax 317-572-4002.

For sales inquiries and resellers information, including discounts, premium and bulk quantity sales and foreign language translations please contact our Customer Care department at 800-434-3422, fax 317-572-4002 or write to Hungry Minds, Inc., Attn: Customer Care department, 10475 Crosspoint Boulevard, Indianapolis, IN 46256.

For information on licensing foreign or domestic rights, please contact our Sub-Rights Customer Care department at 650-653-7098.

For information on using Hungry Minds' products and services in the classroom or for ordering examination copies, please contact our Educational Sales department at 800-434-2086 or fax 317-572-4005.

Please contact our Public Relations department at 212-884-5174 for press review copies or 212-884-5000 for author interviews and other publicity information or fax 212-884-5400.

For authorization to photocopy items for corporate, personal, or educational use, please contact Copyright Clearance Center, 222 Rosewood Drive, Danvers, MA 01923, or fax 978-750-4470.

Hungry Minds™ is a trademark of Hungry Minds, Inc.

About the Authors

Jim and Cynthia Tunstall are the dummies behind this guide.

Jim has been an editor and writer for The Tampa Tribune since 1978. Cynthia is a freelance writer and photographer whose work has appeared in *Better Homes & Gardens, Elegant Bride,* and the *Atlanta Journal-Constitution*, among others. Together, they've authored six travel guides, including *Frommer's Walt Disney World & Orlando 2002* and *Florida For Dummies, 1st Edition.*

The Tunstalls are native Floridians who live in Lecanto, Florida — a radar blip that's 70 miles west of the Magic Mickey. They currently share space with two horses, two dogs, two cats, a parrot, and a lot of cranky wildlife, including a gopher tortoise named Ike.

Authors' Acknowledgments

Now we know why those folks babble on so much at the Academy Awards.

Angie Ranck at the Orlando/Orange County Convention & Visitors Bureau and Sandra Robert and Donna Jones at Walt Disney World make sure that we survive our time in the trenches.

Our grandsons, Joshua Jacob Tourigny (whom you'll meet later in the book as "J.J.") and Andrew Aden Tourigny, give us a youthful perspective as well as the energy to attack the theme parks time after time.

And Naomi Kraus, lord high czarina and our editor at Hungry Minds, Inc., has soft hands. She keeps our style intact, while saving us, in a literary sense, from wearing the emperor's clothes.

And the editorial staff at Hungry Minds would like to thank Linda Tibbetts Buckley at Universal Orlando for lending a helping hand when and where we needed it.

Publisher's Acknowledgments

We're proud of this book; please send us your comments through our Online Registration Form located at www.dummies.com.

Some of the people who helped bring this book to market include the following:

Editorial

Editors: Kathy Cox, Project Editor; Naomi Kraus, Development Editor

Cartographer: Elizabeth Puhl

Editorial Manager: Jennifer Ehrlich

Editorial Assistant: Michelle Hacker

Senior Photo Editor: Richard Fox

Assistant Photo Editor: Michael Ross

Cover Photos:

   Front Cover: M. Timothy O'Keefe Photography

   Back Cover: Jeff Hunter/The Image Bank

Production

Project Coordinator: Maridee Ennis

Layout and Graphics: Sean Decker, Joyce Haughey, LeAndra Johnson, Betty Schulte, Julia Trippetti, Jacque Schneider

Proofreaders: Laura Albert, Andy Hollandbeck, TECHBOOKS Production Services

Indexer: TECHBOOKS Production Services

General and Administrative

Hungry Minds, Inc.: John Kilcullen, CEO; Bill Barry, President and COO; John Ball, Executive VP, Operations & Administration; John Harris, Executive VP and CFO

Hungry Minds Consumer Reference Group

Business: Kathleen A. Welton, Vice President and Publisher; Kevin Thornton, Acquisitions Manager

Cooking/Gardening: Jennifer Feldman, Associate Vice President and Publisher

Education/Reference: Diane Graves Steele, Vice President and Publisher; Greg Tubach, Publishing Director

Lifestyles: Kathleen Nebenhaus, Vice President and Publisher; Tracy Boggier, Managing Editor

Pets: Dominique De Vito, Associate Vice President and Publisher; Tracy Boggier, Managing Editor

Travel: Michael Spring, Vice President and Publisher; Brice Gosnell, Publishing Director; Suzanne Jannetta, Editorial Director

Hungry Minds Consumer Editorial Services: Kathleen Nebenhaus, Vice President and Publisher; Kristin A. Cocks, Editorial Director; Cindy Kitchel, Editorial Director

Hungry Minds Consumer Production: Debbie Stailey, Production Director

◆

The publisher would like to give special thanks to Patrick J. McGovern, without whom this book would not have been possible.

◆

Contents at a Glance

Cartoons at a Glance

By Rich Tennant

page 7

page 167

page 121

page 257

page 103

page 317

page 41

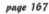

page 337

Cartoon Information:
Fax: 978-546-7747
E-Mail: richtennant@the5thwave.com
World Wide Web: www.the5thwave.com

Maps at a Glance

● ●

Table of Contents

Introduction

● ●

*W*elcome to **Walt Disney World,** a land ruled by a king-sized rodent and one that's a modern utopia to many of the young and young-at-heart. For those of us who have been around a while, **Walt Disney World** is a mystery: Some day, it will run out of gas. (Won't it?) But to the millions who make the pilgrimage here — a group that includes Super Bowl champs, a prince or two, and regular folks — it's a national shrine. That we admit — if a crowded one.

Still, charting a successful course through the home of Mickey Mouse shouldn't be a chore; you are, after all, on vacation. All you need to ensure an enjoyable trip to Orlando is some patience, some advance planning, and a little childlike wonder — now how hard is that?

About This Book

Pay full price? Read the fine print? Do it their way?

Excuse us. There's no need for any of that.

You picked this book because you know the . . . *For Dummies* label and you want to go to **Walt Disney World.** You also probably know how much you want to spend, the pace you want to keep, and the amount of planning you can stomach. You may not want to tend to every little detail, yet you don't trust just anyone to make your plans for you.

In this book, we boil down what has become a world unto itself — **Walt Disney World** — and the surrounding Orlando area. Walt Disney's Florida legacy is still growing 36 years after his death. At current count, **Walt Disney World** includes four theme parks and a dozen lesser attractions, two entertainment districts, tens of thousands of hotel rooms, scores of restaurants, and twin cruise ships.

Universal Orlando and **SeaWorld** add another four theme parks, a pair of resorts, and an entertainment district to the mix. There are also 80 or so smaller attractions nearby, an avalanche of restaurants, and more than 111,000 lodging rooms in Orlando.

How can anyone sort through that kind of mess, you ask?

It takes experience.

After three decades of stomping through the House of the Mouse, we know where to find the best deals (deals that are not rip-offs). In this book, we guide you through **Walt Disney World** and Orlando in a clear, easy-to-understand way, allowing you to find the best hotels, restaurants, and attractions without having to read this book like a novel — cover to cover. Although you can do that if you choose, you can also flip to only those sections that interest you. We also promise not to overwhelm you with choices. We simply deliver the best, most essential ingredients for a great vacation.

Please be advised that travel information is subject to change at any time — and this is especially true of prices. We therefore suggest that you write or call ahead for confirmation when making your travel plans. This is especially important if you have your heart set on visiting a particular attraction, as the theme parks are constantly making changes to their line-ups. The authors, editors, and publisher cannot be held responsible for the experiences of readers while traveling. Your safety is important to us, however, so we encourage you to stay alert and be aware of your surroundings. Keep a close eye on cameras, purses, and wallets, all favorite targets of thieves and pickpockets.

Conventions Used in This Book

In order to make this book an easier reference guide for you, we use some handy abbreviations when we review hotels, dining, and attractions.

You'll probably notice first that we often substitute **WDW** for **Walt Disney World** in order to spare you from having to read those three words over and over again. Another common abbreviation that you'll find is the use of **Universal** in place of **Universal Orlando.** Also, because almost everything in Orlando revolves around its theme parks, you often find that we refer to the section of central Florida that encompasses the theme parks as simply "the parks."

And, because Orlando does its best to make you max them out, we use the following abbreviations for commonly accepted credit cards:

> AE: American Express
>
> CB: Carte Blanche
>
> DC: Diners Club
>
> DISC: Discover
>
> JCB: Japan Credit Bank
>
> MC: MasterCard
>
> V: Visa

We also include some general pricing information to help you as you decide where to unpack your bags or dine on the local cuisine. We have used a system of dollar signs to show a range of costs for one night in a double-occupancy room or a meal at a restaurant. (The main course is included in the cost of each meal; allow for the 6- to 7-percent sales tax as well as any appetizers, drinks, or other extras you desire.) Check out the following table to decipher the dollar signs:

Cost	Hotel	Restaurant
$	$50–$100	$15 and under
$$	$100–$200	$15–$25
$$$	$200–$250	$25–$40
$$$$	$250 and up	$40 and up

Foolish Assumptions

As we wrote this book, we made some assumptions about you and what your needs might be as a traveler. Here's what we assumed about you:

- ✔ You may be an inexperienced traveler looking for guidance when determining whether to take a trip to **Walt Disney World** and Orlando and how to plan for it.

- ✔ You may be an experienced traveler who hasn't had much time to explore Orlando and wants expert advice when you finally do get a chance to enjoy that locale.

- ✔ You're not looking for a book that provides all the information available about Orlando or that lists every hotel, restaurant, or attraction available to you. Instead, you're looking for a book that focuses on the places that will give you the best or most unique experience in Orlando.

If you fit any of these criteria, then *Walt Disney World & Orlando For Dummies 2002* gives you the information you're looking for!

How This Book Is Organized

Walt Disney World & Orlando For Dummies 2002 is divided into eight parts. The chapters in each part lay out the specifics within each part's topic. Likewise, each chapter is written so that you don't have to read what came before or after, though we sometimes refer you to other areas for more information.

Here's a brief look at the parts:

Part 1: Getting Started

Think of this part as the hors d'oeuvres. In this part, we tempt you with the best experiences, hotels, eateries, and attractions at **Disney** and the rest of Orlando. We throw in a weather forecast and a look at special events, and then help you plan a budget. We also provide special tips for families, seniors, travelers with disabilities, and gay and lesbian travelers.

Part 11: Ironing Out the Details

Should you use a travel agent? How about buying a package tour? Where can you find the best airfare? We answer those questions, and then talk about booking tips and online sources in this part. We also give you a menu of area hotels and motels, and we talk about travel insurance, renting a car, and packing tips.

Part 111: Settling into Orlando

After we get you to Orlando, we introduce you to the neighborhoods and explore some of the *modus transporto* (local buses, trolleys, taxis, shuttles, and other vehicles to get from hither to yonder). We also discuss money matters, such as ATMs and taxes.

Part 1V: Dining in Orlando

Yummmmmy. In Part IV, we detail the pros and cons of dining in the parks and related properties, discuss the dress code (clothes are a must, but leave the formal stuff behind), and show you how to save a few bucks. We also rate the restaurants and tell you where you can eat with Disney characters.

Part V: Exploring Walt Disney World

Yippeeee-I-O! In Part V, we push through the turnstiles and drive up the dividends of Disney stockholders. After introducing you to this 47-square-mile fantasyland, we give you a thorough look at the four main theme parks — **Magic Kingdom, Epcot, Disney–MGM Studios,** and **Animal Kingdom** — as well as the **WDW** water parks, Disney Cruise Line, and the rest of the World.

Part VI: Exploring the Rest of Orlando

Part VI explores life outside Mickeyville. **Universal Studios Florida, Islands of Adventure, SeaWorld, Discovery Cove,** and a few of the smaller attractions are worth some of your time and money. There are also some inviting day trips, including **Busch Gardens** and the **Kennedy Space Center.** And don't forget to give yourself time to shop for souvenirs.

Part VII: Living It Up After the Sun Goes Down: Orlando Nightlife

Long considered to be kids' destinations, Disney and the rest of Orlando have discovered that many of you want to party into the night. In Part VII, we explore **Pleasure Island, CityWalk,** and other thriving Orlando hot spots, as well as dinner shows and the performing arts.

Part VIII: The Part of Tens

Every Dummies book offers The Part of Tens. Finding this part in a . . . *For Dummies* book is as certain as annual rate increases at Disney and Universal. In Part VIII, we give you parting knowledge about cheap attractions and places where you can kill an hour of your time.

You'll also find two other elements near the back of this book. We have included an *appendix* — your Quick Concierge — containing lots of handy information you may need when traveling in Orlando, like phone numbers and addresses of emergency personnel or area hospitals and pharmacies, contact information for babysitters, lists of local newspapers and magazines, protocol for sending mail or finding taxis, and more. Check out this appendix when searching for answers to lots of little questions that may come up as you travel.

We have also included *worksheets* to make your travel planning easier — among other things, you can determine your budget, create specific itineraries, and keep a log of your favorite restaurants so you can hit them again next time you're in town. You can find these worksheets easily because they're printed on yellow paper.

Icons Used in This Book

You'll find seven icons throughout this guide:

The Tip icon tells you how to save time (including ways to beat the lines) as well as provides other handy facts.

Watch for the Heads Up icon to identify annoying or potentially danger-ous situations such as tourist traps, unsafe neighborhoods, budgetary rip-offs, and other things to beware.

The Remember icon highlights information that bears repeating. Bears repeating.

We use this icon to identify hotels, restaurants, and other places, that are particularly good for grown-ups. Orlando is exceptionally receptive to small fries, so finding some calm inside the kiddie storm can be quite the challenge.

Keep an eye out for the Bargain Alert icon as you seek out money-saving tips and/or great deals.

You encounter these icons when we start barnstorming through the big parks. Joshua Jacob, also known as J.J., our grandson, has graciously agreed to give you a 9-year-old's perspective on some of the rides, shows, and more.

Where to Go from Here

We've briefed you on what to expect from this book and told you how to use it to plan a magical vacation to **Walt Disney World** — no pixie dust necessary. So start reading; there's a lot to do before you arrive, from arranging a place to hang your Mouse ears each night to exploring the best Orlando's theme parks have to offer. Like the Boy Scouts' creed, the successful Orlando traveler needs to "be prepared"; follow the advice in this book and you will be. And, last but not least, smile — you're going to **Disney World!**

Part I
Getting Started

In this part . . .

To get the most enjoyment out of a vacation — with the least amount of hassle — it helps to know what awaits you in your chosen paradise before the landing gear lowers. Given its popularity, planning a trip to Walt Disney World as far in advance as possible is essential. In this part, we highlight the joys of a trip to Orlando and help you sort out the logistics of planning one, from choosing the best times of the year to go to planning your vacation budget. We also look at some of the best things to do while you're exploring Disney World and its environs.

Chapter 1

Discovering the Best of Walt Disney World and Orlando

● ●

In This Chapter

▶ Checking out must-do experiences and activities

▶ Finding great places to stay

▶ Locating the premier spots for dining

▶ Seeking the top thrill rides

▶ Finding hot things to do at night

● ●

*N*o matter what your interest — be it fine dining or finding out how fast you can travel on a ride before losing your lunch — Orlando has something to offer you. There is a reason, after all, that this city is the number one family tourist destination in the United States. Thanks to its many offerings — theme parks, museums, and world-class resorts, just to name a few — the city manages to be all things to a lot of folks, and consequently attracts visitors of all ages and from all backgrounds and countries. Yes, it gets crowded and, in the summer, it's hot and sticky, but one thing you definitely won't be is bored.

All-Star Experiences

The major players in Orlando's vacation business (no surprise) are its numerous theme parks. You can spend your entire vacation inside these mega-amusement centers without running out of things to do. From *Cinderella's Castle* to *Big Thunder Mountain Railroad,* everyone loves the **Magic Kingdom,** Disney's original park, but you have other great things to try inside Walt's World and around Orlando. Here's a list of exciting places to visit:

  ↙ At **Epcot,** you can travel around the globe in the *World Showcase,* pump up your adrenaline on such thrill rides as *Body Wars* and *Test Track* in *Future World,* and try your hand at the interactive games at *Innoventions.*

- **Disney–MGM Studios** is a ton of fun for all ages. Take a plunge down the *Tower of Terror,* ride the *Rock 'n' Roller Coaster,* and enjoy the spectacle of *Fantasmic!,* an after-dark mix of live-action, waterworks, and fireworks.

- **Universal Studios Florida** and its sister park, **Islands of Adventure,** combine cutting-edge, high-tech effects with great creativity. Their not-to-be-missed attractions include *Back to the Future, Terminator 2: 3-D Battle Across Time,* the *Incredible Hulk Coaster,* the *Amazing Adventures of Spider-Man,* and *Dueling Dragons.*

- With the opening of *Journey to Atlantis* and *Kraken,* **SeaWorld** has made headway in its battle with Disney and Universal. But it's best to come here for the hands-on encounters with critters and the up-close views of polar bears, killer whales, and other creatures.

  SeaWorld's new sister, **Discovery Cove,** offers a chance to swim with dolphins (for a premium) as part of a daylong package.

- If you're a night owl, you'll find it hard to call your trip complete without spending an evening at **Pleasure Island** or **CityWalk.** Dance clubs, jazz halls, covert venues, restaurants, and shopping make these two entertainment districts Orlando's prime places to party the night away.

Put Your Head on These Pillows

In the United States, Orlando is second only to Las Vegas in total number of hotel rooms, and with so many to choose from, no matter what kind of hotel you prefer, you'll find it here.

Walt Disney World has a vast selection of hotels from which to choose. Families find it hard to beat the woodsy **Fort Wilderness Resort & Campground** or the **Wilderness Lodge,** whose features range from bunk beds to a geyser in the lobby. What more can a kid ask for?

Disney's **Port Orleans Resort** is the best choice among the moderately priced **WDW** properties. It has plenty of amenities, including boat shuttles to nearby properties, swimming pools outfitted with a waterfall and water slide, and multiple dining areas.

If you're on a leaner budget or not planning to spend much time in a room, you may prefer Disney's **All-Star Movie, All-Star Music,** and **All-Star Sports resorts.** With rates as low as $77 per night, they're the best bargain on **WDW** soil.

Don't need to stay in the World? Good. Booking a room in nearby Kissimmee, located only 10 to 15 minutes from **WDW,** can save you a lot of money. Although it doesn't have a lot of frills, the **Econo Lodge Maingate Hawaiian** on West Irlo Bronson Memorial Highway has rates as low as $35 per night. (See Chapter 3 for more suggestions on saving money on hotel rooms.)

Walt Disney World & Orlando

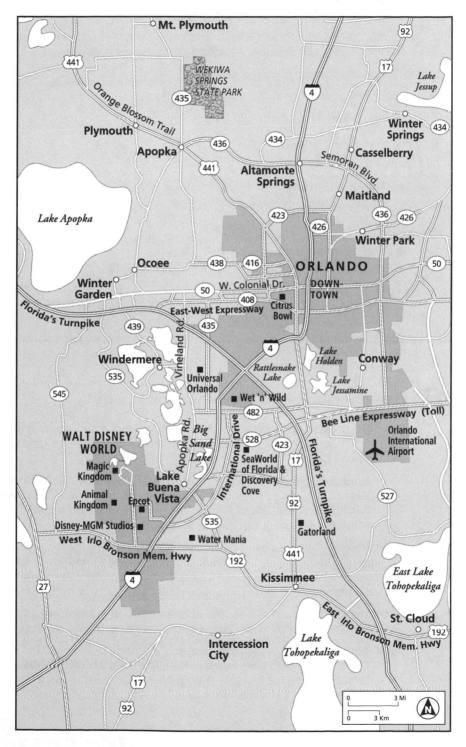

Who's going where?

The number of Florida theme-park visitors rises and falls slightly from year to year, according to *Amusement Business,* a trade magazine that estimates attendance.

Here are its 2000 figures and each park's national ranking:

1. Magic Kingdom, 15.4 million, up 1.3 percent.

3. Epcot, 10.6 million, up 5 percent.

4. Disney–MGM Studios, 8.9 million, up 2 percent.

5. Animal Kingdom, 8.3 million, down 3 percent.

6. Universal Studios Florida, 8.1 million, even.

7. Islands of Adventure, 6 million (first full year).

9. SeaWorld Florida, 5.2 million, up 11 percent.

10. Busch Gardens Tampa, 5 million, up 28 percent.

All of the parks raised adult rates $2 and kids' rates $1–$2 in 2001, the third hike in two years. (*Note:* In 2000, SeaWorld and Busch sold passes to Florida residents that let them pay a single price for unlimited entry throughout the year. These additional "free" entries caused their inflated attendance.)

Here are other great hotels if you have special needs:

- ✔ **Business:** Take advantage of concierge service and an array of free-time ventures such as golf and tennis at **Marriott's Orlando World Center.**

- ✔ **Romance:** Set on 1,500 acres, the **Hyatt Regency Grand Cypress Resort,** with its swan-inhabited lakes, is a scenic place to get away. Better yet, the **Villas of Grand Cypress** offers an even more romantic setting, with fireplaces and whirlpools.

- ✔ **Nothing but Disney:** If you must be on Disney property and in the epicenter of the action, check into the **Grand Floridian Resort & Spa,** the **Polynesian Resort,** or the **Contemporary Resort.** All are on Disney's monorail route, providing easy access to the parks.

- ✔ **Service:** It's hard to beat the elegant **Peabody Orlando's** 24-hour concierge and room service, nightly turndowns, and friendly staff.

- ✔ **Pools:** Disney resorts have terrific swimming pools, usually Olympic-size and based on themes. The pool at the **Caribbean Beach Resort,** for instance, resembles a fort with stone walls, cannons, and a water slide.

> ✔ **Health club:** How can you beat a full Body by Jake club? The **Walt Disney World Dolphin** has one, complete with a weight room, aerobics classes, personal training, massages, body wraps, saunas, and more.

Whet Your Appetite

Whether you prefer French cuisine or Italian, an elegant atmosphere or a rowdy one, there's probably a restaurant in Orlando that will cater to your every dining whim. For a list of our premier dining choices in Orlando, see Chapter 14.

Think kids and it's hard to ignore dining with Donald Duck and other Disney characters at **Walt Disney World** parks and resorts. The best breakfast and dinner venue for character meals is Chef Mickey's at the **Contemporary Resort.**

Do you prefer romance? The hands-down winner for romance-themed restaurants is Victoria & Albert's at **Disney's Grand Floridian Resort & Spa.** Dinner is an intimate, seven-course meal that retails for $85 a head (not including tax, tip, or wine — romance doesn't come cheap).

If you're dying for a view, Arthur's 27, which is on the 27th floor of the **Wyndham Palace Resort** in Lake Buena Vista, is hard to beat. You won't get a better angle for sunsets or Disney fireworks.

Here are some of the area's other bests:

> ✔ **Barbecue:** Bubbaloo's just north of the downtown
>
> ✔ **California cuisine:** Pebbles in Lake Buena Vista
>
> ✔ **Italian chow:** Capriccio in **The Peabody Orlando** and Pacino's Italian Ristorante in Kissimmee
>
> ✔ **Vegetarian fare:** the California Grill at **Disney's Contemporary Resort**
>
> ✔ **Wine list:** Maison & Jardin in Altamonte Springs

Chills and Thrills for Speed Freaks

If you're a speed freak who lives for the ups and downs of a good ride, Disney and the other parks will more than keep you busy.

The *Summit Plummet* water slide at Disney's **Blizzard Beach** starts pretty slow but finishes fast with a 120-foot, bathing suit-ripping free-fall. *The Amazing Adventures of Spider-Man* at **Islands of Adventure** is an amazing 3D simulator that dips and twists through comic-book action. *The Incredible Hulk Coaster* at **Islands of Adventure** launches you from 0 to 40 mph in 2 seconds — and spins you through seven rollovers. *Dueling Dragons,* a set of twin coasters at **Islands of Adventure,** catapults your body through five inversions at 55 to 60 mph while the coasters come within 12 inches of each other three times.

A twin-pack of rides at **Disney–MGM Studios** rounds out the adrenaline-inducing action. First up, *Rock 'n' Roller Coaster* rips from 0 to 60 mph in 2.8 seconds and goes directly into an inversion as 120 speakers blast Aerosmith at (yeeeow!) 32,000 watts in your stretch limo. If that doesn't send you into a tailspin, try the *Tower of Terror,* a free-fall experience that leaves your stomach hanging on several levels.

After the Sun Goes Down

Although Orlando is regarded primarily as a family destination, a red-eye culture has evolved thanks to those people who don't want to go to bed at the same time as the theme parks.

Here's a sampling of attractions that get you out of kids' way and on the town:

- ✔ **Pleasure Island** in **Downtown Disney** is a six-acre complex of clubs and restaurants headlined by the high-energy Mannequins Dance Palace, the country flavor of the Wildhorse Saloon, and the rhythm and blues of the BET Soundstage. The adjoining **Disney West Side** offers the throaty sounds of the House of Blues, the renowned no-animals *Cirque du Soleil,* and the ultimate arcade, **DisneyQuest.**

- ✔ The stars at **CityWalk** — **Universal Orlando**'s chip off the nightlife block — include the whimsical Jimmy Buffett's Margaritaville, the Caribbean-themed Bob Marley — A Tribute to Freedom, the rocking Hard Rock Live, and the groove.

- ✔ In Downtown Orlando, the Sapphire Supper Club is a sophisticated alternative to the usual club scene. One of the top spots in town for cool jazz, this joint caters to the martini-and-cigar crowd.

Chapter 2

Planning Your Trip Schedule

● ●

In This Chapter

▶ Considering the pros and cons of traveling in each season

▶ Checking out Orlando's weather patterns

▶ Consulting a calendar of special occasions

● ●

*A*lthough, by most standards, Orlando is a hive of activity throughout the year, some seasons are definitely busier than others. Deciding when to take your trip may affect what you see, how much you pay, and how long you stand in line. In this chapter, we analyze the advantages and disadvantages of visiting during various times of the year so you can decide the time of year that works best for your dream vacation plans.

The Secrets of the Seasons

In a nutshell, Orlando is Las Vegas for kids, so when they're out of school, the theme parks are a tangle of pushy, sweaty bodies. The busiest times to go are during spring break, summer (late May to Labor Day), and the winter holidays (mid-December to early January).

Obviously, your vacation experience is best when crowds are thinnest and the weather is mild. In some cases, rooms are cheaper in the off-seasons, but unlike traditional vacation destinations, you won't get a major break on prices in Orlando just because fewer people are in town. Business clients, the convention trade, and international visitors keep things busy year-round, so many hotels don't offer a high-low season rate scale. This year-round popularity also means that you need to book as early as possible.

Florida residents often scoot to the parks as a day trip or for a long weekend. Most out-of-state guests don't have that luxury. But if you have kids, take a hint from two families that we know and consider pulling them out of school for a few days during the off-season to avoid lines. Ask their teachers for schoolwork to take with you. You can also suggest that your kids write a report on some educational element of the vacation. (Yes, they will actually learn things while they're traipsing around places such as the *World Showcase* at **Epcot**!)

Even if you come in the off-season, the parks run full tilt (though operating hours may be shorter). Orlando never turns out the lights, and each season has its perks and pitfalls.

Spring: Excitement blooms in Orlando

Spring is sensational in Orlando because

- ✔ The weather is mild.
- ✔ Accommodations that give discounts give them during spring.
- ✔ The lines inside the theme parks are relatively short.

But keep in mind that

- ✔ Without a winter, spring is fleeting. The temperature can get warm and sticky in April.
- ✔ The high pollen count can drive allergy sufferers crazy.
- ✔ Spring break cometh. Avoid this time period unless you're taking a break from the books.

Summer: Have fun in the Orlando sun

Summer is superb in Orlando because

- ✔ Daylight is plentiful, and long days are capped by beautiful fireworks displays.
- ✔ August means back-to-school sales at all Orlando's malls and outlets.
- ✔ All hotels, major restaurants, and indoor tourist attractions in Central Florida have air-conditioning.

However, keep in mind that

- ✔ The heat and humidity are oppressive.
- ✔ Crowds and sweat create a sometimes unpleasant perfume in the air.
- ✔ Discounts? Ha! Why cut prices with these crowds?

Fall: Harvest good times in Orlando

Fall is fabulous in Orlando because

- ✔ Ah, fall foliage. Orlando gets a 17-minute burst of fall colors. It's short but sweet.

> ✔ Accommodations that give discounts offer them in the fall.
>
> ✔ Lines in the parks begin to shrink to reasonable wait times.

But keep in mind that

> ✔ While the weather is cooler, the temperature doesn't get as mild as spring until Thanksgiving or later.
>
> ✔ Once mid-December arrives, so do the high prices.

Winter: You'll be warm and welcome in Orlando

Winter is wonderful in Orlando because

> ✔ Orlando doesn't have a true winter — just a few days at or near freezing, followed by mild, sunny weather.
>
> ✔ Lines at the parks don't get much better than they are during winter.

However, remember that

> ✔ The many conventions held in Orlando throughout the year keep room rates reasonably high.
>
> ✔ During the mid-December to early-January holidays, the parks are just as crowded as in the dead of summer.

Weather Warnings

You don't need to be paranoid, but knowing a little about Florida's weather-related temper tantrums is a good idea. Here's a list of weather events that you may experience during your stay:

> ✔ **Hurricanes:** The Gulf-and-Atlantic hurricane season runs from June 1 to November 30. In an average year, the Atlantic churns out ten of these storms, and one or two touch Florida. The Gulf adds three to five. The good news: Orlando's inland location means the worst a storm will do is ruin a couple days of vacation.
>
> ✔ **Lightning:** This scary but beautiful show courtesy of mother nature makes regular appearances during Orlando's frequent summer thunder storms.
>
> However, don't let the presence of lightning ruin your trip. Unless you're standing in the wrong place (under an oak tree, wading in water, trying to hit a golf ball while wearing metal cleats and holding a metal club, or at the top of a roller coaster) at the wrong time, lightning's wrath is short-lived.

✔ **Sun:** Florida isn't called the Sunshine State without reason. Make sure you bring plenty of sunscreen on your trip. Florida tourism thrives on the sun, but you won't enjoy your vacation much if you're laid up with a painful sunburn or, even worse, sun poisoning.

Preventing your skin from turning a magnificent, and painful, shade of red is simple: Slather yourself with a 25-rated (or higher) sun block. And don't forget to keep re-applying it, especially after you hit the swimming pool. Likewise, remember to bring a wide-brimmed hat and don't forget a Florida native's favorite fashion statement — sunglasses.

Table 2-1 lists, by month, average high and low temperatures recorded in Central Florida.

Table 2-1		Central Florida Average Temperatures									
Jan	Feb	Mar	Apr	May	June	July	Aug	Sept	Oct	Nov	Dec
High °F											
71.7	72.9	78.3	83.6	88.3	90.6	91.7	91.6	89.7	84.4	78.2	73.1
High °C											
22.0	22.7	25.7	28.7	31.3	32.5	33.2	33.1	32.0	29.1	25.7	22.8
Low °F											
49.3	50.0	55.3	60.3	66.2	71.2	73.0	73.4	72.5	65.4	56.8	50.9
Low °C											
9.6	10.0	12.5	15.7	19.0	21.8	22.7	23.0	22.5	18.6	13.8	10.5

Orlando's Calendar: Attractions in Review

In this section, we list (by month) just a few of Orlando's many exciting festivals and special events. Please double-check with festivals and their organizations before planning your vacation around any of these events. Event dates are subject to change.

You can access Orlando's major daily newspaper, the *Orlando Sentinel,* at www.orlandosentinel.com for information about other upcoming events.

January

Zora Neale Hurston Festival. This four-day festival is celebrated in Eatonville, the first incorporated African-American town in America. It highlights the life and works of author Zora Neale Hurston and is usually held the last weekend in January. Eatonville is 25 miles north of the parks. Admission is $5 adults, $3 kids 17 and under. Lectures or seminars require additional fees. Call ☎ **800-352-3865** or 407-647-3307 for details.

February

Mardi Gras at Universal Studios. Authentic parade floats from New Orleans, stilt walkers, and traditional doubloons and beads add to the fun of this event, which is included in the price of admission to the park. This event also includes special entertainment. It's in mid-February. For information call ☎ **800-837-2273** or 407-363-8000; Internet: www. universalorlando.com.

Spring Training. Also in mid-February, welcome the **Atlanta Braves** as they arrive for spring training at **Disney's Wide World of Sports Complex.** They play an 18-game spring season that begins in early March. Tickets are $11– $17.50. For general information, call ☎ **407-939-7810**. To buy tickets, call TicketMaster at ☎ **407-839-3900.** You can also get information online at www.disneysports.com or www. atlantabraves.com.

April

Orlando International Fringe Festival. More than 100 acts from around the world participate in this eclectic event, held for 10 days in April and May at various locations in downtown Orlando. Entertainers perform drama, comedy, political satire, experimental theater, and a seven-minute version of *Hamlet,* all on an outdoor stage. Ticket prices vary, but most performances are under $12. Call ☎ **407-648-0077** for more information.

June

Gay Weekend. The first weekend in June draws tens of thousands of gay and lesbian travelers to Central Florida. This event grew out of "Gay Day," an unofficial event at **Disney World** dating to the early 1990s when it drew 50,000 people. **Universal Orlando** and **SeaWorld** also host this weekend. You can find online information at www.gayday.com.

July

Independence Day. Orlando heats up as July 4th is celebrated with bands, singers, dancers, and unbelievable fireworks displays at

Disney's Star-Spangled Spectacular. The parks stay open late for the occasion (☎ 407-824-4321; Internet: www.disneyworld.com). **SeaWorld** exhibits a dazzling laser/fireworks spectacular (☎ 407-351-3600; Internet: www.seaworld.com), and Orlando's Lake Eola Park shows a free display, too (☎ 407-246-2827).

September

Night of Joy. One weekend each September, the **Magic Kingdom** hosts a contemporary Christian music festival featuring top artists. This is a very popular event, so if it's on your dance card, get tickets ($25–$30) early. Ticket price also includes access to all **Magic Kingdom** attractions. Call ☎ 407-824-4321 for more information.

October

Halloween Horror Nights. Orlando is frightfully fun in October as **Universal Orlando** (☎ 800-837-2273 or 407-363-8000; Internet: www.universalorlando.com) transforms its grounds for 19 nights into a mass of haunted attractions, complete with live bands, special shows, a psychopath's maze, and hundreds of ghouls and goblins roaming the streets. The studio closes at dusk and then reopens in a new, chilling form at 7 p.m. The park charges full admission ($48) for this event and also serves alcohol. Guests aren't allowed to wear costumes so that Universal employees can spot their peers.

Epcot International Food & Wine Festival. Also in October, here's your chance to sip and savor the food and beverages of 30 cultures. For information, call ☎ 407-824-4321.

November

The Walt Disney World Festival of the Masters. On the second weekend in November, **Downtown Disney Marketplace** is home to one of the largest art shows in the South. The exhibition features top artists, photographers, and craftspeople — all winners of juried shows throughout the United States. Admission is free. Call ☎ 407-824-4321 for details, or visit www.disneyworld.com.

December

Christmas at Walt Disney World. During the Disney Christmas festivities, Main Street in the **Magic Kingdom** is lavishly decked out with lights and holly, and carolers welcome visitors. Thousands of colored lights illuminate an 80-foot tree. **Epcot, Disney–MGM Studios,** and **Animal Kingdom** also offer special embellishments and entertainment throughout the holiday season, as do all Disney resorts. Some holiday highlights include *Mickey's Very Merry Christmas Party,* an after-dark ticketed event, which takes place on weekends at the **Magic Kingdom** and offers a traditional Christmas parade and fireworks display. Admission ($35 adults, $26 kids 3 to 9) includes cookies, cocoa, and a souvenir photo. The best part? Shorter lines for rides. The *Candlelight Procession* at **Epcot** features hundreds of candle-holding carolers, a celebrity narrator telling the Christmas story, and a 450-voice choir that's very moving. Call ☎ **407-824-4321** for details concerning all these events.

The Osborne Family Christmas Lights. Also in December, this spectacular display came to **Disney–MGM Studios** in 1995 when the Arkansas family ran into trouble with hometown authorities over their multimillion-light display. In a twinkle, Disney moved the whole shebang to Florida. For online information on all activities, go to www.disneyworld.com.

Chapter 3

Preparing Your Budget

●●

In This Chapter

▶ Managing your dollars and cents

▶ Avoiding surprise expenses

▶ Debating traveler's checks, credit cards, ATMs, and cash

▶ Cost-cutting tidbits

●●

Developing a realistic budget is an important key to enjoying your vacation — the last thing you want to experience when you get to Orlando is sticker shock, and Central Florida is famous for its ability to exact a pound of flesh from even the most cost-conscious traveler. From hotel rooms to meal tabs to admission fees, you can break your bank if you don't do some homework in advance. The good news is that we can help you make sure that you don't bust your bankroll.

Adding Your Costs

Budgeting your **Walt Disney World** vacation is easy, and using the work-sheets that we include in the Appendix of this book gives you a pretty accurate estimate of its cost. The hard part is sticking to the budget that you create. Mickey and his pals are masters when it comes to separating you from your dollars. Vacationing at Walt Disney World makes you feel good, even giddy, and before you know it, you'll be out of dough.

If you avoid impulse bingeing — er, buying — and draft an honest budget, you'll avoid running out of money (or facing shock therapy when your credit-card bills arrive).

Make sure to include everything in your vacation budget. Add the cost of getting to the airport, airport parking (if you're driving yourself), airline tickets (you can find tips for getting the best airfare in Chapter 5), transportation from the Orlando airport to your room, your room rates, meals, shuttle or rental car charges, park admission (multiplied by the number of days you'll visit), the cost of other attractions that you want to explore, entertainment expenses, and tips. Tack on another 15 to 20 percent as a safety net. (How can you turn down your kids when they beg for Goofy slippers?)

Here are some prices to expect when you get to Orlando:

- **Lodging.** The average room in Orlando costs $90–$95 a night; in most cases, that rate includes any children staying in the room. The full range is $35–$300 or more if you prefer suites or condos. If you choose to stay on **Disney** property, the average room will set you back $120–$125 per night; the lowest-priced room costs $77, and prices for the most expensive rooms are in the stratosphere.

- **Transportation.** Some hotels offer free shuttles to the parks; others take you for a fee (see Chapter 8 for more information). If you stay at **Disney,** you can access its free transportation system (though it's plodding). Rental-car rates start at about $35 a day (don't forget to add the $6 daily charge to park your car at the theme parks).

- **Dining.** Chowing down in Orlando costs an average of $60–$80 per person, per day; $100 if you dine mostly in the theme parks or at **Disney's** and **Universal's** resorts (see Chapters 13 and 14 for more information on dining). Keep in mind that food in the parks and resorts is overpriced and occasionally mirrors the same quality as cardboard. Outside the parks, you can find delis for takeout and assorted budget eateries. Also, don't overlook the option of a room with a small kitchen or microwave.

- **Attractions.** Your expenses for attractions will depend on what kind of parks you favor and how often you go. **Disney, Universal,** and **SeaWorld** parks charge $48 for adults and $38–$39 for kids per day (see Chapters 17 though 25 for information on the individual parks). If you're going to visit one of the above several times, buy one of the multiday, multipark passes that we outline in Chapters 17 through 25. Parts V and VI of this book also include some free and inexpensive attractions that you can visit if you want to lower your costs.

- **Shopping and Entertainment.** Orlando is no shopper's paradise, but there are two large malls and some outlets (see Chapter 27) where you may find a bargain. We don't recommend allowing yourself to be gouged by the amusement-park gift shops unless you find a must-have souvenir.

Table 3-1 outlines various vacationing costs in Orlando.

Table 3-1	What Things Cost in Orlando	
Transportation	**U.S.$**	**U.K.£ (As of this writing, $1.47 = 1£)**
Taxi from airport to WDW (4-5 people)	44.00	29.93
Shuttle from airport to WDW (adult fare)	15.00	10.20

Accommodations	U.S.$	U.K.£ (As of this writing, $1.47 = 1£)
Double room at Econo Lodge, Kissimmee	35.00–119.00	23.81–80.95
Double room at Disney's All-Star Resorts	77.00–109.00	52.38–74.15
Double room at Disney's Port Orleans Resort	129.00–209.00	87.76–142.18
Double room at Radisson Hotel Universal Orlando	99.00–199.00	67.35–135.37
Double room at Disney's Grand Floridian	314.00–790.00	213.61–537.42
Food and Beverages	**U.S.$**	**U.K.£ (As of this writing, $1.47 = 1£)**
Coca-Cola (restaurant)	1.25	.85
Bottle of beer (restaurant)	2.50	1.70
All-you-can-eat buffet dinner at Akershus	18.50	12.59
Seven-course fixed-price dinner for one at Victoria & Albert's, not including tip or wine	85.00–160.00	57.82–108.84
Attractions	**U.S.$**	**U.K.£ (As of this writing, $1.47 = 1£)**
Child 1-day, 1-park admission to Walt Disney World & Universal Orlando	38.00	25.85
Adult 1-day, 1-park admission to Walt Disney World & Universal Orlando	48.00	32.65
Child 3-day Universal Orlando Pass	79.95	54.39
Adult 3-day Universal Orlando Pass	99.95	67.99
Child 4-Day Park Hopper admission to Walt Disney World	152.00	103.40
Adult 4-Day Park Hopper admission to Walt Disney World	192.00	130.61

Keeping a Rein on Runaway Expenses

Even the biggest penny pinchers can forget to include certain items in their travel budget, resulting in a much larger tab than expected. A big reason these costs are hidden is that they are almost never quoted to you when you inquire about hotel or car-rental rates, unless you *specifically ask about added charges.* And visitors often underestimate the greed of the theme parks and their own inability to pass up those high-priced Mickey ears.

Look out for these surprises that can wreak havoc on your budget:

- ✔ **Sales tax:** Florida has a 6-percent sales tax that's added to most things except groceries and medical services. In addition, expect another 5 percent, for a total of 11 percent, added to your hotel room in **Walt Disney World** and Orlando; the total is 12 percent in nearby Kissimmee.

- ✔ **Car-rental charges:** Sales tax, surcharges, and various other required add-ons can add 20 to 25 percent to the quoted rates.

- ✔ **Tipping:** A 15-percent tip is the general rule for restaurant service and cab rides. The hotel housekeeper deserves $1 to $2 a day for cleaning your mess, making your beds, and keeping you stocked with towels. Baggage handlers usually receive $1 per bag.

- ✔ **A prisoner of the parks:** Whether you're visiting a theme park for the day or you're trapped for the length of your stay in a **Disney** or **Universal** resort without a car, expect to be charged exhorbitant amounts for meals and more.

Paper, Plastic, or Pocket Change?

There are a number of options you can use to pay for your vacation, including meals, souvenirs, and so on. In this section, we explore available options to help you determine the one that's right for you.

Traveling with traveler's checks

Traveler's checks are a throwback to the days before ATM machines gave you easy access to your money. Because you can replace them if they're lost or stolen, traveler's checks are a sound alternative to stuffing your wallet with cash. However, you may have trouble cashing them in some places. Common issuers include American Express, ☎ **800-221-7282,** and MasterCard, ☎ **800-223-9920.** (See Chapter 9 for more information on acquiring traveler's checks.)

Relying on ATMs

Many folks prefer to use ATMs when on vacation. At **Walt Disney World,** you can find ATMs on Main Street and in *Tomorrowland* in the **Magic Kingdom;** at the entrances to **Epcot, Disney–MGM Studios,** and **Animal Kingdom;** at **Pleasure Island;** and in **Downtown Disney Marketplace.** You can also find ATMs near *Guest Services* at **SeaWorld, Universal Studios Florida,** and **Islands of Adventure** (also at *The Lost Continent* near the bridge leading to *Jurassic Park*).

Outside of the amusement parks, you can find ATMs at most malls, convenience stores, and some grocery and drug stores. But remember that you frequently must pay an extra charge for using non-bank ATMs. In Florida, you're assessed an average charge of $2.60 if you use an ATM that isn't affiliated with your bank.

Cirrus (☎ 800-424-7787) and Plus (☎ 800-843-7587) are the two most popular networks; check the back of your ATM card to find out what network your bank affiliates with. (The 800-numbers also provide ATM locations where you can withdraw money.) Withdraw only as much cash as you need for incidentals — we recommend carrying no more than $50 or $60.

Be extremely careful when using ATMs, especially at night and in areas that are heavily traveled but not well lit. Don't let the land of Mickey lull you into a false sense of security. Donald and Pluto won't mug you — but thieves working the theme parks may.

Charge! Carrying the cards

Traveling with credit cards is a safe alternative to carrying cash. Credit cards also provide you with a record of your vacation expenses once you return home. Most major credit cards are accepted throughout Central Florida. You can get cash advances from your major credit accounts, but make sure that you have your personal identification number (PIN) before leaving home. To get your PIN, call your credit card's issuer and ask them to send it to you.

Tips for Cutting Costs

You can conserve your cash in more than just a couple of ways when you vacation in Orlando. Use these tips to keep your vacation costs manageable:

- ✓ **Consider a package.** This doesn't mean an escorted tour, just a package that includes accommodations, airfare, and in some cases, additional perks. See Chapter 5 for more information on the ins and outs of package tours.

- ✓ **Visit during the off-season.** Hotel prices in the off-season cost can be substantially lower, depending on the property. If possible, travel at non-peak times (September to November or April to June, for example).

- ✓ **Travel during off-days of the week.** Airfares vary depending on the day of the week you fly. You can often cut your airfare in half if you stay over on a Saturday night. Likewise, you may find cheaper flights if you travel on a Tuesday, Wednesday, or Thursday. See Chapter 5 for more tips on getting the best airfare.

- ✓ **Find out if your kids can stay in your room with you free.** A room with two double beds usually doesn't cost more than a room with a queen-size bed. Many hotels don't charge you extra if the third and fourth persons are children. Reserving one room and paying an extra $10 to $15 for a rollaway can save you hundreds over the course of your vacation.

✔ **Reserve a room with a kitchen and do your own cooking.** Although the family chef may disagree with this suggestion, you can limit the amount of times per day that you eat out.

✔ **If you have a multiday pass to a theme park, utilize your in-and-out privileges.** Go back to your hotel for a picnic lunch and a swim or nap. You can eat economically, miss the midday sun, and refuel for an evening at the park.

✔ **Avoid splurging — pace yourself.** Your money goes fastest when you overexert yourself exploring the parks, and you end up too hungry, thirsty, or tired to care about how much you spend. Begin each day with a big breakfast at a fast-food restaurant or an all-you-can-eat buffet (you can find several outside the parks that cost around $3–$5). Also, remember to stop often at drinking fountains, because bottled water and sodas at attractions are extremely overpriced.

✔ **Brown-bag it.** Bringing your own food is extremely cost-effective. Remember, however, that parks are wise to this scheme, so make your operation covert — hide it in a fannypack or backpack.

✔ **Make lunch the most expensive meal of the day.** Trying out expensive restaurants makes more sense at lunch time, rather than dinner. Most restaurants have the same menu at lunch as at dinner, but at lower prices. Make sure that you also check out the early-bird specials.

✔ **Don't spend every day at a theme park.** Discover your hotel's pool, playground, workout room, and other freebies. Also, get out of town and head for one of the lower-priced attractions away from theme-park-central.

✔ **Skip souvenirs.** Make your photographs and memories the best mementos of your trip. If you're worried about money, do without the T-shirts, key chains, salt-and-pepper shakers, mouse ears, and other trinkets. Set a spending limit and stick to it!

✔ **The Disney Club** offers 10- to 30-percent discounts at **WDW** parks, resorts, and restaurants, plus savings on packages deals, car rentals, and merchandise. Added benefits include a members-only Web site that features additional discounts on meals, rooms, and attractions in other cities; special travel packages; and discounts on multi-day theme-park passes. Membership costs $39.95 per year. For more information or to join, call ☎ **800-654-6347** or surf over to www.disneyclub.com.

✔ **Amtrak** (☎ **800-872-7245**; Internet: www.amtrak.com) offers 20-to 30-percent discounts at **WDW** resorts and on related packages and meals in the parks, and up to 30 percent off some rental cars.

✔ **Receive instant discounts with an Orlando Magicard.** Another discount card, the Orlando Magicard is good for up to $500 in discounts on accommodations, car rentals, attractions, and more. Better yet, the card is free. You can get a Magicard from the Orlando/Orange County Convention & Visitors Bureau, 8723 International Dr., Suite 101, Orlando, FL 32819 (☎ **800-643-9492** or 407-363-5872). You may also be eligible for other discounts if you're a member of AARP, AAA, the military, or some service clubs, so don't be bashful — just ask.

Chapter 4

Planning Ahead for Special Travel Needs

● ●

In This Chapter

▶ Travel tips for the whole family

▶ Travel advice for the senior set

▶ Travel tips for people with disabilities

▶ Travel advice for gays and lesbians

● ●

*W*orried that your kids are too young or that you're too old to enjoy **Disney** and beyond? Afraid you may experience barriers blocking your access or lifestyle? In this chapter, we dispense a little advice for travelers with specific needs.

Making Family Travel Fun

Orlando loves kids and welcomes them like no other city in the world. In addition to its theme parks, Orlando has plenty of smaller kid-friendly attractions. All but a few restaurants offer low-priced children's menus (see Chapter 14 for more info on kids and dining), and most hotels go crazy over their younger guests, providing pint-size pools and, in some cases, special gifts and programs (see Chapter 8 for kid-friendly hotels).

However, despite Orlando's reputation as Kidsville, U.S.A., you may find that some attractions are a bit too sophisticated or intense for kids, including most of **Epcot's** exhibits (see Chapter 18) and many of the primo thrill rides at **Islands of Adventure** (see Chapter 24). Likewise, you may find other attractions, such as **Discovery Cove** (see Chapter 25), cost-prohibitive.

Traveling with tots

Traveling with young children can often bring you more stress than relaxation on your vacation. Consider that younger children have special needs. They often eat on a routine basis, require frequent bathroom breaks, and have very short attention spans. (Does the phrase, "Dad, are we there yet?" ring a bell?) Here are a few general suggestions for making travel plans for you and your youngsters:

✔ **Consider age — are your kids old enough?** Do you really want to bring an infant or a toddler to an overcrowded, usually overheated world that he or she may not appreciate because of his or her age? The large number of stroller-pushing, toddler-toting parents in the parks suggests that many people think the experience isn't too terrible, but we're warning you anyway. Our younger grandson, Andy, is 4 and just able to appreciate a few of the parks' offerings, especially those at **Disney's Magic Kingdom** (see Chapter 17). However, some of the costume-wearing characters frighten him, he wants a nap when we want to see the parade, and he's dead weight when we have to carry him when he gets too tired. No matter how organized you are, a little one is going to slow you down. Put your family in our position and ask yourself whether your family will enjoy a trip under such conditions that also costs the equivalent of a developing nation's GNP (gross national product). Think of it this way — would you bring a toddler to the ballet?

✔ **Accommodations for the little ones.** Kids under 12 (and older, in many cases) can stay for free in their parents' room in most hotels. Look for places that have pools and other recreational facilities so your family can spend a no-extra-expense day or two away from the parks. If you want to skip a rental car and aren't staying at Disney, International Drive is the next-best place for centralized rooms, restaurants, and attractions. A trolley runs there frequently, hotels often offer family discounts (see Chapter 8), and many provide free or moderate cost shuttles to **Walt Disney World, SeaWorld,** and **Universal Studios.**

✔ **Select a sitter service.** Most Orlando hotels offer baby-sitting services and several Disney properties operate marvelous child-care facilities with counselor-supervised activity programs on the premises. **Walt Disney World** properties have used **KinderCare** sitters since 1981 (☎ 407-827-5444). All their sitters are very carefully checked out, including a criminal background search, and if you're not staying at a Disney accommodation, you can call KinderCare on your own. In fact, they can even take your kids to the park or to any of the services at your resort, except swimming. Rates for in-room service are $12 per hour for one child, $13 per hour for two children, and $14 per hour for three kids, with a four-hour minimum — the first half-hour of which is travel time for the sitter. Call 24 hours in advance to make a reservation or to check rates for more than four kids.

✔ **Plan ahead for character dining.** If you would like to eat a meal with a cast of Disney characters while at **Walt Disney World,** make character dining priority-seating reservations when you reserve your hotel room. (See Chapter 15 for more details about character dining.) Also, once you're in WDW, check the daily schedule for character appearances (all the major parks post them in handout maps or boards near the entrance) and make sure the kids know when they're going to meet their heroes, because doing so is often the highlight of their day. A little planning can help you avoid running after every character you see, which only tires your little ones and gives you sore feet. And remember — the "in" thing is getting character autographs, so take our advice: Buy an autograph book at home instead of paying premium park prices.

✔ **Establish ground rules.** Being firm when the object is fun is tough, but consider setting ground rules before leaving home on things like bedtime and souvenirs. Your kids will be on something akin to a sugar high while they're on vacation (you may be, too), so don't allow giddiness to take control of your senses.

✔ **Keep tabs on the little ones in the land of Mickey.** Getting lost inside a theme park is as easy as remembering your middle name. Getting found takes a bit more work. For adults and older kids, make sure you arrange a lost-and-found meeting place as soon as you arrive in the park. Attach a name tag to younger kids, and find a park employee as soon as you're separated from your party. We list lost-and-found locations in our descriptions of the major theme parks in Chapters 17 through 25.

✔ **Pack to toddler-proof your hotel room.** Although your home may be toddler-proof, hotel rooms aren't. Bring blank plugs to cover outlets and whatever else is necessary to prevent an accident from occurring in your room.

✔ **Stay safe in the sun.** Don't forget to bring sunscreen for the entire family. If you forget to bring it, buy sunscreen with a 25 or higher rating at a convenience store or a drugstore (some theme-park shops also carry it). Slather your young children — even if they're in a stroller — and make sure you pack a hat for infants and toddlers. Likewise, make sure everyone traveling with you drinks plenty of water to avoid dehydration.

✔ **Remember ride restrictions.** Most parks explain their height restrictions for certain attractions or identify those that may unsettle young children. (We also list these restrictions in our discussions of the major theme parks in Chapters 17 through 25.) Save yourself and your kids some grief before you get in line and experience disappointment. Make your restriction rules firm — a bad trip down a darkened tunnel or a scary loop-de-loop can make your youngster cranky all day (and the fear of such rides can last a long while thereafter).

✔ **Take time out for a show.** Take time for an inside, air-conditioned show two or three times a day, especially during summer afternoons. They're a good way to beat the heat, and you may even get your littlest tykes to nap in the darkened theater. For all shows, arrive at least 20 minutes early to avoid the bad seats, but not so early that the kids go nuts waiting (most of the waiting areas are outside).

✔ **Pack a snack.** When dreaming of your vacation, you probably don't envision hours spent waiting in lines. Unfortunately, doing so is an inevitability you can't avoid. Store some lightweight snacks in an easy-to-carry backpack, especially when traveling with small kids, to save you headaches and save you money over park prices, which are sometimes double those in the free world.

✔ **Rent a stroller.** Unless you're particularly attached to your stroller, or it's specially designed for triplets, you won't have a problem using the ones provided by the parks, most of which charge $6–$7 a day for rentals. Renting a stroller from the parks allows you to avoid hauling yours to and from the car or on and off the trams, trains, or monorails. However, there are exceptions — the most notable being **Universal Studios Florida** and **Islands of Adventure,** where you face a long walk from the parking lot to the ticket booths. For infants and toddlers, you may want to bring a sling or backpack-type carrier to use when traveling to and from the parking lots as well as while you're standing in line for the shows and attractions.

✔ **Take a break.** The **Disney, Universal,** and **SeaWorld** parks maintain play areas that offer parents a rest while their kids continue to have fun. Schedule two or three visits to these spots a day, depending on your stamina. Many of these kid zones include water toys, and some parks have major water-related rides, so packing a change of clothes for the whole family is a good idea. Rent a locker ($5 or less) and store your spare duds until you need them. During summer months, the Florida humidity can keep you feeling soggy all day, so you'll appreciate the fresh clothing. (So will other visitors who enter your air space.)

✔ **Plan playtime for parents. Walt Disney World** and **Universal Orlando** offer a parent-swap program for parents traveling with small children. On many of the "big kid" rides, one parent can ride the attraction while the other stays with the kids, and then the adults can switch places without having to stand in line again. Notify a staff member that you want to take advantage of this program when you get in line.

Finding kid-friendly tours

Many theme parks specially design tours for the younger set that include great sources of age-appropriate entertainment.

SeaWorld has justifiably earned its reputation as a park that makes education fun with a variety of tours. One of the most interesting is the *Polar Expedition Guided Tour.* This hour-long journey gives kids a chance to come face to face with a penguin and get a behind-the-scenes look at "Wild Arctic" support areas. Call ☎ **407-370-1380** to schedule a tour. *To the Rescue,* another hour-long tour, allows you to see some of the park's rescue and rehabilitation work with several species, including manatees and rare sea turtles. Both tours are kid-friendly, though the latter may appeal more to older children.

SeaWorld tours are offered on a first-come, first-serve basis, so reserve a place at the Guided Tour Information desk when you enter the park. They cost $7 for adults and $6 for 3- to 9-year-olds, plus park admission ($47.95 adults, $38.95 kids). Call ☎ **800-406-2244** for more information. In June, July, and August, *Camp SeaWorld* offers 200 classes, including some sleepover programs and family courses. Contact ☎ **407-370-1380** for more details.

At **Walt Disney World,** the *Family Magic Tour* features an interactive scavenger hunt and costs $25 for adults and $20 for kids, plus park admission of $48 and $38, respectively.

Cutting Costs — Savings for Seniors

Although Orlando is a kid- and family-oriented zone, many of its hotels, restaurants, and attractions also roll out the red carpet for older travelers, who in some cases come with grandkids. You can find discounts from several sources, which we list in this section.

Saving money on accommodations

If you're not a member of **AARP (American Association of Retired Persons),** 601 E. St. NW, Washington, DC 20049 (☎ **800-424-3410** or 202-434-2277; Internet: www.aarp.org), do yourself a favor and join. Membership costs $10 per person or couple (you must be 50 or over) and enables you to receive discounts on car rentals and hotels.

Mature Outlook, P.O. Box 9390, Des Moines, IA 50306-9519 (☎ **800-336-6330**), is an organization similar to AARP, offering discounts on car rentals and hotels. The $39.95 annual membership (per person or couple) also gets you $200 in Sears coupons and a bimonthly magazine. Membership is open to anyone 18 and over, but the organization's primary focus is on the 50-and-over crowd.

Money-saving publications

The *Mature Traveler Guide* published by the Orlando/Orange County Convention & Visitors Bureau (☎ **800-643-9492**; Internet: www.orlandoinfo.com) offers $275 in discounts on rooms, attractions, and other items. You can also pick one up at the CVB's office at 8723 International Drive, Suite 101, Orlando, FL 32819 (southeast corner of I-Drive and Austrian Row).

Folks of all ages can obtain 10-to 30-percent discounts at **WDW** parks, resorts, and restaurants as well savings on packages, merchandise, and car rentals through the **Disney Club.** Added benefits include a member's-only Web site that features additional discounts on meals, rooms, and attractions in other cities; special travel packages; and discounts on multi-day theme-park passes. Membership costs $39.95 per year. For more information or to join, call ☎ **800-654-6347** or surf over to www.disneyclub.com.

Additional savings for seniors

If you're a senior, here are some additional ways for you to save money:

✔ Hilton's Senior HHonors Program, available to people 60 and older, provides discounts up to 50 percent off hotel rooms and 20 percent off dinner in hotel restaurants. The annual membership is $51 per person, but because spouses are enrolled for free, only one of you needs to join if you travel together. Call ☎ **800-548-8690** from 7 a.m. to 11 p.m. CST, Monday through Friday, 8:30 a.m. to 5 p.m. most weekends.

✔ Most U.S. airlines sell senior airfare coupons for travelers 62 and older. Each coupon is good for one flight anywhere in the United States. You can buy a packet of four coupons for $542–$596. Each coupon is valid for one-way travel.

✔ Amtrak (☎ **800-872-7245**) offers a 15-percent discount on the lowest available coach fare (with certain travel restrictions) to people 62 and over.

Keep in mind that although some of us may look the part, others don't. If you look younger than your years, consider yourself blessed and always carry some form of photo ID so that you can take advantage of discounts wherever they're offered. Minimum ages for discounts vary from 50 on up, so asking never hurts.

Traveling without Barriers

A disability need not prevent you from savoring the magic of Orlando and **Walt Disney World.** Many of the city's attractions and hotels are designed to accommodate the needs of the disabled, whether they be specially equipped guest rooms or audio aids for the sight impaired. A little advance research and planning, however, is a smart idea.

Finding accommodating lodgings

Every hotel and motel in Florida is required by law to maintain a special room (or rooms) equipped for wheelchairs, but keep in mind that the law is being phased in over time, so some hotels may not yet have rooms for the disabled. A few places, including **Buena Vista Suites** (☎ **407-239-8588**) and **Embassy Suites** (☎ **407-239-1144**), have wheel-in showers. **Walt Disney World's Coronado Springs Resort** (☎ **407-934-7639**), which opened in 1997, maintains 99 rooms that are designed to accommodate guests with disabilities, so make your special needs known when making reservations. For other information about special Disney rooms, call ☎ 407-939-7807.

Getting around

Public buses in Orlando have hydraulic lifts and restraining belts for wheelchairs, and they serve **Universal Orlando, SeaWorld,** shopping areas, and downtown Orlando. When staying on **Disney** property, you can use shuttle buses that accommodate wheelchairs from your hotel.

If you need to rent a wheelchair or an electric scooter for your visit, Walker Medical & Mobility Products will deliver one to your room; it offers a model that accommodates guests weighing up to 375 pounds that fits into Disney's transports and monorails, as well as rental cars. For more information, call ☎ 888-726-6837 or visit Walker's Web site at www.walkermobility.com. You can also rent conventional and electric chairs daily at the theme parks (see Chapters 17 through 25).

Many of the major car rental companies now offer hand-controlled cars for disabled drivers. Avis can provide such a vehicle at any of its locations in the United States with 48-hour advance notice; Hertz requires advance reservations of between 24 and 72 hours at most of its locations. See the appendix in the back of the book for the major rental companies' toll-free numbers and Web sites.

Amtrak (☎ 800-872-7245; Internet: www.amtrak.com) will provide you with redcap service, wheelchair assistance, and special seats if you give them 72 hours notice. Travelers with disabilities are also entitled to a 15-percent discount off the lowest available adult coach fare. Documentation from a doctor or an ID card proving your disability is required, however. Amtrak also provides wheelchair-accessible sleeping accommodations on long-distance trains. Amtrak permits service dogs aboard, and they travel free. TDD/TTY service is also available at ☎ 800-523-6590, or write to P.O. Box 7717, Itasca, IL 60143.

Greyhound (☎ 800-752-4841; Internet: www.greyhound.com) allows a physically challenged passenger to travel with a companion for a single fare. If you call 48 hours in advance, the bus line also arranges assistance along the route of your trip.

Maneuvering through theme parks

Most theme-park rides and shows, especially the newer ones, are designed to be accessible to a wide variety of guests. Likewise, theme parks often give people in wheelchairs (and their parties) preferential treatment so they can avoid long lines. If you need crutches or suffer from some other medical problem that may restrict your mobility in any way, you're probably better off renting a wheelchair; the amount of walking you'll need to do in the parks may wear you down in just a few hours.

Nationwide resources

Mobility International USA, P.O. Box 10767, Eugene, OR 97440 (☎ 541-343-1284; Internet: www.miusa.org), provides accessibility information as well as travel programs for those with disabilities. Membership ($35 a year) includes a quarterly newsletter called *Over the Rainbow.*

The **Society for Accessible Travel for the Handicapped** (SATH, 347 Fifth Ave., Suite 610, New York, NY 10016; ☎ 212-447-7284; Internet: www.trav.org/sath/) is another good information source. You can join for $45 or get information for a $5 charge.

If you're vision-impaired, contact the **American Foundation for the Blind,** 11 Penn Plaza, Suite 300, New York, NY 10001. Call ☎ 800-232-5463 for information on traveling with Seeing-Eye Dogs.

Each park's brochure tells you what to expect when you arrive. All the parks offer parking that is as close as possible to the entrance for people with disabilities. Tell the parking booth attendant about your special needs and he or she will direct you to the appropriate spot. You can rent wheelchairs at most major attractions, but you'll probably be most comfortable in your chair from home (and will save some money, too).

 Keep in mind, however, that wheelchairs wider than 24.5 inches may make navigating through some attractions difficult. And, crowds can make getting around tough for any guest.

The following sections give you information about services for the physically challenged at various parks in Orlando.

Walt Disney World

The Magic Mickster offers a *Guidebook for Guests with Disabilities* that details many services. Disney no longer mails them prior to visits, but you can pick one up at *Guest Services* near the front entrance to any of the four parks. You can also call ☎ 407-824-4321 or ☎ 407-827-5141 (TTY) for answers to any questions regarding special needs. For accessibility issues relating to the **WDW** resorts, call ☎ 407-939-7807 or ☎ 407-939-7670 (TTY). Some examples of Disney services include the following:

- ✔ Almost all **Disney** resort hotels have rooms for people with disabilities.

- ✔ You can find braille directories inside the **Magic Kingdom** in front of the *Main Street* train station and in a gazebo in front of the Crystal Palace restaurant. You can also pick up complimentary guided-tour audiocassette tapes and recorders (a $25 refundable deposit is required) at *Guest Services* to assist visually impaired guests.

✔ All parks maintain special parking areas for the physically challenged.

✔ You can acquire free personal translator units to amplify the audio at selected attractions at **WDW** parks (a $25 refundable deposit is required). Inquire about these units at the *Guest Services* desks inside each park.

✔ You can rent wheelchairs at all the parks.

✔ You can make special arrangements for sign-language interpretation at select live shows in the parks. You need to contact **WDW** at least 7 days in advance of your visit by calling ☎ **407-827-5141** (TTY) or ☎ **407-824-4321.**

Universal Orlando

If you're physically challenged, go to *Guest Services,* located just inside the main entrances of **Universal Studios Florida** and **Islands of Adventure,** to get a *Disabled Guest Guidebook,* a Telecommunications Device for the Deaf (TDD), or other special assistance. You can rent wheelchairs from the concourse area of the parking garage. **Universal** also provides audio descriptions on cassette for visually impaired guests and has sign-language guides and scripts for its shows (advance notice is required; call ☎ **407-363-8000** for details). Call as far in advance as possible and no later than 7 days before arriving for the guides only.

SeaWorld

SeaWorld provides *The SeaWorld Adventure Park Accessibility Guide* for guests with disabilities, although most of its attractions are accessible to people in wheelchairs. You can pick one up at *Guest Relations* inside the park. **SeaWorld** also provides a very basic braille guide for the visually impaired. Sign language interpretation for hearing-impaired people is offered, but arrangements must be made at least 7 days in advance by calling *Guest Services* at ☎ **800-327-2424** or 407-351-3600. You can also call these numbers for more information.

Advice for Gay and Lesbian Travelers

The popularity of Orlando as a destination for gay and lesbian travelers is apparent in the expansion and development of the Gay Day Celebration at **Disney World** into Gay Weekend. Gay- and lesbian-related events are also held at **Universal** and **SeaWorld.** These festivals are held the first weekend in June and draw tens of thousands of gay and lesbian travelers to central Florida. Find information at www.gayday.com or www.gaydays.com.

You also can get information about events for Gay Weekend as well as events that occur throughout the year from Gay, Lesbian & Bisexual Community Services of Central Florida, 934 N. Mills Ave., Orlando, FL 32803 (☎ **407-228-8272;** Internet: www.glbcc.org). Welcome packets usually include the latest issue of *Triangle,* dedicated to gay and lesbian issues, and a calendar of events pertaining to Florida's gay and lesbian community. Though not a tourist-specific packet, the welcome packet includes information and ads for the area's clubs. *Watermark* is another gay-friendly publication that you can find in many Central Florida bookstores (☎ **407-481-224;** Internet: www.watermarkonline.com).

Both the entertainment industry and theme parks have helped build a strong gay and lesbian community in Orlando. Same-sex dancing is acceptable at most clubs at **WDW's Pleasure Island,** especially the large and very popular *Mannequins Dance Club.* Many of **Universal's CityWalk** establishments are similarly gender blind.

If you're interested in sampling some of the other local gay and lesbian hot spots, check out the following places:

- ✔ **The Club at Firestone,** 578 N. Orange Ave. (at Concord Street, in a converted garage that still bears the Firestone sign); ☎ **407-872-0066;** Internet: www.clubatfirestone.com. Go-go boys dance on lifts converted into raised platforms, and a diverse group boogies on the large concrete floor. The Club at Firestone is a serious dance club, with dark lighting, cavernous rooms, and a high-energy atmosphere, which also sometimes features world-renowned DJs. The upper floors, however, were transformed into a separate, more low-key martini bar — The Glass Chamber. Completely enclosed in glass, you can look at the dance floor below while sipping your drink shaken, not stirred. It's open Monday through Sunday, from 9 p.m. to 3 a.m. The cover charge varies from $6–$10. Limited lot parking is available for $3–$5.

- ✔ **Parliament House,** 410 N. Orange Blossom Trail (just west of downtown); ☎ **407-425-7571;** Internet: www.parliamenthouse.com. Attached to a hotel of the same name, this is one of Orlando's wilder, and most popular, gay spots. Not a fancy place, the Parliament House shows the wear and tear of years of hard partying. At the Parliament House, you can drink, dance, and watch shows that include female impersonators and male revues. The dance floor is relatively large, but it gets small quickly as the DJs start spinning and the crowd swells. The Parliament House has five bars. It opens daily at 9 p.m. (there's no specific closing time), except on Sunday, when it opens at 3 p.m. Cover is $5–$8 Friday and Saturday; $3 on Sunday.

- ✔ **Southern Nights,** 375 S. Bumby Avenue (between Anderson Street and Colonial Drive); ☎ **407-898-0424.** Southern Nights has theme nights that pack in women on Saturdays and men on Sundays. Friday nights feature three female-impersonator shows. This club doesn't have a cover and readers of an alternative weekly newspaper voted it "best gay bar in Orlando." It's open daily, but its hours of operation are constantly changing. Call before you go.

Part II
Ironing Out the Details

The 5th Wave   By Rich Tennant

Oh quit complaining. The tickets were a lot less expensive than some of the other attractions, and admit it — when was the last time you saw a really good figure sliding exhibition on an indoor linoleum rink with kitchen dinette obstacles?

In this part . . .

Okay, it's nitty-gritty time. In this section, we chat a little about travel agents, package tours, and how you can get the best airfare. We also help you search for a place to rest your bones: We explore central Florida's neighborhoods, zero in on a room that's right for you, book it, and send you packing.

Chapter 5

Planes, Trains, and Automobiles: Getting to Orlando

· ·

In This Chapter

▶ Using a travel agent — or not

▶ Checking out package tours: the pros, the cons, and the providers

▶ Getting the best airfares

▶ Arriving in Orlando on land

· ·

Getting to your destination *isn't* always half the fun of your trip. But your journey doesn't have to be an expensive hassle or require a master's degree in planning either. In this chapter, we eliminate the travel double-talk, shed the useless options, and make sure you have a fun and easy time planning your getaway.

Acquiring a Travel Agent

The first task you need to complete after you decide where you want to go on vacation is deciding whether you want to book your vacation yourself or use a hired gun. Many Internet-savvy travelers choose to research and book airfares and hotel accommodations online, but if you prefer discussing your options with an expert, working with a travel agent is your best bet.

Finding a good travel agent is hard to do, but they prove invaluable once you find the right one. The best way to find a travel agent is word of mouth. Ask a friend who travels frequently if he or she has a favorite.

All travel agents can find bargain rental-car rates, accommodations, or airfares. Good travel agents stop you from choosing the wrong deal, even if it is cheap. The best travel agents can help you with all aspects of your vacation: arranging decent rental rates, budgeting your time, booking better hotels with comparable prices, finding cheap flights that don't require five connections, and recommending restaurants.

Travel agents work on commission, which is good news and bad news. The good news: You don't have to pay the commission — the airlines, resorts, and tour operators take care of payment. The bad news: Unscrupulous agents will try to persuade you to book vacations that earn them the most commission while at the same time taking the least amount of their time. Unfortunately, the fact that travel agents are paid commission leads to ugly news, too.

Over the past few years, many airlines and some resorts have started eliminating or limiting travel-agent commissions. Therefore, they don't bother to book these services unless you specifically request them. In fact, some travel analysts predict that if more players in the travel industry follow suit, agents may start charging customers for their services. When and if that day arrives — and even now — consider using reservation agents associated with airline frequent-flier clubs. However, make sure you receive a good deal. To do so, call the airlines two or three times (most have toll-free numbers), get a 24-hour confirmation number for any rate that differs from previous quotes, go with the best rate, and cancel the others.

If you want to grade a travel agent, do a little homework. Flip through our sections on accommodations in this book (see Chapter 8) and choose a few that appeal to you. If you have access to the Internet, check prices on the Web (see "Getting the Best Deals on Airfare — Plane and Simple," later in this chapter). You can then take your notes and ask a travel agent to make the arrangements for you. Because they have access to resources better than the most complete travel Web site, travel agents should be able to offer you a price that's better than one you can get yourself. Likewise, travel agents can issue your tickets or vouchers on the spot; if they can't get your No. 1 hotel, they can recommend an alternative.

Travel agents do receive a commission when it comes to **Disney** vacations, and they're usually a better source of information than Disney receptionists, who will answer your questions but, in most cases, won't volunteer money-saving tips. Shop around among the airlines, too (see the Appendix in the back of this book for the toll-free numbers and URLs of the major airlines). Delta is Disney's official airline and a big player in its packages.

After you've digested the information on package tours in the next section, you can ask your travel agent to book the same package (at no added cost to you), plus add-ons such as airport transfers and side trips. Doing so makes life much easier — and cheaper — for you.

Discovering the Ins and Outs of All-in-One Packages

Package tours give you the opportunity to buy airfare, accommodations, and add-ons (if you choose) at the same time. We discuss the ins and outs of package deals in the following sections.

Why buy a package tour?

For popular destinations such as **Walt Disney World,** packages can often help save you money — especially packages that roll your hotel, airfare, and round-trip airport transportation into one mix.

Packages can save you money because they're sold in bulk to tour operators, who resell them to the public. The system resembles shopping at one of those membership discount clubs, except the tour operator is the person who buys 1,000 options (hotel rooms, airline tickets, and so on) in bulk and resells them 10 at a time for a cost that undercuts what you'd normally pay.

Package tours vary as much as salad dressing flavors. Some packages offer flights on scheduled airlines, whereas others book charters. Some offer lower prices rather than a better class of hotel. Likewise, with some packages, you can choose between independent and escorted vacations, or add an escorted side trip to your itinerary. However, with some packages, your choice of accommodations and travel days may be limited.

If you choose to buy a package, think strongly about purchasing travel insurance, especially if the tour operator asks you to pay up front. But don't buy insurance from the tour operator! If they don't fulfill their obligation to provide you with the vacation you've paid for, you have no reason to think they'll fulfill their insurance obligations either. Obtain travel insurance through an independent agency. See Chapter 9 for more information on buying travel insurance.

Where can I find travel packages?

If you've decided that you want to give package tours a try, your next course of action is to find the travel package that fits your needs. To find packages, check the ads in the back of national magazines such as *Travel & Leisure* and *Condé Nast Traveler,* or those magazines that include travel sections, such as *Elegant Bride.* You can also check the travel section of your Sunday newspaper, but your best bets are the choices we outline in this section.

 The Orlando market is ultra competitive, so don't overlook a package because it has features you won't use. You may find you can fly from New York to Orlando and pick up your rental car, while discarding the four hotel nights (to stay with relatives or friends), yet still pay less than if you booked your airfare and rental car separately.

Theme park offerings

Disney offers a dizzying array of packages that include airfare, accommodations on or off Disney property, theme-park passes, a rental car, meals, and a Disney cruise. You can call ☎ **800-828-0228** or 407-828-8101 to find out more information about Disney packages (see Chapter 7).

Disney offers seasonal packages, as well as specially themed vacations, such as golf, honeymoons, spa makeovers, and so on.

Here are some of the positive aspects of booking a Disney package tour:

- ✔ Using **Disney** as your source for an all-Disney vacation is hard to beat, especially if you receive other discounts, such as those associated with the Disney Club card (see Chapter 3). However, if you want to see more of Orlando than **Walt Disney World** (and most people do), you should compare the offerings of a Disney agent with those of a regular travel agent. A motivated travel agent can put together a package of Disney and non-Disney accommodations and attractions for less than the amount Disney charges. Of course, given Mickey's knack for emptying wallets, finding something cheaper is often a no-brainer.

- ✔ Nobody knows the Diz better than its staffers.

- ✔ Disney reps can offer accommodations in all price ranges ($77 and up).

However, be aware of the following drawbacks to Disney package deals:

- ✔ Resort guests receive the same perks, whether you buy your Disney package from **Disney** or someone else.

- ✔ You have to prod Disney reservation agents for details. If you don't ask about them to begin with, the agents usually overlook volunteering suggestions, such as the possibility that you can save money if you start your **Disney** vacation a day earlier or later.

- ✔ Some **WDW** package perks aren't worth a nickel. For example, if they say you get your picture taken with Mickey as part of the deal, expect that you can find a better deal elsewhere and pay for your own photo.

For detailed information on Disney packages, write to **Walt Disney World,** Box 10000, Lake Buena Vista, FL 32830-1000, call ☎ **800-828-0228** or 407-828-8101, or go online to www.disneyworld.com to order a *Walt Disney World Vacations* brochure or video. You'll find a dizzying menu of options from which to choose.

Although not on the same scale as Disney, the packages at **Universal Orlando** have improved greatly since the addition of the **Islands of Adventure** park (see Chapter 24), the **CityWalk** food-and-club district (see Chapters 14 and 29), and the **Portofino Bay** and **Hard Rock hotels** (see Chapter 8). Your package choices include resort stays, VIP access to the parks and rides, and discounts to other non-Disney attractions. **Universal** also offers packages with Carnival Cruise Line out of Port Canaveral, and some include travel and transportation. Contact **Universal Studios Vacations** at ☎ **888-322-5537** or 407-224-7000, or surf online to www.usevacations.com.

SeaWorld also offers two- and three-night packages that include rooms at a handful of Orlando hotels (including the **Renaissance Orlando,** see Chapter 8), car rental, tickets to SeaWorld (see Chapter 25), and in some cases, other theme parks. You can get information at ☎ **800-423-8368**, or online at www.seaworld.com.

Airline packages

You can also tap airlines as a good resource for packages, as well as a reason to shop outside **WDW** parks. Many airlines package their flights with lodging and other accommodations. And, when you pick an airline, you can choose one that offers frequent service to your hometown and allows you to accumulate frequent-flyer miles.

Delta Dream Vacations, the big fish in the pond, is the official **Disney** airline. It offers selections that can include round-trip airfare, lodging (including tax and baggage tips), a rental car with unlimited mileage or round-trip transfers from the airport, admission to some or all Disney parks for the length of your visit, accommodations, and so on.

Cutting ticket costs by utilizing consolidators

Consolidators, also known as bucket shops, can be a good place to find low fares. Consolidators buy seats in bulk and sell them to the public at prices below the airlines' discounted rates. Their small, boxed ads usually run in the Sunday travel sections of major newspapers, at the bottom of the page. Before you pay, however, ask for a confirmation number from the consolidator, then call the airline to confirm your seat. Be prepared to book your ticket with a different consolidator — there are many to choose from — if the airline can't confirm your reservation.

Also, be aware that bucket-shop tickets are usually nonrefundable or rigged with stiff cancellation penalties, often as high as 50 to 75 percent of the ticket price. Among consolidators, **Council Travel** (☎ 800-226-8624; Internet: www.counciltravel.com) and **STA Travel** (☎ 800-781-4040; Internet: www.statravel.com) cater especially to young travelers, but people of all ages can take advantage of their bargain-basement prices. **Travel Bargains** (☎ 800-247-3273; Internet: www.1800airfare.com), formerly owned by TWA, offers deep discounts on many other airlines with a four-day advance purchase. Other reliable consolidators include **1-800-FLY-CHEAP** (☎ 800-359-2432; Internet: www.1800flycheap.com); **Cheap Tickets** (☎ 888-922-8849; Internet: www.cheaptickets); **TFI Tours International** (☎ 800-745-8000 or 212-736-1140), which serves as a clearinghouse for unused seats; or rebators, such as **Travel Avenue** (☎ 800-333-3335 or 312-876-1116) and the **Smart Traveler** (☎ 800-448-3338 or 305-448-3338), which rebate part of their commissions to you.

Prices for Delta Dream Vacations usually vary depending on the package, property, departure city, and season. Call ☎ **800-872-7786,** or visit online at www.deltavacations.com/disney.html.

Continental Airlines Vacations offers several packages that include airfare, car rental, and hotel stays at numerous central Florida hotels and **WDW** resorts. You can apply the airline's frequent-flyer miles to some packages and you can make reservations with or without air service. Call ☎ **800-525-0280** for general information, or check out www. coolvacations.com online.

For other airline-package possibilities, see the phone numbers and Web sites for the various airlines listed in the Appendix in the back of this book.

Other places to find packages

Beside airline and theme park package offerings, you can also find vacation packages elsewhere. One option is American Express, the official credit card of **Walt Disney World. American Express Vacations** (☎ **800-241-1700;** Internet: http://travel.americanexpress.com/travel/personal) allows card holders to book reservations at WDW resorts while throwing in a variety of perks, including discounts on merchandise, dinner shows, and certain Disney tours.

Other package specialists include:

- ✔ **SunStyle** (☎ **888-786-7895;** Internet: www.sunstyle.com) is a wholesale operator that offers a variety of packages targeting **Disney, Universal Orlando, SeaWorld,** and hotels located near those parks. You can buy tickets and book airfare and car rentals through this agency.

- ✔ **Touraine Travel** (☎ **800-967-5583;** Internet: www.tourainetravel. com) offers a wide variety of tour packages to **Disney** and Disney properties, **Universal Orlando, SeaWorld,** and the **Disney Cruise Line.**

- ✔ If you're a linkster, you have several packagers from which to choose. **Golf Getaways** (☎ **800-800-4028;** Internet: www. golfgetaways.com), **Golfpac Vacations** (☎ **800-327-0878;** Internet: www.golfpacinc.com), and **Golf.Com** (Internet: www.golf.com) offer a slate of play-and-stay packages — from the most basic to the extraordinarily comprehensive.

The comfort zone

Flying is fun for some folks, but if you're like us, you consider flying a necessary evil for getting to the real party. Some airlines have been adding an inch or so of legroom, but tourist class remains cramped, the cabin temperature is often too hot or too cold, and the air is dry enough to suck the spit out of a Saint Bernard. However, here are a few things you can do — some while you book your flight — to make your trip more tolerable.

✔ **Bulkhead seats** (the front row of each cabin compartment) have a little more legroom than normal plane seats. However, bulkhead seats also have some drawbacks. For example, bulkhead seats don't provide you with a place to put your carry-on luggage, except in the overhead bin, because there's not a seat in front of you. Likewise, you may find this isn't the best place to see an in-flight movie.

✔ **Emergency-exit row seats** also offer extra room. Airlines usually assign these seats at the airport on a first-come, first-serve basis, so ask when you check in whether you can sit in one of these rows. Remember though, that in the unlikely event of an emergency, you're expected to open the emergency-exit door and help direct traffic. This, of course, doesn't count in-air emergencies. You'll be jeered or even wrestled to the ground by fellow passengers if you try to open the emergency door in mid-flight.

✔ **Wear comfortable clothes.** Be sure to dress in layers, because "climate con-trolled" aircraft cabins vary greatly in temperature and comfort levels. You won't regret taking a sweater or jacket that you can put on or take off as your onboard temperature dictates.

✔ **Bring some toiletries aboard on long flights.** Cabins are notoriously dry places. If you don't want to land in Orlando with the complexion of King Tut, take a travel-size bottle of moisturizer or lotion to refresh your face and hands at the end of your flight. If you're taking an overnight flight (the red-eye), don't forget to pack a toothbrush to combat your breath upon arrival.

Although some toiletries are helpful on airplane trips, some are dangerous. *Never* bring an unsealed container of nail polish remover into an airline cabin, because the cabin pressure causes the remover to evaporate and damage your luggage; the resulting smell won't help you gain any friends on your flight either. Likewise, if you wear contact lenses, wear your glasses for the flight, or at least bring some eye drops. Your don't want to spend your hard-earned cash to have your "soft" lenses surgically removed at an Orlando hospital.

✔ **Jet lag** usually isn't a problem for flights within the United States, but some people coming from the West Coast are affected by the three-hour time change. The best way to combat this time warp is to acclimate yourself to local time as quickly as possible. Stay up as long as you can the first day, and then try to wake up at a normal time the second day. Likewise, drink plenty of water during your first few days in town, as well as on the plane, to avoid dehydration.

✔ **If you're flying with kids,** don't forget chewing gum for ear-pressure problems (adults with sinus problems should chew as well), some toys to keep your angels entertained, extra bottles or pacifiers, and diapers. Even if your kids aren't coming with you, keep in mind that many people on Orlando flights are bringing their little darlings. Inbound, kids are often swinging from overhead compartments, excited about their journey to see Mickey Mouse. Outbound, they can fill all the luggage racks with souvenirs and stuffed toys before you can stow your briefcase.

Getting the Best Deals on Airfare — Plane and Simple

Buying airfare is a lesson in capitalism. Rarely do you pay the same fare for your ticket as the person sitting next to you on the plane. Airline ticket prices are based on the market — that means you — which translates into a roll of the dice, unless you know how to shop.

Business travelers and others who require flexibility usually pay the full fare price. However, if you can book your flight well in advance, don't mind staying over a Saturday night, or are willing to travel on a Tuesday, Wednesday, or Thursday, you will usually pay a fraction of the full fare price. Likewise, if you can fly on only a few days' notice, you can enjoy the benefits of cheaper airfare. On most flights, even the shortest hops, full-price fare is close to $1,000 or more, but an advance-purchase ticket, sometimes purchased as few as 7 or 14 days before the trip, can cut your ticket cost to $200 to $300. Obviously, planning ahead pays.

Periodically, airlines lower prices on their most popular routes. Although these sale-price fares have date-of-travel restrictions and advance-purchase requirements, you can't beat buying a ticket for (usually) no more than $400 for a cross-country flight. To take advantage of these airline sales, watch for ads in your local newspaper and on TV and call the airlines or check out their Web sites (see the Appendix for Web addresses and phone numbers). Keep in mind, however, that airline sales often take place during low-travel-volume seasons. In fact, finding an airline sale around the holidays or around the peak summer vacation months of July and August is rare. On the other hand, November, December, and January (excluding holidays) often bring discounted and promotional fares, with savings of 50 percent or more.

Here are some tips for discovering the best values on airfare to Orlando:

✔ Ask the airlines for their lowest fares and inquire about discounts for booking in advance or at the last minute. Decide when you want to go before you call, because many of the best deals are nonrefundable. Also, call more than once. Yes, being on hold that long is frustrating, but you'll probably get different rates each time, and one may be a bonanza.

✔ The more flexible you are about your travel dates and length of stay, the more money you're likely to save. Flying at off times (at night, for instance) usually saves you money.

✔ Visit a large travel agency to find out about all your available options. Sometimes a good agent knows about fares you won't find on your own. Internet providers offer travel sections that can provide pricing comparisons.

✔ Several so-called no-frills airlines — low fares but no meals or other amenities — fly to Florida. The biggest is Southwest Airlines (☎ **800-435-9792**; Internet: www.iflyswa.com), which has flights from many U.S. cities to Orlando. A recent start-up that has received rave reviews is JetBlue Airways (☎ **800-538-2583**; Internet: www.jetblue.com), a low-cost carrier that operates mostly on the Eastern Seaboard, but does offer a number of routes from the West Coast. Unlike the other airlines in this category, JetBlue offers a number of amenities, including 24-channel satellite TV access, to all of its passengers.

✔ Consider joining a travel club, such as Moment's Notice (☎ **718-234-6295**) or Sears Discount Travel Club (☎ **800-433-9383** for information or 800-255-1487 to join). They supply unsold tickets to their members at discounted prices. (You pay an annual fee to receive the club's hot line number.) Of course, your choices are limited to what's available, so you have to be flexible. Keep in mind, however, that you may not have to join these clubs to get such deals, because some airlines now unload unsold seats directly through their Web sites.

Arriving in Orlando

If you're flying to Orlando, the best place to land is Orlando International Airport (☎ **407-825-2001**; Internet: http://fcn.state.fl.us/goaa/index.htm), unless a rental car and 90 minutes of interstate driving from Tampa is in your game plan). The Orlando airport offers direct or nonstop service from 70 U.S. and 25 international cities. Forty scheduled airlines and as many charters feed 30 million people through its gates annually.

Limit your carry-on luggage

Because lost-luggage rates have reached an all-time high, consumers bring their possessions on board to try to divert disaster. But planes are more crowded than ever, and overhead compartment space is at a premium. Some domestic airlines have started cracking down, limiting you to a single carry-on for crowded flights and imposing size restrictions to the bags that you bring on board. The dimensions vary, but the strictest airlines say carry-ons must measure no more than 22 x 14 x 9 inches, including wheels and handles, and weigh no more than 40 pounds.

Many airports are already furnished with x-ray machines that literally block any carry-on bigger than the posted size restriction. These measures may sound drastic, but keep in mind that many of these regulations are enforced only at the discretion of the gate attendants. If you plan to bring more than one bag aboard a crowded flight, make sure that your medications, documents, and valuables are consolidated in one bag in case you're forced to check the second bag.

Orlando International Airport connects to highways, Interstate 4, and toll roads that get you (whether you're driving or being driven) into the heat of battle within 30 or 40 minutes.

Finding great deals online

On the Internet, you can find great deals not only on airfare, but also on hotels and car rentals. Among the leading travel sites are: **Arthur Frommer's Budget Travel Online** (www.frommers.com); **Lowestfare** (www.lowestfare.com); **Microsoft Expedia** (www.expedia.com); **Priceline** (www.priceline.com); **Travelocity** (www.travelocity.com); and **Smarter Living** (www.smarterliving.com).

Each Web site has its own little quirks, but all provide variations of the same service. Simply enter the dates that you want to fly and the cities that you want to visit, and the computer searches for the lowest fares. Several other features are standard at these sites as well, including the ability to check flights at different times or dates in hopes of finding a cheaper fare; e-mail alerts when fares drop on a route that you've specified; and a database of last-minute deals that advertises super-cheap vacation packages or airfares for those who can get away at a moment's notice.

The latest buzz in the online travel world is about **Orbitz** (www.orbitz.com), a site launched by United, Delta, Northwest, American, and Continental airlines. It shows all possible fares for your desired trip, offering fares lower than those available through travel agents. (Stay tuned: At press time, travel-agency associations were waging an antitrust battle against this site.)

Qixo (www.qixo.com) is another powerful search engine that allows you to search for flights and hotel rooms on 20 other travel-planning sites (such as Travelocity) at once. Qixo sorts results by price, after which you can book your travel directly through the site.

Using Other Methods to Arrive in Orlando

Can't stand to fly? Can't afford the extra expense? You're not alone. Each year, many people drive a car or hop a train to get to Orlando. In this section, we explore the details of taking to the open road or riding the rails.

Driving a car to Orlando

Driving to Orlando is a less expensive and potentially more scenic option, unless the distance is so great that making the road trip eats up too much of your vacation.

Here's how far several cities are from Orlando: Atlanta, 436 miles; Boston, 1,312 miles; Chicago, 1,120 miles; Cleveland, 1,009 miles; Dallas, 1,170 miles; Detroit, 1,114 miles; New York, 1,088 miles; and Toronto, 1,282 miles.

Need directions? No problem.

- ✔ **From Atlanta:** Take I-75 South to the Florida Turnpike to I-4 West.

- ✔ **From Boston and New York:** Yake I-95 South to I-4 West.

- ✔ **From Chicago:** Take I-65 South to Nashville and then I-24 South to I-75 South to the Florida Turnpike to I-4 West.

- ✔ **From Cleveland:** Take I-77 South to Columbia, S.C., then I-26 East to I-95 South to I-4 West.

- ✔ **From Dallas:** Take I-20 East to I-49 South, to I-10 East, to I-75 South, to the Florida Turnpike, to I-4 West.

- ✔ **From Detroit:** Take I-75 South to the Florida Turnpike to I-4 West.

- ✔ **From Toronto:** Take Canadian Route 401 South to Queen Elizabeth Way South to I-90 (New York State Thruway) East to I-87 (New York State Thruway) South to I-95 over the George Washington Bridge, and continue south on I-95 to I-4 West.

AAA (☎ **800-222-4357;** Internet: www.aaa.com) and some other automobile clubs offer free maps and optimum driving directions to their members.

Arriving by train

Amtrak trains (☎ **800-872-7245;** Internet: www.amtrak.com) pull into two central stations: 1400 Sligh Blvd. in downtown Orlando (about 23 miles from **Walt Disney World**), and 111 Dakin Ave. in Kissimmee (about 15 miles from **Walt Disney World**). Amtrak's Auto Train allows you to bring along your car to Florida without having to drive it all the way. The service begins in Lorton, Va. — about a four-hour drive from New York, two hours from Philadelphia — and ends at Sanford, Fla., about 23 miles northeast of Orlando. The Auto Train departs Lorton and Sanford daily at 4:00 p.m., arriving at the other end of the line the next day at 8:30 a.m. Fares for the Auto Train vary according to season and schedule, but the cheapest rate for a car (including one passenger) is $250. Additional passengers pay $118 for a one-way fare.

As with airfares, you can sometimes get discounts if you book train rides far in advance. But you may find some restrictions on travel dates for discounted train fares, mostly around the very busy holiday periods. Amtrak offers money-saving packages, including accommodations (some at **WDW** resorts), car rentals, tours, and so on. For package information, call ☎ **800-321-8684.**

Chapter 6

Finding the Hotel That's Right for You

● ●

In This Chapter

▶ Finding a hotel room that meets your needs

▶ Choosing the neighborhood in which you want to stay

▶ Selecting a hotel that falls in your price range

● ●

*W*here you plant yourself during your vacation helps determine many things about your trip, including your itineraries, how much money you spend, and whether you need to rent a car.

However, you can take one thing to the bank: Unlike the seedier or less competitive areas of Florida, almost every hotel in Orlando has been built or renovated in the past 20 years, so you can expect reasonably modern trimmings. (Hotel appliances won't shock you, and you don't need rabbit ears to see what's on the tube.) Most places in Orlando also try to make kids feel as if they're Mickey's favorite relatives. Therefore, the factors that decide where you rest your head for the night boil down to location and price. Although you'll pay more for the best locations, you may find these hotels worth the convenience. The closer your hotel is to the things you want to do and see, the less time you waste getting to your destination.

In this chapter — and in Chapters 7 and 8 — we help you separate the tacky from the tasteful Orlando accommodations, so sharpen your pencil and read on.

Deciding Where to Stay

Deciding where to stay in Orlando isn't easy, because rooms come in many different flavors: hotels, motels, bed and breakfasts, and so on. Orlando's more than 111,000 rooms make choosing a room seem a bit overwhelming. The following section gives you a profile of the lodging players.

Evaluating chain hotels versus motels

Galactic chains such as **Holiday Inn, Sheraton, Marriott, Hyatt,** and others are a bit like chain restaurants — what you get at one is a lot like what you get at another (the exception being upscale models at the higher end of the **Marriott** and **Hyatt** chains). (See the Appendix at the back of this guide for a list of the major hotel chains' toll-free numbers.)

Independent inns often target select varieties of travelers, such as those traveling with kids, travelers on a budget, or couples who visit friends annually.

Both hotels and motels offer service and amenities. Hotels tend to include more amenities, offer higher-priced rooms, and, in a few cases, feel snobbier than motels, (though that attitude can be a fatal flaw in the competitive Orlando market, where you'll likely see more Goofy hats than Gucci ones). Motels often have a chain or mom-and-pop façade, come in one- to three-story models, include free parking, and some emit a friendly atmosphere that's likely to remind you of home. Those on the lower end of the price scale don't offer many doodads other than soap, towels, and — if you're lucky — coffeemakers, but their rates don't require that you take out a second mortgage, either. And many motels are quite comfortable if you're not spending a lot of time in the room.

Seeking solace from the kids

Orlando swarms with kids, but, as the top honeymoon destination in the United States, plenty of adults visit here as well. Avoiding children for the length of your visit is next to impossible, but if you're childfree and don't relish the prospect of screaming kids in the room next door, you can improve the odds in your favor. The bad news is that the quiet will cost you. As a general rule — **Disney** properties not included — the more expensive a hotel is, the less likely you are to run into children.

Hotels that cater to business travelers, especially those in downtown Orlando, tend to have fewer children as guests, although they still cater to the family market. Most Orlando B&Bs do not allow children under 16 to stay as guests, and some feature luxurious rooms that rival those in the big resorts. A few moderately priced hotels go the distance to keep adults happy (we single these out in Chapter 8), but you won't find any in the budget category.

Finding the Perfect Location

Disney maintains the corner on the Orlando hotel market, boasting a 90 percent occupancy rate (compared to 75 percent elsewhere in town) in its 17 Disney-owned-and-operated resorts (with more to come over the next few years) and nine official hotels located on **WDW** property. A lot of folks stay at Disney, especially if they're toting children to the parks. The other four popular areas for guests are Lake Buena Vista, International Drive, and to a lesser degree, Kissimmee, and downtown Orlando. (See Chapter 10 for specifics about down-town neighborhoods.)

Choosing where to stay in Disney World

Where you stay in the Land of the Mouse will depend on which parks you want to visit and what your budget allows. This section includes some options that should help you whittle your choices.

Most of Disney's pricier accommodations — the **Grand Floridian Resort & Spa, Polynesian Resort, Contemporary Resort,** and **Wilderness Lodge** — are situated on the doorstep of the **Magic Kingdom.** The first three offer the advantage of being on Disney's monorail system, so you can literally park your keister a subway stop from the parks.

Many of the more moderately priced resorts are near **Disney West Side, Pleasure Island, Downtown Disney Marketplace,** and **Typhoon Lagoon.** These resorts include **Port Orleans** and **Old Key West.** The official Disney hotels, including the **Wyndham Palace Resort & Spa, Double-tree Guest Suites,** and **Courtyard by Marriott,** are in the same area, but they're more expensive.

Disney's BoardWalk, Caribbean Beach Resort, and **Yacht and Beach Club Resort** are closest to **Epcot** and **Disney–MGM Studios,** as are the **Walt Disney World Swan and Dolphin.** (In this group of hotels, the **Caribbean** is in the mid-price range, while the others are more expensive.)

The relatively low-priced **All-Star** (with rooms from $77) and **Coronado Springs** resorts are near **Animal Kingdom** and **Blizzard Beach.** However, they're a considerable hike from everything else at **Walt Disney World.**

The perks of staying with Mickey

The **Disney** resorts are a wonderland of creativity, from larger-than-life cowboy boots decorating stairwells and shrubs shaped like dancing hippos to buildings topped with giant birds and fish. Staying on Disney property has benefits and drawbacks.

The benefits of lodging in Mickey's backyard include

- ✔ Unlimited free transportation via the Disney Transportation System's buses, monorails, ferries, and water taxis to and from the four theme parks, resorts, and smaller attractions.

✔ Surprise Mornings, where selected parks open early for resort guests on rotating days.

✔ Free parking inside theme park lots (other visitors pay $6 a day).

✔ Reduced-price children's menus in most restaurants.

✔ A *Guest Services* desk where you can buy tickets to all **WDW** theme parks and attractions to avoid standing in the park lines.

✔ As far as proximity is concerned, you can't get much closer to ground zero.

Drawbacks of staying with the Mouse include

✔ The Walt Disney World Transportation System can be slow.

✔ Resort rates are about 30 percent higher than prices at comparable hotels and motels located farther from the parks.

✔ You may wind up a prisoner of **Disney**'s other stiff pricing schemes for restaurants, trinkets, and so on.

✔ If you don't spend a little time away from the Wizard of Diz, you'll miss the "real" Florida.

✔ Mickey, Mickey, MICKEY . . . *ack!* Living in the Disney Dimension can get old after a few days.

Deciding where to stay in Lake Buena Vista

The Lake Buena Vista area borders **Walt Disney World** from the northeast to the southeast along Highway 535. Hotel Plaza Boulevard in Lake Buena Vista is home to many of the nine official Disney hotels — those that are on Disney property but not owned by Mickey. These hotels are all situated near **Downtown Disney Marketplace, Disney West Side, Pleasure Island,** and **Typhoon Lagoon.** Each has free shuttle service to **WDW** theme parks and some, but not all, of the perks of staying with Mickey. Hotels in the official Disney category have larger rooms, more amenities, and fall in the moderate to expensive range.

Lake Buena Vista also includes major chains like **Hyatt, Best Western,** and **Comfort Inns.** The **Hyatt Regency Grand Cypress Resort** and **Villas of Grand Cypress** are outstanding resorts, with large rooms, patios or balconies, and a ton of amenities, including golf courses, five-star restaurants, and an equestrian center, but they're also on the high end of the price chain. The **Holiday Inn Sunspree,** which caters to families — they even have Kidsuites — is closer to the middle of the price pack (see the index, later in this chapter, for more specific pricing information).

Orlando Hotel Neighborhoods

The perks to staying in the Lake Buena Vista area include

- This area is close to **WDW** but not quite as expensive.
- There are a number of non-Disney restaurants that offer savings but still feature bargain kids' meals.
- If you choose an official property, you receive free transportation to **Disney.**

Drawbacks include

- You don't get all of the perks of staying with Mickey.
- Though a little cheaper than **Disney,** the hotels and motels in Lake Buena Vista are still high.

Determining where to stay in the International Drive area

The hotels and resorts on International Drive (I-Drive) are seven to ten miles north of the Walt Disney World parks (via I-4) and one to three miles from **Universal Orlando** and **SeaWorld.** The northern end of I-Drive is congested and hard to navigate during most seasons and is also covered wall to wall in T-shirt and jeans shops, burger barns, and second- or third-tier attractions. On the other hand, the central and southern portions are more relaxed and less cramped. I-Drive hotels range from low to high priced. This area includes plenty of restaurants (see Chapter 14), shopping (see Chapter 27), and entertainment options (see Chapters 28 and 29).

Advantages to lodging on International Drive include

✔ The area offers something in everyone's price range.

✔ You can stay on International Drive without renting a car if your hotel offers shuttles to the parks that interest you (and most of them do).

Drawbacks include

✔ The area is very congested, and big events at the convention center cause congestion, making it even harder to see the sites.

✔ The area is close to **Universal** and **SeaWorld,** but if you're mainly interested in **Disney,** you're seven to ten miles from the heart of the action.

✔ If you decide not to rent a car and your hotel's shuttle service isn't free, prepare to pay up to get to the parks.

✔ Crooks love working this area.

Figuring out where to stay in the Kissimmee–St. Cloud Area

Kissimmee is east of **Walt Disney World.** The town straddles U.S. 192/Irlo Bronson Memorial Highway and is very family and budget friendly. It has a branch of just about every chain restaurant and fast-food outlet known to civilization. If you're traveling with kids and looking for something special, we suggest the **Holiday Inn Nikki Bird Resort,** which offers specially designed Kidsuites — a space for your little ones that's within your room. Other lodging in Kissimmee includes several **Best Westerns, Comfort Inns,** and **Days Inns.** Rates for these chains run from $50 to $150.

Good reasons to stay in the Kissimmee area include

- ✔ Kissimmee is close to **Disney,** and many of its motels will shuttle you there for a fee.
- ✔ Portions of it have a small-town feel.
- ✔ You can eat and sleep in Kissimmee without blowing your entire bankroll.

Drawbacks include

- ✔ Small-town in the case of Kissimmee sometimes means cow town.
- ✔ Many of the storefronts and some of the motels are a little on the tacky side.
- ✔ Many motels are no-frills.

Staying in downtown O-town

The grande dame of downtown Orlando, the **Church Street Station** entertainment district recently closed, but the area still has some excellent restaurants, shops, and clubs. The quaint **Antique Row** is nearby. Hotels in this area are, on average, moderately priced, catering mostly to business travelers. (See the Index in Chapter 8 for additional pricing information on Orlando's best hotels grouped according to location.)

The upside to staying downtown includes:

- ✔ Unlike some downtowns, Orlando offers loads of entertainment, and it's close to non-glitter attractions, such as museums and sports venues.
- ✔ Shopping in Orlando is far less touristy than in the theme parks.
- ✔ Orlando has a broad selection of cuisine from which to choose.

Drawbacks include

- ✔ Limited hotel choices.
- ✔ You're far from **Universal** and **SeaWorld,** even farther from **Disney,** and the traffic is usually wicked on the way to the parks.
- ✔ A rental car is probably a necessity.

Choosing a Hotel That's Right on the Money

Every hotel, motel, and bed and breakfast listing in Chapter 8 has a $ symbol to help you find your price window. The $ symbols are based on *rack rates* (non-discounted rates) and they usually reflect the upper end of a hotel's high-low rates. Unfortunately, room prices are subject to change without notice (and they often do), so the rates that we quote in this book may change by the time you call the hotel for reservations. Don't be surprised if the rate the hotel offers is lower than the rack rates listed in this book. Likewise, don't be too alarmed if the price has crept up a little.

Here's your scorecard:

- ✔ **$ ($50–$100):** Accommodations at this level generally include basic trimmings and limited space. They also tend to lean toward the no-frills side. Those at the higher end may offer amenities such as hair dryers, coffeemakers, cable TV, a midsize pool, a kids' play area, and Continental breakfast. If they're multistory, they also usually have an elevator.

- ✔ **$$ ($100–$200):** Lodgings in this price range will probably offer you a choice of king-size or double beds, a full range of amenities (coffeemakers, hair dryer, two TVs in the two-room models, multi-line phones and possibly a modem line, VCRs, free daily newspaper), designer shampoos, and room service. Rooms are slightly larger and a Jacuzzi and fitness center may accompany the pool. The Continental breakfast probably includes fresh fruit, granola, and muffins rather than day-old doughnuts and little boxes of cereal. The hotel may also have a palatable on-site restaurant.

- ✔ **$$$ ($200–$250):** Hotels at this level add a guest-services desk for attraction tickets and restaurant reservations. Likewise, they usually include a large, resort-style pool with multiple Jacuzzi tubs (some of the higher-end rooms have their own), a fitness center, and occasionally a small spa. Rooms have multiple phones, beds, and TVs, as well as minibars, a bath, *and* separate shower.

- ✔ **$$$$ ($250 and Up):** Nothing in this price range is outside the realm of possibility, including a Body by Jake gym (the **Walt Disney World Dolphin,** see Chapter 8, has one). In addition to the nicer amenities in the previous categories, many of these hotels offer concierge levels, extra large rooms, 24-hour room service, gorgeous pool bars, and live entertainment in their lounges. Some also include full-service spas, gourmet restaurants, and tight security.

Chapter 7

Booking the Best Hotel Room Your Money Can Buy

* *

In This Chapter

▶ Getting a good deal on your hotel room

▶ Shopping for a hotel on the Internet

▶ Arriving in town without a reservation

* *

Some folks call a hotel, ask for a rate, and pay it — no questions asked. These are also the same people who go to a car lot and pay sticker price. You, however, won't do the same as these people because we're going to show you how to find the best hotel rates.

The Truth about Rack Rates (and Why You Don't Have to Pay Them)

Rack rates are the standard rates that hotels charge for their rooms. If you call a hotel for a rate or walk into a hotel to get a room for the night, you pay the room's rack rate. Hotels also post their rack rates on the backs of room doors (unless the spring breakers took it home as a souvenir).

You don't have to pay rack rates. In fact, hardly anyone does. Perhaps the best way to avoid paying the rack rate is surprisingly simple: Ask for a cheaper or discounted rate. The hotel's answer may pleasantly surprise you.

Room rates usually depend on many factors, not the least of which is how you make your reservation. For example, a travel agent may be able to secure a better price with certain hotels than you can, because hotels sometimes give agents special discounts as a reward for bringing in a lot of return business.

Seasons also affect room rates, especially as occupancy rates rise and fall. If a hotel is nearly full, it's less likely to offer you a discount.

Likewise, if it's nearly empty, the hotel may negotiate a room rate with you. Some resorts offer mid-week specials and downtown hotels often offer cheaper weekend rates.

Orlando, for the most part, doesn't have a normal winter-summer pattern of high- and low-travel seasons. Blame two things for that: Disney's year-round tourist appeal and a convention schedule that takes a breather only in summer — when the family frenzy is going full tilt. These factors especially impact moderately priced accommodations outside **Walt Disney World** (see Chapter 2 for more on this). Many non-Disney hotels and motels, however, tend to offer lower rates from early January through March, from just past Labor Day to just before Thanksgiving, and in the first two weeks of December.

Room prices can change without notice, so the rates we quote in this book may differ from the actual rate you receive when you make your reservation.

Throughout this book, we provide $ symbols for an at-a-glance price comparison of the various hotels (see the Introduction for an explanation of the $ rates). Finding a place to hang your sneakers for $50 is hard. The average rate for hotels in Orlando runs $90–$95 per night for a double. The **Walt Disney World** average is $20–$25 higher ($110–$115).

Getting the Best Room at the Best Rate

Finding the best hotel rate requires a bit of detective work. For example, reserving a room through the hotel's 800-number, rather than calling the hotel directly, may result in a lower rate. However, the central reservations number may not know about discounts at specific locations. Case in point: Some franchises may offer a special group rate for a wedding or family reunion, but they may neglect to tell the central booking line. Your best bet is to call the local number *and* the 800-number to see which one gives you a better deal.

If you're a student, senior, military or government employee (or retiree), or a member of AAA or AARP, ask about discounts. The Orlando/Orange County Convention and Visitors Bureau's free Magicard (☎ 800-551-0181; Internet: www.orlandoinfo.com) is good for a family of six and up to $500 in discounts on accommodations, car rentals, attractions, and restaurants.

As a rule, Disney resorts, villas, and official hotels don't offer regular discounts other than for seasonal variations. One of the best ways to catch a break from Mickey is through a package (see Chapter 5). **Disney** offers numerous vacation plans that can include meals, tickets, recreation, airfare, rentals, dinner shows, and other features. Call the **Walt Disney World Travel Company** (☎ **800-828-0228** or 407-828-4101) or on the Internet go to www.disneyworld.com to book single rooms or resort packages. You can also write to **Central Reservations Operations,** P.O. Box 10000, Lake Buena Vista, FL 32830-1000, or call ☎ **407-934-7639.** This service offers general information about **WDW,** including packages, vacation brochures, and videos.

The Disney Club can be a good investment if you're planning multiple visits or staying at least a week. Check out Chapter 3 for more details on the card.

When booking your room, don't forget to allow for the area's combined sales and bed taxes. In Orange County (Orlando, Winter Park, and Maitland), the *tax equals 11 percent.* In Osceola County (Kissimmee/St. Cloud), the taxes add *12 percent* to your bill.

Once you've made your reservation, asking one or two more pointed questions can go a long way toward making sure you have the best room in the house. For example, always ask for a corner room. They're usually larger, quieter, closer to the elevator, include more windows and light than standard rooms, and don't always cost more. Likewise, ask which floor and side has the best view, if there is one, as well as whether the hotel is renovating (if so, request a room away from the renovation work). You can also ask about the location of the restaurants, bars, and discos in the hotel — these may be a source of irritating noise. If you aren't happy with your room when you arrive, talk to the front desk. If they have another room, they should accommodate you, within reason, of course.

Surfing the Web for Hotel Deals

The Internet offers numerous sites from which you can retrieve information on hotels or resorts in Orlando. The biggest advantage that you get from using the Internet is that you can see the hotel or resort (hopefully, a photo within the last year or two) before you book your trip. Plus, you can book online and save the aggravation of listening to a slew of annoying automated voice systems.

The Disney site, www.disneyworld.com, allows you to click on a link, "Parks & Resorts," to find the resorts, which are divided into five categories: Value, Moderate, Deluxe, Homes Away From Home, and Other Selected Resorts.

Each individual resort link leads you to more information that includes rooms, rates, floor plans, restaurants, recreation, and so on. Select the "book" feature on the main Web page to make reservations online.

Joining a hotel club

Although many travelers participate in the airlines' frequent-flyer programs, not as many take advantage of the major hotel chains' frequent-stay clubs. You should. Even if you don't stay in a hotel for more than the time span of your yearly vacation, you may be able to realize significant savings by joining its program.

Like the airlines' scheme, hotels allow you to accumulate points for staying at a participating property, dining in the hotel's restaurant, or using some other service. Although programs vary, points can be exchanged for free room nights, discounted room rates, special perks and privileges, and, in some cases, frequent-flyer miles. And the price is right — it's free. Unlike the airlines, however, just joining a hotel club may make you eligible for special discounted rates, entitle you to express check-in and checkout privileges, and get you free breakfasts, free local calls, or a free morning newspaper.

Here's a rundown of some frequent-stay programs that offer perks even to not-so-frequent travelers:

- **Bass Hotel & Resorts Priority Club Worldwide** (☎ 800-272-9273; Internet: www.priorityclub.com) covers the Inter-Continental Resorts, the Crowne Plaza hotels and resorts, and all of Holiday Inn's properties. Priority Club members get express check-in privileges, access to discounted rates at select hotels, and several free perks. Freebies vary according to hotel, but often include free breakfast, free local phone calls, and/or free parking.

- **Choice Hotels International Guest Privileges** program (☎ 888-770-6800; Internet: www.guestprivileges.com) covers Sleep, Quality, Comfort, and Clarion properties. Participants receive a number of excellent perks, including express check-in, access to special rates, free room upgrades based on availability, free local calls, complimentary newspapers, and extended checkout times.

- **Hyatt Hotel's Gold Passport** program (☎ 800-304-9288; Internet: www.goldpassport.com) bestows a host of privileges upon its members. Members have access to a private reservation line and receive express check-in, complimentary newspapers, and free access to a hotel's fitness center. You'll also receive special offers and discounted rates from select Hyatt properties.

Other popular frequent-stay programs include **Hilton's HHonors** program (☎ 800-548-8690; Internet: www.hilton.com/hhonors), **Starwood Hotels Preferred Guest** (☎ 888-625-4988; Internet: www.preferredguest.com), **Marriott Rewards** (☎ 801-468-4000; Internet: www.marriottrewards.com), **Club Ramada** (☎ 800-672-6232; Internet: www.clubramada.com), and **Howard Johnson Supermiles** (☎ 800-547-7829; Internet: www.hojo.com).

At the Universal Orlando site, www.universalorlando.com, you can find information on the **Portofino Bay and Hard Rock hotels,** including room rates, packages, amenities, and a room locator. You can also preview the next planned Universal resort, the **Royal Pacific Hotel.**

Although **SeaWorld** doesn't have its own resort, www.seaworld.com features two- and three-night money-saving packages with rooms at a handful of Orlando hotels (including **Renaissance Orlando Resort** at SeaWorld — see Chapter 8), car rental, and tickets.

The **Orlando Convention and Visitors Bureau**'s Web site (www.orlandoinfo.com) supplies visitors with information on finding hotels, family-friendly motels, and resorts in its "Accommodations" section. If you find a hotel you're happy with, you can book it directly on the site.

For an especially good selection of discounted hotel rooms in Orlando, check out the offerings on **Hotel Kingdom.com** (www.hotelkingdom.com). The Web site, a division of Discount Hotels of America, features some of the city's best hotels, often at a steep discount. And though the prices aren't as cheap during high season, we often find they have rooms available when other services are sold out.

Here are a few other sites where you may find discounts:

- ✔ **Orlando.com** (www.orlando.com, then click on the"Travel" link) provides links for reservations, accommodations, and special deals. Use the "accommodations" link to find a list of hotels and resorts from budget places to deluxe vacation rentals and villas.

- ✔ **Florida Travel Online** (www.orlandotravel.com) is a wholesaler for hotel rooms, suites, and homes. Click the "places to stay," which lists prices and other information on approximately 30 hotels and resorts. Clicking the individual hotel links gives you information on each property.

- ✔ **hoteldiscount!com** (www.180096hotel.com) lists bargain room rates at hotels in more than 50 U.S. and international cities, including Orlando. The cool thing is that hoteldiscount!com pre-books blocks of rooms in advance, so sometimes it offers rooms — at discount rates — at hotels that are "sold out." This site is notable for delivering deep discounts in cities where hotel rooms are expensive. The toll-free number is printed all over this site (☎ **800-715-7666**); call it if you want more options than are listed online.

- ✔ **TravelWeb** (www.travelweb.com) lists more than 26,000 hotels in 170 countries, focusing on chains such as Hyatt and Hilton, and you can book almost 90 percent of these online. TravelWeb's Click-It Weekends, updated each Monday, offers weekend deals at many leading hotel chains.

Arriving Without a Reservation

Our first bit of advice: Don't come to Orlando without a reservation. If you do, you're more likely to end up feeling like Grumpy than Happy. This is especially true if it's high-travel season, when rooms are both pricey and scarce. If you do, however, decide to head for Orlando on a spur-of-the-moment inspiration, here are a few tips that will save you from having to camp out in your car.

The **Orlando Information Center** is related to the Orlando/Orange County Convention and Visitors Bureau. These folks find last-minute rooms for non-planners. Room rates, depending on the seasons, can be a bargain. However, you can only get a room for the night you visit the center, and you have to come in person to find out what, if anything, is available. The Information Center is located in Orlando at 8723 International Drive, a mile west of Sand Lake Road. (☎ 407-363-5872 for information only.)

Other reservation services include the **Central Reservation Service** (☎ 407-740-6442); Florida Hotel Network (☎ 800-538-3616); Orlando. com (☎407-999-9800; Internet: www.orlando.com); and Vacation Works (☎ 407-396-1883).

Accommodation Search Engine (www.ASE.net) offers discounts of up to 30 percent off room rates. Fill out a form that records your choices in several categories — rates, types of hotels, facilities, recreation amenities, and so on. After the form is filled out, click the search button on the page, and you receive a list of hotels or resorts that fit your selections.

Chapter 8

Orlando's Best Hotels

• •

In This Chapter

▶ Taking a look at Orlando's best hotels

▶ Exploring some additional lodging choices

• •

*W*e've scouted hundreds of places to stay in Orlando and whittled them down to the best — a few dozen that we mention in this chapter — so you don't have to waste your time wading through reviews of places that aren't worth looking at. You may think we're martyrs to the hotel cause, but that's what we get paid for; thankfully, martyrdom no longer requires getting our heads chopped off or being burned at the stake.

Choosing a Hotel That's within Your Budget

When we mention hotel prices in this book, we refer to the hotels' rack rates, which you should easily be able to beat if you shop for discounts (see Chapter 7 on getting the best hotel room rates for your money). And, to make it easy for you to recognize pricey versus moderately priced hotels, each of the following entries includes one or more $ symbols. The cheapest hotels we list have one $ symbol, and the most expensive have $$$$ symbols. But remember, use our $ symbols only as a general guideline for hotel comparisons. If you visit Orlando in the off-season, buy a package, or find a discount deal, you can stay at $$$$ hotels for $$ rates. Likewise, you can also find $$$$ rooms or suites in $ and $$ hotels.

 All the rates in this chapter are per night double, but many accommodations, including all **Disney** resorts, allow kids to stay free with their parents or grandparents (as long as the number of guests doesn't exceed the maximum occupancy of the room). However, always ask about kid rates when booking your room, just to be safe.

In general, expect higher hotel prices on the more upscale digs as well as those in or near the attractions. Almost every hotel in Orlando caters to families with children, but we've added a *For Grownups* icon to the hotels, resorts, and inns that are an especially good fit for adults looking for some peace and quiet.

Keep in mind, you are going to Florida, so every hotel that we list has air-conditioning and at least one pool (or we will tell you otherwise). They also have television (most have cable and some offer in-room movies for a fee) and telephones. Likewise, many have hair dryers, coffeemakers, and in-room safes. Also, please note that all Disney-owned accommodations offer free access to the Disney transportation system. (See Chapter 11 for more on the transportation system.)

If you're considering booking a room at a Disney resort, be sure to ask when calling **Central Reservations** (☎ 407-934-7639) or the **WDW Travel Company** (☎ 800-828-0228) about any discounts available to members of AAA or other auto clubs, AARP, frequent-flyer programs, or other groups. Also, ask about special days (yes, they have a day for almost everyone, including Florida residents, emergency personnel, fire, police, and others — so ask). And, ask about meal plans — they can save you money — or packages that include a room, tickets, and airfare.

Orlando Hotels from A to Z

Best Western Kissimmee

$ U.S. 192/Kissimmee

This budget inn is close to **Disney.** The rooms are blatantly basic — small, with cramped bathrooms — but the price is hard to ignore. There are two pools and breakfast and dinner buffets are served in a family-style restaurant. There's a free Disney shuttle and transportation to other parks for a fee.

2261 E. Irlo Bronson Memorial Hwy. (U.S. 192, located 15 minutes from Orlando, near the Florida Turnpike). ☎ *800-994-0062 or 407-846-2221. Fax: 407-846-1095. Internet:* http://orlando.hotelguide.net/data/h101504.htm. *282 units. Parking: Free. Rack rates: $45–$60. Check for AAA and package rates. AE, CB, DC, DISC, MC, V.*

Best Western Lake Buena Vista Hotel

$$ Lake Buena Vista/Official WDW Hotel

This 18-story high-rise is a great place to view the Disney fireworks ($10 more for a room with a view) without braving the crowds in the parks. The lakefront hotel is located on prime property along Hotel Plaza Boulevard and is within walking distance of **Downtown Disney Marketplace.** The rooms are about 325 square feet and some come with balconies and views of the lake. Amenities include Nintendo, coffeemakers, free local calls, an on-site restaurant, several pools, a playground, baby-sitting service, free shuttles to Disney parks, and transportation to other parks for a fee.

2000 Hotel Plaza Blvd. (between Buena Vista Dr. and Apopka–Vineland Rd./Hwy. 535, across from Doubletree Hotel). ☎ ***800-348-3765*** *or 407-828-2424. Fax: 407-828-8933. Internet:* www.orlandoresorthotel.com. *325 units. Parking: Free. Rack rates: $89–$199. Ask about AAA discounts and packages. AE, CB, DC, DISC, JCB, MC.*

Blue Tree Resort

$$–$$$ **Lake Buena Vista**

This 16-acre complex is mostly made up of time-share units rented by their owners. Accommodations include one- and two-bedroom units and standard hotel rooms; all come with free local telephone privileges. The one- and two-bedroom units include pull-out sleeper sofas and range from 786- to 987-square feet — perfect for families. There are four pools, recreational and exercise facilities, as well as transportation for a fee to attractions. Larger units come with full kitchens, and the lower floors have patios.

12007 Cypress Run Rd. (located off Hwy. 535 on Palm Pkwy., about ½ mile from the entrance to Downtown Disney Marketplace). ☎ ***800-688-8733*** *or 407-238-6084. Fax: 407-238-6012. Internet:* www.bluetreeresort.com. *390 units. Parking: Free. Rack rates: $119–$250. Discounts including AAA are available. AE, DISC, MC, V.*

Celebration Hotel

$$–$$$ **U.S. 192/Kissimmee**

Located in the Disney-run town of Celebration, this hotel has a three-story, wood-frame design straight out of 1920s Florida. All rooms (350 square feet and up) offer TVs with Nintendo, dataports, safes, hair dryers, and makeup mirrors. Suites and studios have refrigerators and wet bars. Other amenities include a pool, Jacuzzi, and fitness center. Shops, an 18-hole golf course, a movie theater, and several restaurants are within walking distance. There's a free shuttle to **WDW** parks and transportation for a fee to others.

700 Bloom St. (Take I-4 to exit 25A/U.S. 192, go east to second light, then right on Celebration Ave.) ☎ ***888-499-3800*** *or 407-566-6000. Fax: 407-566-6001. Internet:* www.celebrationhotel.com. *115 units. Parking: Free, valet $8. Rack rates: $165–$255 ($205–$470 for studios and suites). AE, DC, DISC, MC, V.*

Courtyard by Marriott

$$ **Lake Buena Vista/Official WDW Hotel**

The Courtyard is a moderately priced hotel located close to the **Downtown Disney Marketplace's** shops and restaurants. Rooms measure 340 square feet — a standard hotel size — and have coffeemakers and hair dryers; most come with balconies. A small reception area is located in a 14-story atrium, a full-service restaurant, a cocktail lounge, and a deli that specializes in pizza. There's free transportation to the **WDW** parks, transportation for a fee to others.

Accommodations in Walt Disney World & Lake Buena Vista

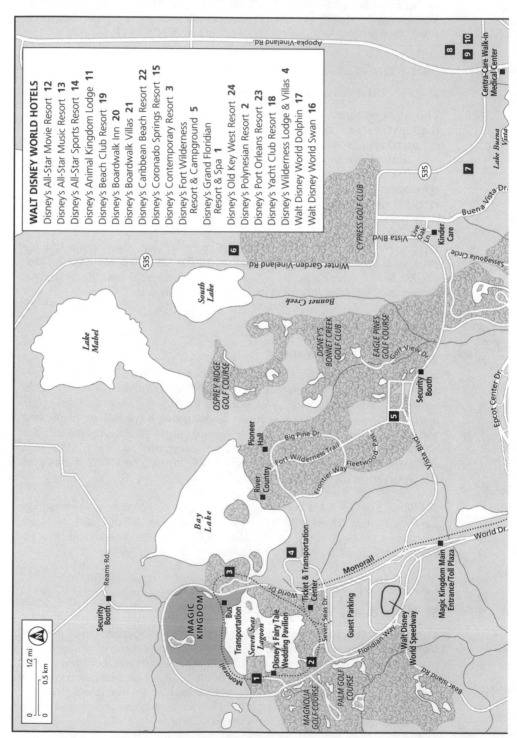

WALT DISNEY WORLD HOTELS

Disney's All-Star Movie Resort **12**
Disney's All-Star Music Resort **13**
Disney's All-Star Sports Resort **14**
Disney's Animal Kingdom Lodge **11**
Disney's Beach Club Resort **19**
Disney's Boardwalk Inn **20**
Disney's Boardwalk Villas **21**
Disney's Caribbean Beach Resort **22**
Disney's Coronado Springs Resort **15**
Disney's Contemporary Resort **3**
Disney's Fort Wilderness
  Resort & Campground **5**
Disney's Grand Floridian
  Resort & Spa **1**
Disney's Old Key West Resort **24**
Disney's Polynesian Resort **2**
Disney's Port Orleans Resort **23**
Disney's Yacht Club Resort **18**
Disney's Wilderness Lodge & Villas **4**
Walt Disney World Dolphin **17**
Walt Disney World Swan **16**

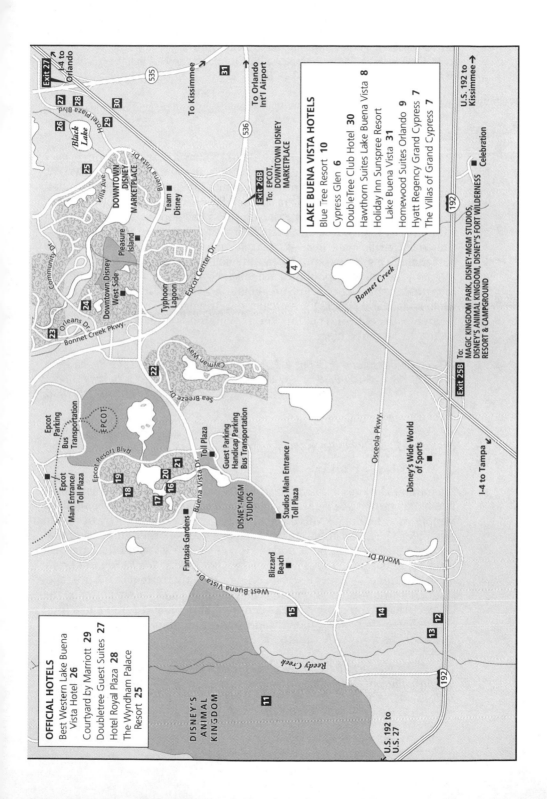

1805 Hotel Plaza Blvd. (between Lake Buena Vista Dr. and Apopka–Vineland Rd./Hwy. 535, close to the Hilton Royal Plaza Hotel). ☎ **800-223-9930** *or 407-828-8888. Fax: 407-827-4626. Internet:* www.courtyardorlando.com. *323 units. Parking: Free. Rack rates: $89–$169. Discounts for AAA members, check for package rates. AE, CB, DC, DISC, JCB, MC, V.*

Cypress Glen

$$$$ Lake Buena Vista

This delightful Art Deco surprise, built in 1992 by a Disney executive, isn't cheap, but you get what you pay for. Only a 10-minute drive from **WDW,** this retreat rents two guest rooms to adults looking for peace and quiet. The traditional accommodation is the 350-square-foot Josephine Baker Suite — named for innkeeper Sandy Sarillo's passion for jazz — equipped with a private entrance and a small private bath. The Sophia Suite — named for Sarillo's mother — is a 1,200-square-foot wonder whose standouts include a sitting room, a beautiful 430-square-foot bath highlighted by a two-person whirlpool tub, a small exercise room, and a magnificent four-poster bed. A bountiful breakfast and stocked mini fridges (beer, wine, sodas, and snacks) are included in the price. This is a smoke-free residence except for The Tap Room, which has a marble-top bar, big-screen TV, and free cigars.

10336 Vista Oaks Court (P.O. Box 2202/Hwy. 535 north of WDW), Lake Buena Vista, FL 32830. ☎ **888-909-0338** *or 407-909-0338. Fax: 407-909-0345. Internet:* www.cypressglen.com. *2 units. Rack rates: $250–$355. Parking: Free. AE, DC, DISC, MC, V.*

Disney All-Star Movie Resort

$ Walt Disney World

Kids aren't the only ones amazed by the, uh, aesthetics of this resort. When did you last see architecture as inspiring as Goliath-size Dalmatians leaping from balconies? If you're not saying "Oh, brother!" by now, you may enjoy the larger-than-life versions of a host of other characters that decorate the buildings here, and the low (by Mickey standards) rates will thrill some parents. *The All-Star resorts that follow this listing are pretty much the same* — expect small rooms (260 square feet) and postage-stamp bathrooms. But you're still "on property," and you're enjoying the lowest prices your Mouse bucks can buy. This All-Star hotel has a food court that serves pizza, pasta, sandwiches, and family-dinner platters. The pool has a *Fantasia* theme.

1991 W. Buena Vista Dr. (Disney All Star Resorts are located close to Animal Kingdom, Blizzard Beach, and Winter Summerland). ☎ **407-934-7639** *or 407-939-7000. Fax: 407-939-7111. Internet:* www.disneyworld.com. *1,900 units. Parking: Free. Rack rates: $77–$109. AE, DC, DISC, MC, V.*

Disney's All-Star Music Resort

$ **Walt Disney World**

If you insist on staying on Disney property and are on a tight budget (or don't care about those few hours of in-room time), beating the All-Star's rates is hard. But you'd better be a fan of family togetherness, because the tiny rooms mean you'll be up close and personal. They start at 260 square feet or about what you get on a cruise ship if you choose a mid-price cabin. (If you've never been on a cruise ship, go to the smallest bedroom in your house and imagine living inside it for seven days.)

1801 W. Buena Vista Dr. (at World Dr. and Osceola Pkwy.). ☎ ***407-934-7639*** *or 407-939-6000. Fax: 407-939-7222. Internet:* www.disneyworld.com. *1,920 units. Parking: Free. Rack rates: $77–$109. AE, DC, DISC, MC, V.*

Disney's All-Star Sports Resort

$ **Walt Disney World**

Adjacent to the **All-Star Music Resort,** this 82-acre property draws sports fans looking for a vacation and visual overload. The 260-square-foot rooms are housed in buildings decorated in football (huge helmets protect stairwells from rain), baseball, basketball, tennis, and surfing motifs. Amenities include a brightly decorated food court, room service (pizza only), babysitting, a guest-services desk, pool, video arcade, and playground.

1701 W. Buena Vista Dr. (at World Dr. and Osceola Pkwy.). ☎ ***407-934-7639*** *or 407-939-5000. Fax: 407-939-7333. Internet:* www.disneyworld.com. *1,920 units. Parking: Free. Rack rates: $77–$109. AE, DC, DISC, MC, V.*

Disney's Animal Kingdom Lodge

$$$–$$$$ **Walt Disney World**

Disney's newest arrival offers the feel of a game-preserve. The rooms follow a *kraal* (semicircular) design, giving guests a hit-or-miss view of 130 bird species and 75 giraffes, gazelles, and other grazing animals in a 30-acre savanna. (You get the same view through large picture windows in the lobby.) The rooms are 344 square feet, easily one-third larger than the "tomb rooms" at WDW's all-star resorts (see earlier in this chapter). All rooms have hair dryers and dataports and the lodge rooms have a balcony. Not surprisingly, this is the closest you can stay to **Animal Kingdom,** but almost everything else on **WDW** property is quite a distance away.

2901 Osceola Parkway, Bay Lake, FL 32830. ☎ ***407-934-7639*** *or 407-938-3000. Fax: 407-939-4799. Internet:* www.disneyworld.com. *1,293 units. Parking: Free, valet $6. Rack rates: $199–$510 double, $380–$565 concierge, $600–$2,350 suites. AE, DC, DISC, MC, V.*

Disney's Beach Club Resort

$$$$ **Walt Disney World**

Members of the health-and-fitness set can walk to **Epcot** from the Beach Club, which has a quintessential Victorian Cape Cod theme and a posh atmosphere. Kids and adults love the 3-acre, free-form swimming pool, Stormalong Bay. Guest rooms are about 400 square feet and come with one king-size or two queen beds. All units come with dataports, hair dryers, double vanities, a tub/shower combination, ceiling fans, and balconies. This is a nice upscale resort destination, especially if you want to stay very close to the Disney parks. For eats, the Cape May Café offers character breakfasts and New England clambake buffet dinners.

1800 Epcot Resorts Blvd. (The Beach Club is off Buena Vista Dr., west on Epcot Resorts Blvd.). ☎ *407-934-7639 or 407-934-8000. Fax: 407-934-3850. Internet:* www. disneyworld.com. *597 units. Parking: Free, valet $6. Rack rates: $279–$610. AE, DC, DISC, MC, V.*

Disney's BoardWalk Resort & BoardWalk Villas

$$$$ **Walt Disney World**

More than any other Disney property, the BoardWalk Inn appeals to couples and singles looking for a sliver of yesterday. The 1920s "seaside" resort overlooks a village green and lake. The accommodations are larger than those in the moderate Disney resorts (360 square feet and up), with two queen beds, a child-size daybed, a midsize bathroom, dataports, hair dryers, and balconies. There are two pools, and recreational facilities include tennis, fishing, boating, bike rental, and even a moonlight cruise. The villas sleep up to 12 and some have kitchens, washer-dryers, and whirlpool baths. The resort has a quarter-mile boardwalk that offers shops, restaurants, and street performers, which means there's plenty to do after the sun goes down. There are two restaurants. *Note:* Rooms overlooking the boardwalk have the best views, but tend to be noisy thanks to the action below.

2101 N. Epcot Resorts Blvd. (north of Buena Vista Dr., on Epcot Resorts Blvd.). ☎ *407-934-7639 or 407-939-5100. Fax: 407-934-5150. Internet:* www.disneyworld.com. *378 units, 532 villas. Parking: Free. Rack rates: $279–$630, villas $375–$1,800. AE, DC, DISC, MC, V.*

Disney's Caribbean Beach Resort

$$ **Walt Disney World**

This moderately priced hotel's amenities aren't as extensive as those at some of **Disney**'s higher-end properties (or those in the same class outside the **World**), but it's still offers good value for families. Units are grouped into five villages, some with water views. The 314-square-foot rooms feature two double beds, ample-sized bathrooms, hair dryers, and double vanities. The swimming pool resembles a Spanish-style fort, and there's a nature trail, small aviary, and a picnic area. There's one restaurant and a food court.

900 Cayman Way. (off Buena Vista Dr. toward Epcot on Sea Breeze Dr. and Cayman Way). ☎ *407-934-7639 or 407-934-3400. Fax: 407-934-3288. Internet:* www. disneyworld.com. *2,112 units. Parking: Free. Rack rates: $122–$209. AE, MC, V.*

Disney's Contemporary Resort

$$$–$$$$ **Walt Disney World**

If location is a priority, the Contemporary has one of the best in the **World** because the monorail literally runs through the hotel, allowing you a fast track to **Epcot** or the **Magic Kingdom.** The 15-story A-frame resort — Disney's first in Florida — overlooks the manmade Seven Seas Lagoon. At nearly 400 square feet, the standard rooms are among Disney's biggest, a plus for families. Most accommodations come with two queen-size beds, a daybed, dataports, hair dryers, and views of the lake and Magic Kingdom. The pool area is virtually a mini water park. There are three restaurants, including one that offers character meals (see Chapters 14 and 15), a health club, and a marina.

4600 N. World Dr. (the Contemporary is located at the far northern end of Mickeyville, close to the Magic Kingdom off World Dr.). ☎ *407-934-7639 or 407-824-1000. Fax: 407-824-3535. Internet:* www.disneyworld.com. *1,041 units. Parking: Free, valet $6. Rack rates: $224–$370, suites $289–$1,610. AE, DC, DISC, MC, V.*

Disney's Coronado Springs Resort

$$ **Walt Disney World**

This moderate resort has an American Southwest theme and a slightly more upscale feel than the others in this class. Rooms (314 square feet) are housed in four- and five-story hacienda-style buildings with terracotta tile roofs and palm-shaded courtyards. Some overlook the 15-acre Golden Lake; the better your view, the higher the price. Rooms feature two double beds (the décor differs in each section, but the layout is the same), with coffeemakers, hair dryers, and dataports. Ninety-nine rooms are specially designed to accommodate travelers with disabilities, and nearly three-fourths of the rooms are nonsmoking. If you like to swim, you'll delight in the Mayan temple-inspired main pool. Dining options include a restaurant and a food court.

1000 Buena Vista Dr. (Disney's Blizzard Beach off Buena Vista Dr.). ☎ *407-934-7639 or 407-934-6632. Fax: 407-939-1001. Internet:* www.disneyworld.com. *1,967 units. Parking: Free. Rack rates: $129–$$209 , suites $258–$1,010. AE, DC, DISC, MC, V.*

Disney's Fort Wilderness Resort and Campground

$–$$$ **Walt Disney World**

This woodsy, 780-acre resort delights campers, but it's quite a hike from most of the Disney parks, except the **Magic Kingdom.** Even so, there's more than enough to keep you busy at the resort. Guests enjoy extensive recreational facilities, ranging from a riding stable to a nightly campfire. Secluded campsites offer 110/220-volt outlets, barbecue grills, picnic tables, and children's play areas. There are wilderness cabins and rustic one-bedroom cabins (504 square feet) that can sleep up to six people, with living rooms, fully equipped eat-in kitchens, coffeemakers, hair dryers, and barbecue grills. Nearby Pioneer Hall hosts the rambunctious *Hoop-Dee-Doo Musical Revue* (see Chapter 29) nightly.

3520 N. Fort Wilderness Trail (located off Vista Blvd., on Fort Wilderness Trail). ☎ *407-934-7639 or 407-824-2900. Fax: 407-824-3508. Internet:* www.disneyworld. com. *784 campsites, 408 wilderness cabins. Parking: Free. Campsites: $34–$77; Cabins: $184–$254. AE, DC, DISC, MC, V.*

Disney's Grand Floridian Resort & Spa

$$$$ **Walt Disney World**

You won't find a more luxurious address — in a Victorian sense anyway — than this 40-acre *Great Gatsby*-era resort on the shores of the Seven Seas Lagoon. It's a great choice for couples seeking a bit of romance, especially honeymooners who aren't on a tight budget. The Grand Floridian is **Walt Disney World's** upper-crust flagship, and it's as pricey as it is plush. The opulent, five-story domed lobby hosts afternoon teas accompanied by piano music. In the evenings, an orchestra plays big-band tunes. A typical guest room measures 400 square feet and is equipped with dataports and hair dryers. Most rooms overlook a garden, pool, courtyard, or Seven Seas Lagoon. The hotel is one of three on the Disney monorail line. The resort also has a first-rate health club and spa, as well as five restaurants, including Victoria & Albert's (see Chapter 14).

4401 Floridian Way (northwest corner of the WDW property, just north of the Polynesian Resort). ☎ *407-934-7639 or 407-824-3000. Fax: 407-824-3186. Internet:* www.disneyworld.com. *933 units. Parking: Free, valet $6. Rack rates: $314–$790, suites $810–$2,175. AE, DC, DISC, MC, V.*

Disney's Old Key West Resort

$$$$ **Walt Disney World**

If you can swallow the price, the reward is some peace and quiet away from the Disney insanity. This is a timeshare property that mirrors turn-of-the-century Key West. Units are rented to tourists when their owners are not using them, and they're a good choice for large families or long stays. The accommodations include standard rooms, studios, and one- and two-bedroom villas (ranging in size from 376 to 1,333 square feet) that have full kitchens or kitchenettes, coffeemakers, and hair dryers. There's a restaurant, playground, video arcade, and four pools.

1510 N. Cove Rd. (off Bonnet Creek Pkwy. on Community Dr.). ☎ *407-934-7639 or 407-827-7700. Fax: 407-827-7710. Internet:* www.disneyworld.com. *709 units. Parking: Free. Rack rates: $244–$349, villas $330–$730. AE, DC, DISC, MC, V.*

Disney's Polynesian Resort

$$$$ Walt Disney World

The Polynesian was built when Disney first opened its doors. Though it has aged, it still offers a good location — near the **Magic Kingdom** and on the monorail line. Rooms here are reasonably large (400 square feet), and most have balconies or patios, hair dryers, and canopied beds with bamboo and rattan furnishings. Numerous recreational activities are available from which to choose, including fishing and boat rentals.

1600 Seven Seas Dr. (off Floridian Way across from Shades of Green and Magnolia Palm Dr.). ☎ ***407-934-7639*** *or 407-824-2000. Fax: 407-824-3174. Internet:* www. disneyworld.com. *853 units. Parking: Free, valet $6. Rack rates: $289–$520 and up. AE, DC, DISC, MC, V.*

Disney's Port Orleans Resort

$$ Walt Disney World

The old Dixie Landings Resort was merged into this neighboring hotel, which offers good value. As is the case with the resorts at this level, it's pretty much a clone of the other moderate resorts — perhaps a touch nicer. The midsize rooms have small bathrooms, two double beds, hair dryers, and wrought-iron balconies. Kids love the larger-than-Olympic-size Doubloon Lagoon swimming pool and its serpent-shaped waterslide. Gardeners will appreciate the landscaping, which features stately oaks, formal boxwood hedges, azaleas, and jasmine. Boatwright's Dining Hall (see Chapter 14) serves New Orleans-style cuisine; there's also a food court.

2201 Orleans Dr. (off Bonnet Creek Pkwy., next to the Dixie Landings Resort). ☎ ***407-934-7639*** *or 407-934-5000. Fax: 407-934-5353. Internet:* www.disneyworld.com. *3,056 units. Parking: Free. Rack rates: $129–$209. AE, DC, DISC, MC, V.*

Disney's Wilderness Lodge

$$–$$$$ Walt Disney World

Here's an option for those who like the great outdoors but prefer the comfort of an indoor resort. The Wilderness Lodge reminds most folks of a rustic, national park lodge, in part because it's patterned after the one at Yosemite. Its main drawback: It's difficult and time-consuming to get to other areas via the free WDW Transportation System. There are several plusses, including a lakefront sand beach and a large serpentine swimming pool, seemingly excavated out of the rocks. The modestly sized rooms are 344 square feet, with two queen-size beds, hair dryers, and views of the lake, woods, or a meadow. The lodge also added 181 villas (measuring 356 to 1,080 square feet) in 2000. Continuing the Yellowstone theme, a geyser shoots water into the sky every hour, on the hour — just like Old Faithful. There are two restaurants and a plethora of water-related activities.

901 W. Timberline Dr. (on Seven Seas Dr., south of the Contemporary Resort on the southwest shore of Bay Lake east of the Magic Kingdom). ☎ *407-934-7639 or 407-824-3200. Fax: 407-824-3232. Internet:* www.disneyworld.com. *909 units. Parking: Free, valet $6. Rack rates: $189–$475, villas $264–$895. AE, DC, DISC, MC, V.*

Disney's Yacht Club Resort

$$$$ Walt Disney World

The resort resembles a turn-of-the-20th-century New England yacht club resort (in a Disney sense) and is located on a 25-acre lake it shares with the Beach Club (also listed in this chapter), which is a notch below it on the resort food chain. The relatively large rooms sleep up to five and are equipped with dataports and coffeemakers; most rooms have patios or balconies, although some views are of the asphalt parking lots. The resort has three restaurants, an eye-popping swimming pool, a marina, and a health club.

1700 Epcot Resorts Blvd. (off Buena Vista Dr.). ☎ *407-934-7639 or 407-934-7000. Fax: 407-924-3450. Internet:* www.disneyworld.com. *642 units. Parking: Free, valet $6. Rack rates: $279–$480, suites $490–$2,080. AE, DC, DISC, MC, V.*

Doubletree Guest Suites Resort

$$–$$$$ Lake Buena Vista/WDW Official Hotel

This seven-story, all-suite hotel is a good choice for large families. Young patrons get their own check-in desk, where they receive a chocolate-chip cookie. There's also a children's theater, game room, and video arcade. The one-bedroom suites (643 square feet) can sleep up to six adults and include a refrigerator, microwave oven, coffeemaker, and hair dryer. You'll also find several recreational facilities, including a pool, whirlpool, fitness room, and two tennis courts. Bus service to **WDW** parks is free; you can hitch a ride to other parks for a fee.

2305 Hotel Plaza Blvd. (just west of Apopka–Vineland Rd./Hwy. 535; turn into the entrance to Downtown Disney Marketplace). ☎ *800-222-8733 or 407-934-1000. Fax: 407-934-1011. Internet:* www.doubletreeguestsuites.com. *229 units. Parking: Free. Rack rates: $129–$249. AE, CB, DC, DISC, JCB, MC, V.*

Econo Lodge Maingate Hawaiian Resort

$–$$ Kissimmee

Location and price are the perks at this inn, located 1.2 miles from the **WDW** entrance. Standard rooms have about 280 square feet and beds for four or five. The rooms are clean and the price is great for the budget-conscious, but you get few frills other than a free shuttle to Disney parks. You'll pay to get to the other theme parks.

U.S. 192/Kissimmee Hotels

Best Western Kissimmee **6**
Celebration Hotel **4**
Econo Lodge Maingate Hawaiian Resort **3**

Holiday Inn Nikki Bird Resort **2**
Renaissance Worldgate **1**
The Unicorn Inn **5**

7514 W. Irlo Bronson Memorial Hwy./U.S. 192 (2 miles from I-4). ☎ *800-356-6935, 407-390-9063, or 407-396-2000. Fax: 407-390-1226. Internet:* www.enjoyfloridahotels.com. *445 units. Parking: Free. Rack rates: $35–$119. AE, DC, DISC, MC, V.*

Four Points By Sheraton Orlando Downtown

$$ Downtown Orlando

This recently renovated Sheraton offers a conventional (by modern standards) and business-class home base. The hotel has a number of rooms with great views of Lake Eola, and the location isn't bad if you're inclined toward the downtown area. It's 25 minutes from **Disney** and 10 to 15 minutes from **Universal, SeaWorld,** and Orlando International Airport (if the traffic gods are smiling). Standard rooms have about 300 square feet of living space and feature dataports, coffeemakers and hair dryers. You can arrange transportation to the parks for a fee. To see the location of this hotel on a map, check out the "Downtown Orlando Nightlife" map in Chapter 28.

151 E. Washington St. (from I-4 take the Anderson St. exit; the hotel is located off Rosalind directly across from the entrance to Lake Eola Park). ☎ *800-325-3535 or 407-841-3220. Fax: 407-422-7074. Internet:* www.sheraton.com. *250 units. Parking: Valet $9. Rack rates: $89–$219. AE, MC, V.*

Hampton Inn at Universal Studios

$ International Drive

It ain't fancy but it's close (two blocks) to **Universal Studios Florida** and **Islands of Adventure,** a mile from the heat of International Drive's tourist traps, and four miles from **SeaWorld.** The rooms measure 300 square feet and have dataports and coffeemakers; microwaves and refrigerators are available in some units. Although no restaurant is on the premises, several are within walking distance. You can get a ride to the theme parks for a fee, but in this neck of the woods, it's probably cheaper to rent a car.

5621 Windhover Dr. (Take I-4 to Exit 30B. Go through two traffic lights; turn right at Shoney's Restaurant. The hotel is a five-story white building). ☎ *800-426-7866 or 407-351-6716. Fax: 407-363-1711. Internet:* www.hamptoninn.com. *120 units. Parking: Free. Rack rates: $79–$99. Ask about special discounts. AE, DISC, DC, MC, V.*

Hard Rock Hotel

$$$ International Drive Area/Universal Orlando

You can't get rooms closer to **CityWalk** or **Universal Studios Florida** than those at this Loews hotel. It opened in January 2001 with rack rates a shade cheaper than its sister, the **Portofino Bay,** listed later in this chapter. This resort is on par with WDW's **Animal Kingdom Lodge,** though at 400 square feet, its rooms are 15 percent larger. Rooms come with two queens or one king, and feature safes, irons, and hair dryers. Unfortunately, though the rooms are pretty soundproof, a few notes do seep through the walls, so ask for a room that's situated away from the lobby area. There's free transportation to the **Universal** and **SeaWorld** parks. As for **Disney,** you're on your own. The biggest perk: *Guests get no-line access to almost all rides at Universal's theme parks.*

5000 Universal Blvd. (off Kirkman Road/Hwy. 435). ☎ *888-322-5541 or 407-363-8000. Fax 407-224-7118. Internet:* www.universalorlando.com. *654 units. Parking: Free, valet $8. Rack rates: $185–$315. AE, CB, DC, DISC, MC, V.*

Holiday Inn Family Suites Resort

$$ International Drive

This all-suite property opened in 2000 and does a fantastic job catering to a diverse clientele. Families will appreciate the two-bedroom Kidsuites that feature a second semiprivate bedroom equipped with bunk beds and a theme (room themes range from Disney to space exploration). The resort's other suites cater to everyone from honeymooners (suites feature a two-person heart-shaped whirlpool tub) to movie buffs (suites offer a private screening room equipped with 60-inch televisions and DVD player). All suites measure 485 square feet and sleep up to seven people. Most come with small kitchenettes, although some come with a full kitchen. The recreational facilities are excellent and the location — only a mile away from **Walt Disney World** — is great. **Note:** Adults seeking peace and quiet should ask to stay in the West Track Courtyard section, which features an adults-only lap pool and whirlpool.

13351 Lake Buena Vista (located off Fla. 535 near the Crossroads Shopping Center). ☎ *800-366-6299 or 407-239-4500. Fax: 407-239-7713. Internet:* www.kidsuites. com. *507 units. Parking: Free. Rack rates: $89–$159, Kidsuites, $109–$179. AE, DISC, JCB, MC, V.*

Holiday Inn Nikki Bird Resort

$–$$ U.S. 192/Kissimmee

Here's another great family base and the closest Holiday Inn to **Walt Disney World's** main gate. The resident mascot, Nikki, wanders the resort, where kids 12 and under eat free at a breakfast buffet next door. Other kid-friendly treats include nightly entertainment featuring songs, puppet shows, and games. The standard rooms are a shade under 325 square feet and sleep four, while the spacious Kidsuites add 75 more square feet and have a separate area for youngsters. Varying suite themes include a circus tent. All accommodations feature dataports, refrigerators, coffeemakers, and hair dryers. There's free transportation to the **WDW** parks and transportation for a fee to the others.

7300 Irlo Bronson Memorial Hwy. (located on U.S. 192 just west of I-4). ☎ *800-206-2747 or 407-396-7300. Fax: 407-396-7555. Internet:* www. holidayinnsofcentralflorida.com. *530 units. Parking: Free. Rack rates:*

$89–$139, Kidsuites $119–$229. Discounts for AAA, AARP, and corporate. AE, DISC, DC, MC, V.

Holiday Inn Sunspree Resort Lake Buena Vista

$-$$ Lake Buena Vista

Also close to the Disney parks, this Holiday Inn also caters to kids in a big way. They get their own check-in desk and a personal welcome from raccoon mascots Max and Maxine. The hotel's 231 spacious Kidsuites offer 405 square feet, beds for up to six, and a theme (a space capsule, igloo, clown tent, treehouse, jail, and more). Standard rooms are somewhat smaller and sleep four. All accommdations feature refrigerators, coffee-makers, and hair dryers. If you like sleeping in, ask for a room that doesn't face the pool area. Kids under 12 get to eat free in their own restaurant, and, if you want some time to yourself, the resort has one of the best child activity centers around.

13351 Lake Buena Vista (located off Fla. 535 near the Crossroads Shopping Center). ☎ *800-366-6299 or 407-239-4500. Fax: 407-239-7713. Internet:* www.kidsuites. com. *507 units. Parking: Free. Rack rates: $89–$159, Kidsuites, $109–$179. AE, DISC, JCB, MC, V.*

Homewood Suites Orlando

$$ Lake Buena Vista

These moderately priced family suites are two miles from **Disney** and loaded with such amenities as kitchenettes, refrigerators, coffeemakers with coffee, microwaves (they even give you a bag of popcorn), stoves, utensils, and hair dryers. The one-bedroom suites come with a king-size bed or two doubles, and the living area has a sleeper sofa. A free continental breakfast is served daily. Disney transportation is complimentary (you pay to get to others). Pets are welcome.

8200 Palm Pkwy. (located off So. Apopka-Vineland Road/Hwy. 535 near Lake Buena Vista). ☎ *800-225-5466 or 407-465-8200. Fax: 407-465-0200. Internet:* www. homewood-suites.com. *Parking: Free. Rack rates: $119–$159. AE, CB, DC, DISC, MC, V.*

Hotel Royal Plaza

$$ Lake Buena Vista/Official WDW Hotel

Another of the Disney "official hotels," its standard rooms (a bit tight at 300 square feet) remain one of the best deals this close to the Magic Mickey. The rooms are outfitted with VCRs, safes, minibars, dataports, coffeemakers, and hair dryers. The hotel's staff is one of the friendlier ones in Orlando. Other amenities include a large swimming pool, a sauna, four tennis courts, and a video game arcade. Despite its age (25, which is old by Disney-area standards), it's in good shape. Transportation to the **Disney** parks is included, but you'll pay to go elsewhere.

1905 Hotel Plaza Blvd. (between Buena Vista Dr. and Apopka-Vineland Rd./ Fla. 535). ☎ ***800-248-7890*** *or 407-828-2828. Fax: 407-827-6338. Internet:* www. orlandotravel.com/hotels/royal.htm. *394 units. Parking: Free, valet $8. Rack rates: $109–$215. AE, CB, DC, DISC, JCB, MC, V.*

Hyatt Regency Grand Cypress

$$$$ Lake Buena Vista

A resort destination in and of itself, this is a great place to get away from the Disney crowd frenzy, which is still only a mile away. You need deep pockets to stay here, but the reward is a palatial resort with a Thai theme. The hotel's 18-story atrium has inner and outer glass elevators, which provide a unique thrill. The beautifully decorated rooms measure 360 square feet and offer minibars, safes, irons, dataports, and hair dryers. Recreational facilities include golf (45 holes), 12 tennis courts (5 lighted), two racquetball courts, a spa, an adjoining equestrian center, and more. The property's half-acre, 800,000-gallon pool has caves, grottoes, and waterfalls. There's free transportation to **WDW,** and you can pay to go elsewhere. When hunger strikes, try the Black Swan (see Chapter 14). Also, see **The Villas of Grand Cypress,** later in this section.

1 N. Jacaranda (Hwy. 535 north of Disney's Lake Buena Vista entrance or Hotel Plaza Boulevard). ☎ ***800-835-7377*** *or 407-239-1234. Fax: 407-239-3800. Internet:* www. grandcypress.com. *750 units. Parking: Free, valet $10. Rack rates: $325–$400, $450–$1,500 suites. AE, CB, DC, DISC, JCB, MC, V.*

Marriott Village at Little Lake Bryan

$$ Lake Buena Vista

The December 2000 christening of this enterprise brought together three properties in a cluster just east of Lake Buena Vista, less than three miles from WDW. The fully gated resort features a 400-room **SpringHill Suites,** a 388-room **Fairfield Inn,** and a 312-room **Courtyard by Marriott** surrounding a central courtyard. In-room space ranges from a low of 350 square feet up, and all accommodations have refrigerators and hair dryers. The property offers a food court, a video arcade, several pools, a fitness center, and a convenience store. There's also a free shuttle to the **Disney** parks.

8623 Vineland Ave. (off Hwy. 535). ***877-682-8552*** *or 407-938-9001. Fax: 407-938-9002. Internet:* www.marriott-village.com. *1,100 units. Parking: Free. Rack rates: Courtyard by Marriott, $139–$165; SpringHill Suites, $129–$155; Fairfield Inn, $119–$145. AE, MC, V.*

The Peabody Orlando

$$$$ International Drive

Welcome to the home of the famous — drum roll, maestro, *s'il vous plait* — Marching Mallards. Their home is in the thick of all the action I-Drive has to offer, including attractions, restaurants, and shopping. These real ducks march into their luxury pool each morning at 11 — no kidding! — through the lobby, accompanied by — what else? — John Philip Sousa's marching music and a red-coated duck master, then back out at 5 p.m. You don't have to be a guest to enjoy the fun, so if you're in the neighborhood, drop in for the show.

The Peabody Hotel is located across from the Convention Center, which makes this hotel especially popular with business travelers. Guest rooms, even the standard ones (500 square feet), are lavishly furnished and come with numerous amenities, including dataports, minibars, and hair dryers. The Peabody offers some of the best hotel dining in town — look for its signature restaurant, Dux, in Chapter 14. You'll have to pay for transportation to all of the theme parks, so a rental car is a good idea if you want to stay here.

9801 International Dr. (between the Bee Line Expressway and Sand Lake Rd., across the street from the Orange County Convention Center). ☎ *800-732-2639 or 407-352-4000. Fax: 407-354-1424. Internet:* www.peabody-orlando.com. *891 units. Parking: Free, valet $8. Rack rates: $330–$1,500 and up. Ask about packages, holiday/summer discounts, and senior rates for those over 50. AE, CB, DC, DISC, JCB, MC, V.*

Portofino Bay Hotel

$$$$ International Drive Area/Universal Orlando

Some folks thought Universal wouldn't enter the hotel fray, but in 1999 it made quite a splash with this Loews property, which really delivers for those with deep pockets. It offers eight restaurants/lounges, a spa, and a fitness center in a package designed to look like the Mediterranean seaside village of Portofino, Italy. The accommodations (450 square feet) offer four-poster beds with cloud-soft pillows, and bathrooms outfitted with marble tubs, hair dryers, and tiled foyers. Rooms are state-of-the-art "smart rooms" that provide security, adjust room temperature, and report malfunctions as they occur. Butlers are available in some of the villas and all of the rooms in this category include complimentary cocktails and hors d'oeuvres nightly, access to a separate pool, and use of the bocce ball courts. There's free transportation to **Universal** and **SeaWorld** parks, but not the **Disney** ones. *Guests get no-line access to almost all rides at Universal's theme parks.*

5601 Universal Blvd. (Located off I-4, take Apopka-Vineland Rd. west to Universal Orlando, where the resort is located). ☎ *888-322-5541 or 407-503-1000. Fax: 407-224-7118. Internet:* www.universalorlando.com. *750 rooms. Parking: Free, valet $8. Rack rates: $235–$395, suites $395–$2,320. AE, CB, D, DC, MC, V.*

International Drive Area Accommodations

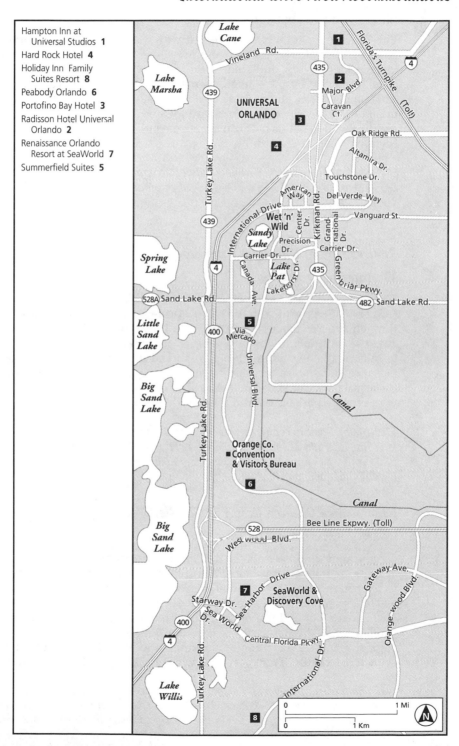

Hampton Inn at
  Universal Studios **1**
Hard Rock Hotel **4**
Holiday Inn Family
  Suites Resort **8**
Peabody Orlando **6**
Portofino Bay Hotel **3**
Radisson Hotel Universal
  Orlando **2**
Renaissance Orlando
  Resort at SeaWorld **7**
Summerfield Suites **5**

Radisson Plaza Hotel Orlando

$$ Downtown Orlando

This downtown hotel is very popular with the business set, but offers a good deal for the leisure traveler as well. The 330-square-foot rooms include hair dryers, and some offer views of the Orlando skyline. The hotel has a restaurant, lounge, two tennis courts, a pool with a Jacuzzi and tanning decks, and a fitness center. You have to pay for transportation to all of the theme parks, which are located 15 to 25 minutes away. To see the location of this hotel on a map, check out the "Downtown Orlando Nightlife" map in Chapter 28.

60 S. Ivanhoe Blvd. (downtown near College Park area north of Colonial Dr.). ☎ *800-333-3333 or 407-425-4455. Fax: 407-425-7470. Internet:* www.radissonorlando.com. *337 units. Parking: self $6, valet $7. Rack rates: $105–$300. Ask about special packages. AE, CB, DC, DISC, MC, V.*

Radisson Hotel Universal Orlando

$$ International Drive

This is a great location if you'll be spending all or most of your time at **Universal, SeaWorld,** and the other I-Drive attractions (see Chapters 23 through 26). You can't get any closer to Universal — it's right across the street — without staying in one of its pricier resorts. Renovated just a few years ago, everything looks fresh and up-to-date. Standard rooms measure 300 square feet and have dataports; some offer views of the Universal parks and **CityWalk.** A restaurant is on site, and transportation to the theme parks is offered for a fee.

5780 Major Blvd. (directly across the street from Universal Orlando on Vineland Rd.). ☎ *800-327-2110 or 407-351-1000. Fax: 407-363-0106. Internet:* www.radissonuniversal.com. *760 rooms. Parking: Free. Rack rates: $99–$199. AE, CB, DC, DISC, MC, V.*

Renaissance Orlando Resort at SeaWorld

$$–$$$ International Drive

Large rooms, good service, and luxurious surroundings are this hotel's calling cards. Its most valuable feature, however, is a location that's perfect if you're going to **Universal, SeaWorld** (it's right across the street), and to a lesser degree, the second-tier I-Drive attractions. The large rooms (385 square feet and up) offer marble baths, safes, dataports, and Sony PlayStations. The Renaissance has four lighted tennis courts, a health club, spa and sauna, three restaurants, and arguably the best Sunday brunch in Orlando. Transportation to the parks is available for a fee.

6677 Sea Harbour Dr. (From I-4 follow signs to SeaWorld; the hotel is across from the attraction). ☎ *800-468-3571 or 407-351-5555. Fax: 407-351-4618. Internet:* www.renaissancehotels.com. *778 units. Parking: Free, valet $9. Rack rates: $169–$289. AE, DISC, DC, MC, V.*

Renaissance Worldgate

$$ U.S. 192/Kissimmee

The Renaissance version of a budget hotel, it's a cut below the standard in price and quality, although certainly above average in comfort and appearance. Converted from a Doubletree in the fall of 2000, it's located two miles west of **WDW.** The midsize rooms come with mini fridges, hair dryers, coffeemakers, and irons. There's free transportation to the **Disney** parks. The biggest minus: Rooms need better soundproofing. You can hear your neighbor's phone and, if you're near enough, the thunder of the ice machine.

3011 Maingate Lane (on the north side of U.S. 192). ☎ *800-468-3571 or 407-396-1400. Fax: 407-396-1171. Internet:* www.renaissanceworldgate.com. *Parking: Free self, valet $8. Rack rates: $99–$159. AE, DC, DISC, MC, V.*

Summerfield Suites

$$–$$$ International Drive

These one- and two-bedroom suites offer 400 and 550 square feet, respectively, in a neat-as-a-pin package. Some rooms sport open-air balconies overlooking a courtyard; all come with kitchens, refrigerators, and coffeemakers. Units also feature such homey touches as an iron and ironing board, a TV in the living room and bedrooms, and multiple telephones. A daily continental breakfast is free, and there's a pool and a fitness center where you can work off the calories. A shuttle to **WDW** is available for a fee.

8480 International Dr. (between the Bee Line Expwy. and Sand Lake Rd.). ☎ *800-833-4353 or 407-352-2400. Fax: 407-238-0778. Internet:* www.summerfields-orlando.com/. *Parking: Free. Rack rates: $129–$259. AE, CB, DC, DISC, MC, V.*

The Villas of Grand Cypress

$$$–$$$$ Lake Buena Vista

Meet the sister site to the Hyatt Regency Grand Cypress (listed earlier in this chapter). The villas, a short drive from the larger hotel, offer privacy not found in most resorts, great views of the golf courses and canals, and resident ducks that wander onto your patio when they hear the door open (so be prepared with crackers or bread crusts). You can play 45 holes of golf on Jack Nicklaus-designed courses or take lessons at the golf academy. The horse crowd loves the top-of-the-line equestrian center; riding lessons and packages are available. The Mediterranean-style villas, which range from junior suites to four-bedroom affairs (425–1,100 square feet), have patios or balconies, dataports, hair dryers, and Roman tubs. The larger villas have full kitchens. Dining is available in the elegant Black Swan Restaurant (see Chapter 14). There's free shuttle service to the Hyatt Grand, all of the resort's recreational facilities, and to the **WDW** parks.

1 N. Jacaranda (off Hwy. 535, past the Disney entrance on Hotel Plaza Blvd., about a mile on the right). ☎ *800-835-7377 or 407-239-4700. Fax: 407-239-7219. Internet:* www.grandcypress.com. *146 villas. Parking: Free, valet $10. Rack rates: $215–$1,800. Ask about golf, equestrian, family, and getaway packages. AE, CB, D, DC, MC, V.*

Walt Disney World Dolphin

$$$$ Walt Disney World/Official WDW Hotel

What a wonderful place for folks a) not on a budget, b) wanting to be close to **Epcot** and **Disney–MGM Studios,** and c) desperate to stay in a place that answers the question: What kind of buildings would Dali have created if he were an architect?

It's hard not to notice the massive, 56-foot twin dolphins on the roof of this resort, which some people feel is unfortunate. Once inside the lobby, you'll encounter prints from the likes of Matisse and Picasso. The rooms are 400 square feet and offer Nintendo, dataports, and hair dryers; some come with balconies. The Dolphin suffers from Four Fever: it has four restaurants, four pools, and four lighted tennis courts. There's also a health club, a jogging trail, and a lounge. It shares many of its facilities with its sister hotel, the **Walt Disney World Swan** (listed later in this chapter). There's free transportation to the **WDW** parks, but you have to pay for a ride to the others.

1500 Epcot Resorts Blvd. (off Buena Vista Dr., next to Walt Disney World Swan). ☎ *800-248-7926, 800-227-1500, or 407-934-4000. Fax: 407-934-4884. Internet:* www. swandolphin.com. *1,509 units. Parking: Free, valet $8. Rack rates: $295–$3,100. Inquire about packages. AE, CB, DC, DISC, JCB, MC, V.*

Walt Disney World Swan

$$$$ Walt Disney World/Official WDW Hotel

Located on the same property as the Dolphin, the Swan offers another chance to stay on the Magic Mickey's property without being bombarded by rodent decor. This 12-story hotel is topped with dual 45-foot swan statues and seashell fountains. The Swan and Dolphin hotels are connected by a canopied walkway. The luxurious rooms are a shade smaller (360 square feet) than those in the Dolphin, but have the same Nintendo, dataports, and hair dryers. This hotel also has four restaurants, four pools, and four lighted tennis courts. You can get a free ride to the **Disney** parks and transportation for a fee to the other theme parks.

1200 Epcot Resorts Blvd. (off Buena Vista Dr., next door to the Walt Disney World Dolphin). ☎ *800-248-7926, 800-228-3000, or 407-934-3000. Fax: 407-934-4499. Internet:* www.swandolphin.com. *758 units. Parking: Free, valet $8. Rack rates: $295–$3,100. Inquire about packages. AE, CB, DC, DISC, JCB, MC, V.*

The Unicorn Inn

$ Kissimmee

Here's a rarity — an Orlando B&B that allows kids. The Unicorn, a blue-clapboard house in downtown Kissimmee, celebrated its sixth year as an inn in 2001. The inn has basic but clean and cozy rooms ranging in size from 200 to 275 square feet. All are individually decorated in period styles and offer a private bathroom and dataports. Several of the rooms can be doubled up to create a suite large enough for a four-member family. Rates include a free continental breakfast, and guests can make use of the inn's shared kitchen facilities, a boon for budget travelers. There's no pool. Located 12 miles east of **Disney,** the inn is a 20-minute drive from the parks; there's no transportation to the parks, so you'll need a car.

8 S. Orlando Ave. (From Disney go east on U.S. 192, right on Bermuda Ave., left on Emmett St. past the courthouse, right on South Orlando Ave.). ☎ *800-865-7212 or 407-846-1200. Fax: 407-846-1773. Internet:* www.bnbweb.com/unicorn.html. *5 units. Parking: Free. Rack rates: $85. Ask about AARP and AAA discounts and other packages. MC, V.*

Veranda Bed & Breakfast

$$ Downtown Orlando

Located in Thornton Park, this inn is near scenic Lake Eola and is an option if you want to stay near the downtown museums but not in a motel or hotel. Its four buildings date to the early 1900s. All units (ranging from studios to suites that are 250 to 350 square feet) include private baths and entrances; some have garden tubs, balconies, kitchenettes, and four-posters. The two-bedroom, two-bath Key Lime Cottage ($199) sleeps four and has a full kitchen. Rates include a continental breakfast. The B&B doesn't offer transportation to the parks, making this another spot where a rental car is a necessity. To view the location of this hotel on a map, check out the "Downtown Orlando Nightlife" map in Chapter 28.

115 N. Summerlin Ave. ☎ *800-420-6822 or 407-849-0321. Fax: 407-849-0321, ext. 18. Internet:* www.theverandabandb.com. *9 units. Parking: Free. Rack rates: $99–$199. AE, DC, DISC, MC, V.*

Wyndham Palace Resort & Spa

$$$–$$$$ Lake Buena Vista/Official WDW Hotel

The hotel's spacious accommodations — most with lake-view balconies or patios — are within walking distance of **Downtown Disney Marketplace.** It's an ideal spot for honeymooners or those looking for a romantic weekend getaway. The appealing rooms are equipped with minirbars, irons, dataports, coffeemakers, and hair dryers. Sixty-five of the rooms are billed as eco-friendly (they have special air-conditioner filters, filtered water, and are odor-free) and 20 special-needs rooms (rooms with roll-in showers, higher sinks, lower light fixtures, and larger doorways). Amenities include three pools, a fully equipped spa, a sauna, a video arcade, and two restaurants, including the 27th-floor Arthur's 27 (see Chapter 14). Rates include free transportation to Disney; you pay a fee for transportation to the other theme parks.

1900 Buena Vista Dr. (off Hwy. 535, turn in the entrance to Downtown Disney Marketplace; the hotel is on Hotel Plaza Blvd.). ☎ *800-327-2990 or 407-827-2727. Fax: 407-827-6034. Internet:* www.bvp-resort.com. *1,014 units. Parking: Free, valet $9. Rack rates: $209–$718. AE, CB, DC, DISC, MC, V.*

No Room at the Inn?

Okay, some of you hate organization and love spontaneity. You're not going to plan a trip in any way, shape, or fashion. There are rooms available and you're going to find them, come hell, high water, or all of our warnings to plan ahead.

Well, bully for you. You probably can find a place to stay, though you'll almost certainly not get pick of the litter.

If you insist on arriving without a reservation and don't want to wear out a set of knuckles on motel doors, the official **Orlando Visitors Center** (☎ **407-363-5872**, but only call for information; you must show up to get a room) at 8723 International Dr., Suite 101, may be able to help you. The Center is open 8 a.m. to 8 p.m. daily, except Christmas. The Center can usually point you to available rooms, sometimes at a discount, but these rates are usually only good for the night you arrive.

You also should try the **Central Reservation Service**, ☎ **407-740-6442**, Internet: www.reservation-services.com; and **Discount Hotels of America**, ☎ **407-294-9600**; Internet: www.discounthotelsamerica.com.

Accommodations Indexes

The following section presents a listing of hotel recommendations by neighborhood and price. Use the maps in this chapter to get a more specific fix on where each hotel is located in relation to what you want to see and do while you're in Orlando.

Hotel Index by Location

Downtown Orlando
Four Points By Sheraton Orlando
    Downtown ($$)
Radisson Plaza Hotel Orlando ($$)
Veranda Bed & Breakfast ($$)

International Drive Area/Including Universal Orlando
Hampton Inn at Universal Studios
    ($)
Hard Rock Hotel ($$$)

Holiday Inn Family Suites Resort ($$)

The Peabody Orlando ($$$$)

Portofino Bay Hotel ($$$$)

Radisson Hotel Universal Orlando ($$)

Renaissance Orlando Resort at SeaWorld ($$–$$$)

Summerfield Suites ($$–$$$)

Lake Buena Vista (including Official WDW Hotels)

Best Western Lake Buena Vista Hotel ($$)

Blue Tree Resort ($$–$$$)

Courtyard by Marriott ($$)

Cypress Glen ($$$$)

Doubletree Guest Suites Resort ($$–$$$$)

Holiday Inn Sunspree Resort Lake Buena Vista ($–$$)

Homewood Suites Orlando ($$)

Hotel Royal Plaza ($$)

Hyatt Regency Grand Cypress ($$$$)

Marriott Village at Little Lake Bryan ($$)

The Villas of Grand Cypress ($$$–$$$$)

Walt Disney World Dolphin ($$$$)

Walt Disney World Swan ($$$$)

Wyndham Palace Resort & Spa ($$$–$$$$)

U.S. 192/Kissimmee

Best Western Kissimmee ($)

Celebration Hotel ($$–$$$)

Econo Lodge Maingate Hawaiian Resort ($–$$)

Holiday Inn Nikki Bird Resort ($–$$)

Renaissance Worldgate ($$)

The Unicorn Inn ($)

Walt Disney World

Disney's All-Star Movie Resort ($)

Disney's All-Star Music Resort ($)

Disney's All-Star Sports Resort ($)

Disney's Animal Kingdom Lodge ($$$–$$$$)

Disney's Beach Club Resort ($$$$)

Disney's BoardWalk Resort & BoardWalk Villas ($$$$)

Disney's Caribbean Beach Resort ($$)

Disney's Contemporary Resort ($$$–$$$$)

Disney's Coronado Springs Resort ($$)

Disney's Fort Wilderness Resort and Campground ($–$$$)

Disney's Grand Floridian Resort & Spa ($$$$)

Disney's Old Key West Resort ($$$$)

Disney's Polynesian Resort ($$$$)

Disney's Port Orleans Resort ($$)

Disney's Wilderness Lodge ($$–$$$$)

Disney's Yacht Club Resort ($$$$)

Hotel Index by Price

$$$$ ($250 and up)

Cypress Glen (Lake Buena Vista)

Disney's Beach Club Resort (Walt Disney World)

Disney's BoardWalk Resort & BoardWalk Villas (Walt Disney World)

Disney's Contemporary Resort (Walt Disney World)

Disney's Grand Floridian Resort & Spa (Walt Disney World)

Disney's Old Key West Resort (Walt Disney World)

Disney's Polynesian Resort
(Walt Disney World)
Disney's Wilderness Lodge
(Walt Disney World)
Disney's Yacht Club Resort (Walt
Disney World)
Hyatt Regency Grand Cypress
(Lake Buena Vista)
The Peabody Orlando
(International Drive area)
Portofino Bay Hotel (International
Drive Area/Universal Orlando)
The Villas of Grand Cypress (Lake
Buena Vista)
Walt Disney World Dolphin
(Lake Buena Vista/Official
WDW Hotels)
Walt Disney World Swan (Lake
Buena Vista/Official WDW
Hotels)

$$$ ($200 to $250)

Celebration Hotel (U.S.
192/Kissimmee)
Disney's Animal Kingdom Lodge
Disney's Fort Wilderness Resort &
Campground (Walt Disney
World)
Hard Rock Hotel (International
Drive Area/Universal Orlando)
Summerfield Suites (International
Drive area)
Wyndham Palace Resort & Spa
(Walt Disney World)

$$ ($100 to $200)

Best Western Lake Buena Vista
Hotel (Lake Buena
Vista/Official WDW Hotel)
Blue Tree Resort (Lake Buena
Vista)
Courtyard by Marriott (Lake
Buena Vista)
Disney's Caribbean Beach Resort
(Walt Disney World)
Disney's Coronado Springs Resort
(Walt Disney World)

Disney's Port Orleans Resort
(Walt Disney World)
Doubletree Guest Suites Resort
(Lake Buena Vista/Official
Disney Hotel)
Four Points By Sheraton Orlando
Downtown (Downtown
Orlando)
Holiday Inn Family Suites Resort
(International Drive)
Holiday Inn Nikki Bird Resort
(Kissimmee)
Holiday Inn Sunspree Resort
(Lake Buena Vista)
Homewood Suites Orlando (Lake
Buena Vista)
Hotel Royal Plaza (Lake Buena
Vista/
Official Disney Hotel)
Marriott Village at Little Lake
Bryan (Lake Buena Vista)
Radisson Plaza Hotel Orlando
(Downtown)
Radisson Hotel Universal Orlando
(International Drive area)
Renaissance Orlando Resort at
SeaWorld (International Drive
area)
Renaissance Worldgate
(Kissimmee)
Veranda Bed & Breakfast
(Downtown Orlando)

$ ($50 to $100)

Best Western Kissimmee
(U.S.192/Kissimeee)
Disney's All–Star Movie Resort
(Walt Disney World)
Disney's All–Star Music Resort
(Walt Disney World)
Disney's All–Star Sports Resort
(Walt Disney World)
Econo Lodge Maingate Hawaiian
Resort (Kissimmee)
Hampton Inn at Universal Studios
(International Drive area)
The Unicorn Inn (Kissimmee)

Chapter 9

Tying Up the Loose Ends

● ●

In This Chapter

▶ Buying travel and medical insurance

▶ Dealing with illness away from home

▶ Renting a car (or why you shouldn't)

▶ Making reservations and getting tickets in advance

▶ Packing tips

● ●

*Y*ou're almost ready to leave for Orlando. All you need to do is take care of a few last-minute details, plan an itinerary, put the dog in the kennel, stuff your bags with everything that's clean, water the geraniums, pay the mortgage, and finish 50 other eleventh-hour musts.

The information in this chapter will save you from wasting precious vacation hours while you wait in line, call around town, and buy the dental floss you forgot to pack. We also help you make decisions on whether to rent a car and give you advice on what to do if you get sick.

For more information about money issues, discounts, and budget matters, check out Chapter 3. Now, put your seat and tray-table in an upright position.

Buying Travel Insurance: Good Idea or Bad?

There are three primary kinds of travel insurance: trip cancellation, lost luggage, and medical. Trip cancellation insurance is a good idea for some, but lost luggage and additional medical insurance don't make sense for most travelers. Be sure to explore your options and consider the following advice before you leave home:

✔ **Trip cancellation insurance.** Cancellation insurance is a good idea if you've paid a large portion of your vacation expenses up front. If you've bought a package trip, cancellation insurance comes in handy if a member of your party becomes ill or if you experience a death in the family and aren't able to go on vacation.

✔ **Lost luggage insurance.** Your homeowner's insurance should cover stolen luggage if your policy encompasses off-premises theft, so check your existing policies before you buy any additional coverage. Airlines are responsible for up to $2,500 on domestic flights, but that may not be enough to cover your sharkskin suit. Our best advice: Wear it on the plane, and if you're carrying anything else of substantial value, stow it in your carry-on bag.

✔ **Medical insurance.** Your existing health insurance should cover you if you get sick while on vacation. (However, if you belong to an HMO, check to see whether you're fully covered when away from home.)

Some credit cards (American Express and certain gold and platinum Visas and MasterCards, for example) offer automatic flight insurance against death or dismemberment in case of an airplane crash. If you still think you need more insurance, make sure you don't pay for more insurance than you need. For example, if you need only trip cancellation insurance, don't purchase coverage for lost or stolen property. Trip cancellation insurance costs approximately 6 to 8 percent of your vacation's total value. Here's a list of some of the reputable issuers of travel insurance:

✔ **Access America**, 6600 W. Broad St., Richmond, VA 23230 (☎ **800-284-8300;** Fax 800-346-9265; Internet: www.accessamerica.com)

✔ **Travelex Insurance Services,** 11717 Burt St., Suite 202, Omaha, NE 68154 (☎ **888-457-4602**; Fax: 800-867-9531; Internet: www.travelex-insurance.com)

✔ **Travel Guard International,** 1145 Clark St., Stevens Point, WI 54481 (☎ **877-216-4885;** Internet: www.travel-guard.com)

✔ **Travel Insured International, Inc.,** P.O. Box 280568, 52-S Oakland Ave., East Hartford, CT 06128-0568 (☎ **800-243-3174;** Fax: 860-528-8005; Internet: www.travelinsured.com)

Combating Illness Away from Home

Finding a doctor you trust when you're out of town is hard. And getting a prescription refilled is no piece of cake, either. So, here are some travel tips to help you avoid a medical dilemma while you're on vacation:

✔ If you have health insurance, carry your identification card in your wallet. Likewise, if you don't think your existing policy is sufficient, purchase medical insurance for more comprehensive coverage.

✔ Bring all your medications with you as well as a prescription for more if you think you'll run out.

✔ Bring an extra pair of contact lenses or glasses in case you lose them.

✔ Don't forget to bring over-the-counter medicines for common travelers' ailments such as diarrhea or stomach acid.

✔ If you suffer from a chronic illness, talk to your doctor before taking your trip. For conditions such as epilepsy, diabetes, or a heart condition, wear a *MedicAlert* identification tag to immediately alert any doctor about your condition and give him or her access to your medical records through MedicAlert's 24-hour hotline. Participation in the MedicAlert program costs $35, with a $20 renewal fee. Contact the MedicAlert Foundation, 2323 Colorado Ave., Turlock, CA 95382 (☎ **888-633-4298;** Internet: www.medicalert.org).

If your ailment isn't a life-threatening emergency, use a walk-in clinic. You may not get immediate attention, but you'll probably pay around $60 rather than the $300 minimum for just signing in at an emergency-room counter.

Disney offers in-room medical service 24 hours a day by calling ☎ **407-238-2000. Doctors on Call Service** (☎ **407-399-3627**) is a medical group that makes house and room calls in most of the Orlando area. **Centra-Care** operates several reputable walk-in clinics throughout the Orlando area. Branches are listed in the Yellow Pages, including ones on International Drive (☎ **407-370-4881**) and at Lake Buena Vista, near Disney (☎ **407-934-2273**).

You can get a reputable referral from **Ask-A-Nurse.** Ask-A-Nurse asks whether you have insurance, but that's for information purposes only, so they can track who uses their system. Ask-A-Nurse is a free service open to everyone. In Kissimmee call ☎ **407-870-1700;** in Orlando call ☎ **407-897-1700.**

You can fill your prescriptions at 24-hour pharmacies, including Walgreen's, 1003 W. Vine St. (Hwy. 192), just east of Bermuda Avenue (☎ **407-847-5252**), and Eckerd Drugs, 7324 International Drive (☎ **407-345-0491**). Other pharmacies are listed in the Yellow Pages of the phone book.

To find a dentist, call **Dental Referral Service** (☎ **888-343-3440**). They can tell you the nearest dentist who meets your needs. Phones are staffed daily from 8 a.m. to 8 p.m.

Weighing Your Rental-Car Options

First off, you have to decide whether you'll need a car for your Orlando vacation (see Chapter 11 for more information about renting a car in Orlando). If you're going to spend most of your time at a resort, especially **Walt Disney World,** you may not need a car. Disney has its own transportation system; its buses and monorails are free, but you'll be a prisoner of **WDW's** often slow and indirect schedule.

If you plan to visit **Universal Orlando, SeaWorld,** and other attractions or areas of central Florida, you'll need to either rent a car or choose an alternate form of transportation, such as one of a number of hotel shuttles (some are free; others charge an average of $7–$10 per person). Mears Transportation, which is a shuttle service, and taxis are other options (see Chapter 11 for more information on transportation options in Orlando). Getting several people to the parks on a daily basis can be expensive if you choose these routes, but you'll save on car-rental rates, gas, and the $6- or $7-per-day parking fee at the major attractions if you take advantage of Orlando's transit system. You need to decide if the added convenience and mobility of a rental car is worth the added expense. Keep in mind that most car rentals are worth at least 500 miles on your frequent-flier account!

Adding up the cost of renting a car

On top of the standard rental prices, other optional charges apply to most car rentals. The *Collision Damage Waiver (CDW),* which requires you to pay for damage to the car in a collision, is charged on rentals in most states, but is covered by many credit card companies. Check with your credit card company before you go so that you can avoid paying this hefty fee (as much as $15–$20 a day).

Car-rental companies also offer additional liability insurance (if you harm others in an accident), personal accident insurance (if you harm yourself or your passengers), and personal effects insurance (if your luggage is stolen from your car). If you have insurance on your car at home, you're probably covered for most of these unlikelihoods. If your own insurance doesn't cover you for rentals, or if you don't have auto insurance, consider buying additional coverage (car-rental companies are liable for certain base amounts, depending on the state). But, weigh the likelihood of getting into an accident or losing your luggage against the cost of extra coverage (as much as $20 a day combined), which can significantly add to the price of your rental.

Some companies also offer refueling packages, in which you pay for an entire tank of gas up front. The price is usually fairly competitive with local gas prices, but you don't get credit for any gas remaining in the tank. If you reject this option, you pay only for the gas you use, but you have to return the vehicle with a full tank or face charges of $3 to $4 a gallon for any shortfall. If a stop at a gas station on the way to the airport will make you miss your plane, by all means take advantage of the fuel purchase option. Otherwise, skip it.

Booking a rental car on the Internet

As with other aspects of planning your trip, using the Internet can make comparison shopping and reserving a car rental much easier. All the major booking sites — **Travelocity** (www.travelocity.com), **Expedia** (www.expedia.com), **Yahoo! Travel** (http://travel.yahoo.com), and **Cheap Tickets** (www.cheaptickets.com), for example — offer search engines that can dig up discounted car-rental rates. Enter the size of the car you want, the pickup and return dates, and the city where you want to rent, and the server returns a price. You can then make your reservation through these sites.

An excellent Web site, **BreezeNet's Guide to Airport Rental Cars** (www.bnm.com), offers tips and sample rates for car rentals at airports around the world. It also features destination-specific discount specials, including many for Orlando.

If you want information about specific rental-car companies serving Orlando, see the Appendix in the back of this book.

Ask the right questions before renting a car

Car-rental rates vary even more than airline fares. The price depends on the size of the car, the length of time you keep it, where and when you pick it up and drop it off, where you travel with it, and a host of other factors. Asking a few key questions can save you hundreds of dollars. Ask the following questions to help save money when renting a car:

✓ **Is the weekend rate lower than the weekday rate?** Ask if the rate is the same for pickup Friday morning as it is Thursday night. If you're keeping the car five or more days, a weekly rate may be cheaper than the daily rate.

✓ **Will I be charged a drop-off fee if I return the car to a location that's different from where it was rented?** Some companies may assess a drop-off charge, others do not. Ask if the rate is cheaper if you pick up the car at the airport or a location in town.

✓ **May I have the price I saw advertised in the local newspaper?** Be sure to ask for that specific rate; otherwise you may be charged the standard (higher) rate. Don't forget to mention membership in AAA, AARP, frequent-flyer programs, and trade unions. These usually entitle you to discounts ranging from 5 to 30 percent. Ask your travel agent to check any and all of these rates.

Making Reservations and Getting Tickets in Advance

Because time is at a premium in Orlando, and you'll be spending enough of it on attraction lines, the last thing you want to do is wile away precious hours waiting for a restaurant table or a theater ticket. Although, in most cases, an advance reservation is not the mandatory item it is in other cities, having one in hand will certainly make your day run more smoothly.

Reserving a table

Compared to New York and San Francisco, where tables at the best restaurants are snapped up weeks in advance, securing reservations in Orlando is easy. In most instances, you can wait until you get to Florida to make dining reservations. Eateries on the "exceptions" list include Emeril's in **CityWalk** and Victoria & Albert's at **Walt Disney World** (see Chapter 14 for more information about Orlando's fantastic dining scene), where reservations need to be made at least a month in advance. Your hotel's concierge or front desk can help with reservations.

 Most **Walt Disney World** restaurants use a system called *Priority Seating*. With Priority Seating, you make a reservation that ensures you'll get the next available table after your arrival at the restaurant. Priority Seating reservations differ from a traditional reservation, where an empty table is held for you, but it's far better than just show-ing up and waiting your turn. For more details on this reservation system, see Chapter 13. You can arrange for Priority Seating for restau-rants, including character meals and dinner shows, up to 60 days in advance by calling ☎ **407-939-3463.** You can also make arrangements near the entrances to the theme parks (see Chapters 17 through 20 for detailed park information) or at Disney resorts.

Reserving a ticket and getting event information

Ticketmaster is the key reservations player for most major events in Orlando, including concerts, shows, and pro sports events. If you know of an event that's happening while you're in town, check first with your hometown Ticketmaster outlets to see whether they sell tickets for the event. (If you live as close as Miami or Atlanta, they probably do.) Other-wise, call the Ticketmaster outlet in Orlando at ☎ **407-839-3900,** or go to its Web site at www.ticketmaster.com. Ticketmaster is open from 9 a.m. to 9 p.m. Monday through Friday and 9 a.m. to 7 p.m. Saturday and Sunday.

Dozens of rock, rap, jazz, pop, country, blues, and folk stars are in town during any given week in Orlando. After you're in town, you can find schedules in the *Orlando Sentinel's* **Calendar** section, published every Friday. The newspaper also includes information about local attractions, hotels, restaurants, cultural events, and so on. To get information before you arrive, you can find the newspaper online at www. orlandosentinel.com.

You can also get additional event information from the **Orlando/ Orange County Convention & Visitors Bureau** (☎ 407-363-5872; Internet: www.orlandoinfo.com).

See Chapters 28 through 29 for information about making advance reservations for some of Orlando's best after-dark fun.

Reserving a green

Disney has 99 holes of golf (five regulation, par-72 courses and a nine-hole, par-36 walking course) that are open to the public as well as resort guests. For tee times and information, call ☎ 407-824-2270 up to seven days in advance. (Disney resort guests can reserve up to 30 days in advance.) Golf packages are available, and reservations can be made in advance by calling ☎ 407-934-7639. Get online details at www. disneyworld.com. (See Chapter 21 for more information.)

You can get information on and make reservations at other non-Disney courses through **Golfpac** (☎ 800-327-0878 or 407-260-2288; Internet: www.golfpacinc.com) or contact **Tee Times USA** (☎ 800-465-3356; Internet: www.teetimesusa.com).

Gearing Up: Practical Packing Advice

To start packing for your trip, take everything you think you'll need and lay it out on the bed. Now get rid of half of it. It's not that the airlines won't let you take it all — they will, with some limits — but why do you want to get a hernia from lugging half your house around with you? Remember, suitcase straps are particularly painful to sunburned shoulders. Use the tips in this section to avoid renting a truck to move your luggage around Orlando.

Florida is a laid-back place. Therefore, you can leave your formal wear — even your tie — at home unless you're planning a special night out. Instead, bring casual clothes, including some comfortable walking shoes (a must) and airy shirts, blouses, shorts, skirts, or pants. If you're coming during the Sunshine State's microscopic winter (that's mainly January and February), you may need to layer your clothing. In fact, bringing a light jacket or sweater and a thin rain poncho anyway is smart. And don't forget all the necessary toiletries, medications (pack these in your carry-on bag so that you have them if the airline loses your luggage), and a camera.

Some airlines allow two pieces of carry-on luggage per person, both of which must fit in the overhead compartment or the seat in front of you, but others restrict passengers to one. (Ask when making your reservation.) Use carry-ons for valuables, medications, and vital documents first. You can then add a book, breakable items you don't want to put in your suitcase, and a snack if you have room. Also, carry the sweater or light jacket with you — cabins can feel like the Arctic one minute and a sauna the next.

Here are some other essential packing tips:

- ✔ You can leave the snowshoes, ski masks, and thermal underwear at home; some winter mornings in central Florida do get brisk. Therefore, *layered clothing* (a sweater, light jacket, and a sweatshirt) is a good idea. You might also want to bring along a pair or two of long pants if you are visiting in winter— shorts and 50-degree temperatures don't mix well.

- ✔ The most common sign welcoming diners to Florida's restaurants states "Shirt and Shoes Required." It summarizes the Floridian way of life: casual, but not gross. Please, no short-shorts, tank tops, outer-underwear, or see-throughs in the dining room. (You may not care, but the rest of us are trying to eat.) Beyond those, you won't encounter many rules for attire. Classier joints may insist on a coat, fewer yet a tie, but sport coats or — heaven forbid! — suits are pretty much a waste of time and luggage space. Slacks and a nice shirt or blouse are sufficient for almost everywhere and nice shorts show up everywhere, even at night.

- ✔ Sun cover-ups are essential. You can get a blistering burn on the coolest and cloudiest of days in Florida. Bring a hat (preferably one with a 360-degree brim) and sunglasses, too. Don't forget to bring sunscreen with a 25-rating or higher. Better still, get a waterproof one so you don't lose its benefits to sweat or the water in the hotel pool. Kids especially need protection from the sun.

- ✔ Don't forget an umbrella or poncho, regardless of the season. Florida is as wet as it is warm and the umbrella and poncho prices in theme parks can cause an anxiety attack.

- ✔ Bring at least two pairs of shoes and plenty of socks so you can start each day with fresh, dry footwear. Your standby pair of shoes will be invaluable after a visit to one of the many theme parks that have water rides. Likewise, waiting in line on hot days is tougher on the tootsies than keeping ice cream from melting on the equator. Many theme-park veterans carry extra shoes and socks with them, changing footwear midway through their day.

- ✔ If you're visiting Florida from early spring to late fall, bring a lot of lightweight shirts (T-shirts work very well) and shorts to stay cool during the days. And for the sake of your fellow patrons, don't forget an extra swipe of deodorant.

Part III
Settling into Orlando

The 5th Wave   By Rich Tennant

"The hotel said they were giving us the 'Indiana Jones' suite."

In this part . . .

Orlando isn't New York or London, but it can seem overwhelming at first. Getting around the tourist areas and downtown Orlando can be quite intimidating. Don't worry, though — it's not as complicated as it looks. In this part, we walk you through the city's neighborhoods, tell you where to catch local transportation, and erase any confusion you may have.

Chapter 10

Orienting Yourself in Orlando

● ●

In This Chapter

▶ Landing at the airport

▶ Exploring Orlando's neighborhoods

▶ Getting information when you arrive

● ●

*A*lthough it may seem that way to first-time visitors, all roads in Orlando do not lead to **Disney.** Yes, you would be hard-pressed to get lost on a street or highway without coming across a sign directing you to **WDW,** but this doesn't mean that navigating the rest of the city won't drive you to distraction. We start off by getting you from the airport to the parks and then clue you in about Orlando's major neighborhoods.

Arriving on the Orlando Scene

While other travelers who didn't read this book are lost in the black hole known as Orlando International Airport (☎ **407-825-2001;** Internet: `http://fcn.state.fl.us/goaa/index.htm`), you'll whiz on to baggage claim and your chariot of choice. Our best words of advice: Heads up! You're going to need to pay attention to get out of the airport in a timely fashion.

If you can run a direct route, just follow the signs to baggage claim. (You land at Level 3, so you need to take a shuttle to the main terminal, and then go to Level 2 for your bags. You can catch hotel shuttles or taxis on the ground level; rental-car desks are at Level 1.) **Note:** If you're arriving from a foreign country, you have to go through Immigration before baggage claim and then through Customs after picking up your luggage.

If you need cash, ATMs are located in the arrival and departure terminals near the three pods of gates (1–29, 30–59, and 60–99). There are also ATMs located where the shuttles deposit you in the main terminal. If you need to convert your pounds, francs, and so on to U.S. dollars, you can find currency exchanges (open 9:30 a.m. to 9:00 p.m.) opposite the ATMs at gate pods 1–29 and 60–99 in the air terminal. In the main terminal, they're located where shuttles arrive from gates 1–29.

All major car-rental companies are located at the airport (on Level 1) or nearby. (See the Appendix in the back of this book for the toll-free numbers of the major rental companies.)

Finding Your Way to Your Hotel

The airport is a 25-minute hop, skip, and long jump from **Walt Disney World** and 15 to 20 minutes from Universal Orlando and downtown. **Mears Transportation Group** (☎ 407-423-5566; Internet: www. mears-net.com) is the major shuttle player. It runs vans between the airport (you board at ground level) and all Disney resorts and official hotels, as well as most other area properties, every 15 to 25 minutes. Round-trip to downtown Orlando or International Drive is $23 for adults ($16 for kids 4 to 11); it's $27 for adults ($19 for kids) to **Walt Disney World/Lake Buena Vista** or Kissimmee/U.S. 192.

QuickTransportation/Orlando (☎ 888-784-2522 or 407-354-2456; Internet: www.quicktransportation.com) is more personal. You're greeted on the ground level with a sign bearing your name. They cost more than Mears, but they're coming for you, not other travelers, too. And they're only going to your resort. It's a good option for four or more people. Rates are from $70 (up to six, round-trip) to I-Drive/Universal Orlando and $130 to Disney.

Taxis are another option if your party has enough people. The standard rates for **Ace Metro, ☎ 407-855-0564,** and **Yellow Cab, ☎ 407-699-9999,** are $2.50 for the first mile and $1.50 a mile thereafter. The one-way charge from the airport to **Disney** for up to five people in a cab or seven in a van is about $44. A trip to International Drive is $26; to downtown, it's $20. Vans and taxis load on the ground level of the airport.

Some hotels offer free shuttle service to and from the airport, so make sure to ask when booking your room.

If you're driving a rented car from the airport, take the north exit out of the airport to 528 West (a toll road also known as the Bee Line Expressway). Follow the signs to I-4, then go west to Exit 26B (marked Epcot/Disney Village) and follow the signs toward the **Disney** attractions. Your ride takes about 25 minutes if traffic isn't too heavy. This and other **WDW** exits are clearly marked.

Exploring Orlando by Neighborhood

Orlando's major artery is Interstate 4. Locals call it I-4 or that #@$*%^#!! road, because it's often congested, especially during the weekday rush hour (7 to 9 a.m. and 4 to 6 p.m.). I-4 runs diagonally across the state from Tampa to Daytona Beach. Likewise, exits from I-4 lead to all **WDW**

properties, **Universal, SeaWorld,** International Drive, U.S. 192, Kissimmee, Lake Buena Vista, downtown Orlando, and Winter Park. Most of the exits are well marked, but construction is common, and exit numbers often change. Keep this in mind when you're traveling along I-4, so that you don't end up in the Bahamas.

Orlando Neighborhoods

The Florida Turnpike crosses I-4 and links with I-75 to the north. U.S. 192, a major east-west artery, reaches from Kissimmee to U.S. 27, crossing I-4 near the **WDW** entrance road. Farther north, the Bee Line Expressway toll road (or Hwy. 528) goes east from I-4 past Orlando International Airport to Cape Canaveral and the **Kennedy Space Center.** The East-West Expressway (also known as Hwy. 408) is another toll road that bypasses the tourist meccas.

Walt Disney World

The empire, its big and little parks, resorts, restaurants, shops, and assorted trimmings are scattered across 30,500 acres. The thing that you may find most surprising is that **WDW** isn't even in Orlando. It's southwest of the city, off I-4 on West U.S. 192. Stay in this area, and you'll learn that convenience has its price. Accommodations here run as much as double the price in nearby Kissimmee.

Downtown Disney West Side and **Pleasure Island** are Disney's two nighttime entertainment areas. **Downtown Disney Marketplace** is the nearby shopping complex. Combined, they're filled with restaurants, shops, and dance clubs of all types and prices. They're actually in Lake Buena Vista, although it's a part of **Walt Disney World.**

Even if you're not staying or driving in Mickeyville, it's a good idea to get a Walt Disney World Transportation Guide Map to see where everything is. It's free and available at the main parking booths, resort security booths, or *Guest Services* desks inside the hotels.

Lake Buena Vista

Lake Buena Vista is **Disney**'s next-door neighborhood. It's where you'll find "official" (though not Disney-owned or located) hotels, and it's close to **Downtown Disney.** This charming area has manicured lawns, tree-lined thoroughfares, and free transportation throughout the realm, though it may take a while to get from Point A to Point B because of a combination of slow shuttle service and heavy traffic.

Celebration

Imagine living in a Disney world. Celebration is an attempt to re-create a squeaky-clean, Mickey magic town. It will eventually have thousands of residents living in Disney homes, which start at about $200,000. Celebration's downtown area is, however, designed for tourists. It has a hotel and some first-rate, if pricey, shops and restaurants.

Orlando Neighborhoods

Kissimmee

Kissimmee has a tacky side: It's loaded with T-shirt shops and every burger barn known to Western civilization. But Kissimmee is just a short drive (roughly 10-15 miles) from the Wizard of Disney and, with plenty of modest motels, it's a good choice for those on a budget. The town centers on U.S. 192/Irlo Bronson Memorial Highway.

International Drive (Highway 536)

Known as I-Drive, this tourist mecca extends seven to ten miles north of the Disney kingdom between Highway 535 and the Florida Turnpike. From bungee jumping and ice skating to dozens of themed restaurants, this stretch of road is *the* tourist strip in central Florida. I-Drive also offers numerous hotels and shopping areas. It's home to the Orange County Convention Center and offers easy access to **SeaWorld** and **Universal Orlando.** The northern half of I-Drive is already packed, and developers continue to eat up space in the southern half.

Downtown Orlando

Right off I-4 East, Downtown Orlando is home to loads of clubs, shops, and restaurants. Dozens of antique shops line Antique Row on Orange Avenue near Lake Ivanhoe.

Winter Park

Just north of downtown Orlando, Winter Park offers Park Avenue, a collection of upscale shops and restaurants along a cobblestone street. Winter Park has little, if any kid-appeal, and it's too far north to use as a home base if you plan on spending much time at the Disney parks.

Information, Please

After you've landed, one of the best places for up-to-date information is the concierge or the front desk at your hotel (and they're even better if you're staying on Disney soil).

If you're in the International Drive area, stop for information at the official Orlando Visitors Center, 8723 International Drive (four blocks south of Sand Lake Road); ☎ **407-363-5872**

Friday's **Calendar** section in the *Orlando Sentinel* also includes a lot of tourist-friendly information on dining and entertainment.

At Orlando International Airport, arriving passengers can find information at **The Magic of Disney** and **Disney's Flight of Fantastic,** two shops located in the A and B terminals, respectively. They sell Disney multiday park tickets, make dinner show and hotel reservations, and provide brochures. Facilities are open daily from 6 a.m. to 9 p.m.

The airport's **Universal Studios Store,** which is open daily from 6:30 a.m. to 10:00 p.m., provides similar services, as do the **SeaWorld** stores in the A and B terminals, which are open daily from 6:30 a.m. to 10:00 p.m.

Chapter 11

Getting Around Orlando

- -

In This Chapter

▶ Exploring Orlando's transportation options

▶ Driving in Orlando

▶ Strolling around the city

- -

*O*rlando feeds on adventurers like you. Tens of millions of travelers arrive every year, and Orlando's tourism czars (prompted by Disney's dollars) want to make getting from Point A to Point B as easy as possible. The faster you can get around town, the more time (and money) you can spend in the attractions, clubs, and restaurants.

However, unless you volunteer for incarceration in Mickeyville, you may have to deal with slowdowns such as rush hour, which runs from 7 to 9 a.m. and 4 to 6 p.m. weekdays, so allow a cushion in your travel plans. During the week, tourist traffic heightens commuter traffic. Most of the parks don't open until 9 a.m. (except **WDW's Animal Kingdom,** see Chapter 20), so you won't miss much if you arrive a little late. Traffic is just as bad on weekends because more vacationers are on the roads, as well as nearly as many commuters, because the parks are open daily.

Relying on Orlando's Transportation Network

Your major decision regarding Orlando transportation will be whether to use **Walt Disney World's** transportation network (which is truly useful only to those staying at a **WDW** resort), to rent a car, or to stick to other means. What system will work best for you depends on what you want to see, where you are staying, and how much time you want to spend getting around the city.

Traveling with Disney's transportation system

If you plan to stay at a Disney resort or an official hotel (see Chapter 8 for more information on Disney hotels) and will spend the majority of your time visiting Disney parks, you can probably skip a rental car — at least for most of your stay. A free transportation network runs through **Disney World.** Buses, ferries, water taxis, and monorails operate from two hours prior to the parks' opening until two hours after closing. Likewise, Disney offers service to **Downtown Disney, Typhoon Lagoon, River Country, Blizzard Beach, Pleasure Island, Fort Wilderness,** and other Disney resorts. Disney properties also offer transportation to other area attractions, but you'll have to pay extra.

The advantages of using Disney's transportation system include:

- ✔ It's free.
- ✔ You save on car rental and gas charges.
- ✔ You don't have to pay $6 a day to park in the theme park lots.
- ✔ If your party wants to split up, you can board a transport to different areas.

Disadvantages include:

- ✔ You're at the mercy of Disney's schedule.
- ✔ Sometimes you have to take a ferry to catch a bus to get on the monorail to reach your hotel. The system makes a complete circuit, but does not necessarily travel the most direct route for you. It can take an hour or more to get somewhere that's right across the lagoon from you. Use this book's maps (see *Maps at a Glance,* just before the Table of Contents) to show you what's where and where you want to be.
- ✔ You have to endure multiple stops, particularly on buses, and at peak periods crowds may force you to wait for the next bus.

If you plan to travel on the Disney transportation network, verify with the driver or someone at your hotel's information desk that you're taking the most direct route. Keep asking questions along the way. Unlike missing a highway exit, missing a stop on the bus route means you'll have to take another ride on the Mickey-go-round.

Getting around by bus

Lynx (☎ **407-841-2279** or 407-841-8240; Internet: www.golynx.com) bus stops are marked with a paw print. The buses serve **Disney,**

Universal, and **International Drive** ($1 for adults, 25 cents for kids 8 to 18), but their routes are not very visitor-oriented.

Touring by trolley

The I-Ride Trolley on International Drive (☎ 407-354-5656; Internet: www.iridetrolley.com) runs every 15 minutes, 7 a.m. to midnight (75 cents for adults, 25 cents for seniors, kids under 12 ride free). Due to I-Drive's heavy traffic, this is the best way to get around if you're staying in this area or at least spending the day. It cuts down on the hurry-up-and-wait frustration of bumper-to-bumper traffic.

Using a taxi

Yellow Cab (☎ 407-699-9999) and Ace Metro (☎ 407-855-0564) are among the taxicab companies serving the Orlando area. But for day-to-day travel to and from the attractions, cabs are expensive unless your group has five or more people. Rates cost $2.50 for the first mile, $1.50 per mile thereafter.

Traveling by shuttle

Mears Transportation Group (☎ 407-423-5566; Internet: www.mears-net.com) operates shuttle buses to all major attractions, including **Cypress Gardens** (Lakeland), **Kennedy Space Center** (Cape Canaveral), **Busch Gardens** (in Tampa), **Universal Orlando, SeaWorld,** and **Disney,** among others. Rates vary by destination. For more on great attractions just outside of Orlando, see Chapter 26.

Maneuvering through town on a motorcycle

If you have a motorcycle license, you can rent bikes at American V Twin, 5101 International Drive (☎ 888-268-8946) or 407-903-0058; Internet: www.amvtwin.com), and Iron Horse Rentals, 4380 L.B. McLeod Road (☎ 800-946-4743 or 407-426-7091; Internet: www.hogride.com). Their inventories can be in short supply, so call ahead. You must be at least 21 years old, have a valid motorcycle license, and have a major credit card. Rentals range from $800 to $1,200 per week and include helmets, locks, and a brief orientation.

Plan months in advance if you're visiting during Bike Week — late February and early March — or Biketober Fest in mid-October. (Both events are in Daytona Beach, but many bikers stay in Orlando.)

Touring Orlando by Car: Expanding Your Sightseeing Horizons

If you're on an extended stay — more than a week — you probably want to rent a car for at least a day or two to venture beyond the tourist areas. (Yes, there *is* life beyond the theme parks.) See the Appendix at the back of this book for toll-free numbers of various car rental agencies.

Here are a few additional (in some cases redundant) tips for driving in Orlando.

✔ Remember to allow for rush hour traffic between 7 to 9 a.m. and 4 to 6 p.m. on weekdays.

✔ I-4 may look like it runs north and south on most maps, but Orlando's sign painters say otherwise. To them, you drive west toward **Disney** or Tampa and east toward downtown Orlando and Daytona Beach.

✔ In Florida, you can make a right turn on red after coming to a full stop and making sure the coast is clear (unless signs say otherwise). Consider yourself warned: If you're sitting at a red light with your blinker on and not turning right, you'll probably hear horns blaring. Chances are, the drivers are saluting you — make sure your path is clear, and then *move it.*

✔ Posted speed limits are enforced pretty vigorously. Fines for speeding begin at more than $150. Pay particular attention to road construction and school zones, where speed limits are reduced and signs warn about speeding fines being doubled — they're not kidding.

✔ Remember the Name Game: International Drive is called I-Drive. Irlo Bronson Memorial Highway is U.S. 192 or just 192. Florida Route 528 is the Bee Line Expressway. State Road 50 is more commonly called Colonial Drive.

✔ You must have a Florida handicap permit to park in handicap parking places. Handicap permits from other states are honored, but a disabled license plate alone won't do.

✔ Along a 12-mile stretch of U.S. 192 in Kissimmee, there are periodic, 25-foot-high markers, brightly marking the area's many points of interest. The westernmost marker is Marker 4 (planners expect to add three, two, and one due to future growth in that direction). The remaining pairs are numbered eastward in sequence. If you phone for directions to a restaurant, hotel, or attraction along this stretch of road, you'll likely be told the destination's location in relation to these markers. (It's "just past Marker" so and so.) The turnoff for **Walt Disney World** is right around Marker 7.

> ✔ Buckle Up: Florida law says both front- and back-seat passengers must wear a seat belt.
>
> ✔ In an emergency, dial ☎ **911,** or you can reach the Florida Highway Patrol on a cell phone by dialing ☎ ***FHP.**

Watch Your Step: Strolling the Streets of Orlando

 We don't recommend traveling on foot anywhere in Orlando, but you occasionally will have to walk across a parking lot or street. *Be very careful.* This city isn't conducive to strolling. Within the safe confines of the theme parks, you will have no problems hoofing around (in fact, you'll be on your feet quite a bit), but walking anywhere outside the theme parks is a thrills-and-chills experience most people want to avoid. Orlando is among the most dangerous cities in the country for pedestrians, according to a Washington, D.C.-based research group. Wide roads that are designed to move traffic quickly and a shortage of sidewalks, streetlights, and crosswalks are to blame.

Chapter 12

Keeping Your Cash in Check

. . . .

In This Chapter

▶ Accessing cash in Orlando

▶ Dealing with a robbery

. . . .

*T*ake a moment to ponder the meaning of the most important word in Orlando's economic vocabulary.

Tourism (tooo' riz-um): n. 1. travel, particularly the kind that brings two sides together, one giving food, shelter, and entertainment in exchange for payment from the other; 2. a game of chance in which a bunch of business bigwigs attempt to relieve the unsuspecting of their assets; 3. a puzzling phenomenon in which visitors pay to do things that natives leave town to avoid.

With that in mind, read this chapter for advice on accessing and guarding your money to keep the good times rolling in Orlando.

Finding Funds in Orlando

Even the most thrifty travelers usually find themselves forking out more money than usual during their Orlando visit, and carrying a fully loaded wallet isn't always the most convenient, or the safest, way to go. Cash, credit, or check; Orlando makes it easy for visitors to access and spend their vacation dollars.

Banking on credit

Disney parks, resorts, shops, and restaurants (but not most of its fast-food counters) accept five major credit cards: American Express, Diners Club, Discover, MasterCard, and Visa. Most other theme parks, attractions, accommodations, and restaurants accept those, too, and in some cases others.

You can also receive cash advances off your credit card at any bank. Keep in mind that you'll start paying interest the moment you receive the cash and you won't get frequent-flyer miles on an airline credit card. At most banks, you don't need to go to a teller; you can get a cash advance at the ATM if you know your personal identification number (PIN). If you've forgotten your PIN or didn't even know you had one, call the phone number on the back of your credit card and ask the bank to send it to you. It usually takes five to seven business days, though some banks will give it to you over the phone if you tell them your mother's maiden name and the number of freckles on your right shoulder or pass some other kind of security clearance.

SunTrust Bank, at 1675 Buena Vista Drive, across from **Downtown Disney Marketplace,** will give you a cash advance on your Master-Card or Visa. It will also cash traveler's checks or personal checks of $25 or less (if drawn on a U.S. bank and if you have a driver's license and major credit card). The bank also exchanges non-U.S. currency. The bank is open 9 a.m. to 4 p.m. weekdays, and until 6 p.m. Thursdays (☎ **407-828-6106**).

Dealing with Disney dineros

Walt Disney World theme parks and some resorts offer their own way of paying. The Disney debit card can be used in shops and restaurants. This is sometimes referred to as a Disney credit card, but it isn't a credit card in the true sense of the word. Items are actually charged to your room and you have to settle up before checking out (sigh, another line).

Although we don't recommend doing so, you can buy Disney Dollars (currency with cute little pictures of Mickey, Goofy, or Minnie on it) at the guest-services desk in each of the parks. The bills come in $1, $5, and $10 denominations, and they're good at shops, restaurants, and resorts throughout **Walt Disney World** and in Disney stores elsewhere on the planet. This currency provides no real benefit other than its negligible souvenir value. If you want to trade Disney Dollars for real currency upon leaving, you end up facing — you guessed it! — another line.

Refunds for deposits on wheelchairs, strollers, and such in the theme parks are usually paid in Disney Dollars. If you're persistent, you can get your refunds in Uncle Sam's dollars, instead of Mickey's.

Locating ATMs

Central Florida is literally peppered with 24-hour automatic teller machines linked to a national network that most likely includes your bank at home, including those using the Cirrus, Honor, MasterCard, and Plus systems. (The back of your ATM card should list its affiliation.) The 800-numbers provide ATM locations where you can withdraw money while on vacation. There's frequently an extra charge for using non-bank ATMs. In Florida, the average is $2.60 if the ATM isn't affiliated with your bank.

In Central Florida, ATMs are about as common as corner phone booths used to be. You can find them on *Main Street* and in *Tomorrowland* in the **Magic Kingdom,** in the *Disney Crossroads Shopping Center,* and at the **WDW All-Star Sports Resort, Disney–MGM Studios, Epcot, Animal Kingdom,** and **Pleasure Island.** They're also located near *Guest Services* at **SeaWorld, Universal Orlando,** and **Islands of Adventure.** You also can find them at most of the area's Circle K and 7-Eleven convenience stores and in most major malls.

Maps that the theme parks give you as you enter also show you where to find an ATM. Some practically beckon ATM locations in neon. After all, the object is to get you to spend, Spend, SPEND!

If you need to make an eye-to-eye transaction, most local banks are open 9 a.m. to at least 3 or 4 p.m. Monday through Friday, and many drive-ins are open 9 a.m. to noon on Saturdays.

Keeping Your Money Safe (And What to Do If It's Stolen)

Orlando's wholesome, friendly image persuades many travelers to drop their guards, often with disastrous results. If you're a tourist, you're easy pickings for thieves and tourist-related crimes are one of Orlando's biggest problems, much as they are in destinations such as New York, Las Vegas, and London. To reduce your chances of losing your cash to a thief, take the following precautions:

✔ Use ATMs only in well-lighted areas, making sure to shield your access numbers from prying eyes. Never put anything in the trash that has your account number or other personal information on it.

✔ Women should keep their purses slung diagonally across their chests. The best kind of purse to take is one that folds over, rather than one that has just a zipper on top. Do not sling your camera or purse over your chair when in a restaurant.

✔ If your hotel has an in-room safe, use it. Stash excess cash, traveler's checks, and any other valuables that you don't need for immediate use. Better yet, leave any valuables you won't need at home. If your hotel room doesn't have a safe, put your valuables inside the hotel's safety deposit box.

If you are robbed, keep the following in mind:

✔ Almost every credit-card company has a toll-free emergency number that you can call if your wallet or purse is stolen. The credit-card company may be able to wire you a cash advance off your credit card immediately, and, in many places, get you an emergency credit card in a day or two.

✔ The issuing bank's 800-number is usually on the back of the credit card. Make note of this number before you leave on your trip and stash it somewhere other than your wallet. If you forget to write down the number, you can call ☎ **800-555-1212** — that's 800 directory assistance — to get the number. And because thieves may not swipe this guidebook — though it's worth its weight in gold — **Citicorp Visa's** U.S. emergency number is ☎ **800-336-8472**. **American Express** cardholders and traveler's check users need to call ☎ **800-221-7282** for all money emergencies. **MasterCard** holders must call ☎ **800-307-7309**.

✔ If you opt to carry traveler's checks, make sure that you keep a record of their serial numbers in a safe location so you can handle an emergency. Good hiding places for the serial numbers include your hotel safe *and* a close relative's house.

Odds are that if your wallet is gone, you've seen the last of it and the police aren't likely to recover it for you. However, after you realize it's gone and you cancel your credit cards, you should still call the police. You may need their report number for credit card or insurance purposes later.

For more monetary information, see Chapter 3.

Part IV
Dining in Orlando

The 5th Wave   By Rich Tennant

In this part . . .

Few cities offer as many dining options as O-Town.
Some of the city's menus feature innovative chefs,
clever themes, and snappy service. (We'll leave out the
others.) And, because central Florida attracts visitors
from every corner of the planet, you're assured of finding
literally any kind of cuisine that tickles your taste buds.

In this part, we explore the vast array of dining options
Orlando offers, including the kids' favorite, character
dining.

Chapter 13

The Scoop on Orlando Dining

In This Chapter
▶ Making reservations, dressing to dine, and paying the check
▶ Choosing a restaurant by price, location, and cuisine

*T*oday there are almost 4,000 restaurants to choose from in Orlando, with new restaurants opening all the time. And most of the restaurants you'll find are surprisingly decent (this is, after all, a city where food tends to be viewed merely as fuel); some can even stake a claim to greatness. To ensure you the best possible dining experience, in this chapter, we provide general pointers about dining in the land of Diz, the dress code, and making reservations. In Chapter 14, we detail Orlando's A-List eateries and also give you lists of Orlando's best restaurants by price, location, and cuisine. And, in Chapter 15, we discuss the quintessential Orlando food experience — character dining.

Making Reservations

Reserving a table is a bright idea for some of Orlando's finest restaurants (see Chapter 14 for a list of the best places to eat), but in most cases, you don't need to make reservations before you leave home or right after you land. There are, of course, some notable exceptions to this rule.

Priority Seating is the buzz word at **Disney** properties. This practice is the Magic Mickster's way of saying you get the next available table after you arrive. (Be warned, however. You'll probably have to wait after you get to the restaurant.) We recommend that you always call ahead and make a Priority Seating reservation. If you try walking in off the street to find a table, chances are slim that you will succeed before your stomach starts growling at you. Call ☎ **407-939-3463** to stake a claim to a Disney table. If you're staying at a **WDW** resort, you can make a reservation at the hotel's concierge desk.

You can also make Priority Seating reservations after you're inside the Disney parks. We suggest you do this immediately upon your arrival. At **Epcot,** visit the WorldKey Information Satellite on the main concourse at *World Showcase.* You can also talk to the *Guest Services* desk at **Epcot.**

In the **Magic Kingdom,** make reservations in person at the individual restaurants — the same holds true for **Disney–MGM Studios,** located on Hollywood Boulevard. At **Animal Kingdom,** visit *Guest Services* to make reservations.

Worried **WDW** can't entertain your vegetarian taste buds? Looking for kosher food? Disney can usually handle those diets and other special ones (people who need fat-free or sugar-free meals, folks who have allergies or a lactose intolerance, for instance) as long as guests give Disney advance notice – usually no more than 24 hours. It's a good idea to do this when you make Priority Seating arrangements. If you're not staying at **WDW,** call ☎ **407-824-2222.**

Dressing to Dine

You must wear clothes to dine, except, perhaps, at Orlando's one or two nudist resorts. You can, however, leave the penguin suits and long gowns at home. Florida is casual; it doesn't have the same dress codes as Monaco, on the *Queen Elizabeth II,* or at the New York Philharmonic. In most cases, people don't get gussied up to go to dinner in Florida unless they're celebrating a special event or dining at a high-end restaurant that requires formal or semiformal attire. For example, if you eat at Disney's Victoria & Albert's, you need a coat and tie or dressy dress — gender doesn't matter. Likewise, Dux at the **Peabody Hotel** on I-Drive is another restaurant that requires a little more than casual wear. (See Chapter 14 for details.)

Trimming the Fat from Your Dining Budget

If you're staying in the parks until closing, you may find it more convenient to eat there, but you'll probably pay an average of 25 percent more than in the outside world. If you don't mind ditching Mickey every now and again, you can lower your dining costs.

Here are a few suggestions to help you get the most out of your dining dollars:

✔ We won't list all of them, but if you spend any time on International Drive or U.S. 192/Irlo Bronson Memorial Highway between Kissimmee and Disney, you'll see all sorts of billboards peddling all-you-can-eat breakfast buffets for $3.99 to $4.99. This is a good way to fill your tanks early and skip or at least go easy on lunch, especially if your day is in the parks, where lunches are overpriced. Breakfast buffets are served by **Golden Corral,** 8033 International Dr. (☎ 407-352-6606); **Ponderosa Steak House,** 6362 International Dr. (☎ 407-352-9343), and 7598 U.S. 192 W. (☎ 407-396-7721); and **Sizzler Restaurant,** 9142 International Dr. (☎ 407-351-5369), and 7602 U.S. 192 W. (☎ 407-397-0997).

✔ Make sure you pick up the free magazines and ad books that you see everywhere in Orlando hotels, tourist information centers, most convenience stores, newspaper racks, and so on. These publications include coupons good for a second meal free, discount prices, or a free dessert with a meal. Also, watch for ads from restaurants that offer kids-eat-free specials.

✔ Inexpensive kids' menus (usually $5 and under) are common at most of Orlando's moderately priced and family-style restaurants. Many also offer distractions such as place mats with mazes or pictures to color.

✔ If you enjoy a cocktail before or after dinner, you've probably been to those places that charge almost as much for a drink as liquor stores charge for a bottle. If you want to save a few clams, bring or buy your own stash and have your drink in your hotel room or by the pool instead of paying restaurant prices.

That said, don't ignore places with happy-hour specials, including two-for-one drinks — some at bargain rates. You can find listings in free, handout newspapers in hotel lobbies and other places throughout Orlando.

Cutting food costs inside WDW

Eating at Disney can set you back more than a few bucks. For example, a 20-ounce bottle of cola is $2.25 or more and a like-size bottle of water is $2.50. To save money, buy a bottle of water from a local grocery, which likely costs less than $1, and take it with you to the park, refilling it at water fountains. Also, in **Animal Kingdom** you can belly up to the bar at the Rainforest Café, order a pop for $2, and get a free glass of water. If you're eating lunch, the average price per person is under $10 If you eat at the counter service-style fast food areas. The cheapest entrée at the park is a smoked turkey drumstick for $4.75; ice cream bars are $2, and a pineapple float is $2.50.

Some of the resorts at Disney offer a refillable mug, which is good for refills there for the duration of your WDW visit. The cost for the glass varies from place to place, ranging from $7.50 to $10. At most resorts, the refills are free, though a few charge $1. Some of Disney's water parks have refillable glasses, but refills are limited to the day you're in the park. (If you hear that you can use your glass for more than one day in some water parks, don't believe it. It's not true.) For more information, call Disney at ☎ 407-824-4321.

Tackling Tipping and Taxes in Orlando

Sales tax on restaurant meals and drinks ranges from 6 to 7 percent throughout the Orlando area. (These taxes don't apply to groceries.) In addition, the standard tip in full-service restaurants is 15 percent, and a 12-percent tip is usually warranted at a buffet where a server brings your drinks, fetches condiments, and cleans the table. If you have a pre-dinner drink, leave a small tip to reward the server. The practice of tipping the head waiter has all but disappeared, but if you want a special table in a crowded restaurant, money can talk.

Make sure you look over your check because some restaurants have started automatically tacking on a gratuity to your bill, especially for larger groups. Examine your check before coughing up more cash. There's no sense in doubling a tip for routine service.

Chapter 14

Orlando's Best Restaurants

● ●

In This Chapter

▶ Checking out Orlando's restaurants by the ABCs

▶ Reading full reviews of our favorite Orlando restaurants

● ●

*B*arnstorming through the attractions in and around Orlando can leave you as hungry as an alley cat. You can get so hungry walking around the parks that you find yourself willing to eat food no sane person would consider, like pickled eggs and pork rinds. Relax. You don't have to resort to such desperate measures as pickled cuisine. In this chapter, we give you our picks for what we think are Orlando's best restaurants and review them in alphabetical order. We also throw in some handy indexes at the end of the chapter to help you narrow down your choices.

Because you may spend a lot of time in the **Walt Disney World** area, we've given special attention to dining choices there. (Don't worry. We haven't forgotten to toss in a lot of worthwhile restaurants outside of Mickey's realm — including some newer kids under the **Universal Orlando** umbrella and some old standards elsewhere around town.)

All sit-down restaurants in the Disney theme parks require admission, with one exception: the Rainforest Café at **Animal Kingdom.** Also, alcohol isn't served in the **Magic Kingdom;** if you need a drink at the end of the day (and if you have kids, you may), you're out of luck if you stay.

Orlando Restaurants from A to Z

'50s Prime Time Café
$$ Disney–MGM Studios American   AMERICAN

Servers deliver family favorites, including Mom's meatloaf, chicken and biscuits, and turkey sandwiches. The food isn't the best, but the place is so much fun, you may love it anyway. Black-and-white TVs air shows such as *Topper* and *I Love Lucy* as servers zap you back to the days when you

Walt Disney World & Lake Buena Vista Restaurants

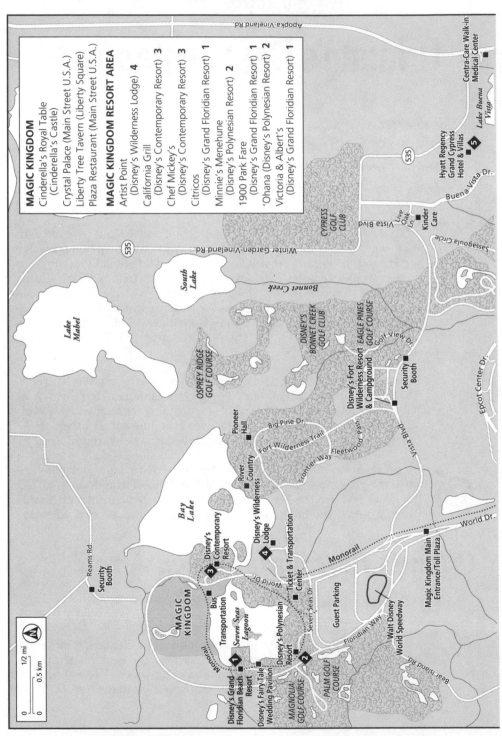

MAGIC KINGDOM

Cinderella's Royal Table
(Cinderella's Castle)
Crystal Palace (Main Street U.S.A.)
Liberty Tree Tavern (Liberty Square)
Plaza Restaurant (Main Street U.S.A.)

MAGIC KINGDOM RESORT AREA

Artist Point
(Disney's Wilderness Lodge) **4**
California Grill
(Disney's Contemporary Resort) **3**
Chef Mickey's
(Disney's Contemporary Resort) **3**
Citricos
(Disney's Grand Floridian Resort) **1**
Minnie's Menehune
(Disney's Polynesian Resort) **2**
1900 Park Fare
(Disney's Grand Floridian Resort) **1**
'Ohana (Disney's Polynesian Resort) **2**
Victoria & Albert's
(Disney's Grand Floridian Resort) **1**

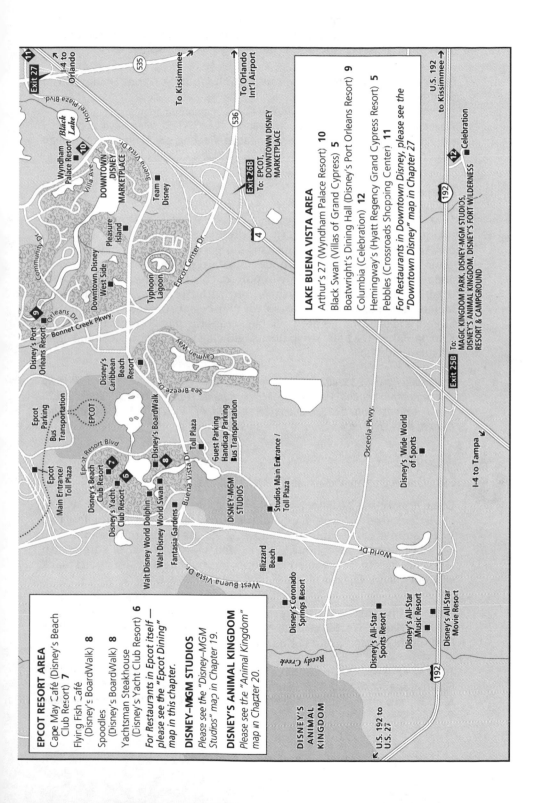

EPCOT RESORT AREA

Cape May Café (Disney's Beach Club Resort) **7**

Flying Fish Café (Disney's BoardWalk) **8**

Spoodles (Disney's BoardWalk) **8**

Yachtsman Steakhouse (Disney's Yacht Club Resort) **6**

For Restaurants in Epcot itself — please see the "Epcot Dining" map in this chapter.

DISNEY-MGM STUDIOS

Please see the "Disney-MGM Studios" map in Chapter 19.

DISNEY'S ANIMAL KINGDOM

Please see the "Animal Kingdom" map in Chapter 20.

LAKE BUENA VISTA AREA

Arthur's 27 (Wyndham Palace Resort) **10**

Black Swan (Villas of Grand Cypress) **5**

Boatwright's Dining Hall (Disney's Port Orleans Resort) **9**

Columbia (Celebration) **12**

Hemingway's (Hyatt Regency Grand Cypress Resort) **5**

Pebbles (Crossroads Shopping Center) **11**

For Restaurants in Downtown Disney, please see the "Downtown Disney" map in Chapter 27 had to finish your vegetables if you wanted dessert. Mom — a.k.a. your server — will scold you if put your elbows on the table or don't clean your plate. Desserts include a pretty good banana split.

Note: All **Disney–MGM** restaurants can be found on the "Disney–MGM Studios" map in Chapter 19.

Near the Indiana Jones Stunt Spectacular. ☎ *407-939-3463. Internet:* www.disney world.com. *Priority Seating recommended. Parking: $6. Main courses: Lunch $10–$17, dinner $11–$19. AE, DC, DISC, MC, V. Open: 11 a.m. to park closing.*

Akershus

$$ Epcot   NORWEGIAN

A large table spills over with the traditional *smarvarmt* (hot) and *koldt-bord* (cold) dishes of a Scandinavian smorgasbord: venison stew, steamed whitefish, smoked pork with honey mustard sauce, Norwegian herring, and *gravlax* (for the culturally impaired, this is a cured salmon whose itty-bitty bones have been yanked out with tweezers). The trimmings include red cabbage, potato salad, Norwegian breads, and cheeses. Sweets and sandwiches are available across the pavilion courtyard at the Kringla Bakeri Og Kafé. Crisp linens, glowing woods, and gleaming crystal surround you.

In Norway Pavilion. ☎ *407-939-3463. Internet:* www.disneyworld.com. *Priority Seating recommended. Parking: $6. Main courses: Lunch buffet: $12 adults, $5.25 kids 3–9; dinner buffet: $18.50 adults, $8 children. AE, DC, DISC, MC, V. Open: Daily noon to 3:30 p.m. and 4:30 p.m. to park closing.*

Arthur's 27

$$$ Lake Buena Vista   INTERNATIONAL

Come first for the 27th-floor sunsets and a spectacular view of the Wizard of Disney's fireworks. Romantic and mellow, this place has the feel of a 1930s supper club, minus the billowing clouds of cigarette smoke. You can choose from selections such as pan-seared breast of squab with chestnut risotto or steamed scallops and poached oysters with black capellini pasta. There's also an impressive wine list.

Note: To find this and other restaurants in Lake Buena Vista, as well as in **Walt Disney World,** see the "Walt Disney World & Lake Buena Vista Restaurants" map earlier in this chapter.

1900 Lake Buena Vista Dr., just north of Hotel Plaza Blvd. In the Wyndham Palace Resort & Spa. ☎ *407-827-3450. Reservations required. Parking: Free. Main courses: $20–$30; fixed-price menu $49–$60. No kids' menu. AE, DC, DISC, MC, V. Open: Daily 6–10 p.m.*

Artist Point

$$ Disney's Wilderness Lodge   AMERICAN NORTHWEST

The smell of fresh baked bread greets you upon entering, but eat the hazelnut and sunflower specialties sparingly so you will have room for the main meal. The specialty here is Pacific Northwest cuisine, specifically seafood, and the menu changes frequently. You might find breaded and pan-fried halibut, maple-glazed king salmon, or a grilled bison rib-eye steak. The game, steaks, and marine cuisine are grilled over an open, hardwood fire. The restaurant caters to the health-conscious and also has a decent wine list.

901 W. Timberline Dr. ☎ *407-939-3463 or 407-824-1081. Internet:* www.disney world.com. *Priority Seating suggested. Parking: Free. Main courses: $14–$32. AE, DC, DISC, MC, V. Smoke-free. Open: Daily 5:30–10 p.m.*

Atlantis

$$$ International Drive Area   SEAFOOD

Although a tad pricey for the quality, this is one of the better seafood restaurants in Orlando. The periodically changing menu offers treats such as a Mediterranean seafood medley (Florida lobster, black grouper, shrimp, and scallops), grilled sea bass, and pan-seared duck and rock shrimp. But the Sunday brunch served in the **Renaissance Orlando Resort's** huge atrium is the real crowd-pleaser. Themes change, but the buffet tables are usually laden with quail, mandarin duck, lamb chops, Cornish hen, clams, mussels, snapper, sea bass, and sushi. A reservation for the brunch is recommended, given the dining room's relatively small size.

Note: This and other International Drive restaurants can be found on the "International Drive Restaurants" map, later in this chapter.

6677 Sea Harbour Dr., off International Drive. In Renaissance Orlando Resort at SeaWorld. ☎ *407-351-5555. Internet:* www.renaissancehotels.com. *Reservations recommended. Parking: Free, valet $9. Main courses: $24–$34, Sunday brunch $30 adults, $20 kids. AE, DISC, DC, MC, V. Open: Daily 6–10 p.m.*

B-Line Diner

$–$$ International Drive Area   AMERICAN

The décor is straight out of the '50s, with cushioned stool seating at a counter and upholstered booths. Gleaming chrome and tile create a vision of yesterday's roadside diners in this informal and friendly gathering place. Kids have their own menu to choose from and grown-ups can dig into comfort foods such as chicken pot pie or roast pork with apples, or a ham-and-cheese sandwich on a baguette. There are also health foods and vegetarian specials.

9801 International Dr., across from Orlando Convention Center. In Peabody Orlando.
☎ *407-345-4460. Internet:* www.peabodyorlando.com. *Reservations not accepted. Parking: Free self and validated valet. Main courses: breakfast $4–$14, lunch $7–$17, dinner $9–$26. AE, CB, DC, DISC, JCB, MC, V. Open: Daily 24 hours (dinner 5–11 p.m.).*

Bahama Breeze

$–$$ International Drive Area   CARIBBEAN

You don't have to try hard to feel like you're in the Bahamas in this informal eatery's airy, tropical setting. From the people who created The Olive Garden and Red Lobster, this prototype serves paella (rice with shrimp, fish, mussels, and chicken) and fish in a bag (mahimahi strips, carrots, peppers, and mushrooms in a parchment pillow), among other offerings. Choose from one of 50 beer brands or dare a Bahamarita or one of the fruity rum drinks. They help pass the time as you wait for a table, because *just about everyone* waits here.

8849 International Dr. ☎ *407-248-2499. Internet:* www.bahamabreeze.com. *Reservations not accepted. Parking: Free, but finding a space is as bad as finding a table, so arrive early. Main courses: $9–$18, sandwiches, salads, and pizza $8–$15. AE, MC, V. Open: Sun–Thu 4:00 p.m.–1:00 a.m., Fri–Sat 4:00 p.m.–1:30 a.m.*

Bergamo's

$$–$$$ International Drive Area   NORTHERN ITALIAN

Bergamo's is almost always packed and the singing waiters are nearly as much fun as the food. For example, you may find Broadway show tunes and opera mixed with veal T-bones and linguine with shrimp, clams, and mussels. Even if you don't eat, this is a good spot to park your keister and enjoy the show over cocktails.

8445 International Dr., inside Mercado Shopping Village. ☎ *407-352-3805. Internet:* www.bergamos.com. *Reservations suggested. Parking: Free. Main courses: $17–$31. AE, DC, MC, V. Open: Daily 5–10 p.m.*

Black Swan

$$$ Lake Buena Vista   INTERNATIONAL

Here's a perfect place for a quiet romantic dinner accompanied by a fine vintage chosen from an extensive wine list. The lodgelike restaurant overlooks the golf course at the Grand Cypress. Try the veal chop *au jus* with peppercorns, beef tenderloin with caramelized onions and Roquefort cheese, or the banana-and-nut encrusted prawns with pineapple salsa. Save room for one of the restaurant's fabulous desserts.

1 N. Jacaranda (off Hwy. 535). In the Villas of Grand Cypress. ☎ *407-239-1999. Internet:* www.hyattgrandcypress.com. *Reservations recommended. Parking: Free. Main courses: $31–$43. No kids' menu. AE, CB, DC, DISC, JCB, MC, V. Open: Daily 6–10 p.m.*

Boatwright's Dining Hall

$$ Disney's Port Orleans Resort NEW ORLEANS

A family atmosphere (noisy), good food (by Disney standards), and reasonable prices (ditto) make Boatwright's a hit, especially with Port Orleans Resort guests. Dinner has a Cajun/Creole spin in most of the entrees. Sadly, the jambalaya is sans seafood, but it's spicy and does have enough chicken and sausage to rule it out for vegetarians. The rice and seafood dish (lightly blackened catfish, scallops, and shrimp with vegetables, red beans, and rice) is a good choice.

2201 Orleans Dr. (off Bonnet Creek Pkwy.). ☎ *407-939-3463 or 407-824-4321. Internet:* www.disneyworld.com. *Priority Seating recommended. Parking: Free. Main courses $7–$9 at breakfast; $16–$23 at dinner. AE, DC, DISC, MC, V. Open: Daily 7:30–11:30 a.m. and 5–10 p.m.*

Bob Marley – A Tribute to Freedom

$ Universal Orlando CARIBBEAN

Bright reds and yellows adorn the walls of this combination club and restaurant that's a replica of the late reggae singer's home in Kingston, Jamaica, complete with tile roof and green window shutters. There's live reggae nightly, but the decibel level doesn't get as high as at Jimmy Buffett's Margaritaville (find info about his restaurant later in this chapter). The small menu has modestly priced light fare including a jerk snapper sandwich served on coca bread with yucca fries; a tomato-based fish chowder; and grouper fingers lightly breaded, fried, and topped with red and green peppers. Of course, most folks don't leave without sipping at least one Red Stripe — Jamaica's national beer.

Note: All **CityWalk** restaurants can be found on the "CityWalk" map in Chapter 28.

1000 Universal Studios Plaza. In CityWalk. ☎ *407-224-2262. Internet:* www.universalorlando.com. *Reservations not accepted. Parking: $7 (free after 6 p.m.). Main courses: $6–$9. AE, DISC, MC, V. Open: Daily 4 p.m. to midnight.*

Bubbaloo's Bodacious BBQ

$ Near North AMERICAN

Smoke billows from the chimney of this real-pit place. The atmosphere is informal, but watch the sauces. Even the mild may be too hot for tender palates; the killer sauce comes with a three-alarm warning — it's meant for those with asbestos taste buds and a ceramic-lined tummy. The pork platter with fixings is a deal and a half. It comes with beans and slaw. Monday through Friday, you find daily specials that include chicken, meat loaf, and roast-beef sandwiches. And, it wouldn't be a barbecue without plenty of brew on hand.

1471 Lee Rd., Winter Park. ☎ **407-628-1212.** *Reservations not accepted. Parking: Free. Main courses: $5–$10. AE, MC, V. Open: Mon–Thu 10:00 a.m.–9 p.m.; Fri–Sat 10:00 a.m.–10:30 p.m.*

Café Tu Tu Tango

$ International Drive Area   INTERNATIONAL

This colorful eatery reminds many of a loft in Barcelona. The all-appetizer menu features treats from Latin America, Asia, the Caribbean, the Middle East, and the United States. This tapas bar is an ideal spot for sampling different types of cuisine; every order comes in a miniature size and it's a great spot for grazing. Try the Cajun-style egg rolls filled with blackened chicken, pepper-crusted seared tuna sashimi with rice noodles, or alligator bites in pepper sauce. While you eat or wait for your table, you might be entertained by a couple doing a tango, a belly dancer, or a magician. **Note:** Ordering several tapas and drinks can turn this into a $$$ restaurant.

8625 International Dr. (just west of the Mercado Shopping Center.) ☎ **407-248-2222.** *Internet:* www.cafetututango.com. *Reservations recommended. Parking: Free. Main courses: Tapas $3.75–$8.55 (even those with small appetites will want two or three). AE, DC, DISC, MC, V. Open: Sun–Thurs 11:30 a.m.–11:00 p.m.; Fri–Sat 11:30 a.m. to midnight.*

California Grill

$$–$$$ Disney's Contemporary Resort   NEW AMERICAN

The 15th-floor views of the **Magic Kingdom** and environs are stunning, and the food here is pretty good, too. You can sit by the show kitchens and grill (not literally, of course) the chefs, who work magic before your eyes. The constantly changing menu features earth foods blended with pizzas and pastas, and may include such highlights as seared grouper in a noodle bowl with a ginger-crab salad and braised lamb shank with chanterelle risotto. The Grill also has a nice sushi menu (crab, eel, tuna, and more), ranging from appetizers to large platters. The restaurant probably offers the best veggie fare in the World and also sports a grand wine list. Legend has it the Art Deco dining room was inspired by Los Angeles's foodie haven, Spago.

4600 World Dr. ☎ **407-939-3463** *or 407-824-1576. Internet:* www.disneyworld.com. *Priority Seating recommended. Parking: Free. Main courses: $20–$30, sushi $10–$30. AE, DC, DISC, MC, V. Open: Daily 5:30–10:00 p.m.*

Capriccio

$$–$$$ International Drive Area   TUSCAN/NORTHERN ITALIAN

The decor is chic and elegant with a black-and-white tile floor, but the showcase is a kitchen with wood-fired pizza ovens. If you're in the mood for something more substantial than pizza, try the pan-seared tuna with braised fennel and radicchio. The seasonally changing menu also features

Epcot Restaurants

Akershus **2**	Lotus Blossom Café **4**
Chefs de France **8**	Marrakesh **7**
Coral Reef **11**	Nine Dragons **3**
Le Cellier Steakhouse **10**	Rose & Crown Pub **9**
L'Originale Alfredo	San Angel Inn **1**
di Roma **5**	Teppanyaki Dining Room **6**

pasta, chicken, and seafood items. The wine list is extensive. Capriccio also has a substantial Sunday brunch (lamb, prime rib, shrimp, smoked salmon, mussels, eggs Benedict, and champagne).

9801 International Dr., across from the Orange County Convention Center. In Peabody Orlando. ☎ *407-345-4540. Internet:* www.peabodyorlando.com. *Reservations recommended. Parking: Free self and validated valet. Main courses: $18–$36, most pizzas under $15, Sunday brunch $31 adults, $15 kids 5–12. AE, CB, DC, DISC, JCB, MC, V. Open: Tues–Sun 6–11 p.m., Sunday brunch 11 a.m.–2p.m.*

Chefs de France
$$–$$$ Epcot   FRENCH

Three of France's finest chefs supervise the kitchen in this eatery, where the art-nouveau interior is agleam with mirrors and candelabras. Etched-glass and brass dividers create intimate dining areas and tables are elegantly appointed. Dinner choices include a superb grilled salmon, Mediterranean seafood casserole (grouper, scallops, and shrimp), and beef short ribs burgundy with pearl onions and mushrooms.

Note: All **Epcot** restaurants can be found on the "Epcot Restaurants" map, earlier in this chapter.

In France Pavilion, World Showcase. ☎ *407-939-3463 or 407-827-8709. Internet:* www.disneyworld.com. *Priority Seating suggested. Parking: $6. Main courses: Lunch $15–$19 lunch, dinner $20–$30. AE, DC, DISC, MC, V. Open: Daily noon–3:30 p.m. and 5 p.m.– park closing.*

Christini's Ristorante Italiano
$$–$$$ International Drive Area   ITALIAN

Numerous awards and trophies, attesting to restaurateur Chris Christini's high standard of service, line this place's wall. The fact that he's been around since 1984 shows Christini's a survivor. Count on his restaurant for great service and a possible peek at show-biz celebrities from down the road at **Disney–MGM** and **Universal**. It's hard to decide what to get for the main course, but one of the house specialties is a veal chop, broiled and seasoned with fresh sage. Another favorite: linguine and little-neck clams served in a red or white sauce. The dress code leans toward jackets for men and dressy dresses for women.

7600 Dr. Phillips Blvd. ☎ *407-345-8770. Internet:* www.christinis.com. *Reservations suggested. Parking: Free. Main courses: $18–$35. AE, CB, DC, MC, V. Open: Daily 6 p.m. to midnight.*

Cinderella's Royal Table
$$–$$$ Magic Kingdom   AMERICAN

Cinderella may be on hand to greet you before you dine in Gothic splendor under knights' banners hanging from a vaulted ceiling. Your meal is delivered by servers who address you as "M'Lord" or "M'Lady." You can order spice-crusted salmon, roast chicken, or a tenderloin of beef with shallot sauce. Lunch offers surprisingly tasty prime-rib slices submerged in cabernet sauce under a pastry crust. Keep in mind, though, that this is the same inside-the-park fare found in all the other Disney parks.

Inside Cinderella's Castle on Main Street. ☎ *407-939-3463. Internet:* www.disney world.com. *Priority Seating recommended. Parking: $6. Main courses: Lunch $12–$16, dinner $20–$29. AE, DC, DISC, MC, V. Open: Daily 11:30 a.m.–3 p.m. and 4 p.m.– park closing.*

Citricos
$$$ Disney's Grand Floridian Resort & Spa   NEW FRENCH

The chef of this bright and airy restaurant makes a statement with French, Alsatian, and Provençal cuisine with California and Florida touches. Depending on when you visit, the menu might include rack of lamb with black olives, pan-seared salmon in a mildly tart citrus beurre blanc, grilled Cornish game hen with mustard-oil drizzle, or braised veal shank with orzo pasta, toasted sesame seeds, and soy glaze. The desserts are definitely worth a look. Citricos has one of the better stocked wine cellars in **WDW**.

4401 Floridian Way. ☎ *407-939-3463 or 407-939-7707. Internet:* www.disney world.com. *Priority Seating urged. Parking: Free. Main courses: $24–$38. AE, DC, DISC, MC, V. Open: Daily 5:30– 10 p.m.*

Columbia
$$ Celebration/South Orlando   CUBAN

A large horse stands sentinel inside the dining room of this newest in the small chain of Columbia restaurants. The original was founded in Tampa in 1905 by the great-grandfather of the present operators (and, frankly, it's by far the best). You dine in a bright room decorated with splashes of old Tampa and Havana: tiles, shiny woodwork, wrought iron, and bent-wood chairs. The 1905 Salad (ham, Swiss cheese, tomatoes, green olives, and grated Romano cheese in a garlicky dressing), paella, and snapper Alicante (baked in a casserole with sweet onions, peppers, olive oil, and sauterne wine) are the signature dishes. Cigar smokers are welcome.

649 Front St. ☎ *407-566-1505. Internet:* www.columbiarestaurant.com. *Reservations recommended. Parking: Free. Main courses: Lunch $9–$22, dinner $13–$27. AE, DC, DISC, MC, V. Open: Daily 11:30 a.m.–10 p.m.*

Coral Reef
$$–$$$ Epcot   SEAFOOD

Seafood rules at this restaurant that offers fabulous views of the Living Seas aquarium and a dash of classical music to transport diners to a romantic spot under the sea. Despite the ambiance, the menu is somewhat overpriced and unimaginative. Entrées include pan-seared tuna, whole roasted snapper, and sautéed rock shrimp. And, no, the aquarium isn't a holding pond for the kitchen. The critters you see won't end up on a plate–high, dry, and cooked.

In Future World's Living Seas Pavilion. ☎ *407-939-3463. Internet:* www.disney world.com. *Priority Seating recommended. Parking: $6. Main courses: Lunch $16–$21, dinner $18–$29. AE, DC, DISC, MC, V. Open: Daily 11:30 a.m.–3:00 p.m. and 4:30 p.m. to park closing.*

Delfino Riviera

$$–$$$ Universal Orlando   ITALIAN

Located above a piazza overlooking the other Portofino Bay (not the one in Italy, alas), the atmosphere here is pretty romantic. This is the hotel's signature ristorante, complete with strolling musicians and crooners. The chef's table has eight seats, and 20 more can dine on a balcony that offers a view of the commoners sitting below. There's also a terrace for outdoor dining. If pasta's your thing, try the scrumptious black-olive pasta with monk fish or the pesto-stuffed ravioli. Meat-eaters should consider the veal roasted with porcini mushrooms, while fish fans will love the sea bass and mushrooms in a chianti sauce. Delfino's wine list is second only to Emeril's (see listing later in this section) among **Universal Orlando's** restaurants.

Note: This restaurant can be found on the "International Drive Restaurants" map, later in this chapter.

5601 Universal Studios Blvd. In Portofino Bay Hotel. ☎ *407-503-3463. Internet:* www. universalorlando.com. *Reservations recommended. Parking: Free, valet $8. Main courses: $25–$42. AE, MC, V. Open: Tue–Sat 5–10 p.m.*

Dux

$$$ International Drive Area   INTERNATIONAL

Think posh with a capital P — that's what comes to mind when you slip inside these walls. The restaurant's name honors the mallards that splash all day in the marble fountains in the Peabody's grandly formal lobby. (You can be sure that birds of the quacking variety will not be on the menu.) This is a favorite of celebrities, who dine here after shooting (movies, not tourists, of course) at **Universal Orlando** and **Disney–MGM.** Its eclectic and diverse menu changes with the seasons. Possibilities include oven-roasted grouper with bok choy, mushrooms, and ginger sauce; pan-seared scallops with lentil stew and chive-and-garlic sauce; and a medium-rare veal chop delivered with an artichoke-basil fricassee and garlic *au jus.* Choose a wine from their long, inspired list. The service is impeccable; for most people, however, the prices here make Dux a choice only for special nights or expense-account meals.

International Drive Restaurants

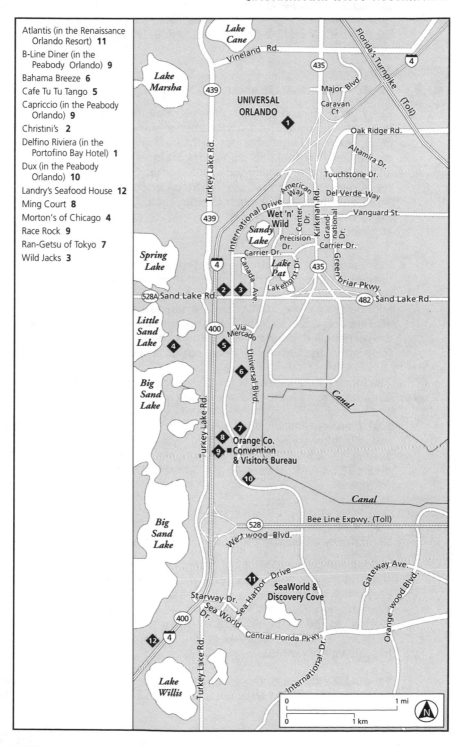

Atlantis (in the Renaissance Orlando Resort) **11**

B-Line Diner (in the Peabody Orlando) **9**

Bahama Breeze **6**

Cafe Tu Tu Tango **5**

Capriccio (in the Peabody Orlando) **9**

Christini's **2**

Delfino Riviera (in the Portofino Bay Hotel) **1**

Dux (in the Peabody Orlando) **10**

Landry's Seafood House **12**

Ming Court **8**

Morton's of Chicago **4**

Race Rock **9**

Ran-Getsu of Tokyo **7**

Wild Jacks **3**

9801 International Dr., across from the Orlando Convention Center. In Peabody Orlando. ☎ **407-345-4550.** *Internet:* www.peabodyorlando.com/. *Reservations recommended. Parking: Free self and validated valet. Main courses: $26–$45. AE, CB, DC, DISC, JCB, MC, V. Open: Mon–Thu 6:00–10 p.m., Fri–Sat 6–11 p.m.*

Emeril's

$$–$$$ Universal Orlando   NEW ORLEANS

Get a mouthful and eyeful in this ultra-modern showplace, the Florida home of culinary genius Emeril Lagasse, star of *Emeril Live* on cable TV's Food Network. Large abstract paintings cover the walls of a two-story restaurant that looks like an old warehouse. The second floor has a 12,000-bottle wine gallery and a cigar room. If you want a show, we highly recommend trying to get one of the eight counter seats where you can watch the chefs working their Creole magic, but to get one you'll need to make reservations *excruciatingly* early (reserve at least a month in advance).

Best bets include andouille-crusted redfish with roasted pecan-and-vegetable relish, half a citrus-glazed duck with walnut-pear chutney and dirty rice, and quail stuffed with Louisiana oyster dressing and served with a ragout of vegetables and cornmeal-crusted oysters. The kitchen also serves pizzas, including one topped with barbecued salmon. Jackets are recommended for gents at dinner, though you'll find a lot of diners, fresh out of the **Universal** theme parks, far less dressy.

The lunch menu is cheaper but has many of the same items as the one at dinner. Plus, it's much easier to get a table.

6000 Universal Studios Blvd. In CityWalk. ☎ **407-224-2424.** *Internet:* www.emerils.com *or* www.universalorlando.com. *Reservations far in advance are a must. Parking: $7 (free after 6 p.m.). Main courses: $17–$26 lunch, $18–$38 dinner. AE, DISC, MC, V. Open: Daily 11:30 a.m.–2:30 p.m., 5:30–10:00 p.m. (11:00 p.m. Fri–Sat).*

Flying Fish Café

$$ Disney's BoardWalk Resort   SEAFOOD

Welcome to Coney Island à la Disney. The decorations here are almost as elaborate as the show kitchen, which puts chefs center stage where everyone can see meals being prepared. All seafood — which reigns supreme here (are you surprised?) — is as fresh as it gets in central Florida, so the menu changes frequently. High points include potato-wrapped red snapper and oak-grilled scallops. There are also beef, poultry, and veggie options.

☎ **407-939-3463** *or 407-939-2359. Internet:* www.disneyworld.com. *Priority Seating recommended. Parking: Free. Main courses: $18–$26. AE, DC, DISC, MC, V. Open: Daily 5:30–10:00 p.m.*

Fulton's Crab House

$$–$$$ **Downtown Disney   SEAFOOD**

Lose yourself in a world of brass, shining mahogany, and river charts while you dine inside a Mississippi Delta-style paddlewheeler. The catch of the day can be presented charcoal-grilled, broiled, fried with a dusting of cornmeal, blackened, or steamed. The grilled tuna mignon is served rare, with lemon-grass dipping sauce, steamed bok choy, and a jasmine rice cake. There's also a dinner for two that combines Alaskan king crab and lobster. You'll find a comprehensive wine list. In addition to the indoor dining room, there's a deck for fair-weather visits.

Note: All **Downtown Disney** restaurants can be found on the "Downtown Disney" map in Chapter 28.

Aboard the riverboat at Pleasure Island next to the Lego store. ☎ **407-934-2628.** *Internet:* www.levyrestaurants.com. *Priority Seating recommended. Parking: Free; valet $6. Main courses: Lunch $11–$37, dinner $17–$44. AE, DC, DISC, MC, V. Open: Daily 11:30 a.m.– 4 p.m. and 5 p.m.–midnight.*

Hemingway's

$$ **Lake Buena Vista   SEAFOOD**

If Papa were to eat at his namesake, he might dive into the beer-battered coconut shrimp with horseradish sauce and orange marmalade or the blackened swordfish with Cajun tartar sauce. No doubt, he would skip the wine list (there is a decent one) and opt for a few *Papa Dobles,* a potent rum concoction he invented and, according to legend, once downed 16 at one sitting! The interior of Hemingway's has a Key West air, and the walls are hung with several sepia photographs of the famous author and his fishing trophies. The eatery has a romantic indoor dining room lighted by hurricane lamps, and there's a wooden deck near a waterfall. It's usually child-free, although there is a kids' menu.

1 Grand Cypress Blvd. (off Hwy. 535). In Hyatt Regency Grand Cypress Resort. ☎ **407-239-3854.** *Internet:* www.hyattgrandcypress.com. *Reservations recommended. Parking: Free self and validated valet. Main courses: Lunch $10–$20, dinner $22–$32. AE, CB, DC, DISC, JCB, MC, V. Tue–Sat 11:30 a.m.–2:30 p.m.; daily 6–10:30 p.m.*

Hollywood Brown Derby

$$ **Disney–MGM Studios   AMERICAN**

It's tough for your eyeballs to dodge the huge derby that marks this restaurant as you square dance into and around **Disney–MGM.** This re-creation of the restaurant where Hollywood's stars gathered in the '30s and '40s is decorated with caricatures of the regulars on its walls. The vittles aren't the best in the solar system, but there's a respectable skillet-seared grouper with red onions, chick peas, and a lemon-tomato-butter sauce, and a grilled salmon with minestrone and pasta. The restaurant's two signatures are the Cobb salad, invented by then-owner Bob Cobb in the 1930s, and grapefruit cake with cream-cheese frosting.

Hollywood Boulevard. ☎ *407-939-3463. Internet:* www.disneyworld.com. *Priority Seating recommended. Parking: $6. Main courses: Lunch $14–$20, dinner $17–$26. AE, DC, DISC, MC, V. Open: Daily 11 a.m. to park closing.*

House of Blues
$$ Downtown Disney   AMERICAN/MISSISSIPPI DELTA

Inside this Louisiana clapboard building you find hearty portions of down-home Southern food served in an atmosphere literally shaking with rhythm and blues. Exceedingly crowded on days of big concerts, the music in the nightclub next door is as much a draw as the food. Funky folk art covers the rustic walls from floor to ceiling. The back patio has seating and a nice view of the bay. Food-wise, the spicy jambalaya (shrimp, chicken, ham, and andouille sausage) and shrimp etouffee are good bets. Sunday's Gospel Brunch is a ton of foot-stomping fun, but the food is not a highpoint (the beef is tough and the fish is dry, among other flaws). Brunch is the only time you can make reservations and it sells out fast, *so make them early.*

Located under the old-fashioned water tower on Disney's West Side. ☎ *407-934-2583. Internet:* www.hob.com. *Reservations not accepted (except for Gospel Brunch). Parking: Free. Main courses: $13–$24; brunch $28 adults, $15 kids 4-12. AE, DC, DISC, MC, V. Open: Daily 11 a.m.–2 a.m.*

Jimmy Buffett's Margaritaville
$–$$ Universal Orlando   CARIBBEAN

After the parrotheads have enough to drink, the noise can make it hard to hear your stable mates, but most folks come to Margaritaville to sing and get rowdy, not to gab. There are three watering holes: the Landshark Bar, the 12-Volt Bar, and the Volcano Bar, which comes complete with a two-story, margarita-spewing mini mountain. Despite the renowned cheeseburgers in paradise (yes, they're on the menu at $8), the food has Caribbean leanings. And, although it's not contending for a critic's choice award, it's fairly tasty. Hot numbers include jerk chicken, jambalaya, and a Cuban meat loaf survival sandwich that's a cheeseburger of another kind.

But, watch your tab. At up to $8 a pop for margaritas, the bill can climb to $60 or more for a routine lunch.

1000 Universal Studios Plaza. In CityWalk. ☎ *407-224-2155. Internet:* www.universalorlando.com. *Reservations not accepted. Parking: $7, free after 6 p.m.. Main courses: $8–$17. AE, DISC, MC, V. Open: Daily 11:30 a.m. to midnight.*

L'Originale Alfredo di Roma

$$ Epcot   ITALIAN

Sample southern Italian cuisine in a seaside Italian palazzo lined with huge murals. Alfredo's servers can be snooty and its pasta is certainly over-priced (many dishes top the $20 mark). Your best bets include the signature fettucine Alfredo, and the thinly sliced veal combined with prosciutto, peppers, mozzarella, potatoes, and veggies. An exhibition kitchen, allowing you to observe the chefs at work, helps pass the time while you wait. This is the *World Showcase*'s most popular restaurant, so Priority Seating is a must.

In Italy Pavilion, World Showcase. ☎ *407-939-3463. Internet:* http://asp. disney.go.com/. *Priority Seating urged. Parking: $6. Main courses: Lunch $10.25–$23, dinner $17–$38 (most under $25). AE, DC, DISC, MC, V. Open: Daily noon to park closing.*

Landry's Seafood House

$$$ International Drive Area   SEAFOOD

The staff here usually rolls out a warm welcome, while the kitchen makes seafood specialties with Cajun and Caribbean touches. The catch of the day may be grouper, mahi-mahi, or snapper. There's also an assortment of other seafood, steak, chicken and pasta dishes.

8800 Vineland Ave. (Hwy. 535, east of I-4.) ☎ *407-827-6466. Internet:* www.landrys seafoodhouse.com. *Reservations for parties of eight or more. Parking: Free. Main courses: $15–$19. AE, DC, DISC, MC, V. Open: Mon–Fri 4:00–11:00 p.m., Sat–Sun 11:30 a.m.–11:00 p.m.*

Le Cellier Steakhouse

$$ Epcot   STEAKS

You'll feel welcome in this cozy steak house, which tends to be less crowded — and less manic — than some of **Epcot's** other restaurants. Although it doesn't compete with outside-world steak-and-chop houses, it has a nice selection of Midwest, corn-fed beef in the usual cuts: fillet, porterhouse, prime rib, rib-eye, and so on. For a different twist, there's also venison osso buco (a cabernet-braised shank accompanied by potatoes and vegetables). You can wash down your meal with a Canadian wine or beer.

In Canada Pavilion, World Showcase. ☎ *407-939-3463. Internet:* www.disney world.com. *Priority Seating recommended. Parking: $6. Main courses: $9–$15 lunch; $15–$20 dinner. AE, DC, DISC, MC, V. Open: Daily noon to park closing.*

Downtown Orlando Restaurants

Le Coq Au Vin	**6**
Le Provence	**3**
Little Saigon	**2**
Manuel's on the 28th	**1**
Numero Uno	**5**
Pebbles	**4**

Le Provence

$$–$$$ **Downtown Orlando** **CLASSIC FRENCH**

Lace in the windows adds to this restaurant's French motif, but regulars know that the food — not the décor — is the highlight. Duck, veal, lobster, scallops, and tuna headline the menu, but if you're in the mood for creative seafood try the snapper stuffed with shrimp mousse, then wrapped in phyllo with smoked tomato compote and braised cabbage. If you order à la carte, try the authentic foie gras or terrine, then lobster bisque, and then a fish, game, meat, or vegetarian main dish. There are also seven fixed-price options ranging from three to six courses. An adjacent cocktail lounge, Monaco, offers live jazz entertainment.

50 E. Pine St. (one block north of Church St. and just east of Court.) ☎ **407-843-1320.** *Internet:* www.cenfla.com/res/leprovence. *Reservations strongly recommended. Parking: Valet $4. Main courses: Lunch $7–$10, dinner $18–$34 (most* *under $25), fixed-price $28–$58. Open: Mon–Fri 11:30 a.m.– 2 p.m. and 5:30–9:30 p.m., Sat 5:30–10:30 p.m.*

Le Coq Au Vin

$–$$ South Orlando FRENCH

Affordability and good food make this a solid choice for French cuisine if you're on a budget. Owner-chef Louis Perrotte loves country cooking and changes his menu seasonally to include dishes such as a grouper fillet encrusted with toasted pecans bathed in citrus beaurre blanc or a center-cut Black-Angus steak served with a dollop of peppercorn sauce. You may also run into rack of lamb, braised rabbit, or grilled salmon depending on when you touch down. (If you want to eliminate the mystery, call first.) This restaurant has a bistro atmosphere and regulars who attest to its staying power. Some insist this is Florida's best French restaurant, especially if you're after a bargain.

4800 So. Orange Ave. ☎ 407-851-6980. Reservations required. Parking: Free. Main courses: $15–$28. AE, DC, MC, V. Open: Tue–Fri 11:30 a.m.–2:00 p.m. and 5:30–10:00 p.m.; Sat–Sun 5:30–10:00 p.m.

Liberty Tree Tavern

$$ Magic Kingdom AMERICAN

This sit-down restaurant's 18th-century pub atmosphere and good service help make it one of the better places to dine in the **Magic Kingdom,** but few will be compelled to a second or third visit. The cuisine is traditional American and the vittles are basic: roasted turkey, marinated flank steak, and honey-mustard ham with trimmings. There's a la carte service at lunch and a buffet for dinner. Visitors watching their cholesterol will appreciate the restaurant's limited heart-healthy options.

In Liberty Square, Magic Kingdom. ☎ 407-939-3463 or 407-824-6464. Internet: www . disneyworld.com. Priority Seating recommended. Parking: $6. Main courses: Lunch $10–$17, dinner buffet $20 adults, $10 kids 3-11. (See Chapter 15 about Disney character dining). AE, DC, DISC, MC, V. Open: Daily 11:30 a.m.–3:00 p.m. and 4:00 p.m. to park closing.

Little Saigon

$ Downtown Orlando VIETNAMESE

Situated in the heart of a tiny Vietnamese neighborhood, this ethnic eatery has been open for more than 13 years and thrives on its regulars. The menu offers everything from appetizers to noodle dishes to stir-fries that mix and match pork, beef, seafood, and vegetables. The combo plates are a good deal. Service and attention depend on the traffic. Order food by number; if you need a description of a dish, you may need to ask for the manager, whose English is better than that of some of the servers. Don't miss the summer rolls with peanut sauce.

1106 E. Colonial Dr., just west of I-4 on Hwy. 50 ☎ *407-423-8539. Reservations not accepted. Parking: Free. Main courses: Lunch under $5, dinner $5–$8. AE, DISC, MC, V. Open: Daily 10 a.m.–9 p.m.*

Lotus Blossom Café
$ Epcot   CHINESE

The grub in this open-air café is much like what you find in Chinese restaurants located in mall food courts. Don't expect anything out of the ordinary from the stir fry, sweet and sour, or pork-fried rice. That said, it's still a bargain in pricey **Epcot**.

In China Pavilion, World Showcase. ☎ *407-939-3463. Internet:* www.disney world.com. *Priority Seating not accepted. Parking: $6. Main courses: Most are $4–$8. AE, DC, DISC, MC, V. Open: Daily 11 a.m. to park closing.*

Maison & Jardin
$$$ Near North   INTERNATIONAL

Formal and romantic, Maison & Jardin (*House and Garden* just sounds so much prettier in French, doesn't it?) is a time-honored local favorite and a consistent award winner. Alas, this can be a healthy trek, depending on where you're staying (15 minutes from downtown, 30 minutes from **Disney**). The reward is an atmosphere that's refined for its mature customers (in other words, leave the kids home). Prices are up there on the Richter scale (expect at least $100 for dinner for two, including liquid libations, starters/finishers, tax, and tips), but the vittles are grand and the service matches. The menu has the right blend, including beef Wellington, veal tenderloin with Maine lobster and morel sauce, and a seared quail-and-ostrich combo. The wine list is also pretty impressive.

430 Wymore Rd. (Altamonte Springs/Exit 48 off I-4 to Hwy. 436, left at top of ramp, go to second light, left on Wymore Rd. a half-mile on right.) ☎ *407-862-4410. Internet:* www.maison-jardin.com. *Reservations recommended. Parking: Free. Main courses: $22–$34, fixed price $45–$62. AE, CB, DC, DISC, MC, V. Open: Mon–Sat 6–10 p.m.; Sun brunch 11 a.m.–2 p.m. and dinner 6–9 p.m.*

Mama Melrose's Ristorante Italiano
$–$$ Disney–MGM Studios   ITALIAN

The specialty at this cheery Italian trattoria is brick-oven baked pizza and the menu is fleshed out marginal pastas, chicken entrées, and seafood dishes. The food isn't very exciting, but it's a notch above fast food.

(Close to the Muppet*Vision 3D adventure show). ☎ *407-939-3463. Internet:* www. disneyworld.com. *Priority Seating recommended. Parking: $6. Main courses: Lunch $8–$15, dinner $12–$22. AE, DC, DISC, MC, V. Open: Daily 11:30 a.m. to park closing.*

Manuel's on the 28th

$$$ Downtown Orlando   INTERNATIONAL

Manuel's is literally the pinnacle of elegance, situated in a posh, panoramic enclave on the 28th floor of a downtown bank. Come here for a stunning after-dark view of the sparkling, sprawling metropolis that Orlando has become. At most view restaurants, the food can't match the scenery; Manuel's, despite a small kitchen, is an exception. The dozen or more appetizers and entrées hit high notes with duck, lamb, yellowfin tuna, lobster, and filet mignon. One popular dish is the phyllo-wrapped lamb loin stuffed with spinach and topped with a rosemary-shallot sauce. The service is very professional, and there's a great wine list.

390 N. Orange Ave. ☎ *407-246-6580. Internet:* www.manuelsonthe28th.com. *Reservations required. Parking: Free. Main courses: $29–$45. AE, DC, DISC, MC, V. Open: Tues–Sat 6–10 p.m.*

Marrakesh

$$ Epcot   MOROCCAN

For a spot of romance and truly authentic flavor, head for Marrakesh. Of all the Epcot eateries, this venue best typifies the international spirit of the park. Hand-laid mosaics in intricate patterns set the scene for lavish North African dining, complete with belly dancers (Walt may be turning over in his grave). Marrakesh uses a long list of spices including saffron to enhance flavorful specialties. The menu features couscous with chicken, lamb, or a variety of garden vegetables. Entrees include marinated shish kabob, lamb roasted in its own juices, and a seafood medley.

In Morocco Pavilion, World Showcase. ☎ *407-939-3463. Internet:* www.disney world.com. *Priority Seating recommended. Parking: $6. Main courses: Lunch $14–$17, dinner $16–$28. AE, DC, DISC, MC, V. Open: Daily noon–park closing.*

Ming Court

$$ International Drive Area   CHINESE

Dine in an ethereal setting, graced by lotus ponds filled with colorful koi while you're entertained by — get this — zither music. One of O-Town's favorite Chinese restaurants, you'll rub elbows with more locals than tourists and find innovative twists on traditional oriental cuisine. The flavors are delicate and probably more balanced than at your neighborhood Chinese place. Try the grilled filet mignon with Szechuan seasoning or the lightly battered and deep-fried chicken breast with lemon-tangerine sauce.

9188 International Dr. (between Sand Lake and Bee Line Expressway). ☎ *407-351-9988. Internet:* www.ming-court.com. *Reservations recommended. Parking: Free. Main courses: Lunch $3–$10, dinner $13–$33. AE, CB, DC, DISC, JCB, MC, V. Open: Daily 11:00 a.m.–2:30 p.m. and 4:30 p.m. to midnight.*

Morton's of Chicago

$$–$$$ International Drive Area STEAKS

Steak-stuffers may be more inclined to go to a Kansas City steak joint, but Morton's is pretty respected locally. Maybe they don't grow the hoofers here, but they know beef, which is served in straightforward meat-and-potatoes style. The cuts are costly, but they're tender and well aged. Side dishes are à la carte, which can add up to an expensive evening if you go overboard. The no-smoking section could be larger — and more smoke-free — but there's a full bar.

7600 Dr. Phillips Blvd. (In the Dr. Phillips Marketplace). ☎ *407-248-3485. Internet:* www.mortons.com. *Reservations recommended. Parking: Free. Main courses: $17–$30. AE, DC, MC, V. Open: Mon–Sat 5:30–11:00 p.m.; Sun 5–10 p.m.*

Nine Dragons

$$ Epcot CHINESE

Carved rosewood paneling and an amazing dragon-motif ceiling add nice visual touches to this restaurant. Portions tend to be smaller than what most expect in a Chinese restaurant, but there isn't a shortage of taste. Regional dishes include spicy squid deep-fried in basil, soy, and Shao Xing wine. There's also a flavorful dish of sliced beef in bamboo shoots, snow peas, and zucchini. The menu also has familiar standbys such as moo goo gai pan and sweet and sour pork.

In China Pavilion, World Showcase. ☎ *407-939-3463. Internet:* www.disney world.com. *Priority Seating recommended. Parking: $6. Main courses: Lunch $10–$25, dinner $12–$30. AE, DC, DISC, MC, V. Open: Daily 11:30 a.m.–park closing.*

Numero Uno

$–$$ Downtown Orlando CUBAN

Some see this family-run Cuban joint as a hole in the wall, but you won't notice the décor after the paella hits your table. If that doesn't appeal to you, order *ropa vieja* (literally "old clothes," because the beef is so tender), roast pork, or a remarkable *arroz con pollo* (chicken and rice, usually served with saffron). The trimmings include a lot of Latin favorites such as plantains.

2499 S. Orange Ave. ☎ *407-841-3840. Reservations recommended. Parking: Tight, but free. Main courses: $8–$20. AE, DC, DISC, MC, V. Open: Mon.–Fri. 11 a.m.–3 p.m.; Mon–Sat 5:30–9:00 p.m.*

'Ohana

$$ Disney's Polynesian Resort POLYNESIAN

Think fun. The whole family will find something to like about 'Ohana's pig-out specials. You're welcomed to island hospitality by a server who addresses you as "cousin." That fits, because 'Ohana means *family* in

Hawaiian. Located in the Polynesian's main dining room, this nightly luau gives you a chance to see your food being prepared over an 18-foot fire pit. While you wait, someone blows a conch shell and a storyteller arrives on the scene. Then, there are coconut races in the center aisle, you can shake it in hula lessons, and those with birthdays are urged to work out a hula hoop while everyone sings "Happy Birthday" in Hawaiian.

Kids like the hoopla; those seeking intimacy don't.

Soon after you're seated, the feeding frenzy begins in rapid succession (ask your waiter to slow down if the pace is too fast). The vittles include salad, fruit, fresh-baked bread, grilled salmon, turkey, shrimp, steak, and pork sausage. A full bar offers tropical drinks.

1600 Seven Seas Dr. ☎ *407-939-3463 or 407-824-2000. Internet:* www.disney world.com. *Parking: Free. Main courses: Fixed-price family feast, $23 adults, $10 kids 3–11 (see Chapter 15). AE, DC, DISC, MC, V. Daily 7:30–11:00 a.m. and 5:00– 10:00 p.m.*

Pacino's Italian Ristorante
$$ South Orlando   ITALIAN

The hand-painted ceiling of this restaurant contains fiber optics that create an aura of dining under the stars, but there's also a patio if you want the real thing. Some servers can be a little aloof, but the price and taste make up for it. Pacino's serves twin veal chops that are usually fork tender, a challenging 32-ounce porterhouse steak, and *fruitti di mare* (shrimp, calamari, clams, and scallops sautéed with white wine and herbs and heaped onto a mound of linguine).

5795 W. Hwy. 192/Irlo Bronson Memorial Pkwy. (2 miles east of I-4). ☎ *407- 396-8022. Internet:* www.pacinos.com. *Reservations accepted. Parking: Free. Main courses: $12–$27 (most are under $20), pizza $9–$11. AE, MC, V. Open: Daily 4–11 p.m.*

Park Plaza Gardens
$$ Near North   INTERNATIONAL

The garden-like atmosphere (look, up in the sky, a glass roof!) is an elegant touch that goes with the cuisine, which is sophisticated and health-conscious. Since 1979, Chef Clair Epting and his pampering staff have been serving up such treats as red snapper sautéed in sweet brown butter and crimini mushrooms, veal medallions in a date-and-cider demiglaze, cedar plank-roasted salmon with grilled asparagus. The restaurant has an extensive selection of domestic, French, and Italian wines.

319 Park Ave. S., Winter Park. ☎ *407-645-2475. Internet:* www.parkplaza gardens.com. *Reservations suggested. Parking: Free. Main courses: Lunch $8–$19, dinner $16–$28. AE, CB, DC, DISC, MC, V. Open: Mon–Thurs 11:30 a.m.–2 p.m. and 6–10 p.m.; Fri–Sat 11:30 a.m.–2 p.m. and 6–11 p.m.; Sun 11 a.m.–9 p.m.*

Near North Restaurants

Bubbaloo's Bodacious
BBQ **2**
Maison & Jardin **1**
Park Plaza Gardens **4**
Rolando's **3**

Pastamore Ristorante
$$ Universal Orlando   ITALIAN

Just inside the door you find large display cases full of fresh mozzarella, eggplant, olives, and more that you can order to go or enjoy alfresco on Pastamoré's outdoor patio. This family-style restaurant greets you with statues and Italian artifacts that are scattered about and the kitchen is open, allowing you a view of the cooks at work. The antipasto primo is a meal in itself. The mound includes bruschetta, eggplant Caponata, melon con prosciutto, grilled portobello mushrooms, olives, plum tomatoes with fresh mozzarella, a medley of Italian cold cuts, and more. The menu also has traditional features such as veal marsala, chicken parmigiana, shrimp scampi, fettuccine alfredo, lasagna, and pizza.

1000 Universal Studios Plaza. In CityWalk. ☎ *407-363-8000. Internet:* www.universalorlando.com. *Reservations accepted. Parking: $7, free after 6 p.m. Main courses: $7–$20. AE, DISC, MC, V. Open: Daily 5 p.m. to midnight.*

Pebbles

$–$$ Downtown Orlando   AMERICAN

This is as close as Orlando gets to a hometown chain. Classy and casual, Pebbles features a menu that ranges from a create-your-own burger (price negotiable) to filet mignon and honey-roasted spare ribs. Owner Manny Garcia offers affordability in the Pebbles line with entrées such as duck, lamb, and pasta dishes, as well as tapas (appetizers), burgers, and soups. If they're available, don't miss the chevre-coated lamb chops. Many entrees come with three-cheese mashed potatoes and zucchini wedges. The restaurant has a bar, a respectable wine list (order by the glass), and a fun atmosphere.

There are two other branches of Pebbles located at 2110 W. Hwy. 434 (☎ **407-774-7111**) and 12551 Hwy. 535 (☎ **407-827-1111**).

17 W. Church St., ☎ *407-839-0892. Internet:* www.pebblesworldwide.com. *Reservations not accepted. Parking: Free. Main courses: $10–$23. AE, DC, DISC, MC, V. Open: Sun–Thurs noon–11 p.m.; Fri–Sat 11 a.m. to midnight.*

Planet Hollywood

$–$$ Dowtown Disney   AMERICAN

If you go to **Pleasure Island,** you can't help but see the giant globe with the lettering screaming *Planet Hollywood* at you. Your kids already know about it — and they're probably clamoring to go, especially if they're teens. This place is part restaurant and part showcase for Hollywood memorabilia. Diners are surrounded by movie clips and some 300 show-biz artifacts ranging from Peter O'Toole's *Lawrence of Arabia* costume to the front end of the bus from *Speed!* The food leans toward the mediocre. You can gnaw on such appetizers as hickory-smoked buffalo wings, pot stickers, or nachos, or try out the selection of burgers, sandwiches, pastas, and pizzas. The menu also has fajitas, ribs, and marginal steaks.

1506 E. Buena Vista Dr. In Pleasure Island. ☎ *407-827-7827. Internet:* www.planet hollywood.com. *Reservations not accepted. Parking: Free. Main courses: $6–$17 (most under $13). AE, DC, DISC, JCB, MC, V. Open: Daily 11 a.m.–2 a.m.*

Plaza Restaurant

$ Magic Kingdom   AMERICAN

Take a breather from the hot sun and teeming crowds in the **Magic Kingdom** and have lunch at this hometown-style restaurant, located appropriately enough at the end of Main Street. The menu offers plain and fancy burgers, hot and cold sandwiches (try the Reuben or the double-decker hot roast beef), salads, and milk shakes in three flavors. Or skip the shakes and leave room for a hot-fudge sundae — the **World's** best.

On Main Street. ☎ *407-939-3463. Internet:* www.disneyworld.com. *Priority Seating recommended. Parking: $6. Main courses: $9–$11; ice cream: $3.25–$10. AE, DC, DISC, MC, V. Open: Daily 11 a.m. to park closing.*

Portobello Yacht Club

$$–$$$ Downtown Disney   CONTEMPORARY ITALIAN

A lively atmosphere makes this a good place for a casual bite. Crispy, thin-crusted pizzas, cooked in wood-burning ovens, are one of the signatures at this restaurant. The club is a floating trattoria that bills itself as serving nouveau Old World cuisine. That sounds a bit bizarre, but it works thanks to creative chefs and an attentive staff. Try dining on the patio overlooking the water if the weather is good. Inside or out, expect crowds and a changing menu that may include roasted pork loin with garlic whipped potatoes or pasta with pieces of Alaskan king crab, scallops, shrimp, and clams.

1650 Buena Vista Dr. In Pleasure Island. ☎ *407-934-8888. Internet:* www.levyrestaurants.com. *Priority Seating recommended. Parking: Free, valet $6. Main courses: Lunch $10–$18, dinner $15–$40 (pizzas from $9). AE, DC, DISC, MC, V. Open: Daily 11:30 a.m.–midnight.*

Race Rock

$–$$ International Drive Area   AMERICAN

In case you couldn't guess the theme, it's NASCAR. There are cars and trucks all over the place, and the TV monitors show taped race action. It's *LOUD*. Between the music and racing sounds, it's hard to complete a thought, much less a sentence. But gearheads of all ages love this infield-like pit stop, which features a so-so prime rib, big burgers, pizza, egg rolls, soups, salads, and sandwiches. Race Rock's eye candy also includes some dragsters and hydroplanes. Kids have their own Quarter Midget Menu, complete with games and coloring. Speaking of kids, keeping the sugar away from them here isn't a bad idea; this place lights their little fuses without any ingested assistance.

8986 International Dr., just south of Sand Lake Rd. ☎ *407-248-9876. Internet:* www.racerock.com. *Reservations only accepted for groups. Parking: Free. Main courses: $7–$18. AE, DC, DISC, MC, V. Open: Daily 11 a.m.–11 p.m. and later if it's crowded.*

Rainforest Café

$–$$ Downtown Disney & Animal Kingdom   AMERICAN

Set amid a jungle with tropical sounds of birds and waterfalls, this is a place to eat that kids love! The food's pretty respectable, but it's really the decor that makes this restaurant. As its name suggests, entering the Rainforest Café is like walking into a jungle — there are lifelike silk plants all over, Animatronic monkeys chattering, and occasional rain and thunder rumblings. The menu offers California-influenced house specialties such as Mojo Bones (barbecued pork ribs), Rumble in the Jungle Turkey Pita, and Mixed Grill (barbecued ribs, steak skewers, chicken breast, and peppered shrimp). The barstools resemble zebras, giraffes, and other wild-and-crazy critters.

1800 E. Buena Vista Dr. (in Downtown Disney Marketplace). ☎ *407-827-8500. Internet:* www.rainforestcafe.com. *Reservations not accepted. Parking: Free. (Also just outside entrance to Animal Kingdom.* ☎ *407-938-9100. Parking: $6.) Main courses: $10–$23. AE, DISC, MC, V. Open: Sun–Thurs 10:30 a.m.–11:00 p.m.; Fri–Sat.10:30 a.m. to midnight.*

Ran-Getsu of Tokyo
$$–$$$ **International Drive Area** **JAPANESE**

Oriental tourists flock to this restaurant for both the authentic cuisine and the sushi bar. *Tekka-don,* tender slices of tuna that are mild enough for first-timers, is a refreshing choice on the sushi side. Ditto for the sashimi. *Yosenabe* is a bouillabaisse with an offbeat though savory twist — duck and chicken are added to the seafood mix. Speaking of seafood, *una-ju* delights eel lovers; the fillets are grilled in kabayaki sauce. Less adventurous palates may prefer shrimp tempura or a steak served in teriyaki sauce.

8400 International Dr., near Orlando Convention Center. ☎ *407-345-0044. Internet:* www.rangetsu.com. *Reservations recommended. Parking: Free. Main courses: $14–$35 (most under $25); sushi entrees $14–$41. AE, DC, MC, V. Open: Daily 5–11:30 p.m.*

Rolando's
$–$$ **Near North** **CUBAN**

It isn't big on aesthetics — it has plain tables and chairs and a sparse collection of photos of Cuba on the walls — but large platters of Cuban food make it memorable. Order traditional items such as pork, red snapper, tamale pie, or chicken. House specialties *arroz con pollo* (chicken and rice) and *ropa vieja* (shredded beef). *Paella* (fish and shellfish over rice) is an option *if* you call a day in advance and order dinner for two. Standard Cuban sandwiches come with black-bean soup. Entrées are served with freshly baked rolls, salad, rice, and plantains or yucca.

870 E. Semoran/Hwy. 436, between Red Bug Rd. and U.S. 17–92. ☎ *407-767-9677. Reservations not accepted. Parking: Free. Main courses: Lunch $4–$6, dinner $8–$17. AE, CB, DC, MC, V. Open: Tues–Thu 11 a.m.–9 p.m., Fri–Sat 11 a.m.–10 p.m., Sun noon–8 p.m.*

Rose & Crown Pub & Dining Room
$–$$ **Epcot** **BRITISH**

You can order ale, lagers, and stouts by the pint or (designated-driver alert!) half yard. The Rose & Crown has dark-oak wainscoting, a beamed

Tudor ceiling, English folk music, and saucy servers. British visitors flock here to dine on such traditional dishes as London-style fish (cod) and chips, prime rib with Yorkshire pudding, bangers and mash, and an English sampler (cottage pie, steak and mushroom pie, and chicken and leek pie). On the lighter side, bar food includes sausage rolls, Cornish pasties (meat pies), and a Stilton cheese and fruit plate.

The restaurant's outdoor seating (weather permitting) offers a fantastic view of IllumiNations (see Chapter 18 for more information), making this an excellent spot for a late dinner. Request one of these tables when making your Priority Seating reservation, and make it early (we were told at least 30 days in advance during busy periods). **Note:** If you only want to grab a pint or a snack at the bar, you don't need Priority Seating.

In United Kingdom Pavilion, World Showcase. ☎ *407-939-3463. Internet:* www. disneyworld.com. *Priority Seating recommended for dining room. Parking: $6. Main courses: Lunch $10–$15, dinner $14–$21 at dinner. AE, DC, DISC, MC, V. Open: Daily 11 a.m. until one hour before park closes.*

San Angel Inn
$–$$ Epcot MEXICAN

It's always night inside the inn, where you'll eat at one of several romantic candlelit tables located in a hacienda courtyard that is surrounded by dense jungle foliage. The shadow of a crumbling Yucatán pyramid looms in the distance and you hear the sound of faraway birds while you dine. The ambiance of this restaurant, located inside the Mexico Pavilion, is exotic, and the fare is traditional — that's why you won't find nachos or Mexican pizza on the menu. Entrées include *mole poblano* (chicken simmered with more than 20 spices and a hint of chocolate) and *filete motuleno* (grilled tenderloin of beef served over black beans, melted cheese, pepper strips, and plantains). There are also combination platters. Your drinking options include Dos Equis beer and margaritas.

In Mexico Pavilion, World Showcase. ☎ *407-939-3463. Internet:* www.disney world.com. *Priority Seating recommended. Parking: $6. Main courses: Lunch $9–$17, dinner $17–$22 at dinner. AE, DC, DISC, MC, V. Open: Daily 11 a.m. to park closing.*

Sci-Fi Dine-In Theater Restaurant
$$ Disney–MGM Studios AMERICAN

Horror flicks (which are too hokey to be scary) play on the screen while you dine in a replica of a 1950's Los Angeles drive-in movie emporium, complete with tables ensconced in flashy, chrome-trimmed convertible cars. Alas, the food isn't as fun as the surroundings. The kitchen turns out basic beef, pork, poultry, tuna, and pasta. That said, the fun factor may lead you to give this experience a thumb's up.

☎ *407-939-3463. Internet:* www.disneyworld.com. *Priority Seating recommended. Parking: $6. Main courses: Lunch $8–$15, dinner $11–$20. AE, DC, DISC, MC, V. Open: Daily 11 a.m. to park closing.*

Spoodles
$$ Disney's BoardWalk Resort   MEDITERRANEAN TAPAS

Tapas, pizza, and pasta are the main items on the menu at this Mediterranean-style restaurant. The barbecued Moroccan beef skewers with raisins, toasted almonds, and couscous are drenched in a hot, tangy sauce. The artichoke ravioli with garlic, cherry tomatoes, and arugula is a vegetarian treat. Or try the oven-roasted snapper with artichokes, fennel, and oven-dried tomatoes. There also are several conventional entrees featuring shrimp, scallops, fish, lamb chops, and steaks. Table-side sangria presentations add something special to the evening. During the height of the summer, Spoodles gets crowded and the wait can be long even with Priority Seating, so this isn't a good choice for famished families coming straight from the parks.

☎ *407-939-3463 or 407-939-2380. Internet:* www.disneyworld.com. *Priority Seating recommended. Parking: Free. Main courses: Lunch $5–$11, dinner $15–$26. AE, DC, DISC, MC. V. Open: Daily 7–11 a.m., noon to 2 p.m., and 5–10 p.m.*

Teppanyaki Dining Room
$$–$$$ Epcot   JAPANESE

The restaurant centers on a steak house where diners sit at grill tables and chefs rapidly dice, slice, stir-fry, and propel cooked food onto your plate with amazing dexterity. Kids especially enjoy watching the chef wield his or her cleaver and utensils. Several parties are seated at teppanyaki tables, which makes for sociable dining, especially for single travelers looking for conversation. Expect the entrees to have chicken, steak, scallops, lobsters, or a combination. Alas, the culinary acrobatics are better than the food. Kirin beer, plum wine, and sake are served.

The adjoining Tempura Kiku offers sushi, sashimi, and tempura-battered shrimp and chicken.

In Japan Pavilion, World Showcase. ☎ *407-939-3463. Internet:* www.disney world.com. *Priority Seating recommended for Teppanyaki; reservations not accepted at tempura counter. Parking: $6. Teppanyaki main courses: Lunch $10–$20, dinner $15–$30; Tempura Kiku lunch $9–$18, dinner $16–$30. AE, DC, DISC, MC, V. Open: Daily 11 a.m. until one hour before park closes.*

Victoria & Albert's
$$$$ Disney's Grand Floridian Resort & Spa   INTERNATIONAL

The setting is Victorian and a nostalgic reminder that dining out was once a treat to be savored in an evening-filling, relaxed, and stylish manner.

The chef works wizardry with food from a diverse marketplace. This is the most memorable (and memorably expensive) restaurant in **WDW.** But if money's no object and you're serious about food and romance going hand in hand, head here. The intimate dining room has exquisitely appointed tables. The food is impeccable and presented with a flourish by an attentive and professional staff (each table has servers named Victoria and Albert). The seven-course menu changes nightly. You may begin with Beluga caviar with toast points or apple-smoked Colorado bison, then have a Dungeness crab cake as a hot appetizer. Antelope consommé may follow, preceding a main course of black bass with toasted couscous or a beef tenderloin with Cipollini onion risotto. Your faithful servers may then bring out English Stilton served with pine-nut bread, port wine, and a pear poached in burgundy, cognac, and cinnamon sugar as a set-up for a dessert of vanilla bean *crème brûlée* or white chocolate and raspberry Chambord soufflé. (At this point, you explode.) Dinners are usually a two and a half- to three-hour affair, though the later sitting can run longer. If you're inclined to try the chef's table option (you actually dine in the kitchen and watch them prepare your meal), make sure to reserve it weeks, if not months, in advance.

4401 Floridian Way. ☎ *407-939-7707 or 407-939-3463. Internet:* www.disney world.com. *Reservations required well in advance. Jackets required for men. Not recommended for children. Parking: Free self and validated valet. Main courses: Fixed-price $85 per person, $120 with wine pairing; chef's table $115, $160 with wine. AE, DC, DISC, MC, V. Open: Sittings at 5:45 and 9:00 p.m.; chef's table 6:00 p.m.*

Wild Jacks

$–$$ International Drive Area   AMERICAN

You sit family-style at picnic tables with checkered tablecloths while you chow down at this chuckwagon-style eatery. The atmosphere includes mounted buffalo heads, long-dead jack-a-lopes, and more dying-calf-in-a-hailstorm, twitch-and-twang country-western music than an average city slicker ought to have to endure in a lifetime. The kitchen is bursting with steaks on an open-pit grill. In addition to the Texas-size hunks of beef served with jalapeño smashed potatoes and corn on the cob, the menu offers a selection of skewered shrimp, tacos, chicken, or pasta, though it's not a good idea to order experimental stuff in a beef house. Jacks isn't one of Orlando's finest steak houses, but it's successful enough to have other locations in Altamonte Springs and Kissimmee.

7364 International Dr., between Sand Lake Rd. and Carrier Dr. ☎ *407-352-4407. Internet:* www.wildjacksteaks.com. *Reservations accepted. Parking: Free. Main courses: $10–$20. AE, CB, DC, DISC, JCB, MC, V. Open: Sun–Thurs 4–10 p.m., Fri–Sat 4–11 p.m.*

Wolfgang Puck Café

$$–$$$ Downtown Disney   AMERICAN/CALIFORNIA

Avant-garde chef Wolfgang Puck brings his West Coast creations to the heart of Florida. You can eat gourmet pizza with a thin, crisp crust and exotic toppings, either on an outdoor patio or inside. You can follow an appetizer of vegetable spring rolls or a sampling from the sushi bar with the fresh-grilled chicken. The restaurant is busy and often noisy, so conversation may be difficult. For a lot of folks, the food's taste doesn't match its eye appeal.

1482 Buena Vista Dr. In Disney's West Side. ☎ *407-938-9653. Reservations not accepted. Parking: Free. Main courses: $15–$29 (many under $20). AE, DC, DISC, MC, V. Daily 11 a.m.–1 a.m.*

Yachtsman Steakhouse
$$$ Disney's Yacht Club Resort   STEAKS

This restaurant is regarded as one of Orlando's top steak-and-chop houses, a place where diners select their own steaks. It's *the* place to come if you love red meat and are too young or too carefree to worry about arterial blockage. The steaks are aged, the cattle from which they came were grain-fed, and a staff butcher carves the beef. (The porterhouse is tender enough to cut with a fork.) The menu also includes wood-grilled mahi-mahi, a filet and lobster tail combo, and seared salmon. The full bar offers daily specials. The Steakhouse is prone to crowds, but most folks say that it's worth the wait.

1700 Epcot Resorts Blvd. ☎ *407-939-3463. Internet:* www.disneyworld.com. *Priority seating recommended. Parking: Free. Main courses: $20–$55. AE, DC, DISC, MC, V. Open: Daily 5:30–10 p.m.*

Index by price

Maison & Jardin (International, Near North)

Manuel's on the 28th (International, Downtown Orlando)

Morton's of Chicago (Steaks, International Drive Area)

Portobello Yacht Club (Italian, Downtown Disney)

Ran-Getsu of Tokyo (Japanese, International Drive Area)

Teppanyaki Dining Room (Japanese, Epcot)

Wolfgang Puck Café (American, Downtown Disney)

Yachtsman Steakhouse (Steaks, Disney's Yacht Club Resort)

$$

Akershus (Norwegian, Epcot)

Artist Point (American, Disney's Wilderness Lodge)

B-Line Diner (American, International Drive Area)

Bahama Breeze (Caribbean, International Drive Area)

Boatwright's Dining Hall (New Orleans, Port Orleans)

Columbia (Cuban, Celebration)

'50s Prime Time Café (American, Disney–MGM Studios)

Flying Fish Café (Seafood, Disney's BoardWalk Resort)

Hemingway's (Seafood, Lake Buena Vista)

Hollywood Brown Derby (American, Disney–MGM Studios)

House of Blues (American, Downtown Disney)

Jimmy Buffett's Margaritaville (Caribbean, Universal Orlando)

Le Cellier Steakhouse (Steaks, Epcot)

Le Coq Au Vin (French, South Orlando)

Liberty Tree Tavern. (American, Magic Kingdom)

L'Originale Alfredo di Roma (Italian, Epcot)

Mama Melrose's Ristorante Italiano (Italian, Disney–MGM Studios)

Marrakesh (Moroccan, Epcot)

Ming Court (Chinese, International Drive Area)

Nine Dragons (Chinese, Epcot)

Numero Uno (Cuban, Downtown Orlando)

'Ohana (Polynesian, Disney's Polynesian Resort)

Pacino's Italian Ristorante (Italian, South Orlando)

Park Plaza Gardens (International, Near North)

Pastamore Ristorante (Italian, Universal Orlando's Universal Orlando)

Pebbles (American, Downtown Orlando)

Planet Hollywood (American, Downtown Disney)

Race Rock (American, International Drive Area)

Rainforest Café (American, Downtown Disney & Animal Kingdom)

Rolando's (Cuban, Near North)

Rose & Crown Pub & Dining Room (British, Epcot)

San Angel Inn (Mexican, Epcot)

Sci-Fi Dine-In Theater Restaurant (American, Disney–MGM Studios)

Spoodles (Mediterranean, Disney's BoardWalk Resort)

Wild Jacks (American, International Drive Area)

$

Bob Marley — A Tribute to Freedom (Caribbean, Universal Orlando)

Bubbaloo's Bodacious BBQ (American, Near North)

Cafe Tu Tu Tango (International, International Drive Area)

Little Saigon (Vietnamese, Downtown Orlando)

Lotus Blossom Café (Chinese, Epcot)

Plaza Restaurant (American, Magic Kingdom)

Index by location

L'Originale Alfredo di Roma
(Italian, $$)
Lotus Blossom Café (Chinese, $)
Marrakesh (Moroccan, $$)
Nine Dragons (Chinese, $$)
Rose & Crown Pub & Dining Room
(British, $–$$)
San Angel Inn (Mexican, $–$$)
Teppanyaki Dining Room
(Japanese, $$–$$$)

Magic Kingdom

Cinderella's Royal Table
(American, $$–$$$)
Liberty Tree Tavern (American,
$$)
Plaza Restaurant (American, $)

Walt Disney World Resorts

Artist Point (American, $$)
Boatwright's Dining Hall (New
Orleans, $$)
California Grill (American,
$$–$$$)
Citricos (French, $$$)
Columbia (Cuban, $$)
Flying Fish Café (Seafood, $$)
'Ohana (Polynesian, $$)
Spoodles (Mediterranean, $$)
Victoria & Albert's (Inter-
national, $$$$)
Yachtsman Steakhouse (Steaks,
$$$)

Index by cuisine

American

Artist Point (Disney's Wilderness
Lodge, $$)
B-Line Diner (International Drive
Area, $–$$)
Bubbaloo's Bodacious BBQ (Near
North, $)
California Grill (Disney's
Contemporary Resort, $$–$$$)
Cinderella's Royal Table (Magic
Kingdom, $$–$$$)
'50s Prime Time Café
(Disney–MGM Studios, $–$$)
Hollywood Brown Derby
(Disney–MGM Studios, $$)
House of Blues (Downtown
Disney, $$)
Le Cellier Steakhouse (Epcot, $$)
Liberty Tree Tavern (Magic
Kingdom, $$)
Pebbles (Downtown Orlando,
Near North, Lake Buena Vista,
$–$$)
Planet Hollywood (Downtown
Disney, $–$$)

Plaza Restaurant (Magic
Kingdom, $)
Race Rock (International Drive
Area, $–$$)
Rainforest Café (Downtown
Disney Marketplace & Animal
Kingdom, $–$$)
Sci-Fi Dine-In Theater Restaurant
(Disney–MGM Studios, $$)
Wild Jacks (International Drive
Area, $–$$)
Wolfgang Puck Café (Downtown
Disney, $$–$$$)

British

Rose & Crown Pub & Dining Room
(Epcot, $–$$)

Caribbean

Bahama Breeze (International
Drive Area, $–$$)
Bob Marley — A Tribute to Free-
dom (Universal Orlando, $)
Jimmy Buffett's Margaritaville
(Universal Orlando, $–$$)

Chinese
Lotus Blossom Café (Epcot, $)
Ming Court (International Drive Area, $$)
Nine Dragons (Epcot, $$)

Cuban
Columbia (Celebration, $$)
Numero Uno (Downtown Orlando, $-$$)
Rolandos (Near North, $-$$)

French
Chefs de France (Epcot, $$-$$$)
Citricos (Disney's Grand Floridian Resort & Spa, $$$)
Le Coq Au Vin (South Orlando, $-$$)
Le Provence (Downtown Orlando, $$-$$$)
Maison & Jardin (Near North, $$$)

International
Arthur's 27 (Lake Buena Vista, $$$)
Black Swan (Lake Buena Vista, $$$)
Café Tu Tu Tango (International Drive Area, $)
Dux (International Drive Area, $$$)
Manuel's on the 28th (Downtown Orlando, $$$)
Park Plaza Gardens (Near North, $$)
Victoria & Albert's (Disney's Grand Floridian Resort & Spa, $$$$)

Italian
Bergamo's (International Drive Area, $$-$$$)
Capriccio (International Drive Area, $$-$$$)
Christini's (International Drive Area, $$$)
Delfino Riviera (Universal Orlando, $$-$$$)

L'Originale Alfredo di Roma (Epcot, $$)
Mama Melrose's Ristorante Italiano (Disney–MGM Studios, $-$$)
Pacino's Italian Ristorante (South Orlando, $$)
Pastamore Ristorante (Universal Orlando, $$)
Portobello Yacht Club (Downtown Disney, $$-$$$)

Japanese
Ran-Getsu of Tokyo (International Drive Area, $$-$$$)
Teppanyaki Dining Room (Epcot, $$-$$$)

Mediterranean
Spoodles (Disney's BoardWalk Resort, $$)

Mexican
San Angel Inn (Epcot, $-$$)

Moroccan
Marrakesh (Epcot, $$)

New Orleans
Boatwright's Dining Hall (Disney's Port Orleans Resort, $$)
Emeril's (Universal Orlando's Universal Orlando, $$-$$$)

Norwegian
Akershus (Epcot, $$)

Polynesian
'Ohana (Disney's Polynesian Resort, $$)

Seafood
Atlantis (International Drive Area $$$)
Coral Reef (Epcot, $$-$$$)

Flying Fish Café (Disney's
BoardWalk Resort, $$)
Fulton's Crab House (Downtown
Disney, $$–$$$)
Hemingway's (Lake Buena
Vista, $$)
Landry's Seafood House
(International Drive Area, $$$)

Steaks

Le Cellier Steakhouse (Epcot, $$)
Morton's of Chicago (Inter-
national Drive Area, $$–$$$)

Yachtsman Steakhouse (Disney's
Yacht Club Resort, $$$)

Vietnamese

Little Saigon (Downtown, $)

Chapter 15

Disney Character Dining

● ●

In This Chapter

▶ Budgeting for character dining

▶ Finding the best character meals

● ●

*T*he 8-and-under crowd usually gets starry-eyed when characters show up to say howdy, sign autographs, pose for photos, and encourage them to eat their okra. Character turn-outs at mealtimes at several Disney parks, attractions, and resorts are incredibly popular. Translation: One-on-one interaction is somewhat brief, so be ready for that Kodak moment or hope a **WDW** photographer captures the moment (for a premium price).

You may not find a seat if you show up to a character appearance unannounced, so call to make Priority Seating arrangements as far in advance as possible.

The Cost of Catching Characters

Prices for Disney character meals are pretty much the same no matter where you dine. Breakfast (most serve it) averages $14–$16 for adults and $8–$10 for children 3 to 11. Dinners, which are only available in some places (see the listings later in this chapter), run $19–$22 for adults and $9–$13 for children 3 to 9. In general, presentation at all the character meal listings here is high on the fun front and middle-of-the-road when it comes to the vittles. The character luau at **WDW's Polynesian Resort** (see Chapter 29 for information on this meal and other Disney dinner shows) is a bit better in both categories, so naturally it costs you a few more clams.

To make Priority Seating reservations (these reservations don't lock down a table, but they do give you the next available table after you arrive) for any Disney character meal, call ☎ **407-939-3463**. Character meals accept American Express, Diners Club, the Discover Card, MasterCard, and Visa.

You can find most of the restaurants mentioned in this chapter on the map "Walt Disney World & Lake Buena Vista Restaurants" located in Chapter 14. You can also find in-depth reviews of most of their non-character meals and cuisine in that chapter. Additionally, if you're a cyber-sleuth, you can get information at www.disneyworld.com.

The Most Characters Money Can Buy

Although we mention specific characters here, be advised that **WDW** frequently changes its lineups, so don't promise the kids a specific character or you may get burned. Also, keep in mind that you'll have to *add the price of park admission ($48 adults, $38 kids)* to character meals that are held inside the theme parks.

Artist Point

Winnie the Pooh, Tigger, and all their friends from the Hundred Acre Wood host an all-you-can-eat breakfast of scrambled eggs, potatoes, sausage, and bacon. (If you prefer to go with less protein and cholesterol, they also offer a fruit plate in lieu of traditional breakfast fare.) The rustic, lodge-like dining room has a high-beamed ceiling supported by tree-trunk beams and large windows providing scenic lake views.

In Disney's Wilderness Lodge, 901 Timberline Dr. $14.50 adults, $8.75 children 3–9. Open: Daily 7:30–11:30 a.m.

Cape May Café

The Cape May Café is a delightful New England-themed dining room that serves lavish buffet character breakfasts hosted by Admiral Goofy and his crew: Chip 'n' Dale and Pluto (Minnie Mouse occasionally makes an appearance). The buffet is traditional American fare: eggs, pancakes, bacon, and pastries.

In Disney's Beach Club Resort, 1800 Epcot Resorts Blvd. $15.95 adults, $8.95 children 3–9. Open: Daily 7:30–11:00 a.m.

Chef Mickey's

The whimsical Chef Mickey's is the home of buffet breakfasts (eggs, breakfast meats, pancakes, fruit, and so on) where you can meet and be greeted by the Magic Mouse and various pals. Chef Mickey's character buffet dinners come with a salad bar, you-peel-'em-you-eat-'em shrimp, soups, hot entrees, breads, prime rib, vegetables, and an ice cream bar with a great variety of toppings.

In Disney's Contemporary Resort, 4600 North World Dr. Character breakfast $14.95 adults, $7.95 children 3–9; Character dinner $19.95 adults, $8.95 children 3–9. Open: Daily 7:00–11:30 a.m. and 5:00–9:30 p.m.

Cinderella's Royal Table

This Gothic castle — the focal point of the park — is the setting for daily character breakfasts. The menu has standard fare: eggs, bacon, Danish, and fresh breads. Hosts vary, but Cinderella always makes an appearance. This is one of the most popular character meals in the park, so reserve far in advance. This meal is a great way to start your day in the **Magic Kingdom.**

In Cinderella's Castle, The Magic Kingdom. $14.95 adults, $7.95 children 3–9. Open: Daily 8–10 a.m.

Crystal Palace

The real treats here are the characters, Pooh and his pals, who are on location throughout the day. The early menu is typical breakfast fare (omelets, French toast, pancakes, breakfast meats, and — wowser! — breakfast lasagna). Winnie the Pooh holds center stage while the other characters circle the restaurant, providing a lot of love and photo opportunities. At lunch and dinner, standards include fried chicken, macaroni and cheese, and a variety of veggies and desserts. This is one of the worst places to come if you're in dire need of a quiet meal. Pooh and his crew attract jabbering, squealing kids like lovebugs on a wide windshield.

Priority Seating reservations are almost a must here thanks to the crowds.

On Main St., The Magic Kingdom. Breakfast $14.95 adults, $7.95 children 3–9; lunch $15.95 adults, $8.25 children 3–9; dinner $19.95 adults, $9.95 children 3–9. Open: Daily 8:00–10:30 a.m., 11:30 a.m.–3:15 p.m., and 4 p.m. to park closing.

Donald's Prehistoric Breakfastosaurus

Here's another all-you-can-shove-in buffet of eggs, bacon, and French toast. Donald Duck, Mickey Mouse, Goofy, and Pluto are on hand to entertain the little ones while they almost eat. **Note:** This is the only place in **Animal Kingdom** that offers a character breakfast.

In Animal Kingdom, Restaurantosaurus, Dinoland U.S.A. Breakfast $13.95 adults, $7.95 children 3–9. Open: Daily opening–10 a.m.

Garden Grill

This revolving restaurant has comfortable, semicircular booths. As you dine, your table travels past desert, prairie, farmland, and rain-forest environments as only Disney imagineers can design them. There's a Mom's-in-the-kitchen theme here: You're given a straw hat as you enter, and the just-folks service staff speaks in country lingo. Hearty family-style meals are hosted by Mickey, Minnie, and Chip 'n' Dale. (Boy, that Mickey sure gets around.) The American breakfast includes scrambled eggs, potatoes with cheese, sausage, ham, biscuits, fresh fruit, and cinnamon rolls. Lunch and dinner offer rotisserie chicken, fish, steak, potatoes, vegetables, salad, and dessert.

In The Land Pavilion, Epcot. Breakfast $14.95 adults, $8.25 children 3–9; lunch $16.95 adults, $9.95 children 3–9; dinner $18.95 adults, $9.95 children 3–9. Open: Daily 8:30 a.m.–8:10 p.m.

Hollywood & Vine Character Dining

Minnie, Goofy, Pluto, and Chip 'n' Dale host buffet breakfasts (eggs, pancakes, French toast, bacon, sausage, ham, smoked salmon, fajitas) and lunches (turkey, flank steak, chicken, sausage and peppers, fish, pasta).

At Hollywood & Vine, in Disney MGM–Studios. Breakfast $14.95 adults, $7.95 children; lunch $16.50 adults, $8.95 kids. Daily 8:15–11:30 a.m. and 11:30a.m.–3:30 p.m.

Liberty Tree Tavern

This colonial-style, 18th-century pub offers character dinners hosted by Mickey, Goofy, Pluto, Chip 'n' Dale, and Tigger (some or all of them). Meals are fixed-price and offer a salad of mixed greens, roast turkey with mashed potatoes, cornbread, and warm apple crisp with vanilla ice cream for dessert.

Food-wise, this is the best character meal in the **World.**

In Liberty Square, The Magic Kingdom. Dinner $19.95 adults, $9.95 children 3–9. Open: Daily 4 p.m. to park closing.

Minnie's Menehune

Traditional breakfast foods (eggs, pancakes, bacon, and more) are prepared on an 18-foot fire pit and served family-style. Minnie, Goofy, and Chip 'n' Dale appear, and there are parades for children to participate in with Polynesian musical instruments.

In Disney's Polynesian Resort, 1600 Seven Seas Dr. $15.95 adults, $8.95 children 3–9. Open: Daily 7:30–11:00 a.m. at the Polynesian-themed 'Ohana restaurant. (See Chapters 14 and 29 for more details.)

1900 Park Fare

The exquisitely elegant Grand Floridian resort hosts character meals in the festive exposition-themed 1900 Park Fare. Big Bertha — a 100-year-old French band organ that plays pipes, drums, bells, cymbals, castanets, and the xylophone — provides music. Mary Poppins, Winnie the Pooh, Goofy, Pluto, Chip 'n' Dale, and/or Minnie appear at the elaborate buffet breakfasts of traditional eggs, French toast, bacon, and pancakes. Disney villains appear at nightly buffets, which have prime rib, pork loin, fresh fish, and more.

In Disney's Grand Floridian Beach Resort, 4401 Floridian Way. Breakfast $15.95 adults, $9.95 children 3–9; dinner $21.95 adults, $12.95 children 3–9. Open: Daily 7:30–11:30 a.m. and 5:15–9:00 p.m.

Part V
Exploring Walt Disney World

The 5th Wave   By Rich Tennant

"I _know_ these are your character's names, but when you're around guests at the theme park, you're neither sleepy, dopey, nor grumpy."

In this part . . .

You've made travel plans, picked a hotel, and you know where to eat. At last, you're going to Disney World!

However, the Super Bowl champs and half of their fans, thousands of conventioneers and vacationers, and many locals are going to Disney World, too.

Every year, more than 43 million sweaty bodies invade Disney's four major theme parks, and all of them are hell-bent on riding the same rides and eating in the same restaurants as you are. You'll have a lot more fun if you arrive knowing which parks and attractions suit your tastes as well as knowing which parks you should avoid. In this section, we help you rank the parks' amenities so you can determine where you want to spend the majority of your time.

Chapter 16

Getting Acquainted with Walt Disney World

*W*hen the **Magic Kingdom** first opened its gates in 1971, we made the pilgrimage with our 1-year-old daughter, Chris, and wandered in slack-jawed awe among the many marvels of Mickeyville.

Today, as our grandsons Jake and Andy enter the mix, we marvel at a different wonder: growth. Walt Disney's legacy has exploded in the last three decades. It has truly become a world, with four theme parks, nearly a dozen smaller parks and attractions, nightclubs, hotels, restaurants, shopping districts, and two cruise ships. It's enough to fog your mind, so we're here to put the fun back in your vacation planning.

In this chapter, we introduce you to the parks, tantalize you with ride descriptions, and offer you some suggested itineraries. We also use the JJSays ratings system to give you a pint-size view of the rides and shows in the parks.

Of course, don't think ours is the only way to do Disney. We've done it enough times that we know the shortcuts, the duds, and the all-stars. But maybe you can afford a more leisurely pace or prefer a quiet jungle cruise instead of a rock-and-roller coaster. So, make sure that you use this chapter and the rest of Part V to fill in your own dance card.

Introducing Walt's World

Disney's four main theme parks line the western half of this 30,500-acre world. The **Magic Kingdom** is the original attraction; with 15.4 million visitors in 2000, it was busier than any other U.S. theme park. **Epcot**

The Lands

was the third busiest theme park, welcoming 10.6 million visitors, followed by **Disney–MGM Studios** at 8.9 million, and **Animal Kingdom** with 8.3 million visitors a year. Here's a quick look at what you can find in all four Disney parks:

> ✔ **Magic Kingdom:** Built as Disney's flagship park, the **Magic Kingdom** is divided into seven themed lands. They're laid out like the spokes of a wheel, with the park's icon — *Cinderella's Castle* — at the hub. Anyone with kids or who is just young at heart should give the Magic Kingdom at least one full day. It offers more for younger children than any other Orlando theme park, but it has broad appeal for first-timers and Disney fans, too. If you fall into these categories, we recommend two days or more, provided you have the time and budget. (See Chapter 17 for more details about the **Magic Kingdom.**)

✔ **Epcot:** Built as an exposition of human achievement and new technology, **Epcot** is symbolized by *Spaceship Earth,* an item usually described as "that big silver golf ball." *Future World,* the first of Epcot's two sections, has innovative exhibits and rides. The other side of the park, *World Showcase,* has pavilions surrounding a lagoon and showcases the culture of a dozen countries. Allowing two days for the shows, rides, shops, and ethnic restaurants in Epcot is a good idea. (See Chapter 18 for more details about **Epcot.**)

This is the least attractive park for young kids, but the best one for inquiring minds.

✔ **Disney–MGM Studios:** WDW's third-to-evolve park is reminiscent of the Tinseltown of the '30s and '40s. It blends working studios with shows such as *Indiana Jones Stunt Spectacular* and thrill rides such as the *Twilight Zone Tower of Terror* and *Rock 'n' Roller Coaster.* You can tackle this part of **WDW** in one day. (See Chapter 19 for more details about **Disney–MGM Studios.**)

✔ **Disney's Animal Kingdom:** The newest Disney kid on the block is symbolized by the 14-story *Tree of Life,* which is to this park what *Cinderella's Castle* is to the **Magic Kingdom.** This wildlife exhibit, zoo, and theme park has shows such as *It's Tough to Be A Bug!* and *Tarzan Rocks* as well as rides such as *Kilimanjaro Safaris* and *Dinosaur.* You won't have trouble touring this park in one day. (See Chapter 20 for more details about **Disney's Animal Kingdom.**)

Have time for more?

In addition to the big four, other parks and attractions fill in the Disney empire, including the following:

✔ **The Walt Disney Wide World of Sports** complex has a 7,500-seat baseball stadium that's the spring training home of the Atlanta Braves. It also has facilities for 30 other sports, including soccer, softball, basketball, and football.

✔ **Walt Disney World Speedway** has a stock car racing track that hosts the *Richard Petty Driving Experience,* where you can ride shotgun or even drive a car at 145 mph. (If you're from Talladega or Darlington, you probably already know how.)

✔ **Three splashy parks** let you float along lazy streams, scream down waterslides, and more. They're especially appealing in summer, when it's 90 degrees and the humidity is 90 percent. The parks are **Blizzard Beach, River Country,** and **Typhoon Lagoon.**

We give you more info about these spots in Chapter 21.

Happy Birthday Walt!

Disney loves a celebration. In 1996–97, the resort marked the **Magic Kingdom's** 25th anniversary with tons of special events. In 1999–2000, WDW heralded the Millennium. And beginning in October 2001, Mickey will begin a year of "high fives" in honor of the 100th anniversary of Walt Disney's 1901 birth in Chicago. The events will be smaller in scope than earlier celebrations, and details were still being firmed when this book went to press. You can, however, expect things to focus on **Disney–MGM Studios** and include plenty of gingerbread, four new parades, and some small attractions.

Planet Disney also has several shopping (see Chapter 22) and nightlife (see Chapter 28) venues. For example:

- ✔ **Disney's BoardWalk** is a good place to stroll the waterfront, dine, dance, or catch a game in the sports bar.

- ✔ **Downtown Disney** comprises **Pleasure Island,** an adult nightclub district; **Downtown Disney Marketplace,** which features dining and shopping; **Downtown Disney West Side,** with more shopping, dining, *Cirque du Soleil,* the *House of Blues,* and **DisneyQuest.**

You can get additional information about all **WDW** properties by calling ☎ **407-824-4321** or visiting its Web site at www.disneyworld.com.

For a peek at the layout of **Walt Disney World's** various theme parks and other "lands," consult "The Lands" map earlier in this chapter.

Want to go behind the scenes?

If you'd like to get an insider's look at how the Wizards of Diz make magic, *Behind-The-Scenes Tours* are the way to go. So many options are available that the Disney folks sometimes have trouble remembering them all.

Here's a sampling. (**Note:** Unless otherwise noted, all of these tours require park admission, $48 for adults, $38 kids 3 to 9.)

- ✔ **Family Magic Tour:** This two-hour scavenger hunt brings you face to face with Disney characters at the **Magic Kingdom** ($25 adults, $20 kids 3 to 9). It kicks off at 9:30 and 11:30 a.m. daily.

- ✔ **Hidden Treasures of World Showcase:** This 3½-hour tour lets you explore the architectural and entertainment offerings at **Epcot.** It's for ages 16 and older and begins at 9 a.m. Tuesdays, Thursdays, and Saturdays ($49).

✔ **Keys to the Kingdom:** Receive a 4½-hour orientation to the **Magic Kingdom** and a glimpse into the high-tech systems behind Mickey's magic. It's $58 and includes lunch. The tour starts at 8:30, 9:30, and 10 a.m., and 1 p.m. daily.

✔ **Backstage Magic:** At the top of the price chain — $199 per person — *Backstage Magic* is a seven-hour, self- and bus-propelled tour through areas of **Epcot,** the **Magic Kingdom,** and **Disney–MGM Studios** that aren't seen by mainstream guests. If you must know how things work, this tour is for you. You see mechanics repairing and building animatronic beings, and you also venture into **Magic Kingdom** tunnels that aren't only work areas but also paths for the cast to get from one area to another without fighting tourist crowds. It is offered at 9 a.m. weekdays and is limited to 20 adults, so book early. *Park admission isn't required.*

Reservations are recommended, and in many cases essential, for behind-the-scenes tours. You can call ☎ **407-939-8687** to make your reservations.

Finding Your Way to the Fun

If you're driving, Interstate 4's three Disney exits are clearly marked (though the exit numbers periodically change thanks to construction). You can't miss them unless you close your eyes.

Interstate 4 is woefully crowded, especially during rush hour (7 to 9 a.m. and 4 to 6 p.m. weekdays). In addition to the thousands of people heading for a day at the parks, thousands of locals are heading to work at them. So remember to factor possible delays into your time schedule.

Parking in the theme park lots costs $6 per day and is a snap. Just do what the people in the yellow-striped shirts ask you to do. In the Size XXXL **Magic Kingdom** lot, you'll probably want to ride the tram to the front gate (the trams are a hoot — the seats are made out of petrified plastic so if you lack posterior padding, you'll probably remember the ride for a while).

Getting from the parking lot to the action can take as much as an hour at the **Magic Kingdom,** so pack a helping of patience before you begin the day.

At **Epcot, Disney–MGM,** and **Animal Kingdom,** trams are available, but walking can be faster (unless you have small children or sore feet), depending on where you park.

Don't forget to make a note of your parking area and row. After a day spent standing in line, listening to screaming kids, and being tapped out by cash registers, you'll have a hard time remembering your name, not to mention where you parked.

Traveling the World

If you don't have a car or prefer to skip the drive, many area accommodations offer shuttles that are sometimes free but usually carry a fee (check the listings in Chapter 8 for hotels that offer shuttle service).

If you're staying at a **WDW** resort, you can take the Walt Disney World Transportation System to get to the parks. It's a thorough system that includes buses, monorails, ferries, and water taxis serving the major parks from two hours prior to opening until two hours after closing, though it's not always a direct route. The system also serves **Downtown Disney, Typhoon Lagoon, River Country, Blizzard Beach, Pleasure Island, Fort Wilderness,** and other Disney resorts. Disney properties offer transportation to other area attractions as well, but you have to pay for it.

The **Walt Disney World Transportation Guide Map** is a handy-dandy way to see just about everything in the entire World. Disney no longer mails them to you in advance, but you can see one online at www. disneyworld.com or can pick one up inside **WDW** at hotels, guard stations, and the *Guest Services* desks inside the parks. The map shows you everything in the empire and helps give you an idea of where your hotel is in relation to places that you want to visit. You can also look at the map of WDW's areas in this chapter to help orient yourself.

Preparing for Park Admission Costs

The number of admission options — from one- to multiday tickets — offered at **Walt Disney World** is staggering, and they're all expensive (not college-fund decimating, but close to it). Deciding which option will work best for you depends on the number of days you plan to spend in the parks, what parks and attractions you want to see, and whether you're staying at a WDW resort.

If you choose to buy a single-day admission pass, you're limited to seeing one **Disney** park; you can't hop to another one in the middle of the day without paying a separate admission. Most people get the best value from four- and five-day passes.

If you're staying at any **WDW** resort or official hotel (see Chapter 8 for a list of official WDW hotels), you're also eligible for a money-saving *Unlimited Magic Pass,* which is priced according to the length of your stay. The pass also offers special perks, such as early park admission.

If you plan on visiting **Walt Disney World** more than one time during the year, inquire about money-saving annual passes ($349–$459 adults, $295–$399 children 3 to 9). For information on a host of WDW passes, see Table 16-1.

WDW considers everyone 10 and older an adult, and the prices that we give you don't include 6-percent sales tax. Also, know that fluctuating attendance figures and new mega-bucks rides have prompted **Disney** (as well as **Universal** and **SeaWorld**) to bump the single-day admission fee (it's now $48 for adults, $38 for kids 3 to 9) three times in the last two years. And there's no guarantee it won't rise again by the time you arrive. You can get discounts on admission and other things if you're a member of the Disney Club (see Chapter 3 for more information on these discount options).

The average family will spend $100 to $125 per person per day on park admissions, food, and souvenirs alone.

Table 16-1	Walt Disney World Prices	
Admission Option	*Adults*	*Kids (3–9)*
One-day, one-park admission	$48	$38
Four-day Park Hopper Pass (unlimited admission to **Magic Kingdom, Epcot, Animal Kingdom,** and **Disney–MGM)**	$192	$152
Five-day Park Hopper Plus Pass (unlimited admission as above, plus your choice of two admissions to **Typhoon Lagoon, River Country, Blizzard Beach, Pleasure Island,** or **Disney's Wide World of Sports)**	$247	$197
Six-day Park Hopper Plus Pass (unlimited admission as above, plus your choice of three admissions to **Typhoon Lagoon, River Country, Blizzard Beach, Pleasure Island,** or **Disney's Wide World of Sports)**	$277	$222
Seven-day Park Hopper Plus Pass (unlimited admission as above, plus your choice of four admissions to **Typhoon Lagoon, River Country, Blizzard Beach, Pleasure Island,** or **Disney's Wide World of Sports)**	$307	$247
One-day Pass to **Typhoon Lagoon** or **Blizzard Beach**	$30 adults	$24 kids
One-day Pass to **River Country**	$16	$12.50
One-day Pass to **Pleasure Island** Children are not admitted after 7 p.m.	$21, including tax	

Getting the Most Out of Your Trip to the World

The **Magic Kingdom, Epcot,** and **Disney–MGM Studios** usually open at 9 a.m. (sometimes up to 30 minutes earlier) throughout the year. They're open at least until 6 p.m. and often as late as 11 p.m. or midnight during peak periods (holidays and the summer months). **Animal Kingdom** opens at 7 or 8 a.m. and closes at 6 p.m. (slightly later during summer). It's a safe bet that the longer a park stays open, the more people will be visiting that day, so planning your schedule before you get to the park is essential. Unfortunately, hours of operation tend to vary, so it's always wise to call ☎ **407-824-4321** ahead of time or to check the official calendar on Disney's Web site at www.disneyworld.com.

Beat the lines

Everyone's looking for a shortcut and no wonder — lines at Disney and the other big parks can be incredibly long and irritating if you come at the wrong time. Twenty minutes is considered cruising when it comes to line time and 45 minutes to one hour is common at the primo rides. In peak periods — summer, holidays, and other times kids are out of school — it can take longer than an hour to reach the front of the line and, in three or four minutes, the ride is over.

Here are the best tips we can give you to beat the long lines:

✔ Come during off periods.

✔ Plan to spend the morning in one section, the afternoon in another. That way you won't waste time and energy running back and forth.

✔ Spend *two* days in the park if time and budget allow.

✔ Ask about or read the health and height restrictions before you get in line in order to avoid wasting time on a ride that isn't for you.

✔ Disney parks have tip boards that provide up-to-the-minute information on show times and ride waits. You can find the boards at *Main Street,* U.S.A. near Coke Corner in the **Magic Kingdom,** on Hollywood Boulevard near the entrance to Sunset Boulevard in **Disney–MGM Studios,** in the southwest quadrant of Innoventions Plaza near **Epcot's** *Future World Fountain,* and in *Safari Village* at **Animal Kingdom.** Most rides and shows have signs telling you the length of the wait.

Don't want to stand in line as long as other guests, yet not flush enough to hire a stand-in? Disney parks have installed a ride-reservation system called **FASTPASS** where you go to the primo rides, feed your theme-park ticket into a small ticket taker, and get an assigned time to return. When you do, you get into a short line and climb aboard. Here's the drill:

Hang onto your ticket stub when you enter and head to the hottest ride on your dance card. If it's a FASTPASS attraction (they're noted in the guide map you get when you enter), feed your stub into the waist-level ticket taker. Retrieve your ticket stub and the FASTPASS stub that comes with it. Look at the two times stamped on the latter. You can return during that one-hour window and enter the ride with almost no wait. In the meantime, you can do something else until the appointed time.

Note: Early in the day, your one-hour window may begin 40 minutes after you feed the FASTPASS machine, but later in the day it may be hours. Initially, Disney only allowed you to do this on one ride at a time, but you can now get a pass for a second attraction two hours after your first assigned time.

Use E-Ride tickets

The **Magic Kingdom's** *E-Ride Nights* are a bargain for travelers persistent enough to track them down. Only offered in the off season and with little advance notice, E-Ride Tickets cost $10 and give Disney resort guests three hours to ride the nine most popular rides — *Big Thunder Mountain Railroad, Space Mountain,* and *ExtraTERRORestrial Alien Encounter,* to name a few — as many times you can. Better still, they only let 5,000 guests into the park during E-Ride Nights. The tickets are sold on a first-come, first-serve basis at the *Guest Services* desks in the Disney hotels and at the **Magic Kingdom** ticket window (you will be required to show a Disney Resort Guest ID and a valid multiday admission pass). Call ☎ **407-824-4321** for details.

Get a show schedule as soon as you enter the park

Getting a show schedule (it's part of the handout guide map) as soon as you enter the park is essential. Spend a few minutes looking over the schedule, noting where you need to be and when. Many of the attractions in **Walt Disney World** are nonstop, but others occur only at certain times or once a day. You can find maps and schedules at counters on one side or the other of the turnstiles, sometimes at both. They're also at most Disney shops.

Avoiding the Crowds

Crowds are a fact of life at **Walt Disney World,** but that doesn't necessarily mean you'll have to stand in long lines at all the rides and attractions. Forward thinkers can definitely decrease their risk of encountering a major swarm of tourists. In addition to FASTPASS (see "Beat the lines," earlier in this chapter), here are some facts to keep in mind as you plan your crowd-avoiding strategy:

- Mondays, Thursdays, and Saturdays are the busiest days in **The Magic Kingdom.** Tuesdays, Fridays, and Saturdays are the busy days at **Epcot.** Sundays and Wednesdays are crowded at **Disney–MGM Studios** and **Animal Kingdom.**

- Although it's not guaranteed, the parks tend to be less crowded during parts of April to May and October to November. You also have a better chance of avoiding crowds if you go in the middle of the week. Also, while most people steer clear on rainy days, the parks can be less crowded and you won't miss much other than parades (most of the good stuff is indoors).

- Guests at **Disney** hotels get into some of the parks 90 minutes before the swarm during surprise mornings. Ask at your front desk, but these generally occur on each park's busiest days, except **Animal Kingdom,** which doesn't offer this feature.

- If you do dine at **Disney,** make Priority Seating arrangements early in the day to lock in the time you want to eat. (See Chapter 13 for more reservation information.)

- Before you leave home, prepare yourself for the long waits in line. Practice standing for an hour at a time, half of it in the sun, shuffling 30 inches every 2½ minutes.

Speaking of lines, while you're standing in them with nothing else to do, look at the faces around you. All of a sudden it doesn't look like magic, does it?

Chapter 17

The Magic Kingdom

* *

In This Chapter

▶ Locating resources and services in the Magic Kingdom

▶ Checking out the fun: rides, shows, and attractions

▶ Planning for the parades and fireworks

▶ Setting your sights with a suggested itinerary

* *

*I*f you have young kids or a soft spot for vintage Disney, make your way to this **WDW** signature park first. The **Magic Kingdom** is the most popular of Mickey's enterprises, attracting more than 40,000 people a day! (If you've stood in the beer or bathroom lines at Soldier Field or Yankee Stadium, you have a good idea of what you're in for — although Disney lines can be worse.)

Proof of the staying power of the **Magic Kingdom** lies in the fact that the park has changed little over the years. Even newer attractions, such as *ExtraTERRORestrial Alien Encounter,* fall short of the 3D virtual dynamics you encounter at other theme parks, but the kingdom remains the fairest of them all.

Finding Out More about the Magic Kingdom

Yes, there are rides, shows, and characters galore, but there are also some practical items you'll need to know about the **Magic Kingdom.**

Arriving early and staying late

Although they say the **Magic Kingdom** is open every day from 9 a.m. to 7 p.m., there are exceptions. In fact, the gates almost always open earlier than the official opening time. We recommend trying to get to the park early, but not just because of the bonus opening hours. Plotting an early arrival helps counter morning traffic and allows you a more relaxed pace to get from the parking lot to the fun, which can take as much as an hour. At the end of the day, closing usually is later than

7 p.m., especially in summer and during holidays. The **Magic Kingdom** may be open as late as midnight for certain special events. Call ☎ **407-939-7639** or 407-824-4321 for more details.

Locating special services and facilities

In case you forgot to bring essential items or need special assistance while at the park, here's a list of services and facilities that you may need:

- ✔ **ATMs** are located at the main entrance, *Adventureland*, and in *Tomorrowland.* They honor cards from banks using the Cirrus, Honor, and Plus systems.

- ✔ **Baby-changing facilities,** which include rocking chairs and toddler-size toilets, are located next to the *Crystal Palace* at the end of *Main Street.* Of course, it's not the most cost-effective place to buy them, but you can purchase disposable diapers, formula, baby food, and pacifiers in the Gerber Baby Center. Changing tables are also located in the center as well as in all women's rest rooms and some of the men's.

- ✔ **Disposable cameras and film** are available throughout the park. Although once available, you can no longer rent 35-mm cameras and camcorders at Disney parks.

- ✔ You can find **some of your favorite characters** at **Mickey's Toontown Fair.** In *Fantasyland,* look for them in the Fantasyland Character Fest and the Mad Tea Party (on the guide map and schedule that you get when entering the park). Characters also appear in *Frontierland* (the Splash Mountain Courtyard), *Main Street* (Town Square), and *Adventureland.*

- ✔ **The First Aid Center,** staffed by registered nurses, is located alongside *Crystal Palace* and the Gerber Baby Center.

- ✔ You can call ☎ **407-824-4321** or visit Disney's Web site, `www.disneyworld.com` to obtain additional information about **WDW** properties.

- ✔ You can access lockers in an arcade underneath the Main Street Railroad Station. They cost $5, including a $2 refundable deposit.

- ✔ **Lost children** are often taken to City Hall or the Baby Care Center, where lost children logbooks are kept. Making kids under 7 wear name tags is a smart idea, because reading name tags is often easier for park staffers than trying to drag a name from a frightened, crying youngin'.

✔ You can send packages from any store to *Guest Services* in the Plaza area so that you can pick them up at the same place at day's end instead of hauling souvenirs around with you. If you're staying at the Disney resorts, you can have your packages sent straight to your rooms.

✔ **Pets,** except service animals, are prohibited in the parks, but you can board yours for the day or overnight at the Transportation and Ticket Center's kennels. Day rates are $6, overnighters cost $11.

✔ Make your **Priority Seating** arrangements when you enter the park if you care about having a sit-down meal at a special venue. See Chapter 13 for details.

✔ You can find a list of special shows at counters just inside the park entrance. There's also an *entertainment show schedule* in the park guide map you get upon entering. It lists all the events of the day. You may find special concerts, otherwise unannounced visits from Disney characters, and information about fireworks and parades.

✔ **Rent strollers** at the Stroller Shop near the entrance for $7 a day, including a $1 deposit.

✔ **Ticket prices** (at printing time) for a one-day admission are $48 for adults, $38 for kids 3 to 9. See Chapter 16 for more information on park admission prices.

✔ **Rent wheelchairs** at the gift shop to the left of the ticket booths at the Transportation and Ticket Center, or at the Stroller and Wheelchair Shop inside the main entrance to your right. Cost is $7 plus a $1 deposit; $30 and a $10 deposit for battery-run chairs.

✔ The prices of consumables are pretty much standard among Disney parks. The **Magic Kingdom** nails you to the tune of $1.75 or more for a soda, $2.50 for bottled water, $2.35 for an ice-cream bar, $1.55 for a cup of coffee, and $1.35 for a cup of cocoa. Many of these are common prices at **Universal** and **SeaWorld,** as well.

Making the Rounds: The Magic Kingdom's Top Attractions

More than three dozen attractions, plus shops and restaurants, are included in this 107-acre package. The following description tour moves counterclockwise from the front gate, going through each of **Magic Kingdom's** seven lands. To find all of the listed attractions, see "The Magic Kingdom" map, earlier in this chapter.

The Magic Kingdom

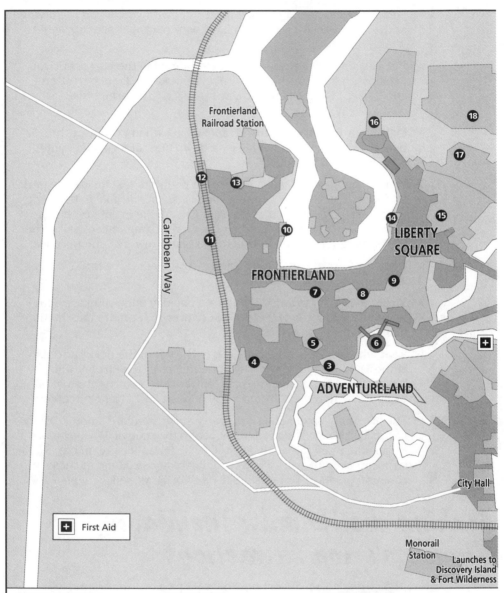

Frontierland
Railroad Station

LIBERTY
SQUARE

FRONTIERLAND

ADVENTURELAND

City Hall

First Aid

Caribbean Way

Monorail
Station   Launches to
Discovery Island
& Fort Wilderness

MAIN STREET U.S.A.	FRONTIERLAND	LIBERTY SQUARE
Main Street Cinema **2**	Big Thunder Mountain Railroad **13**	The Diamond Horseshoe Saloon Revue **9**
Walt Disney World Railroad **1**	Country Bear Jamboree **7**	The Hall of Presidents **15**
ADVENTURELAND	Frontierland Shootin' Arcade **8**	The Haunted Mansion **16**
Jungle Cruise **3**	Splash Mountain **11**	Liberty Belle Riverboat **14**
Pirates of the Caribbean **4**	Tom Sawyer Island **10**	**FANTASYLAND**
Swiss Family Treehouse **6**	Walt Disney World Railroad **12**	Castle Forecourt Stage **19**
Enchanted Tiki Room **5**		Cinderella's Castle **20**
		Cinderella's Golden Carousel **22**

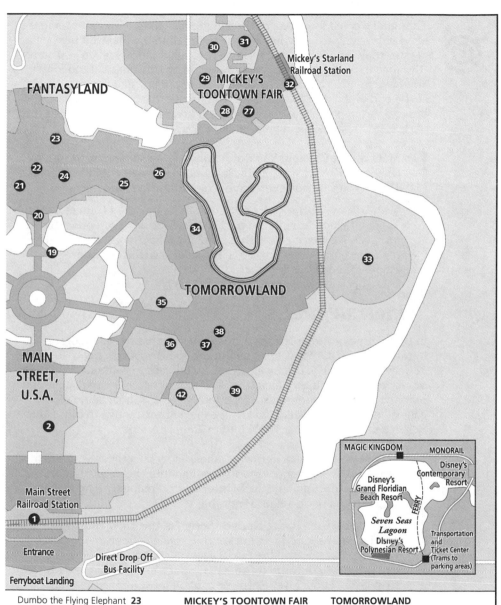

FANTASYLAND

MICKEY'S TOONTOWN FAIR

Mickey's Starland Railroad Station

TOMORROWLAND

MAIN STREET, U.S.A.

Main Street Railroad Station

Entrance

Direct Drop Off Bus Facility

Ferryboat Landing

MAGIC KINGDOM · MONORAIL

Disney's Contemporary Resort

Disney's Grand Floridian Beach Resort

FERRY

Seven Seas Lagoon

Disney's Polynesian Resort

Transportation and Ticket Center (Trams to parking areas)

Main Street, U.S.A.

Though it's considered one of the kingdom's lands, *Main Street* is more of an entry zone where you can lose yourself in the pleasant nostalgia of yesterday. We recommend passing through it quickly when you arrive. (Get thee to the popular stuff right away before the lines get too long!) You have to make a return voyage on *Main Street* when you cry "uncle" at the end of the day. At that time, stamina permitting, so you can browse through the shops at a more leisurely pace before you exit the park. Here are a few highlights of *Main Street, U.S.A.:*

- **Main Street Cinema:** You don't have to pay admission to watch the theater's cartoons, including vintage films like 1928's *Steamboat Willie*. You will, however, have to stand — there are no seats.

- **Walt Disney World Railroad:** This steam-powered train makes a 15-minute loop around the park, with stops in *Frontierland* and at *Mickey's Toontown Fair*. Other transportation along *Main Street* includes horse-drawn trolleys, horseless carriages, jitneys, fire engines, and shoes — yours.

Tomorrowland

In 1994, Disney overhauled *Tomorrowland,* because its vision of the future when the park was designed in the 1960s was starting to look like Yesterville. Originally, Disney imagined a 21st century without computers or answering machines. Thanks to *Star Wars* director George Lucas and others, today's version is more high tech (aliens, robots, and video games, for example), which makes it especially attractive to older kids. Here's a sampling of what you'll find in *Tomorrowland:*

- **Astro Orbiter:** Astronaut wannabes, especially those who are 6 years old and under, love whirling high into the galaxy in colorful rockets. Unfortunately, the orbiter has ridiculously long lines, so skip it if you're on a tight timetable.

- **Buzz Lightyear's Space Ranger Spin:** On this ride, you go to infinity and beyond in an interactive space adventure in which you help Buzz defend the Earth's supply of batteries from the evil Emperor Zurg. You fly an XP-37 space cruiser armed with twin lasers and a joystick that's capable of spinning the craft. (Space Rangers who get motion sickness should sit this attraction out. There's enough space debris flying around without your help.) While you cruise through space, you collect points by blasting anything that smells remotely like Zurg. Your hits trigger light, sound, and animation effects. This ride is similar to, but not as much fun as, the newer *Men in Black Alien Attack* at **Universal Studios Florida** (see Chapter 23).

- **ExtraTERRORestrial Alien Encounter:** George Lucas helped design this extremely popular ride, which is another white-knuckle treat. After you're locked and loaded, something goes terribly wrong with your teletransporter's aim and it sucks in a disgusting meat-eating creature from somewhere in deep space. The lights alternate on and off, but mainly off, and the alien busts loose. Then, with only a strobe light showing you the way, you're treated to down drafts from its flapping wings, liquid spritzes (mucus if you'd prefer to think that way) on your face, and a little blast of hot breath on the back of your neck near the end.

"Uh, no thanks. You guys have fun." No wonder JJ passed. This attraction has a legitimate child warning about it being dark and confining. The recommended age is 10 and older, and although some younger ones may like it, the ride has a *44-inch height minimum.* the age limit is a fair recommendation. Riders are confined by a hard shoulder plate that lowers over your head to lock you into your tomb, er, seat.

- **Space Mountain:** Imagine a roller coaster. Then imagine it in the dark. This ride, *ExtraTERRORestrial Alien Encounter,* and *Big Thunder Mountain Railroad* (we talk about it in the "Frontierland" section, later in this chapter) are the three **Magic Kingdom** attractions that teens and other thrill junkies bolt for first, so get here early or save it for off hours, such as lunch or parade time. It's a classic roller coaster with plenty of plunging and spinning (though it seems faster, it never tops 28 mph). Grab a front seat for the best ride.

Wow, that's double awesome!" It's recommended for those 10 and older, but it's a bit tamer than some of the more modern thrill rides at **Disney–MGM Studios.** However, *you must be 44 inches or taller* to ride it, and there's a bailout area for those who decide to ditch at the last minute.

- **Tomorrowland Speedway:** Kids, especially those ages 4 to 9, like slipping into these Indy-car knockoffs; but older children, teens, and adults find the lines and the steering less than stellar — especially those who are used to go-karts or Malibu Grand Prix. The top speed is 7 mph and there's a thick iron bar separating your tires, so you're pretty much kept on track. You have to be a *minimum of 52 inches tall to drive alone.*

- **Tomorrowland Transit Authority:** This elevated people-mover winds around *Tomorrowland* and into *Space Mountain* on a lazy ride that encourages you to nod off if it's late in the day and you've covered 4 or 5 miles on the old pedometer. There's usually no wait, but this is another one to blow off if you're in a hurry.

- **Walt Disney World Carousel of Progress:** A Disney oldie retooled in 1993, this 22-minute show takes up way too much time and space for its missing wow power. It uses audio-animatronics to trace the technological progress humanity made since the Gas Light era.

Mickey's Toontown Fair

Head off cries of "Where's Mickey?" by taking young kids (2 to 8) to this two-acre site as soon as you arrive. *Toontown* gives kids a chance to meet Disney characters, including Mickey, Minnie, Donald Duck, Goofy, and Pluto. The **Magic Kingdom's** smallest land is set in a whimsical collection of candy-striped tents.

The Barnstormer at Goofy's Wiseacres Farm is a mini roller coaster designed to look and feel like a crop duster that flies slightly off course and right through the Goofmeister's barn. It has a *35-inch height minimum* and its tight turns and small dips will give some adults a rush.

The *S.S. Miss Daisy* is an interactive fountain with enough surprises to win squeals of joy (and relief on hot days).

Minnie's Country House gives kids a chance to play in a kitchen where appliances and utensils do strange things, while *Mickey's Country House* features garden and garage playgrounds, plus a chance to meet the big cheese himself. The *Toontown Hall of Fame* offers continuous meetings with characters.

Fantasyland

The rides and attractions in *Fantasyland* are based on the Disney movies you grew up with way back when, as well as some of the more recent additions to the Disney treasure chest of films. Young kids will want to spend lots of time here, and the lines ensure that you will. Here's a list of attractions in *Fantasyland:*

- ✔ **Cinderella's Castle:** This symbol of the **Magic Kingdom** sits at the end of *Main Street* in the center of the park. It's a favorite for family photos and, if you land at the right time, you can meet Cinderella. The interior has a lot of lovely murals and mosaics, but the attraction is visual — there's really nothing to do here but gawk or go upstairs to eat at Cinderella's Royal Table (see Chapter 14).

- ✔ **Cinderella's Golden Carousel:** In the late 1960s, Disney imagineers found this old beauty — it was built in 1917 — and brought it to the **Magic Kingdom,** where it was restored in time for the park's opening. It's a delight for kids as well as carousel lovers of all ages. The organ plays — what else? — Disney classics such as "When You Wish Upon a Star" and "Twist and Shout."

- ✔ **Dumbo, the Flying Elephant:** This attraction doesn't do much for adrenaline-addicted older kids, but it's a favorite for ages 2 through 6. Dumbo's ears keep them airborne for a gentle, circular flight with some little dips. Most kids older than 6 will be humiliated if you even suggest they ride it. If your little ones are dying to ride

Dumbo, get here as soon as you enter the park — the wait times for this ride are brutal!

✔ **It's a Small World:** Young kids and most parents love this attraction; teens and other adults find it a real gagger. Nevertheless, pay your dues — every Disney visitor ought to be required to ride it at least once. You glide around the world in small boats, meeting Russian dancers, Chinese acrobats, and French cancan girls — and every one of them sings a tune that eats its way into your brain and refuses to stop playing for months.

✔ **Legend of the Lion King:** Simba and friends star in this jungle stage show. Kids under 4 may get fussy; those over 10 may find it child-ish. If the wait isn't bad, it's a good place to park yourself for 30 minutes on a hot day. Show times are listed outside the theater and on the guide map that's available at the park entrance. But a far better rendition of this theme is *Festival of the Lion King* at Disney's **Animal Kingdom** (see Chapter 20).

✔ **Mad Tea Party:** You make this tea party wild or mild, depending on how much you choose to spin the steering wheel in the teacup that's your chariot. The ride is based on *Alice in Wonderland* and is suitable for ages 4 and up.

✔ **The Many Adventures of Winnie the Pooh:** Pooh inadvertently created a small storm of protest and plenty of media coverage when the Wizards of Diz picked this ride to replace the popular *Mr. Toad's Wild Ride* in 1999. *The Many Adventures of Winnie the Pooh* features the cute-and-cuddly little fellow along with Eyeore, Piglet, and Tigger. You board a golden honey pot and ride through a storybook version of the Hundred-Acre Wood, keeping an eye out for heffalumps, woozles, blustery days, and the floody place. This has become a favorite of kids 2 to 8 and their parents.

✔ **Peter Pan's Flight:** Another popular ride among visitors under 8, it begins with a flight over London — adults find the nighttime tableau almost worth the line's long waits — in search of Captain Hook, Tiger Lily, and the Lost Boys. It's one of the old glide rides heralding the technology that was available when the **Magic Kingdom** was born in 1971.

✔ **Snow White's Scary Adventure:** Your journey takes you to the dwarfs' cottage and the wishing well, ending with the prince's kiss to break the evil spell. It's less scary now than it was years ago, when it was really dark, menacing, and surprisingly void of its namesake. She now appears in several friendly scenes, though kids younger than 5 still may get scared.

Liberty Square

Located between *Fantasyland* and *Frontierland,* this re-creation of Revolutionary-era America will infuse you with Colonial spirit shortly after you arrive. Younger guests may not appreciate the historical touches (such as the 13 lanterns symbolizing the original 13 colonies), but they'll delight in seeing a fife-and-drum corps and the opportunity to pose for a picture while locked in the stocks. Here are some other features of *Liberty Square:*

✔ **Boat Rides:** A steam-powered sternwheeler called the *Liberty Belle* departs *Liberty Square* for scenic cruises along the Rivers of America. The passing landscape sort of looks like the Wild West. It makes a restful interlude for foot-weary park-stompers.

✔ **Diamond Horseshoe Saloon Revue:** Fancy ladies, honky-tonk pianos, and gamblers entertain you in a several-times-a-day show that's fun for ages 5 and up. Marshall John Charles sings and banters with the audience, Jingles the Piano Man plays honky-tonk, and there's a magic act — all with lots of humor and audience partici-pation (sit in the balcony if you're not the participating sort). The air-conditioned theater is a great place to dodge the heat and at lunch there's a sandwich menu.

✔ **Hall of Presidents:** American-history buffs age 10 and older most appreciate this show, which can be a real squirmer for young children. The Hall is an inspiring production based on painstaking research. Pay special attention to the roll call of presidents. The animatronic figures are incredibly life-like — they fidget, whisper, and talk to the audience. As of printing time, this attraction had been closed for refurbishment — no reopening date has been announced.

✔ **Haunted Mansion:** Although the mansion has changed little over the years, it continues to be a park favorite and has attracted some-thing of a cult following. It has reasonably good special effects and a fun atmosphere. You may chuckle at the corny tombstones lining the entrance, but the ride doesn't get much scarier than spooky music, eerie howling, and things that go bump in the night. (J.J. declined to rate this attraction, but he jumped at the pop-up ghosts.) The ride is best for those 6 and older.

Frontierland

Rustic log cabins, wooden sidewalks, swinging saloon doors, and other Old West trimmings are featured in *Frontierland,* located behind *Adventureland* and adjacent to *Liberty Square.* Attractions in *Frontierland* include the following:

✔ **Big Thunder Mountain Railroad:** The lines don't lie: This rocking railroad is a favorite of the **Magic Kingdom.** The ride is something of a low-grade roller coaster with speed and a lot of corkscrew action. It has enough of a reputation that even first-time visitors make a beeline for it. So, if you can't get to it as soon as the park opens, FASTPASS (see Chapter 16 for more information on beating the long lines) is your best bet. Or, give it a try late in the day (many coaster veterans maintain the ride is even better after dark) or when a parade pulls most visitors away from the rides.

"Yeeeee-haw!!" Then, "That was awesome!!!" *Thunder Mountain* bounces you around an old mining track, where you barely escape floods, a bridge collapse, rock slides, and other mayhem. (J.J. insists on riding it until everyone in the family turns green or at least begs for a change of scenery.) The ride can be too intense for kids under 6; riders *must be at least 40 inches* tall.

✔ **Country Bear Jamboree:** The stars of this 15-minute animatronic show are bears that croon country-and-western tunes. The Jamboree is a park standard — a show that's been around since Disney invented dirt. The audience gets caught up in the hand-clapping, knee-slapping, foot-stomping fun as Trixie, decked out in a satiny skirt, laments lost love as she sings "Tears Will Be the Chaser for Your Wine." Teddi Barra descends from the ceiling in a swing to perform "Heart We Did All That We Could," and Big Al moans "Blood in the Saddle."

"Pretty neat." (He was probably just happy to be out of the sun for a while.) He also couldn't resist the Disney vending machines that suckered us out of 50 cents for a flattened penny with a Disney logo. These folks are geniuses at getting everything out of your pockets except the lint. All in all, this attraction works best for the over-age-4 set.

✔ **Frontierland Shootin' Arcade:** Combining state-of-the-art electronics with a traditional shooting-gallery format, this arcade presents an array of 97 targets (slow-moving ore cars, buzzards, and gravediggers) in an 1850s boomtown. If you hit a tombstone, it may spin around and mysteriously change its epitaph. To keep things authentic, newfangled electronic firing mechanisms loaded with infrared bullets are concealed in genuine buffalo rifles. When you hit a target, you set off elaborate sound and motion gags. Fifty cents fetches 25 shots.

✔ **Splash Mountain:** If we had to pick one ride as the **Kingdom's** most popular, *Splash Mountain* is it. It's on par with **SeaWorld's** *Journey to Atlantis* (see Chapter 25), though not quite up to *Jurassic Park River Adventure* in **Universal's Islands of Adventure** (see Chapter 24). Still, *Splash Mountain* is a nifty voyage on a flume that has a substantial vertical drop with a good splash factor (around 200 megatons worth of wet). If you're lucky enough to have some real heavyweights in the front seat, look for a little extra explosion on the 40 mph, five-story downhill.

In summer, this ride can provide sweet relief from the heat and humidity, but in cool weather, parents may want to protect their kids (and themselves) from a chill. *Splash Mountain* is recommended for ages 8 and older. *Riders must be at least 40 inches tall.*

✔ **Tom Sawyer Island:** You can explore *Injun Joe's Cave* and tackle swinging bridges that threaten to throw you into a gaping chasm.

> It's a good place for kids to lose a little energy and for moms and dads to relax and maybe indulge in a lunch or a snack at Aunt Polly's, which overlooks the river.

Adventureland

Adventureland is a left-turn off the end of *Main Street*. Kids can engage in swashbuckling behavior while walking through dense tropical foliage (complete with vines) or marauding through bamboo and thatch-roofed huts. Little has changed in this land since the park opened in 1971. The most notable exception is *Magic Carpets of Aladdin*, set to debut about the time this guide reaches bookstores. Its four-passenger carpets will circle a giant genie's bottle while camels spit water at riders. The fiberglass carpets will spin and move up, down, forward, and back. Here's a list of some of the other attractions in *Adventureland:*

- **Enchanted Tiki Room:** Upgraded over the years, the show's newest cast member is Iago of *Lion King* fame. This attraction is set in a large, hexagonal, Polynesian-style dwelling with a thatched roof, bamboo beams, and tapa-bark murals. Other players include 250 tropical birds, chanting totem poles, and singing flowers that whistle, tweet, and warble. The nine-minute show runs continuously throughout the day. Young children are most likely to appreciate this one, but so will nostalgic adults.

- **Jungle Cruise:** This ten-minute, narrated voyage on the Congo, Amazon, and Nile offers glimpses of animatronic animals, foliage, a temple-of-doom-type camp, and lots of surprises. The ride passes animatronic pygmies, pythons, elephants, rhinos, gorillas, and hippos that pop threateningly out of the water and blow snot — well, it could've been snot if they weren't robots — on you. This exhibit is nearly 30-years-old, which means it's pretty hokey sometimes.

- **Pirates of the Caribbean:** In this oldie-but-goodie, after walking through a long grotto, you board a boat headed into a dark cave. Therein, elaborate scenery and hundreds of animatronic figures re-create a Caribbean town overrun by a boatload of buccaneers. To a background of cheerful yo-ho-ho music, the sound of rushing waterfalls, squawking seagulls, and screams of terror, passengers pass through the line of fire into a raging raid and panorama of almost fierce-looking pirates swigging rum, looting, and plundering.

"I *don't* like that ride." We don't know what scared him when he was 3 or so (it's a pretty slow, calm, and tame attraction), but something did and stuck with him like flies on fried chicken. Therefore, we think kids 5 and under may find a pirate's life a bit too scary. Most kids 6 or older, though, will like it.

✔ **Swiss Family Treehouse:** The story of the shipwrecked Swiss Family Robinson comes alive in this attraction made for swinging, exploring, and crawling fun. It's simple and void of all that high-tech stuff that's popular in today's parks. Be prepared to stand on busy days in a slow-moving line. The attraction is also hard for travelers with limited mobility to navigate. Kids 4 to 12 have a blast.

Parades and fireworks

During fireworks and parades, Disney ropes off designated viewing spots for travelers with disabilities and their parties. Consult your park map or a park employee at least an hour before the parade or you may have trouble making it through the crowds to get to the designated spots.

Grab a guide map when you arrive in the kingdom. It includes an entertainment schedule that lists all kinds of special goings-on for the day. These include concerts, encounters with characters, holiday events, and other major happenings.

Disney excels at producing fanfare and the parades and fireworks displays listed here are among the best of their kind in the world.

✔ **Disney's Magical Moments Parade:** With relatively few floats, all showcasing Disney movies, your interest in this parade depends on how much time you're willing to take away from the attractions. The parade includes lots of dancers and extras, but here's a chance to dodge the mainstream and hit a primo ride while the crowds are thin. If you decide to go, go early — seats on the curb disappear fast. Also, don't forget something soft for your fanny. *Magical Moments* is at 3 p.m. year-round. It runs from *Main Street* to *Liberty Square* and *Frontierland*.

✔ **Fantasy in the Sky Fireworks:** This is an explosive display that's held nightly during the summer and on holidays, as well as selected evenings the rest of the year (consult your schedule). Before the display, Tinker Bell flies her magical flight from *Cinderella's Castle*. Suggested viewing areas are *Liberty Square, Frontierland,* and *Mickey's Toontown Fair.* Disney hotels close to the park (**Grand Floridian, Polynesian, Contemporary,** and **Wilderness Lodge**) also offer excellent views.

✔ **SpectroMagic:** This after-dark display replaces the *Main Street Electrical Parade,* a Disney classic that racked up 500 performances during its most recent — and final — **Walt Disney World** run. The *SpectroMagic* production combines fiberoptics, holographic images, clouds of liquid nitrogen, old-fashioned twinkling lights, and classic Disney tunes. Show times vary with seasons. The 20-minute parade is held every night during summer and other peak times, and Thursday through Saturday in the off-season.

Suggested Itineraries

We provide these itineraries to give you a couple ways of seeing the park. They're designed to be time efficient, but you can add or subtract rides and shows based on your tastes.

Planning a day in the Magic Kingdom with kids

Here's an itinerary for a day in the **Magic Kingdom** with your young ones.

- ✔ Consider making a Priority Seating reservation at Cinderella's Royal Table (☎ **407-939-3463**) if you want to have a sit-down dinner in the park (see Chapter 14 for more details about this restaurant).

- ✔ If you have very young kids, take the first train out of the Walt Disney World Railroad Station on **Main Street** and get off at Mickey's Toontown Fair, where tots can meet Mickey and the gang, ride *The Barnstormer at Goofy's Wiseacres Farm*, and visit the houses where Mickey and Minnie live.

- ✔ Go west to **Fantasyland.** Ride *Dumbo the Flying Elephant, Peter Pan's Flight, It's a Small World, The Many Adventures of Winnie the Pooh,* and *Cinderella's Golden Carousel.* If you're in the mood for a show, see *Legend of the Lion King.*

- ✔ At lunchtime, you can stop at Cosmic Ray's Starlight Café for chicken, a burger, or soup before taking in the stage show.

- ✔ If you have preteens, skip **Fantasyland** or at least delay it in favor of **Tomorrowland,** where older kids will love thrill rides such as *The ExtraTERRORestrial Alien Encounter, Buzz Lightyear's Space Ranger Spin,* and *Space Mountain.*

- ✔ If the *Hall of Presidents* and *Haunted Mansion* appeal to you, go to **Liberty Square**; otherwise, head to **Frontierland** for *Splash Mountain* and *Big Thunder Mountain Railroad.*

- ✔ If time permits, most ages will enjoy a trip to **Adventureland** for *Pirates of the Caribbean, the Jungle Cruise,* and the *Swiss Family Treehouse.*

- ✔ Watch the *SpectroMagic* and *Fantasy in the Sky Fireworks* to end your day.

Planning a day in the Magic Kingdom for teenagers and adults

If you no longer belong to the kiddie set, here's a game plan for touring the best the park has to offer you.

✔ Consider making a Priority Seating reservation at **Cinderella's Royal Table** (☎ **407-939-3463**) if you want a sit-down dinner in the park (see Chapter 14).

✔ Beat a path for **Tomorrowland** to ride *Space Mountain, Buzz Lightyear's Space Ranger Spin,* and *The ExtraTERRORestrial Alien Encounter.*

✔ Cut through the center of the park to **Frontierland,** where *Splash Mountain, Big Thunder Mountain Railroad,* and *Country Bear Jamboree* are crowd pleasers.

✔ The Liberty Tree Tavern is a good lunch stop. Before leaving **Liberty Square,** visit *The Haunted Mansion* and *The Hall of Presidents.*

✔ In **Adventureland,** ride *Jungle Cruise* and *Pirates of the Caribbean,* then watch the show in the *Enchanted Tiki Room.*

✔ Bring the day to a rousing conclusion with the *SpectroMagic* and *Fantasy in the Sky Fireworks.*

Index of Attractions by Land

The following section lists all of the fun and exciting attractions housed in the Magic Kingdom by land.

Adventureland

Enchanted Tiki Room
Jungle Cruise
Magic Carpets of Aladdin
Pirates of the Caribbean
Swiss Family Treehouse

Fantasyland

Cinderella's Castle
Cinderella's Golden Carousel
Dumbo the Flying Elephant
It's a Small World
Legend of the Lion King
Mad Tea Party
The Many Adventures of Winnie the Pooh
Peter Pan's Flight
Snow White's Scary Adventures

Frontierland

Big Thunder Mountain Railroad
Country Bear Jamboree
Frontierland Shootin' Arcade
Splash Mountain
Tom Sawyer Island

Liberty Square

Boat Rides
Diamond Horseshoe Saloon Revue
The Hall of Presidents
The Haunted Mansion

Main Street, U.S.A.

Main Street Cinema
Walt Disney World Railroad

Mickey's Toontown Fair

The Barnstormer at Goofy's Wiseacres
   Farm
Mickey's Country House
Minnie's Country House
S.S. Miss Daisy
Toontown Hall of Fame

Tomorrowland

Astro Orbiter
Buzz Lightyear's Space Ranger Spin
The ExtraTERRORestrial Alien Encounter

Space Mountain
Tomorrowland Speedway
Tomorrowland Transit Authority
Walt Disney World Carousel of Progress

Chapter 18

Epcot

· ·

In This Chapter

▶ Highlighting Epcot basics

▶ Experiencing *Future World*

▶ Planning for the *World Showcase*

▶ Examining suggested itineraries

· ·

Grab a big pot. Start with a theme-park foundation, then stir in a heaping helping of technology and add splashes of the movies, street performers, and interactive exhibits. What do you have? **Epcot.** Think of it as a science field trip combined with a whirlwind tour of the world — without the jet lag, though some say it's just as draining if you try to experience it in one day.

Walt Disney wanted his "Experimental Prototype Community Of Tomorrow" to be a high-tech city of 20,000 residents. But, when it was built 15 years after his death, it was more theme park than community and the name was shortened to an acronym, **Epcot,** because, well, it fits on one line in the snazzy brochures that Disney hands out.

 If the **Magic Kingdom** is every kid's dream, **Epcot** isn't. It's more specialized. **Epcot** is suited for older children and adults with a vivid imagination, a need to see the world on a limited budget, or a craving to know how things work — or will work in the future. It's the least friendly Disney park for those under 8–10. If you have wee ones, we recommend skipping it. If, on the other hand, you have older kids or an inquiring mind yourself, we suggest at least a two-day visit because it's so big and varied. *World Showcase* lets you experience exotic, far-flung lands without a passport; you can stroll St. Mark's Square in Venice or dine at a sidewalk cafe while munching some of the best pastries this side of Paris. In *Future World,* you can touch, taste, and catch a wave into the third millennium as you find out about cutting-edge technology and the latest thrill rides.

Epcot

Discovering Epcot's Essentials

Before helping you dive into **Epcot**'s attractions, we should get a few practical matters out of the way.

- ✔ **ATM machines** accept cards from banks using Cirrus, Honor, and Plus. You can find them at the front of the park, in *Germany,* and on the bridge between *World Showcase* and *Future World.*

- ✔ **The baby-changing area** for Epcot is located in the Baby Care Center near the Odyssey Center in *Future World.* It sells disposable diapers, formula, baby food, and pacifiers. There are changing tables in all women's rest rooms and some men's rooms.

- ✔ You can buy **disposable cameras and film** throughout the park. Although once available, you can no longer rent 35-mm cameras and camcorders at Disney parks.

- ✔ Registered nurses staff the **First Aid Center.** It's located near the Odyssey Center in *Future World.*

- ✔ **Epcot's hours** are usually 9 a.m. to 9 p.m., but it's open as late as midnight sometimes.

- ✔ You can call ☎ **407-824-4321** or visit Disney's Web site, www. disneyworld.com, to obtain additional information about **WDW** properties.

- ✔ **Lockers** are located west of *Spaceship Earth,* outside the Entrance Plaza, and in the Bus Information Center by the bus parking lot. The cost is $5 a day, including a $2 deposit.

- ✔ **Lost children** are usually taken to Earth Center or the Baby Care Center. Kids under 7 should wear name tags.

- ✔ You can **send packages** from any store in the park to *Guest Services* in the Plaza area, allowing you to pick them up all at once at the end of the day. This service is free. Allow three hours for delivery. If you're staying at a Disney resort, you can have your packages sent directly to your rooms.

- ✔ You can arrange **pet care** accommodations for $6 a day at kennels just outside the Entrance Plaza at **Epcot.** The Transportation and Ticket Center at the **Magic Kingdom** has overnight boarding available for $11. You must show proof of vaccination.

- ✔ You can make **Priority Seating** arrangements (see Chapter 13) at the World Key Terminals just inside the entrance. If you know where you want to eat ahead of time, call ☎ **407-939-3463.**

- ✔ **Rent strollers** from stands east of the Entrance Plaza and at World Showcase's International Gateway. The cost is $7, including a $1 refundable deposit.

- ✔ **Tickets to Epcot** cost $48 for a one-day adult admission, $38 for kids 3 to 9. See Chapter 16 for other options.

✔ **Rent wheelchairs** inside the Entrance Plaza to your left, to the right of ticket booths at the Gift Shop, and at *World Showcase's* International Gateway. They cost $7, including a $1 refundable deposit. Electric chairs cost $40 a day, including a $10 deposit.

✔ The prices of **consumables** are pretty much standard among Disney parks. **Epcot** will nail you to the tune of $1.55 and up for a soda, $2.50 for bottled water, $2.00 for an ice cream bar, $2.50 for a pineapple float, and $1.15 for a cup of cocoa. Many of these are common prices at **Universal** and **SeaWorld,** as well.

Touring Epcot's Top Attractions

Epcot's 260 acres are vibrantly landscaped, so stop and smell the roses on your way through its two major sections, *Future World* and *World Showcase.*

Epcot is big enough that walking around it can be exhausting (the *World Showcase* semicircle alone is 1.3 miles). That's why some people say **Epcot** stands for "Every Person Comes Out Tired." If you don't spend much time lingering in the *World Showcase,* you can see all of Epcot in one day. A boat launch runs from the edge of *Future World* to *Germany* or *Morocco.* There are also double-decker buses circling the *World Showcase Promenade,* making stops at *Norway, Italy, France,* and *Canada.*

To locate the attractions we discuss in the following sections, check out the "Epcot Map," at the beginning of this chapter.

Future World

Most visitors enter **Epcot** through *Future World,* the northern section of the park (although it appears on the bottom of your guide map, and in the "Epcot" map earlier in this chapter). *Spaceship Earth,* that thing that looks like a giant, silver golf ball meant for a club to fit Paul Bunyon, centers *Future World.* Exhibits in this section focus on discovery, scientific achievements, and technology in areas spanning from energy to undersea exploration.

The crescent-shaped buildings to your right and left, just beyond Spaceship Earth, showcase cutting-edge technology and future products. The building to the left **(Innoventions East)** as you enter the park headlines *House of Innoventions,* which has a preview of tomorrow's smart house (a refrigerator that can itemize and order groceries, a picture frame that can store and send photos to other "smart frames," and a toilet that does everything from warm your tush to eliminate the need for toilet paper). There's also an exhibit on *Future Cars.* Across the way at **Innoventions West,** Sega is the major player, sponsoring dozens of stations with *Video Games of Tomorrow.* Nearby, *Medicine's New Vision* goes behind the scenes with exhibits such as 3D body imaging.

Imagination

Even the fountains at this attraction are magical — shooting water snakes through the air.

Journey into Your Imagination takes a look at how gravity, sound, and other things affect your imagination. This gentle ride takes you to a series of labs where you explore gravity in a world that's been turned upside down, sound in a dark chamber, and illusion with now-you-see-them, now-you-don't animals. Afterward, you're given the opportunity to exercise your imagination in a series of interactive exhibits.

The pavilion's main attraction is the 3D *Honey I Shrunk the Audience* show, based on the Disney film *Honey I Shrunk the Kids.* Inside, mice terrorize you and, after you're shrunk, a large cat adds to the trauma; then, a giant 5-year-old gives you a good shaking. Vibrating seats and creepy tactile effects enhance the dramatic 3D action. Finally, everyone returns to proper size — everyone, that is, but the dog, which should be named Whizzer, creates a final surprise.

"I liked that part where the dog sniffed us and acted like he was going to . . ." Well, that's enough from J.J. on that front. We'll save the surprise.

The Land

If agriculture doesn't interest you, skip *Living with the Land,* a 13-minute boat ride through a simulated rain forest, an African desert, and the American plains. New farming methods and experiments ranging from hydroponics to plants growing in simulated Martian soil are showcased in real gardens. A 45-minute *Behind the Seeds* walking tour is also offered daily and costs $6 for adults and $4 for kids 3 to 9. Sign up at the Green Thumb Emporium near the entrance to Food Rocks.

Live footage and animation mix in *Circle of Life,* a 15-minute, 70-mm motion picture based on *The Lion King.* According to the story line, Timon and Pumbaa are building a monument to the good life called Hakuna Matata Lakeside Village, but their project, as Simba points out, is damaging the savanna for other animals. The environmental message of the film is delivered in an enjoyable manner.

Mock rock performers serenade you with songs about nutrition in *Food Rocks.* Neil Moussaka sings "Don't Take My Squash Away from Me," the Peach Boys harmonize in "Good Nutrition," and Excess, a trio of obnoxious hard rockers, counters by extolling the virtues of junk food.

The Living Seas

The Living Seas pavilion has a 5.7-million-gallon aquarium filled with more than 4,000 sharks, barracudas, rays, dolphins, and other reef fish. You start off with a film demonstrating the formation of the Earth and the seas as a means to support life. You also can see exhibits ranging from a diving barrel used by Alexander the Great in 332 B.C. and Sir Edmund Halley's first diving bell (1697). You then make a simulated dive to *Seabase Alpha,* where a too-short ride offers you views of the pavilion's marine residents. After the ride, you're free to explore an ocean research base of the future that has some hands-on exhibits. *The Living Seas* also has two manatees living in terribly tight quarters.

Children under 12 soon lose interest at this attraction, unless they're intensely fascinated by the sea.

Epcot's DiveQuest program allows certified divers to take part in a 3 ½-hour program that includes a 30- to 45-minute scuba dive in the *Living Seas* aquarium for $140. For information, call ☎ **407-937-8687.**

Spaceship Earth

Epcot's icon houses an attraction of the same name. It includes a slow-track journey back to the roots of communications. The 15-minute ride begins with an audio-animatronic Cro-Magnon shaman recounting the story of a hunt while others record it on cave walls. It advances to ancient Egypt, where hieroglyphics adorn temple walls, then to the Phoenician and Greek alphabets, the Gutenberg printing press, the Renaissance, and eventually you're beamed into outer space.

"What's next?" Our sentiments, exactly. This is a real yawner. A lot of folks stop at Spaceship Earth first thing in the morning as they arrive. If you decide you must do it, you can avoid long lines by saving it until later in the day, when, in most cases, you can walk right in.

Test Track

General Motors and Disney sank $60 million into this long-time-coming marvel of GM engineering and Disney imagineering. You can wait in line for more than an hour during peak periods, so consider the FASTPASS option (see Chapter 16 for more information about beating the long lines). During the last part of your wait, you snake through displays about corrosion, crash tests, and more. The five-minute ride follows a track that looks like an actual highway. It includes braking tests, a hill climb, and tight S-curves in a six-passenger "convertible." There's also a 12-second burst of speed that gets your heart pumping to the tune of 65 mph. It's the best thrill ride in Epcot.

Coming Soon

Disney is working with Compaq and NASA on a new out-of-this-world attraction called Mission: Space. Located to the left of Innoventions East, its headliner will be a motion simulator like those used by astronauts training for missions. (Think liftoff, g-force, and weightlessness as you visit another planet.) The $150- to $200-million exhibit, not scheduled to open until 2002–2003, will also feature interactive games and programs about space exploration.

"That was way fast. Maybe we can do it again, but not this time." In fact, it may be a bit too intense for those under 10. The ride has a *40-inch height minimum.*

Universe of Energy

Ellen's Energy Adventure, a 32-minute ride, features comedian Ellen DeGeneres as an energy expert tutored by Bill Nye the Science Guy to be a *Jeopardy!* contestant. An animated movie depicts the Earth's molten beginnings, its cooling process, and the formation of fossil fuels. You then move back — in solar-powered cars that seat dozens, no less — 275 million years into an eerie, storm-wracked landscape of the Mesozoic Era, a time of violent geological activity. Giant audio-animatronic dragonflies, pterodactyls, dinosaurs, earthquakes, and streams of molten lava threaten before you enter a misty tunnel deep in the bowels of a volcano. The show ends on an upbeat note — a vision of an energy-abundant future and Ellen as a new *Jeopardy!* champion.

Wonders of Life

The *Making of Me,* starring Martin Short, is a captivating 15-minute motion picture combining live action with animation and spectacular in utero photography to create the sweetest introduction imaginable to the facts of life. Short travels back in time to witness his parents as children, their meeting at a college dance, their wedding, and their decision to have a baby. Along with him, we view his development inside his mother's womb and witness his birth.

The presentation may prompt some questions from young children; therefore, we recommend it for ages 10 and up. And, on a different note, the wait to get into the tiny theater may feel like nine months!

Didn't get your fill of being shrunk in *Imagination?* Step into *Body Wars,* where you're reduced to the size of a cell for a medical rescue mission inside the human immune system. This motion-simulator takes you on a wild ride through gale-force winds in the lungs and pounding heart chambers.

Engineers designed this ride from the last row of the car, so that's the best place to sit to get the most bang for your buck.

(Upon seeing his first white-blood cell) "That's disgusting." Then, near the end of the first half, "Mayday, Mayday." Finally, "That was pretty neat." He was luckier than one of our co-pilots. At the first shake, she giggled. At the first rattle, it became a nervous laugh. At the roll, she started frantically fanning herself. At the exit doors, she looked ready to lose her lunch. Riders must be *at least 40 inches tall* to climb aboard.

In the funny *Cranium Command,* Buzzy, an audio-animatronic brain-pilot-in-training, is charged with the seemingly impossible task of controlling the brain of a typical 12-year-old boy during traumas that include meeting a girl and a run-in with the school principal. The boy's body parts are played by well-known actors and comedians, including Charles Grodin, Jon Lovitz, and Dana Carvey.

At *Coach's Corner,* you can have your tennis, golf, or baseball swing analyzed by experts, while the *Sensory Funhouse* offers you a chance to test your perceptions. You can also work out on a video-enhanced exercise bike, get a computer-generated evaluation of your health habits, and take a video voyage to investigate the effects of drugs on your heart.

World Showcase

Those who like *World Showcase* (J.J. isn't among them) are mainly adults or older kids with an appreciation of world history and cultural shows. Its 11 miniature nations open at 11 a.m. daily and surround a 40-acre lagoon. All the countries have authentic, indigenous architecture, land-scaping, background music, restaurants, and shops. Art exhibits, dance performances, and films are among the area's strongest selling points. All the employees in each pavilion are natives of the country represented.

Most of these nations offer some kind of live entertainment throughout the day. You may see Chinese lion dancers and acrobats, Caledonian bagpipers, Mexican mariachi bands, Moroccan storytellers and belly dancers, Italian stilt walkers, and colonial fife-and-drum groups. Check your guide map/show schedule when you enter the park.

You can also find schedules posted near the entrance to each country.

The American Adventure

The American Adventure's 29-minute short-course in U.S. history utilizes a 72-foot rear-projection screen, rousing music, and a large cast of lifelike audio-animatronic figures, including narrators Mark Twain and Ben Franklin. You follow the voyage of the *Mayflower,* watch Jefferson writing the *Declaration of Independence,* and witness Matthew Brady photographing a family that the Civil War is about to divide. You can also witness the stock market crash of 1929, Pearl Harbor, and the *Eagle* heading toward the moon. Teddy Roosevelt discusses the need for national parks; Susan B. Anthony speaks out on women's rights; Frederick Douglass discusses slavery; and Chief Joseph remarks on the situation of Native Americans. The *Voices of Liberty* singers perform folk songs in the Main Hall while you're waiting for the show.

Canada

The pavilion's highlight attraction is *O Canada!* — a dazzling, 18-minute, Circle-Vision 360-degree film that shows our northern neighbor's scenic wonders, from sophisticated Montréal to the thundering flight of thousands of snow geese departing the St. Lawrence River.

The architecture and landscape in *Canada* include a mansard-roofed replica of Ottawa's 19th-century French-style Château Laurier (here called the Hôtel du Canada) and an Indian village complete with a rough-hewn log trading post and 30-foot totem-pole replicas. A steep mountain, cascading waterfall, and forest of evergreens, stately cedars, maples, and birch trees reflect the Canadian wilderness. Tuesday through Saturday, *Off Kilter* entertains visitors with New Age Celtic music.

China

Epcot's version of this Asian land includes a half-size replica of Beijing's *Temple of Heaven,* a summer retreat for Chinese emperors. Gardens simulate Suzhou, with miniature waterfalls, fragrant lotus ponds, and bamboo groves.

The highlight is *Wonders of China,* a 20-minute, Circle-Vision 360-degree film that explores 6,000 years of dynastic and communist rule as well as the breathtaking diversity of China's landscape. The show also includes scenes of the Great Wall, a performance by the Beijing Opera, the Forbidden City, the rice terraces of Hunan Province, the Gobi Desert, and the tropical rain forests of Hainan Island. There's also a gallery of Chinese art, *The House of the Whispering Willows.* The *Dragon Legend Acrobats* perform daily.

France

This pavilion focuses on France's *Belle Époque* (Beautiful Age) — 1870 to 1910 — when French art, literature, and architecture ruled. You enter the pavilion via a replica of the beautiful cast-iron Pont des Arts footbridge over the Seine, and the grounds include a ⅒-scale model of the Eiffel Tower, which was built from Gustave Eiffel's original blueprints.

The premiere event in the *France* pavilion is *Impressions de France*. Shown in a palatial, sit-down theater à la Fontainebleau, this 18-minute film is a scenic journey through diverse French landscapes projected on a vast, 200-degree wraparound screen and enhanced by the music of French composers. Outside, *The Statues*, seemingly lifeless marble forms, pose daily except Friday.

Germany

Enclosed by castle walls, *Germany* offers 'wursts, oompah bands, and a rollicking atmosphere. The clock tower is embellished with whimsical glockenspiel figures that herald each hour with quaint melodies. The pavilion's outdoor Biergarten was inspired by medieval Rothenberg and features a year-round Oktoberfest, while 16th-century building facades replicate a merchant's hall in the Black Forest and the town hall in Frankfurt's Römerberg Square.

If you're a model-train fanatic or visiting with young kids, don't miss the exquisitely detailed version of a small Bavarian town, complete with working train station, located between *Germany* and *Italy.*

Italy

One of the prettiest *World Showcase* pavilions, *Italy* lures you over an arched stone footbridge to a replica of Venice's intricately ornamented pink-and-white Doge's Palace. Other architectural highlights include the 83-foot bell tower of St. Mark's Square, Venetian bridges, and a central piazza enclosing a version of Bernini's Neptune Fountain.

Japan

The central pagoda is modeled after Nara's Horyuji Temple, built in A.D. 700. The building to its right is a replica of Kyoto's Imperial Palace. If you have some leisure time, enjoy the pebbled footpaths, and other traditional touches. Exhibits ranging from 18th-century Bunraki puppets to samurai armor are displayed in the *White Heron Castle,* a replica of the Shirasagi-Jo, a 17th-century fortress.

Make sure that you include a performance of the drums of *Matsuriza,* which entertain guests daily.

Mexico

The music of marimbas and mariachi bands hits you as you approach this festive showcase, fronted by a towering Mayan pyramid modeled on the Aztec temple of Quetzalcoatl (God of Life) and surrounded by dense Yucatán jungle landscaping. Inside the pavilion, you find a museum of pre-Columbian art and artifacts.

El Rio del Tiempo (River of Time) is an eight-minute cruise through Mexico's past and present. Passengers get a close-up look at the Mayan pyramid and the erupting Popocatepetl volcano, which has been doing the real thing in the other Mexico. *Mariachi Cobre*, a 12-piece band, performs Tuesday through Saturday.

Morocco

The *Medina* (old city), entered via a replica of an arched gateway, leads to a traditional Moroccan home and the narrow, winding streets of the *souk,* a bustling marketplace where handcrafted merchandise is on display. The *Medina's* rectangular courtyard centers on a replica of the ornately tiled Najjarine Fountain in Fez, the setting for musical entertainment. There's also a replica of the Koutoubia Minaret, the prayer tower of a 12th-century mosque in Marrakesh.

The *Royal Gallery of Arts and History* contains an ever-changing exhibit of Moroccan art, and the Center of Tourism has a continuous, three-screen slide show. A guided tour of the pavilion, *Treasures of Morocco,* runs from noon to 7 p.m. daily.

Norway

The *Norway* pavilion's stave church, styled after the 13th-century Gol Church of Hallingdal, features changing exhibits. A replica of Oslo's 14th-century Akershus Castle, next to a cascading woodland waterfall, is the setting for the pavilion's featured restaurant, Akershus. Other buildings simulate the red-roofed cottages of Bergen and the timber-sided farm buildings of the Nordic woodlands.

Norway includes a two-part attraction. *Maelstrom,* a boat ride in a dragon-headed Viking vessel, travels Norway's fjords and mythical forests to the music of Peer Gynt. Along the way, you see polar bears prowling the shore and are then turned into frogs by trolls that cast a spell on your boat. The watercraft crashes through a narrow gorge and spins into the North Sea, where a storm is in progress (don't worry — this is a relatively calm ride). The storm abates, a princess's kiss turns you into a human again, and you disembark at a 10th-century Viking village to view the 70-mm film *Norway.* It's an excellent historical and cultural lesson.

United Kingdom

The *U.K.* pavilion evokes Merry Olde England through its *Britannia Square* — a formal London-style park complete with copper-roofed gazebo bandstand, a stereotypical red phone booth (it really works!), and a statue of the Bard. Four centuries of architecture are represented along quaint cobblestone streets.

Don't miss *The British Invasion,* a group that impersonates the Beatles (daily except Sunday), and pub pianist Pam Brody (Tuesday, Thursday, Friday, and Sunday).

Ending Your Day

Epcot's Millennium Celebration didn't end as billed on Dec. 31, 2000. The popular end-of-day fanfare is continuing indefinitely. The show includes the gala *Tapestry of Nations* parade and *IllumiNations,* a blend of fireworks, lasers, and fountains in a display that's signature Disney. The show is well worth suffering the crowds that flock to the parking lot after the show.

 This display is very popular and draws a lot of people, but there are tons of good viewing points around the lagoon. However, it's best to stake your claim to a primo place a half-hour or so before show time, which is listed in your entertainment schedule.

Making the Most of Your Day (s) at Epcot

There's no *one way* to see **Epcot,** and the two itineraries that we offer you in this section are merely options. You can ad lib the following itineraries based on the activities that most appeal to you.

Barnstormer's special: Experiencing Epcot in one day

What an adventurer (or masochist) you are — tackling *Future World* and *World Showcase* in a single bound! Because **Epcot** truly needs two days, you have to move fast and avoid loitering. Here are some tips to help you do so:

✔ As you enter the park, consult the guide map handout or ask which rides accept FASTPASS (see Chapter 16 for details about bypassing the long lines) and go straight to any that you're dying to ride. If the lines are short, don't bother with FASTPASS.

✔ Consider making a Priority Seating reservation for lunch and dinner at the World Key terminals in Innoventions East. If you want to arrange seating in advance, call ☎ **407-939-3463.** We suggest the Coral Reef restaurant in *The Living Seas* or the San Angel Inn in the *World Showcase's Mexico* exhibit for lunch; Akershus in *Norway* or the Rose & Crown Pub in the *United Kingdom* for dinner (see Chapter 14 for more options).

✔ *Future World,* near the front of the park, is the first of **Epcot's** two areas to open in the morning, so start your day there. Skip *Spaceship Earth* at least for now. It's closest to the entrance and that big golf-ball attracts most guests as they enter. Go straight to *Body Wars,* which is in the *Wonders of Life* pavilion to the left of *Spaceship Earth,* and *Test Track,* the newest thrill ride, which is just beyond it. Then do a buttonhook west to *Imagination* and see *Honey, I Shrunk the Audience.*

✔ Visit the *Living Seas,* where you can watch the huge aquarium forever. But don't. You picked the one-day option and there isn't time.

✔ Head to *World Showcase* next. In our opinion, it's the best part of **Epcot.** *China* has a fabulous 360-degree movie, *Germany's* Biergarten blares with oompah music, and *Norway* delivers a history lesson and boat ride called *Maelstrom.* Also, take in the show and concerts at the *American Adventure.*

✔ Don't forget *IllumiNations* to cap your evening.

Whew! You made it in record time.

Stop to smell the roses: Exploring Epcot in two days

Ignore the one-day itinerary covered in the previous section, but consider our advice about making Priority Seating reservations and eating at our in-park dining suggestions.

The basic plan of attack for a two-day visit is to hit *Future World* and all of its rides and exhibits on your first day, and then cruise to *World Showcase* the next.

Be sure to consult your handout guide map or ask which rides have FASTPASS (see Chapter 16).

Day one

✔ Skip *Spaceship Earth,* because that's where 75 percent of the park's visitors go first. Head to *Body Wars,* which is in the *Wonders of Life* pavilion to the left of *Spaceship Earth,* and then visit the *Cranium Command* and *The Making of Me* shows in the same area. *Test Track,* the park's newest thrill ride, is just beyond the pavilion; it'll be crowded, so go get a FASTPASS and come back later. Double back to *Universe of Energy.*

✔ Spend time in *Innoventions,* with its house-of-tomorrow, medical, communications, and Internet themes. Enjoy the peaceful tours through the *Living Seas* and *The Land,* then cut to *Imagination* for the *Honey, I Shrunk the Audience* ride.

> ✔ If time permits, try *Spaceship Earth* now that the lines are shorter and return to any rides or shows that you really enjoyed.

Day two

> ✔ If you arrive when the park opens, go to any *Future World* rides or shows that you missed on your first day or want to repeat. Or, sleep a little later and arrive in time to take up your position at the Port of Entry to the *World Showcase* (it opens at 11 a.m.).

> ✔ Start in *Canada,* to the far right of the entrance. The movie is uplifting and entertaining. Continue counterclockwise to the *United Kingdom* for the shows, people watching, and a real pub. *France* has a captivating movie and wonderful pastry shop; *Morocco* offers a colorful casbah with merchants, Moorish tile and art, and little passages that put you in Bogartville. (For some, this place is better than the real Casablanca, which is pretty dirty.)

> ✔ Japan has grand architecture but move quickly to *The American Adventure,* a patriotic triumph of audio-animated characters. This is a large theater, so waits are rarely long. Next, head to Italy and St. Mark's Square, which comes complete with a 105-foot bell tower.

> ✔ *Germany* features nonstop Oktoberfest with bands, yodelers, beer, and 'wursts. Don't miss the model railway and the Bavarian-looking shops. Steer yourself to *China,* which offers food, bargain buys, gardens and ponds, and a 36-degree movie. Continuing counter-clockwise, *Norway* features the *Maelstrom* ride. *Mexico* completes the *World Showcase* circle with a boat-ride into its history.

> ✔ End your day with the *IllumiNations* fireworks display.

Index of Attractions by Land

Future World

Imagination
Innoventions
The Land
The Living Seas
Spaceship Earth
Test Track
Universe of Energy
Wonders of Life

World Showcase

American Adventure
Canada
China
France
Germany
Italy
Japan
Mexico
Morocco
Norway
United Kingdom

Chapter 19

Disney–MGM Studios

. . . .

In This Chapter

▶ Discovering Disney–MGM's extras and essentials

▶ Comparing MGM and Universal Studios

▶ Reviewing MGM's main attractions

▶ Catching shows and parades

▶ Planning a day in the park

. . . .

Disney's ad writers tout **Disney–MGM Studios** as "the Hollywood that never was and always will be." Its movie- and TV-themed shows and props are a large part of the mix, but the park has two bowel-tightening thrill rides, too — the *Twilight Zone Tower of Terror* and *Rock 'n' Roller Coaster.* Its neighborhoods include Hollywood and Sunset boulevards, where Art Deco movie sets evoke the golden age of Hollywood. New York Street is lined with miniature renditions of the Empire State and Chrysler buildings. It's also an impromptu stage where street actors perform a range of sidewalk slapstick. Likewise, the park is a working studio where shows are often produced.

Unlike the **Magic Kingdom** and **Epcot,** you can pretty much see **Disney–MGM's** 110 acres of attractions in one day if you arrive early and keep up a brisk pace. If you don't get a *Disney–MGM Studios Guidemap* and entertainment schedule as you enter the park, grab one at Guest Services.

Check show times as soon as you arrive and work out an entertainment schedule that appeals to you. Likewise, take a second to plan ahead for mealtime. We describe the park's best restaurants in Chapter 14.

Acquainting Yourself with Disney–MGM Studios

Before we head off for your close-up with the park's rides and attractions, we need to dispose of some mundane matters.

✔ **ATM machines** accept cards from banks using Cirrus, Honor, and Plus. You can find them on the right side of the park's main entrance and next to Toy Story Pizza Planet Arcade, across from *Jim Henson's Muppet*Vision 3D*.

✔ **The Baby Care Center** in **MGM** is to the left of the main entrance with places for nursing and changing. You can buy disposable diapers, formula, baby food, and pacifiers. Changing tables are also in all women's rest rooms and some men's rooms, and disposable diapers are also available at *Guest Services*.

✔ You can find **disposable cameras and film** throughout the park. Although once available, you can no longer rent 35-mm cameras and camcorders at Disney parks.

✔ **The First Aid Center,** staffed by registered nurses, is in the Entrance Plaza adjoining *Guest Services*.

✔ **Park hours** are generally 9 a.m. to at least 7 p.m., with extended hours — sometimes as late as midnight — during holidays and summer.

✔ You can call ☎ 407-824-4321 or visit Disney's Web site, www.disneyworld.com, to obtain additional information about **WDW** properties.

✔ **Lockers** are located near Oscar's Classic Car Souvenirs, to the right of the Entrance Plaza. They cost $5 a day with a $2 refundable deposit.

✔ **Lost children** at **Disney–MGM Studios** are taken to *Guest Services*. Children under 7 should wear name tags.

✔ Shop clerks can **send your packages** to *Guest Services* in the Entrance Plaza. Allow three hours for delivery. If you're staying at a Disney resort, you can have your package shipped directly to your room.

✔ Disney offers **pet care** accommodations for $6 a day at kennels just outside the park entrance. Proof of vaccination is required.

✔ Make **Priority Seating** arrangements when you enter the park if you care about having a sit-down meal at a special venue. Or, if you know where you want to chow down in advance, call ☎ 407-939-3463. See Chapter 14 for details on restaurants in the park.

✔ You can **rent strollers** at Oscar's Super Service, inside the main entrance, for $7 including a $1 refundable deposit.

✔ **Admission prices** are $48 for a one-day adult ticket, $38 for children 3 to 9. See Chapter 16 for other options.

✔ **Rent wheelchairs** from the gift shop to the left of the ticket booths at the Transportation and Ticket Center, or at the Stroller and Wheelchair Shop inside the main entrance to your right. Your cost is $7 including a $1 deposit; $30 plus a $10 deposit for battery-run chairs.

✔ The prices of **consumables** are pretty much standard among Disney parks. **Disney–MGM Studios** will nail you to the tune of $1.55 and up for a soda, $2.50 for bottled water, $2.00 for an ice cream bar, $2.50 for a pineapple float, and $1.15 for a cup of cocoa. Many of these are common prices at **Universal** and **SeaWorld,** as well.

Disney-MGM Studios

ATTRACTIONS ●

The American Film Institute
Showcase **9**

Backstage Pass **11**

Bear in the Big Blue House **13**

Beauty and the Beast—Live on Stage **18**

Disney-MGM Studios Backlot Tour **10**

Disney's "The Hunchback of Notre Dame:
A Musical Adventure" **8**

Sounds Dangerous Starring
Drew Carey **4**

Fantasmic! **17**

The Great Movie Ride **20**

Indiana Jones Epic Stunt Spectacular **3**

Jim Henson's Muppet*Vision 3D **6**

The Magic of Disney Animation **14**

Rock 'n' Roller Coaster **15**

Star Tours **5**

The Twilight Zone Tower of Terror **16**

Voyage of the Little Mermaid **12**

Who Wants To Be A Millionaire—Play It! **1**

DINING (Full Service) ◆

50s Prime Time Café **2**

Hollywood Brown Derby **19**

Mama Melrose's Ristorante Italiano **7**

Sci-Fi Dine-In Theater Restaurant **21**

Pitting Disney–MGM Studios Against Universal Studios Florida

If you love movies or the golden age of Hollywood, you'll enjoy wandering the realistic streets, shops, sets, and back lots of **Disney–MGM Studios. Universal Studios Florida** (see Chapter 23) caters more to visitors with little children thanks to *Nickelodeon Studios, Fievel's Playland,* and *Woody Woodpecker's KidZone.* But is this town big enough for two studios? We pity the visitor who has time to visit only one of these stellar parks.

Both have good shows and, alas, unavoidably long lines. **Universal** has a slight edge in rides, though *MGM's Rock 'n' Roller Coaster,* is, arguably, the best thrill ride in either park. **Universal** is larger, which means you'll wear out more shoe leather, but it's not as congested. It's also a solid two-day park, whereas you can finish off **Disney–MGM** in a day, although a second day provides a nice comfort zone.

Our overall evaluation is that **MGM Studios** has some great shows, mainly the *Indiana Jones Epic Stunt Spectacular, Star Tours, Jim Henson's Muppet*Vision 3D* adventure, and the *Backlot Tour,* but we give **Universal** an ever-so-slight edge.

The following section divides the rides in **Disney–MGM Studios** into two categories. Rides and attractions that are rated G will assuredly entertain the youngest visitors and, in many cases, the older ones as well. PG-rated rides are those that are geared to adults (and may bore children) and those that young children are not permitted on. For a visual look at the park, turn to the "Disney–MGM Studios" map, earlier in this chapter.

Entertaining for the Whole Family: G-Rated Attractions and Rides

Rides and attractions listed in this category are suitable for everyone, but many are especially geared for young kids and may have little appeal to teens or childless adults.

Backstage Pass

This attraction uses the set from the ABC TV show *Home Improvement* as a major part of a 25-minute walking tour through a working television production facility. Alas, it's a real yawner and should be avoided unless you have time to burn.

Bear in the Big Blue House — Live on Stage!

Younger audiences (2 to 8 years old) love this 15-minute show, where Bear, Ojo, Tutter, Treelo, Pip, Pop, and Luna perform some of their favorite songs from the whimsical Disney Channel series. The show happens several times a day and times are in your show schedule.

Beauty and the Beast Live on Stage

A 1,500-seat, covered amphitheater provides the stage for this 30-minute, live Broadway-style production of *Beauty and the Beast* adapted from the movie version. Musical highlights include the rousing "Be Our Guest" opening number and the poignant title song featured in a roman-tic waltz-scene finale. Sets and costumes are lavish and the production numbers are spectacular. Arrive early to get a good seat. The park usually hosts five or six shows a day.

Honey, I Shrunk the Kids Movie Set

The *Honey, I Shrunk the Kids Movie Set* is an 11,000-square-foot play-ground where everything is larger than life. A thicket of grass is 30 feet tall, mushroom caps are three stories high, and a friendly ant makes a suitable seat. Play areas include a massive cream cookie, a 52-foot garden hose with leaks, cereal loops 9 feet wide and cushioned for jumping, and a waterfall cascading from a leaf to a dell of fern sprouts (the sprouts form a musical stairway, activated when you step from sprout to sprout). There's also a root maze with a flower-petal slide, a filmstrip slide in a giant film canister, and a huge spider web with 11 levels. This attraction is a great place for your kids ages 2 to 8 to work off their excess energy, while you regain some of your sanity.

Hunchback of Notre Dame: A Musical Adventure

Dozens of singers and dancers tell the story of Quasimodo in a 32-minute live performance geared to all ages. The human cast, aided by puppets, follows the Disney-animated score and story line in which Quasimodo ultimately loses more than his beloved Esmerelda. Show up 30 minutes early to ensure a good seat and at least five minutes early to make sure you get one at all during busy seasons, when the theater fills to capacity.

Indiana Jones Epic Stunt Spectacular

Spectacular is a good word for this 30-minute rock'em sock'em extrava-ganza guaran-double-teed to keep you entertained and on the edge of your seat. The show is held in a big, open-air pavilion and uses lots of adult volunteers. It begins with Indy rappelling down from the rafters and the nifty special effects soon have him dodging spikes, falling into a pit of molten something-or-other, surviving two ax-wielding gargoyles, grabbing a priceless amulet, and then outrunning fire, steam, and a large boulder that nearly flattens him — all before the first commercial break. The actors, special effects folks, and director use the breaks to explain what you just saw or are about to see, including stunt secrets. In later scenes, Indy battles the evil Nazis in a Cairo marketplace and at an airport-munitions dump.

"Yeah!" It's definitely an adrenaline booster. Young fans (and most adults) really get into the fun as, true to the film, good triumphs over evil, an airplane propeller chops up a big Nazi, and the ammunition dump does its Fourth of July number. Loud noises, though, may make this show a little too intense for kids under 6. There usually are five or six shows a day.

Jim Henson's Muppet*Vision 3D

Located at *Muppet World Headquarters,* this in-your-face, 25-minute spectacle allows the humor of the late Jim Henson to live on through Miss Piggy, Kermit, and the gang. A delight for all ages, this production is a chuckler that mixes some pretty good 3D effects and sensory gags with puppets and a live-action character or two. In the show, you encounter flying Muppets, cream pies, cannonballs, high winds, fiber-optic fireworks, bubble showers, and even an actual spray of water. Kermit is the host, Miss Piggy sings "Dream a Little Dream of Me," Statler and Waldorf critique the action (which includes numerous mishaps and disasters) from the balcony, and Nicki Napoleon and his Emperor Penguins (a full Muppet orchestra) provide music from the pit. Kids in the first row can interact with the characters.

Sounds Dangerous Starring Drew Carey

Drew Carey provides laughs while dual-audio technology provides some incredible hair-raising effects during a 12-minute mixture of movie and live action at ABC Sound Studios. You feel like you're right in the middle of the action of a TV pilot featuring undercover police work and plenty of amusing mishaps. Even when the picture disappears, you continue the chase via headphones that demonstrate sound effects including a roomful of angry bees, a herd of galloping elephants, and a deafening auto race.

Voyage of the Little Mermaid

Hazy lighting helps paint a picture of an underwater world in a 17-minute show that combines live performances, movie clips, puppetry, and special effects. Sebastian sings "Under the Sea," Ariel performs "Part of Your World," and the evil, tentacled Ursula, 12 feet tall and 10 feet wide, belts out "Poor Unfortunate Soul." The Voyage has some scary scenes, but, just like the movie, the show has a happy ending. You get spritzed with water during the show, making this an especially good experience during hot days.

Exploring PG-Rated Attractions and Rides

Rides and attractions in this category appeal to older children and adults. In some cases, they have age, height, or health restrictions. (**Read:** The shrimp enchiladas you had for lunch may not stay in your stomach.)

Disney–MGM Studios opened its newest attraction — based on the Disney-owned ABC TV's hit show *Who Wants to Be a Millionaire?* — in April 2001. It's like the show in that contestants try to answer up to 15 multiple-choice questions. They get three lifelines, including having two wrong answers removed, asking the audience, and calling a stranger on phones set up along Mickey Avenue and the corridor to the Backlot Tour. The big difference: No millions. The contestants play for points and prizes. "Millionaires" get leather jackets and a trip to New York to meet Regis Philbin.

American Film Institute Showcase

More of a shop than anything, the showcase includes an exhibit area where you can waltz through Hollywood history, learning about those behind the movies — editors, cinematographers, producers, and directors whose names blur by in the credits. It also spotlights some of the institute's lifetime achievement winners, including Bette Davis, Jack Nicholson, and Elizabeth Taylor.

Disney–MGM Studios Backlot Tour

This fun, 35-minute special-effects show starts on foot and finishes in a tram. Two folks out of the audience are outfitted in two-piece rain gear with hoods, then dispatched to a lagoon, where one climbs aboard a tugboat (suitably named Miss Fortune) to endure a rainy, rocky, windy ride, capped by a huge wave that rolls over the pilot house. The footage from that adventure is blended with remote effects on a screen to make it look just like the movies. In real life, the audience member gets a little wet, but rain gear saves him or her from a drenching. The second victim enters a fake submarine where underwater air cannons make you think that depth charges are blowing and machine-gun bullets are riddling across the surface.

After the demonstrations, you board a tram for a ride through Disney's costume department (the world's largest), sets from popular (and not-so-popular) TV shows and movies, and the domain of the special-effects wizards.

Well, his yawns turned to wide eyes and a hearty "WOW!" once we entered *Catastrophe Canyon,* where an "earthquake" causes a tanker truck to explode, rocking the tram. Then a very large, *VERY WET* wave threw 70,000 gallons of water our way. All in all, this ride is in the same class as *Earthquake — The Big One* at **Universal Studios Florida** (see Chapter 23).

The Great Movie Ride

A 22-minute journey down MGM's memory lane, *The Great Movie Ride* starts in the 1930s and moves forward from there, using incredibly lifelike animatronic versions of Jimmy Cagney, John Wayne, and Clint Eastwood to re-create some of their most memorable roles. Live bandits then show up and blow up the bank. One of the bad guys kidnaps you and your mates, but — revenge is so sweet, isn't it? — he goes the wrong way, into alienville, which has an uncanny resemblance to one of the *Raiders of the Lost Ark* sets. The space thing from *Alien* is waiting in the ceiling, then the right wall, and pretty soon your bank-robbing buddy gets incinerated when he tries to steal the sphinx's jewel. You then jaunt off to Bogie's Casablanca, and Oz, where a remarkable likeness of the witch warns, "I'll get you my pretty, ahahahaha!"

Sorry folks — this time J.J.'s eyes glazed early and he napped through the ride, but we loved it. Despite the outlaws and alien (which may frighten some youngsters), the ride doesn't contain much for kids of any age unless they like old movies.

The Magic of Disney Animation

Disney characters come alive at the stroke of a brush or pencil as you tour glass-walled animation studios, where you might see some animators at work. Walter Cronkite and Robin Williams (guess who plays straight man?) explain what's going on via video monitors. They also star in a very funny eight-minute Peter Pan-themed film about the basics of animation. Animation is painstaking work: To produce an 80-minute film, the animation team must create more than one million drawings of characters and scenery! Original cels (drawings/paintings on celluloid sheets) from famous Disney movies of the past and some of the many Oscars won by Disney artists are also on display here. The 35-minute tour, recommended for ages 8 and up, also includes a grand finale of magical moments from Disney classics such as *Pinocchio, Snow White, Bambi, Beauty and the Beast,* and *The Hunchback of Notre Dame.*

Mickey Minutiae

The official scorers at **Disney World** keep track of some pretty odd stuff. Here's a sampling guaranteed to impress the lane lizards at your neighborhood bowling alley when you get back home:

- The four worlds and assorted trimmings of **Walt Disney World** cover 47 square miles, the size of San Francisco or two Manhattan islands. Of **Walt Disney World's** 30,500 acres, only one-quarter is developed; 25 percent of it is a preserve.

- **Disney–MGM Studios'** landmark water tower has its own custom set of mouse ears. They're hat size 342.

- Disney sells enough of those signature ear hats annually to cover the head of every human in Pittsburgh and enough T-shirts to put Mickey's mug on the chest of every man, woman, and child in Chicago.

- WDW gift shops sell 500,000 Mickey watches a year.

- Most folks think *Spaceship Earth,* that far-larger-than-life sphere at **Epcot,** looks like a giant golf ball. If Disney wanted to match it with a scale golfer, he or she would have to be nearly 2½ miles tall.

- Speaking of *Spaceship Earth,* that huge hunk of aluminum and plastic alloy tips the scales at 16 million pounds, more than the weight of three fully fueled space shuttles.

- **The All-Star Sports Resort** (see Chapter 8 for more details about this hotel) loves big icons. Its symbols include a mammoth tennis-ball can that's big enough to hold 9,474,609 real tennis balls and a Coke cup capable of holding 1.9 million gallons of the carbonated beverage.

- **WDW** guests gobble enough hamburgers and hot dogs to reach from Orlando to Philadelphia if you stretched them end to end. Guests also eat 5 million pounds of french fries and guzzle more than 46 million soft drinks a year.

- An average Disney housekeeper makes 11,680 beds a year.

- One hundred sixty of the **Disney characters** have costumes to greet park guests, but not all 'toons are created equal. Minnie owns 200 outfits, from evening gowns to cheerleading skirts. Mickey has 175 in his closet. The other characters usually have only one.

- You won't see many bugs on Disney's public properties, because grounds-keepers release millions of good bugs to beat up the bad bugs.

- Sunglasses are the hottest commodity at Disney lost and founds. About 100 pairs are turned in daily at the **Magic Kingdom** alone. The oddest recovery was a glass eye. (Yes, it was claimed.)

- Disney's parks have six million flowers, trees, and shrubs and three million annuals, which is enough to keep 650 gardeners, pest controllers, and irrigation specialists hopping.

Rock 'n' Roller Coaster

Now it's our turn to say, "WOW!" This inverted roller coaster is one of the best thrill rides that **WDW** has to offer and it's certainly not a ride for younger kids or folks with neck or back problems, faint hearts, or a tendency toward motion sickness.

Rock 'n' Roller Coaster is a fast-and-furious, indoor ride that puts you in a 24-passenger stretch limo, outfitted with 120 speakers that blare Aerosmith at 32,000 watts! A flashing light warns you to "prepare to merge as you've never merged before," and faster than you can scream "Stop the music!" (around 2.8 seconds, actually) you shoot from 0 to 60 mph and into the first gut-tightening inversion at 5Gs. The ride's beginning is a real launch (sometimes of lunch) followed by a wild ride through a make-believe California freeway system. One inversion cuts through an "O" in the Hollywood sign, but you won't feel that you're going to be thrown out, because the ride's too fast for that. The ride is so fast, the Disney hype says, that it's similar to sitting atop an F-14 Tomcat. (We've never been in an F-14, so we can't argue.) The ride lasts 3 minutes and 12 seconds, the running time of Aerosmith's hit, "Sweet Emotion," which is one of the tunes played in the limos. Like *Space Mountain,* all the ride action takes place indoors. *Riders must be at least 48 inches tall.*

Star Tours

Your journey to a place far, far away begins with a winding walk (a line) through a bunch of *Star Wars* 'droids and a pre-ride warning about high turbulence, sharp drops, and sudden turns. By now, though, you're a seasoned pro of such things and laugh in the face of danger. Once you get through the waiting zone, there's roughly a four-minute final wait at the loading dock while the group in front of you finishes the ride. *Star Tours* is a virtual ride where you go nowhere, but you feel like you do. The ride starts kind of slow, but it finishes fast as you soar through space in a good-guy fighter, with R2-D2 and C3PO helping you make passes through the canals of Lord Vader's mother ship. The special effects include hitting warp speed (you feel like you're going up with a very small G-force) and falling. All things considered, though, it's not quite up to modern rides here and at Orlando's other theme parks.

"I loved that!" It's certainly not as threatening or active as *Rock 'n' Roller Coaster,* but *Star Tours* still carries a *40-inch height minimum.*

The Twilight Zone Tower of Terror

If you like leaving your stomach at several levels, you'll love *The Twilight Zone Tower of Terror.* Its legend says that during a violent storm on Halloween night 1939, lightning struck the Hollywood Tower Hotel, causing an entire wing and an elevator full of people to disappear. And you're about to meet them as you star in a special episode of *The Twilight Zone.* En route to this formerly grand hotel, guests walk past overgrown landscaping and faded signs that once pointed the way to stables and tennis courts; the vines over the entrance trellis are dead, and the hotel is a crumbling ruin. Eerie corridors lead to a dimly lit library, where you can hear a storm raging outside. After various spooky adventures, the ride ends in a dramatic climax: a terrifying, 13-story free fall into *The Twilight Zone!* At 199-feet, it's the tallest **WDW** attraction and it's a cut above the rival *Dr. Doom's Fearfall* at Universal's **Islands of Adventure** (see Chapter 24). You *must be 40 inches or taller* to ride.

Taking Time Out for Fantastic Parades and Fireworks

In addition to its assortment of rides, **MGM** also offers a daily parade and an exceptional evening display of fireworks.

Fantasmic!

It's hard not to be in awe of the choreography, laser lights, and fireworks that are the core of this 25-minute extravaganza held once or twice a night, weather permitting. Shooting comets, great balls of fire, and animated fountains are among the special effects that really charge the audience. The cast includes 50 performers, a giant dragon, a king cobra, and one million gallons of water — most of it orchestrated by a sorcerer mouse that looks very familiar. You'll probably recognize other characters as well as scenes and musical scores from such Disney movie classics as *Fantasia, Snow White and the Seven Dwarfs, The Little Mermaid,* and *The Lion King.* You also see Jafar, Cruella de Vil, and Maleficent in a battle of good versus evil.

The ample amphitheater has 6,900 seats and standing room for another 3,000 souls. If you want to avoid a real traffic jam after the show, arrive up to 60 minutes early and sit on the right (the theater empties right to left). When there are two shows per night, especially during peak periods, it's usually easier to find a seat at the later show.

A dinner package available at The Hollywood Brown Derby, Mama Melrose's Italian Ristorante, and Hollywood & Vine Café (see Chapters 14 and 15 for more about the restaurants) allows you preferred seating at *Fantasmic!* There's no extra charge — just eat entrees at one of the restaurants before the show and you can wiggle into a reserved seating area right up until 10 minutes before show time, though it's not a specific seat. You can only make arrangements for the package at *Guest Services* in the park or at a **Disney** resort. We believe that unless you're planning to eat at one of the above anyway the idea lacks merit.

Mulan . . . The Parade

A short parade celebrating *Mulan,* Disney's 36th full-length animated feature, this 3 p.m. daily event is based on the story of a young, high-spirited girl who saves her father's life by disguising herself as a man and joining the Chinese army in his place. It's performed afternoons (weather permitting) along Hollywood Boulevard. This parade doesn't touch **Magic Kingdom** parades in size or scope, so unless you're a big *Mulan* fan, this is a good time to skip over to *Tower of Terror* or *Rock 'n' Roller Coaster,* where the lines are shorter because many guests flock to the parade.

Seeing It All in One Day

Here's a suggested itinerary for helping you make it through **Disney–MGM Studios** in one day:

- ✔ Consider making a Priority Seating reservation (at *Guest Services* or call ☎ **407-939-3463**) if you want to eat dinner in the park. The Hollywood Brown Derby is a decent sit-down option (see Chapter 14 for a list of Orlando's best restaurants).

- ✔ Head to the *Twilight Zone Tower of Terror.* It's a high-voltage ride that's not for the young or faint of heart. This ride is bad for folks with fears of tight or high places, but it's one of the park favorites. The other is the new *Rock 'n' Roller Coaster,* which blends incredible take-off speed with three inversions.

- ✔ **Disney–MGM Studios** is small, so backtracking isn't a concern. Consider passing up attractions that have long lines, or use FASTPASS. You may find long lines at *Twilight Zone Tower of Terror, Rock 'n' Roller Coaster*, and *Star Tours.* All are worth your time, as is the *Indiana Jones Epic Stunt Spectacular.*

- ✔ *Voyage of the Little Mermaid* is a must for the young (in years or yearnings); the same goes for *Jim Henson's Muppet*Vision 3D.*

- ✔ If you're looking for a little lunch action, the '50s Prime Time Café and Sci-Fi Dine-In Theater Restaurant offer fun shows along with staple-though-boring comfort foods or burgers and such.

- ✔ Relax at *The Magic of Disney Animation,* and *Sounds Dangerous Starring Drew Carey;* then go on the ton-of-fun *Backlot Tour.*

- ✔ Check your show schedule for favorites such as *Bear in the Big Blue House, Disney's Hunchback of Notre Dame, Beauty and the Beast,* and, at night, never, Never, NEVER miss *Fantasmic!*

- ✔ Also check the schedule (weather permitting) for the mid-afternoon *Mulan* parade.

Index of Attractions and Rides

G-Rated

Backstage Pass
Bear in the Big Blue House — Live on
   Stage!
Beauty and the Beast Live on Stage
Honey, I Shrunk the Kids Movie Set
Hunchback of Notre Dame: A Musical
   Adventure
Indiana Jones Epic Stunt Spectacular
Jim Henson's Muppet*Vision 3D
Sounds Dangerous Starring Drew Carey
Voyage of the Little Mermaid

PG-Rated

American Film Institute Showcase
Disney–MGM Studios Backlot Tour
The Great Movie Ride
The Magic of Disney Animation
Rock 'n' Roller Coaster
Star Tours
The Twilight Zone Tower of Terror

Chapter 20

Animal Kingdom

● ●

In This Chapter

▶ Acquainting yourself with Animal Kingdom

▶ Comparing Animal Kingdom to Busch Gardens

▶ Exploring the attractions in Animal Kingdom

▶ Setting an Animal Kingdom agenda

● ●

*A*s recently as 1997, what you know as **Animal Kingdom** was a
pasture dotted with cow patties and fire-ant mounds. Since then,
the patties and mounds have been replaced with a forest, rivers, ravines,
savannas, and a ton of non-indigenous animals. If your timing is right,
you can see such critters as African lions, Asian tigers, Komodo dragons,
giraffes, cheetahs, white rhinos, lowland gorillas, and hippos. You can
also bump into a few species that may be new to you, like bongos (the
antelopes, not the drums) and naked mole rats (these cuties are pink,
nearly hairless, buck-toothed, and they love building subterranean
toilets).

Much of this $800 million park opened in 1998; its most recent land,
Asia, was finished in 1999; and designers are still working on the next
one, *Beastly Kingdom,* which could open in 2003–2004. Disney CEO
Michael Eisner swears this is the next best thing to going to Africa, but
don't cancel that safari vacation yet. **Animal Kingdom** is a theme park —
even if the exotic wildlife can move out of your view. In this chapter, we
give you helpful information about **Animal Kingdom** and its marvels,
as well as basic info for visiting the park.

Getting to Know the Kingdom

Before we lead you through the jungle of attractions at **Animal
Kingdom,** we thought we'd shell out some nuts-and-bolts information about the park.

> ✔ You can find **ATMs** in **Animal Kingdom** near Garden Gates Gifts to
> the right of the park entrance. Cards from banks using the Cirrus,
> Honor, and Plus systems are accepted.

✔ **The Baby Care Center** is located near *Creature Comforts* in *Safari Village*. As in the other **Disney** parks, you can also find changing tables in women's rest rooms and some men's. You can also buy disposable diapers at *Guest Services*.

✔ **Disposable cameras and film** are available at the Kodak Kiosk in *Africa* and Garden Gate Gifts near the park entrances, as well as in Disney Outfitters in *Safari Village*. You can drop film off for same-day developing at the Kodak Kiosk and Disney Outfitters as well.

✔ **The First Aid Center,** which is staffed by registered nurses, is located near *Creature Comforts* in *Safari Village*.

✔ **Business hours** at **Animal Kingdom** are 8 a.m. to 6 p.m., but hours are often extended to 7 a.m. to 7 p.m.

✔ You can call ☎ **407-824-4321** or visit Disney's Web site, www. disneyworld.com, to obtain additional information about **WDW** properties.

✔ **Lockers** are located in Garden Gate Gifts to your right as you enter the park. You can also find them to the left, near Rainforest Café. Rent lockers for $5 a day including a $2 deposit.

✔ **A lost children center** is located near *Creature Comforts* in *Safari Village*. This is also the site of same-day lost and found. Making kids 7 and under wear name tags is a good idea.

✔ Shop clerks can **send your packages** (there's no charge for this service) to the front of the park at Garden Gate Gifts. Allow three hours for delivery. As in the other Disney parks, if you're staying at a Disney resort, you can have your packages shipped back to your room.

✔ **Pet care** facilities are located just outside the park entrance to the right. You can board your pet for $6 a day.

✔ You can make **Priority Seating arrangements** (see Chapter 13 for details on call-ahead dining) at *Guest Services* just inside the entrance. If you know where you want to eat in advance, call ☎ **407-939-3463**.

✔ **Rent strollers** at the Garden Gates Gifts shop to the right as you enter the park ($7 with a $1 refundable deposit). There are also satellite locations throughout the park. Ask a Disney employee to steer you in the right direction.

✔ **Tickets** cost $48 for adults, $38 for children 3 to 9. See Chapter 16 for other options.

✔ **Rent wheelchairs** at the Garden Gates Gifts shop that's on your right as you enter the park. Rentals cost $7, including a $1 deposit for a standard wheelchair, and $30 (plus a $10 deposit) for electric carts. Ask Disney employees for other locations throughout the park.

✔ **Consumables** aren't cheap. You'll pay $1.55 and up for a soda, $2.50 for bottled water, $2.00 for an ice cream bar, $2.50 for a pineapple float, and $1.15 for a cup of cocoa.

Animal Kingdom

The Boneyard **13**
Character Greeting Trails **4**
Dinosaur **15**
Festival of the Lion King **3**
Flame Tree Barbecue **11**
Flights of Wonder **10**
Harambe Village **6**
It's Tough to Be a Bug **5**
Tarzan Rocks! **12**
Kilimanjaro Safaris **7**
Pangani Forest
  Exploration Trail **8**
Pocahantas & her
  Forest Friends **2**
Rafiki's Planet Watch **9**
Rainforest Café **1**
Restaurantosaurus **14**

Pangani Forest Exploration Trail

Conservation Station

AFRICA

Wildlife Express

ASIA

**Maharajah
Jungle Trek**

**Kali River
Rapids**

Tree of Life

SAFARI VILLAGE

**DINOLAND,
U.S.A.**

THE
OASIS

**CAMP
MINNIE-
MICKEY**

Main Entrance

PARKING AREA   *PARKING AREA*

Understanding the Differences between Animal Kingdom and Busch Gardens

When Disney's fourth theme park opened, it raised two questions: Is it a front-line park worthy of the same sticker shock as Orlando's other major parks, and when does the area have too many?

Attendance figures may give a clue, if not a solid answer, to the latter. **Animal Kingdom** in 2000 was the only one of Florida's nine theme parks to have sagging attendance. The gate was down 3 percent (in fairness, two of the nine were in their first year of operation and Universal Studios Florida had no gain). Comparing **Animal Kingdom** to Florida's other big-time critter park, **Busch Gardens** in Tampa, may help answer the first question. Although we take a closer look at **Busch Gardens** in Chapter 26, we also take a few paragraphs in this chapter to compare the **Gardens** to the **Kingdom.**

Animal Kingdom is more a park for animals, a conservation venue as much as an attraction. The short of it is that it's not as easy to see its creatures; they're given a lot more cover than at **Busch Gardens,** so when they want to avoid your probing eyes and the heat, they can. The beautiful foliage used to create that cover also means that **Animal Kingdom** is a lot prettier than its Tampa rival.

The best time to catch the animals out and about at **Animal Kingdom** is in the early morning just after the park opens — usually 7 or 8 a.m. (depending on the season) — or try to see them at closing as the day begins to cool. Most animals are on the prowl at those times, not at midday (especially during the summer). **Busch's** animals are far easier to see regardless of the time of day.

Animal Kingdom wins the battle of shows with humdingers such as *Tarzan Rocks!* and *Festival of the Lion King.* However, although **Animal Kingdom** has three thrill rides (and we're being kind calling two of them thrilling), **Busch Gardens** pulls ahead with five roller coasters including *Gwazi,* a set of dueling wooden coasters.

Busch, for our money, is the better all-around park. Geographically speaking, however, you may not have or want a choice between the two parks. **Animal Kingdom** is located right in the center of the Orlando action, where you can find a ton of other things to do. Alas, **Busch Gardens** is at least a 90-minute drive from O-Town, and the Tampa Bay area simply doesn't have as much to see and do unless you're into cultural centers, museums, and beaches. If you're considering a trip to the Tampa Bay area, we recommend buying a copy of *Florida For Dummies* or *Frommer's Florida* (both published by Hungry Minds, Inc.), which have a wealth of information about attractions, accommodations, and restaurants on the state's Sun Coast.

Checking Out Animal Kingdom's Top Attractions

The overall conservation theme in this state-of-the-art park is simple but not subtle. Everywhere you turn, you find an environmental message, including the park's signs and the narratives of the tour guides on rides such as *Kilimanjaro Safaris.* Here, it is the animal's comfort that comes first; they are given plenty of cover, which makes it harder for you to see them. And even in high-profile areas, such as *Pangani Forest Exploration Trail* in Africa, **Disney** goes to great lengths to protect resident lowland gorillas, including a magnificent silverback, from prying minds.

Sometimes criticized for being too passive, **Animal Kingdom** is jumping into the coaster craze, albeit with a tame one for starters. *Primeval Whirl* won't have inversions when it opens in a new area of DinoLand U.S.A. in spring 2002. But it will have a lot of spinning action in family-style, rider-controlled cars that go through curves, short drops, and the jaws of a dinosaur. On a smaller scale, so will *Triceratop Spin,* a kids' ride along the same lines that's set to open about the time this book hits bookstores. There also will be a midway of arcade-style games — part of Disney's way of acknowledging **Animal Kingdom's** need for more kid appeal.

Additionally, the park is expected to dive deeper into the thrill-ride fray with a full-fright roller coaster in the Camp Minnie Mickey area, but in a new land called *Beastly Kingdom,* in 2004. Although details are pretty scarce, this is a land of mythical creatures, so the coaster should fit the theme.

The following sections provide you a closer look at the six lands of **Animal Kingdom.** All of the Kingdom's attractions can be found on the "Animal Kingdom" map, earlier in this chapter.

The Oasis

This is your introduction to **Animal Kingdom,** but a lot of folks, ready to get to the action, launch their way through *The Oasis,* overlooking the fact that this is one of the better places to see not-so-rare animals early in the day. The lush vegetation, streams, grottoes, and waterfalls on either side of the walkway are good places to see wallabies, miniature deer, anteaters, sloths, iguanas, tree kangaroos, otters, and macaws. But a misty fog and the landscaping also give them room to escape your eyes if they choose.

Safari Village

After you pass through *The Oasis,* you head straight into *Safari Village,* which, like WDW's **Magic Kingdom,** is set up on a hub-and-spoke format with the village as the hub and five lands scattered around **Animal Kingdom.** This is another animal-viewing area, though the thick cover will make it hard to spot many creatures. There are wood ducks, flamingos, kangaroos, and small-clawed otters walking around the *Tree of Life,* the Kingdom's 145-foot man-made tree (described in detail later in this chapter).

It's Tough to Be a Bug!

Take the walkway through the *Tree of Life's* 50-foot base, grab a pair of 3D glasses, and settle into a sometimes creepy-crawly seat. Based on the Disney-Pixar film, *A Bug's Life,* the special effects in this multimedia adventure are pretty impressive. Though it may not be a good choice for kids under 4 (it's dark and loud) or bug haters, this attraction is a fun and sometimes poignant look at life from a smaller perspective. After you put on your bug-eye glasses, all your senses are awakened by the stars, including ants, beetles, spiders, and — oh, no! — a stink bug. Although the video isn't quite on par with *Honey, I Shrunk the Audience* (see Chapter 18 on **Epcot** attractions), it has some magic moments.

We're sure that J.J. is going to work in pest control when he grows up. He hates bugs. He wanted no part of the show. He fretted a lot while we stood in line. He even threatened to go AWOL, until we explained that our beloved editor would fire us if he didn't bail us out. So he did, reluctantly, and eventually decided it was "well, pretty fun." Same for us. The show includes some spritzes of water, blasts of air, and a foul smell when the stink bug gets its revenge. The seat crawls under your butt when the on-screen insects run amok, causing screams and howls of laughter.

Tree of Life

Like *Cinderella's Castle* at the **Magic Kingdom** (see Chapter 17 for more details) and *Spaceship Earth* in **Epcot** (described in Chapter 18), the 14-story *Tree of Life* is **Animal Kingdom's** icon. The man-made tree and its carved animals are the work of Disney artists, teams of which worked for more than a year on its carved, free-form animal sculptures. It's not as tall or imposing as other icons, but it is impressive. It has 8,000 limbs, 103,000 leaves, and 325 mammals, reptiles, amphibians, insects, birds, dinosaurs, and Mickeys carved into its trunk, limbs, and roots. The *Tree* seems as if a different animal appears from every angle. One of the creators says he expects it to become one of the most photographed works of art in the world. (He's probably a Disney shareholder.)

Although passing up a detailed survey on your way into the park is hard, we recommended gawking only while standing in line for *It's Tough to Be a Bug!* You have time for a more detailed look at the tree — if you so desire — on the way out.

Camp Minnie–Mickey

Youngsters love this place. It's a favorite hangout for several Disney characters from the forest and jungle, including Simba from *Lion King* and Baloo from *The Jungle Book.* Mickey, Minnie, Goofy, Pluto, Donald, Daisy, and a variety of other stars also make appearances from time to time around this woody retreat, which resembles an Adirondack summer camp.

Character Greeting Trails

If you're traveling with children, this is a must do attraction. A variety of Disney characters, from Winnie the Pooh to Timon and Baloo, greet you. Mickey, in recognition of his star status, gets his own pavilion.

Festival of the Lion King

 Festival of the Lion King at the Lion King Theater is a rousing 28-minute show that's the best in **Animal Kingdom** and one of the top three in all of **Walt Disney World.** The six- to eight-times-per-day extravaganza celebrates nature's diversity with a talented, colorfully attired cast of singers, dancers, and life-size critters that lead the way to an inspiring sing-along. Based loosely on the animated movie, this stage show combines the pageantry of a parade with a tribal celebration. The action takes place both on stage and around the audience. Even though the pavilion has 1,000 seats, it's best to arrive at least 20 minutes early.

Pocahontas and Her Forest Friends

 The wait to see *Pocahontas and Her Forest Friends* can be nightmarish, and the 15-minute show isn't close to the caliber of *Festival of the Lion King* and *Tarzan Rocks!* In this show, Pocahontas, Grandmother Willow, and some forest creatures hammer home the importance of treating nature with respect. If you must go, go early. The theater has only 350 seats, though they do allow standing-room crowds.

Africa

Enter through the town of Harambe, which means "coming together" in Swahili, and it represents what happens in this recreation of an African coastal village poised on the edge of the 21st century. Costumed employees greet you as you enter the buildings. The whitewashed structures, built of coral stone and thatched with reed brought from Africa, surround a central marketplace rich with local wares and colors.

Kilimanjaro Safaris

This attraction is one of the few rides and the best animal-viewing venue in the kingdom. But remember: The animals are scarce during the middle of the day, especially in the heat of summer.

Also, the time that you spend waiting in line at this attraction can reach 45 minutes or more. Yes, using FASTPASS (see Chapter 16) is an option, but it virtually eliminates the chance of riding during the best viewing times. Our best advice: Skip FASTPASS, get to the park at the opening bell and go straight to this ride. If you aren't a morning person, your next best shot is to get a FASTPASS that lets you ride as close to the park's closing as you can get.

After you reach the end of the line, you board a very large truck (if you're familiar with an Army deuce-and-a-half you get the idea). You're then off on a bouncy ride through what pretends to be an African land-scape. (The animals aren't pretending.) Animals in the *Safari* include black rhinos, hippos, antelopes, Nile crocodiles, zebras, wildebeests, and a male lion that, if your timing is right, may offer a half-hearted roar toward some gazelles that are safely out of reach. Predictably, the theme is heavy on the conservation front. There's even a little drama — this is a theme park ride after all — as you and your mates help catch some dastardly poachers.

"I can't wait till we do that again!" But some adults can. You have a ton of fun and gain a lot of knowledge, but during the summer months you're in tight quarters in line and on the ride. And there's always someone who forgot deodorant and whose bouquet saturates the air. Remember to apply an extra swipe and dress for the Florida heat, especially at midday, even though much of the waiting area is covered and dotted with overhead fans to keep you cool.

Pangani Falls Exploration Trail

You can get a good look at hippos, mole rats, and African birds along the trail, but lowland gorillas are the main event. The trail has two areas: One is for a family of six including a 500-pound silverback and his ladies and children; the other has five bachelors. They're not always cooperative, especially in hot weather when they tend to spend most of the day in shady areas out of view. But visitors whose timing is good or who make return visits are truly rewarded with up-close views (through Plexiglas) of these magnificent creatures.

Rafiki's Planet Watch

This area of Africa includes *Conservation Station,* which offers a behind-the-scenes look at how Disney cares for animals inside the park. You walk past a series of nurseries and veterinarian stations. The problem is that these facilities need staff in order to be interesting and that's not always the case. *Affection Section* gives you a chance to cuddle some friendly animals (including goats and pot-belly pigs), while *Eco Heroes* has interactive videos that connect you to endangered animal information and world-famous biologists and conservationists.

Asia

Disney's Imagineers have outdone themselves in creating the mythical kingdom of *Anadapour.* The intricately painted artwork at the front is appealing and it also helps make the lines seem to move a little faster. Also, watch for (with little prior announcement) the appearance of local youngsters performing Asian dances.

Flights of Wonder

Flights of Wonder is a bird show that has changed several times since this land opened (and still hasn't found the right mix). The faces may be a little different, but if you've been to one Florida bird show you know the plot. The birds, predictably, are trained hams, as are the human actors.

Kali River Rapids

Whitewater fanatics will scoff, but for a theme-park raft ride, the *Kali River Rapids* ride is pretty good — slightly better, we think, than *Congo River Rapids* at **Busch Gardens** (see Chapter 28), but not as good as *Popeye & Bluto's Bilge-Rat Barges* in **Islands of Adventure** (see Chapter 24). This ride has churning water that mimics real rapids and optical illusions that make you wonder if you're about to go over the falls. The ride begins with a peaceful tour of lush foliage, but soon you're dipping and dripping as your tiny raft tosses and turns. You *will* get wet. The lines are long, but keep your head up and enjoy some of the marvelous art overhead as well as on the beautiful murals. This ride has a *38-inch height minimum.*

Maharajah Jungle Trek

Disney keeps its promise to provide up close views of animals with this exhibit. If you don't show up in the midday heat, you'll probably see Asian tigers through the thick glass. Nothing but air divides you from dozens of giant Old World fruit bats hanging in what appears to be a courtyard. Some of the bats have wingspans of six feet. (If you have a phobia, you can bypass this, but the bats are harmless.) Guides are on hand to answer questions, and you also get a brochure that lists the animals you may spot; it's available on your right as you enter the attraction. (An employee will likely ask if you'd like to recycle it as you exit.) You also have chances to see Komodo dragons, tapirs, playful gibbons, and acrobatic siamangs, whose calls have been likened to someone in the throes of pain or passion.

DinoLand U.S.A.

Located to the right of *Safari Village* as you enter, *DinoLand U.S.A.* is Disney's attempt to capitalize on the dinosaur craze inspired by *Jurassic Park* and (ugh) *Barney*. You enter under Olden Gate Bridge, a 40-foot-tall Brachiosaurus reassembled from excavated fossils. Speaking of which, until late summer 1999, *DinoLand* had three paleontologists working on the very real skeleton of *Sue,* a monstrously big Tyrannosaurus Rex unearthed in the Black Hills of South Dakota in 1990. The paleontologists patched and assembled the bones here, mainly because **Disney** helped pay for the project. Alas, *Sue* got a permanent home at the Field Museum in Chicago, but a cast replica of her 67-million-year-old bones, called *Dino-Sue* on handout guide maps, is on display.

The Boneyard

The Boneyard is a great place for parents to catch a second wind. Kids love the play area and there are plenty of things to wear them down a little. For example, they can slide and climb over a simulated paleontological site and they can squeeze through the fossils and skeletons of a triceratops and a brontosaurus.

 You have to be vigilant about keeping track of your kids. *The Boneyard* is a large area and, although it's monitored by Disney staff at both ends, kids play in a multilevel arena where tube slides can take them from one level to the next in a heartbeat.

Dinosaur

This ride used to be called *Countdown to Extinction,* but it got a new name to go with the Disney motion picture, *Dinosaur.* The ride hurls you through darkness in a CTX Rover time machine, past an array of snarling dinosaurs that are a little hokey. It's far from a smooth ride, and some kids may find the dinosaurs and darkness frightening. However, *Dinosaur* is as close as **Animal Kingdom** comes to a thrill ride — a herky-jerky, twisting-turning, bouncey-jouncey ride in which you and

20 other passengers try to save the last dinosaur worth saving. Evolution, nature's fragility, and potential catastrophe are the punch lines in this lip-biting, armrest-clenching ride against time and some very large lizards (such as a 33-foot carnotaurus, which is named for its favorite food — meat).

"I think I'm gonna puke." That was J.J's comment about halfway through the ride. However, at the end of the ride, J.J. said, "That's the one I like best (in **Animal Kingdom**). Can we do it again?" Riders *must be at least 40 inches tall* — that's 6 inches less than when it was *Countdown to Extinction. Dinosaur* also has a list of warnings aimed at folks with neck and back ailments.

Tarzan Rocks!

This 28-minute, five-times-per-day show pulses with music and occasional aerial theatrics. Phil Collins' movie soundtrack supports a cast of 27, including tumblers, dancers, and in-line skating daredevils who really get the audience into the act. (Go on, try your Tarzan yell — no one knows you here.) Costumes and music are pretty spectacular, second in **Animal Kingdom** only to *Festival of the Lion King* in *Camp Minnie–Mickey.* Our only criticisms: The story line is pretty thin, Tarzan doesn't appear for 14 minutes, and it's clear by his physique and acting ability that he's there for eye candy more than anything. The show is in the 1,500-seat Theater in the Wild.

Conquering the Kingdom in One Day

The good news is that **Animal Kingdom** is small enough to see in a day. The following itinerary is designed to be time efficient, but you can add or subtract rides and shows based on your tastes.

✔ Be here when the gates open, sometimes as early as 7 a.m., but generally around 8 a.m. (Call Disney information ☎ **407-824-4321** to check the time.) Arriving early gives you the best chance of actually seeing animals, because they're most active in the morning air (the next best time to see them is late in the day). If you want to eat breakfast at the Rainforest Café, make reservations at ☎ **407-939-3463.**

✔ The size of the park (500 acres) means a lot of travel after you pass through the gates. Don't linger in *The Oasis* area or around the *Tree of Life;* instead, head directly to the back of the park to be first in line for the *Kilimanjaro Safaris.* Doing so allows you to see more animals before it gets hot and the lines become monstrous. Work your way back through *Africa,* visiting *Pangani Forest Exploration Trail* and, if you have kids, take the train to *Rafiki's Planet Watch* and *Conservation Station.*

✔ Head to the *Tree of Life* in *Safari Village* next for *It's Tough to Be a Bug!* (Thrill seekers may prefer to start at *Dinosaur* in *DinoLand U.S.A.,* a good choice if you get there before the lines or if you use FASTPASS.) Younger kids deserve some time at *The Boneyard* in *DinoLand* as well as *Camp Minnie–Mickey,* on the other side of the park. Then see the park's two best shows, *Tarzan Rocks!* and *Festival of the Lion King.* If your time allows only one show, *Lion King* is the best choice.

✔ The Tusker House Restaurant in *Africa* is a fair lunch stop.

✔ Unless you must have a bird-show fix, skip *Flights of Wonder* in Asia, but don't miss the *Kali River Rapids* and *Maharajah Jungle Trek.* Late in the day, on your way out, look for smaller animals — iguanas, anteaters, and sloths to name a few — in the foliage at *The Oasis.*

Index of Attractions by Land

The Oasis
Port of Entry and Animal Habitats

Safari Village
It's Tough to Be a Bug!
Tree of Life

Camp Minnie–Mickey
Character Greeting Trails
Festival of the Lion King
Pocahontas and Her Forest Friends

Africa
Kilimanjaro Safaris
Pangani Forest Exploration Trail
Rafiki's Planet Watch

Asia
Flights of Wonder
Kali River Rapids
Maharajah Jungle Trek

DinoLand, U.S.A.
The Boneyard
Dinosaur
Tarzan Rocks!

Chapter 21

Enjoying the Rest of Walt Disney World

*I*n Chapters 17 through 20, you get acquainted with the major parks of **Walt Disney World.** But Walt Disney World also has several small parks and attractions. And while we introduce you to that second tier, we also tell you about a few holiday happenings and the **Disney Cruise Line.**

For a visual look at Disney's second-tier attractions and parks, skip ahead in this chapter to the "Other Disney Attractions" map.

Playing It Up at DisneyQuest

Meet the world's most interactive video arcade.

From kids just reaching video-game age to teens, reactions to **DisneyQuest** are pretty much the same: "Awesome!" And, although adults enter the five-level arcade thinking they're going to find kids' stuff, many bite the hook as hard as their offspring when they get a gander at the electronic wizardry — everything from old-fashioned pinball with a new-fangled twist to virtual rides.

Here are some of the entrées that you can find at **DisneyQuest:**

    ✔ *Aladdin's Magic Carpet Ride* puts you astride a motorcycle-like seat while you fly through the 3D Cave of Wonders.

✔ *Invasion: An Extraterrestrial Alien Encounter* takes you on an intense mission to save colonists from intergalactic bad guys. One player flies the module while up to three others fire an array of weapons. (We feel ethically obligated to tell you that we crashed and burned our Starship Tunstall five times.)

✔ *Pirates of the Caribbean: Battle for Buccaneer Gold* outfits you and up to three mates in 3D helmets so you can battle pirate ships virtual reality-style. One of you volunteers to be the captain, steering the ship, while the others assume positions behind cannons to blast the black hearts into oblivion — maybe. Each time you do, you're rewarded with some doubloons, but beware of sea monsters that can gobble you and your treasure. In the game's final moments, you come face to face with the ghost of Davey Jones. As happened to us in Invasion (see the previous bullet), we lost, and our good ship Miss Fortune sank like a stone. **Note:** This ride replaced *Hercules in the Underworld*.

✔ The *Mighty Ducks Pinball Slam* is an interactive, life-size game in which the players ride platforms and use body language to score points.

✔ If you have an inventive mind, stop in *The Create Zone,* where Bill Nye the Science-Turned-Roller-Coaster Guy helps you create the ultimate loop-and-dipster, which you then can ride in a real-feeling simulator. Bring your own motion-sickness medicine (but you can choose slow, medium, or quick death).

✔ If you need some quiet time, sign up at *Animation Academy* for a mini-course in Disney cartooning. The academy also has snack and food areas; a typical theme-park meal and drink runs about $12 per person.

✔ *Songmaker* is another new area. It has short lines, maybe because there's a $10 charge for the CD you create when you step into one of the tiny booths to create it, karaoke-style.

Crowds are heaviest after dark.

Off Buena Vista Dr., adjacent to Pleasure Island and Downtown Disney. ☎ *407-828-4600. Internet:* www.disneyworld.com. *Open: Daily 10:30 a.m. to midnight. Admission: $29 adults, $23 kids 3–9 for unlimited play.*

Fielding the Fun at Disney's Wide World of Sports

Disney's Wide World of Sports is a 200-acre, mega-complex that has a 7,500-seat baseball stadium, a separate four-field complex, two Little League fields, four softball fields, six basketball courts, 12 lighted tennis courts, a track-and-field complex, a golf driving range, and six sand volleyball courts.

Other Disney Attractions

If you're a true sports fan, write in advance for a package of information about the facilities and a calendar of events. Contact **Disney's Wide World of Sports,** P.O. Box 10,000, Lake Buena Vista, FL 32830-1000 (☎ **407-939-1500;** Internet: www.disneyworld.com.)

Here's a sample of the options at **Disney's Wide World of Sports:**

▸ The *Atlanta Braves* play 18 spring training games in the stadium during a one-month season that begins in March. Tickets for the stadium's two seating areas cost $8.50 and $15.50. For information, call ☎ **407-828-3267.** You can order tickets through Ticketmaster at ☎ **407-839-3900** or online at www.atlantabraves.com.

✔ The *NFL Experience* is open daily from 10 a.m. to 5 p.m. Admission is $9 for adults, $7 for kids ages 3 to 9. Ten drills test running, punting, passing, and receiving skills. You can dodge cardboard defenders and run a pass pattern while a machine shoots you a pass. (A much safer way than risking life and limbs against non-cardboard types.) Depending on your enthusiasm and stamina, the NFL Experience can last 45 minutes to three hours.

✔ The NFL, NBA, NCAA, PGA, and Harlem Globetrotters also host events, sometimes annually and sometimes more frequently, at the complex.

Victory Way, just north of U.S. 192 (west of I-4). ☎ 407-939-1500. Open: Daily, but hours vary by venue. Admission prices vary by venue.

Gearing Up at the Richard Petty Driving Experience

Compared to this ride, **Epcot**'s thriller *Test Track* is for sissies — the *Richard Petty Driving Experience* is your chance to race like a pro in a 600-horsepower NASCAR Winston-Cup racecar. How real is it?

You must sign a two-page waiver with words like DANGEROUS, CALCULATED RISK, and UPDATE YOUR WILL! before getting into a car. At one end of the spectrum, you can ride shotgun for a couple of laps at 145 mph. At the other end, you can spend three hours to two days learning how to drive the car yourself and racing other daredevils in 8 to 30 laps of excitement (for a cool $350 to $1,200). You must be 18 years old to ride in the car.

Walt Disney World Speedway on World Drive at Vista Blvd. just off U.S. 192, south of the Magic Kingdom. ☎ 800-237-3889. Admission varies by seasons and hours, so call ahead. Only adults are allowed in the racecars.

Preparing for the Masters at Disney Golf

The Magic Mickey offers 99 holes of golf: five 18-hole, par-72 courses and a 9-hole par-36 walking course. All **WDW** courses are open to the public and offer driving ranges, equipment rentals, pro shops, locker rooms, snack bars or restaurants, and PGA-staffed teaching and training programs. For tee times and information, call ☎ **407-824-2270** up to seven days in advance. (Disney resort guests can reserve up to 30 days in advance.) Golf packages are available and you can call ☎ 407-934-7639 to make reservations in advance.

Greens fees for Disney hotel guests are $100–$145 per 18-hole round (it's $5 more if you're not a resort guest). Here's a rundown of some of Disney's best courses.

- ✔ **Palm Course (18 holes).** By PGA standards, the Palm is Disney's toughest course. Set among natural Florida woodlands, the elevated greens, water, and sand traps offer more hazards than Interstate 4. Good luck with the 18th hole, it's rated the fourth toughest hole on the PGA Tour.

- ✔ **Magnolia Course (18 holes).** This longest course on Disney property is designed in classic PGA style. Wide fairways are deceiving; you've got to hunker down and whack the ball, but take care: There are 11 holes with water hazards, and 97 bunkers on the course. The sixth hole has a special hazard — a sand trap in the shape of Mickey.

- ✔ **Lake Buena Vista Course (18 holes).** This course has a classic country-club style, with lots of pines spread across a residential area. Well-bunkered, it's also a challenge that demands accuracy. This course is one of a few that have hosted a PGA, LPGA, and USGA event.

- ✔ **Eagle Pines Course (18 holes).** Expansive traps and sloping fairways follow the natural lay of the land. Rough pine straw and sand replace grass rough on this course, along with 16 holes featuring water hazards.

- ✔ **Osprey Ridge Course (18 holes).** This Fazio-designed course combines rolling fairways cut through forests of scrub oak, pine, palmetto, cypress, and bay trees. The Osprey course is ranked as one of the best public and resort places to play golf by *Golf Digest.*

- ✔ **Oak Trail Course (9 holes).** If you can't go a day without getting in a few holes, but don't have time for the 18-hole courses, this is the place to spank the ball. This 9-hole walking course is designed for families, or for a quick golf fix.

Disney occasionally offers discounted tee times after 3 p.m. during the summer high season. To find out if a discount is available during your visit, call ☎ 407-824-2270 up to seven days in advance or consult the golf section on Disney's Web site at www.disneyworld.com.

If you want more golfing options, or want to get out of Disney for a bit, two excellent sources of information and tee time reservations are *Golfpac* (☎ 800-327-0878 or 407-260-2288; Internet: www.golfpacinc.com) and *Florida Golfing* (☎ 866-833-2663; Internet: www.floridagolfing.com).

Puttering Around at Disney Miniature Golf

Those too timid to tee off at Disney's majors — or whose big games aren't yet up to par — can try their putters on the World's miniature golf courses. There are four whimsically themed courses, and everyone, from novices to master mini-golfers, should find at least one to their liking.

Fantasia Gardens

Fantasia Gardens Miniature Golf, located across the street from the **Walt Disney World Swan** hotel off Epcot Resorts Boulevard, offers two 18-hole miniature courses drawing inspiration from the Walt Disney classic cartoon of the same name. On the *Fantasia Gardens* course, hippos, ostriches, and gators appear, and the Sorcerer's Apprentice presides over the final hole. This is a good course for beginners and kids. Seasoned mini-golfers will probably prefer *Fantasia Fairways,* which is a scaled-down golf course complete with sand traps, water hazards, tricky putting greens, and holes ranging from 40 to 75 feet.

Buena Vista Dr., just east of World Drive. ☎ *407-560-8760. Internet:* www.disneyworld.com. *Open: Daily from 10 a.m. Admission: $9.25 adults, $7.50 kids 3–9.*

Winter Summerland

Santa Claus and his elves supply the theme at **Winter Summerland,** a miniature golf spread that opened in 1999 with two 18-hole courses. The *Winter* course takes you from an ice castle to a snowman to the North Pole. The *Summer* course is pure Florida, from sand castles to surfboards to a visit with Santa on the Winternet.

East off Buena Vista Dr., just north of Osceola Pkwy. ☎ *407-560-3000. Internet:* www.disneyworld.com. *Open: Daily from 10 a.m. Admission: $9.25 adults, $7.50 kids 3–9 per round of miniature golf.*

Making a Splash at Disney's Water Parks

Disney has a trio of water parks where you can chill out for all or part of a day.

Here are a few things to keep in mind before you head off for a swim:

- ✔ Go in the afternoons — about 2 p.m., even in summer — if you can stand the heat that long and want to avoid crowds. The early birds are usually gone by then and lines are short.

- ✔ Go early in the week when most week-long guests are filling the lines at the major parks.

- ✔ Kids can get lost just as easily at a water park, and the consequences can be worse. All **Disney** parks have lifeguards, usually wearing bright red suits; but, to be safe, ask how to identify an on-duty lifeguard and keep an eye on your little ones.

- ✔ If modesty is your policy, women should remember to bring a one-piece bathing suit for the more daring slides. All bathers should remember the wedgie factor on the more extreme rides, such as *Summit Plummet.* The wedgie factor is this: You may enter the park wearing baggies and find yourself in a thong.

Blizzard Beach

The newest of Disney's water parks, **Blizzard Beach** is a 66-acre ski resort in the midst of a tropical lagoon set beneath the 90-foot, uh-oh, *Mount Gushmore.* The base of *Mount Gushmore* has a sand beach with several other attractions, including a wave pool and a smaller, kids' version of the mountain.

Here are brief descriptions of other **Blizzard Beach** attractions:

- ✔ **Cross Country Creek** is a 2,900-foot tube ride around the park and through a cave where you get splashed with melting ice.

- ✔ **Runoff Rapids** allows you and your tube to careen down your choice of three twisting-and-turning runs, one of which plunges you into darkness.

- ✔ **Ski-Patrol Training Camp** is designed for preteens. It features a rope swing, an airborne water drop from a t-bar, slides such as the wet and slippery *Mogul Mania,* and a challenging ice-flow walk along slippery floating icebergs.

- ✔ **Slush Gusher** is a speed slide that shoots you along a snow-banked gully. It packs a *48-inch minimum height* requirement.

- ✔ **Meltaway Bay** is a one-acre, relatively calm wave pool.

- ✔ **Tike's Peak** is a mini-version of **Blizzard Beach** for mini-visitors. It offers short slides, a squirting ice pool, a fountain play area, and a snow castle.

- ✔ **Snow Stormers** has three flumes that descend from the top of *Mount Gushmore* along a switchback course through ski-type slalom gates.

✔ **Summit Plummet** is wild! Read *every* speed, motion, vertical-dip, wedgie, and hold-onto-your-breastplate warning in this guide. Then test your bravado in a bull ring, a space shuttle, or dozens of other death-defying hobbies as a warm-up. This puppy starts pretty slow, with a lift ride (even in Florida's 100-degree dog days) to the 120-foot summit. Kiss any kids or religious medal you may carry with you because, if you board, you *will be on the world's fastest body slide*. It's a test of your courage and swimsuit that goes virtually straight down and has you moving, *sans* vehicle, at 60 mph by the time you reach the *catch pool* (the stop zone). Even the hardiest of riders may find this slide hard to handle; a veteran thrill-seeker has described the experience as "15 seconds of paralyzing fear." *Minimum height requirement is 48 inches.*

✔ **Teamboat Springs** is the **World**'s longest white-water raft ride. Your six-passenger raft twists down a 1,200-foot series of rushing waterfalls.

✔ **Toboggan Racers** is an eight-lane slide that sends you racing, head first, over exhilarating dips into a "snowy" slope.

World Drive, north of the All-Star resorts and across from the Winter Summerland miniature golf courses. ☎ **407-560-3400.** *Internet:* www.disneyworld.com. *Open: Daily 10 a.m.–5 p.m., extended to 9 a.m.–8 p.m. during peak times such as summer. Admission: $29.95 adults, $24 kids 3–9.*

Typhoon Lagoon

Typhoon Lagoon is the ultimate in water theme parks. Its fantasy setting is a palm-fringed tropical island village of ramshackle, tin-roofed structures, strewn with cargo, surfboards, and other marine wreckage left by the great typhoon. A storm-stranded fishing boat (the Miss Tilly) dangles precariously atop the 95-foot *Mount Mayday,* the steep setting for several rides. Every 30 minutes, Tilly's stack blows and shoots a 50-foot geyser into the air.

Here are some other sweeteners of the park:

✔ **Castaway Creek** is a 2,100-foot lazy river that circles most of the park. Hop onto a raft or an inner tube and meander along through a misty rain forest, then past caves and secluded grottoes. *Water Works,* its theme area, is where jets of water spew from shipwrecked boats and a Rube Goldberg assemblage of broken bamboo pipes and buckets soak you. Tubes are included in the admission.

✔ **Ketchakiddie Creek** is a kiddie area designed exclusively for kids 2 to 5 years old. An innovative water playground, it has bubbling fountains in which kids can frolic, mini-waterslides, a pint-size white-water tubing run, spouting whales and squirting seals, rubbery crocodiles on which to climb, grottoes to explore, and waterfalls under which to loll. This area is also small enough for you to take good home videos or photographs.

✔ **Shark Reef** includes a very small snorkeling area with a simulated coral reef that's populated by about 4,000 parrot fish, angelfish, yellowtail damselfish, and other cuties, including small rays. Guests are given free equipment (and instruction) for a 15-minute swim. If you don't want to get in, you can observe the fish via portholes in a walk-through area.

✔ **Typhoon Lagoon** is the park's main swimming area. This large (2.75 million gallons) and lovely lagoon is the size of two football fields and is surrounded by a white sandy beach. The chlorinated water has a turquoise hue much like the waters of the Caribbean. Large waves hit the shore every 90 seconds. A foghorn sounds to warn you when a wave is coming. Young children can wade in the lagoon's more peaceful tidal pools — *Blustery Bay* and *Whitecap Cove.*

✔ **Humunga Kowabunga** consists of three 214-foot *Mount Mayday* slides that propel you down the mountain on a serpentine route through waterfalls and bat caves and past nautical wreckage at up to 30 mph before depositing you into a bubbling catch pool; each slide offers slightly different views and thrills. There's also seating for non-Kowabunga folks whose kids have commissioned them to "watch me." Women should wear a one-piece on the slides (except those who don't mind putting on a different sort of show for gawkers). This attraction has a *48-inch height minimum.*

✔ **White-Water Rides,** found in *Mount Mayday,* is the setting for three white-water rafting adventures — *Keelhaul Falls, Mayday Falls,* and *Gangplank Falls* — all of which offer steep drops coursing through caves and passing lush scenery. *Keelhaul Falls* has the most spiraling route, *Mayday Falls* has the steepest drops and fastest water, and the slightly tamer *Gangplank Falls* uses large tubes so that the whole family can pile on.

West of Downtown Disney and south of Lake Buena Vista Dr., between the Disney Village Marketplace and Disney–MGM Studios. ☎ *407-560-4141. Internet:* www. disneyworld.com. *Open: Daily 10 a.m.–5 p.m., extended to 9 a.m.–8 p.m. during peak periods. Admission: $29.95 adults, $24 kids 3–9.*

River Country

One of the many recreational facilities at the **Fort Wilderness Resort** campground, this mini-water park is themed after Tom Sawyer's swimming hole. **River Country** is usually less crowded than the other Disney water parks, making it attractive to those who prefer a less hectic place to swim. Kids can scramble over boulders that double as diving platforms for a 330,000-gallon swimming hole. Two 16-foot slides also provide access to the pool. Here are some other fun features:

- ✔ Attractions on the adjacent **Bay Lake,** which is equipped with ropes and ships' booms for climbing, include a pair of flumes — one 260 feet long, the other 100 feet — that corkscrew through *Whoop-N-Holler Hollow.*

- ✔ **White-Water Rapids** carries inner-tubers along a winding, 230-foot creek with a series of chutes and pools.

- ✔ **The Ol' Wading Pool** is a smaller version of the swimming hole designed for young children.

- ✔ There are pool and beach-side areas for sunning and picnicking, plus a 350-yard boardwalk trail through a cypress swamp. Beach towels ($1) and lockers ($5) are available. Light fare is available at Pop's Place. To get here without a car, take a launch from the dock near the entrance to the **Magic Kingdom** or a bus from its Transportation and Ticket Center.

East of Magic Kingdom, on Seven Seas Dr. east of Frontier Way. ☎ *407-824-2765. Internet:* www.disneyworld.com. *Open: Daily 10 a.m.–5 p.m., and sometimes 10 a.m.–7 p.m. (call the park for details) Admission: $15.95 adults, $12.50 kids 3–9.*

Enjoying the Holiday Season at Disney

Few commercial ventures put folks in the holiday spirit like Disney does. Lights, trees, caroling, and special activities begin around Thanksgiving and last until the end of the year.

Three of the best Yuletide attractions include the following:

- ✔ **Mickey's Very Merry Christmas Party**, an after-dark ticketed event (8 p.m. to 1 a.m.), takes place on weekends at the **Magic Kingdom** and offers a traditional Christmas parade and a breath-taking fireworks display. The additional charge ($36 adults, $26 kids 3 to 9) includes cookies, cocoa, and a souvenir photo. The best part? Shorter lines for the rides.

- ✔ **The Candlelight Procession** at **Epcot** features hundreds of candle-holding carolers, a celebrity narrator telling a Christmas story, a 450-voice choir, and a 50-piece orchestra. Also held on weekends, this is a very moving event that features several celebrities during the run of the event. Normal theme park admission ($48 adults, $38 kids 3 to 9) is charged.

- ✔ The **Osborne Family Christmas Lights** came to **Disney–MGM Studios** in 1995, when an Arkansas family ran into trouble with hometown authorities over their multimillion-light display. It seems they'd committed the ultimate Little Rock sin, taking to heart the old hymn that says, "You can't be a beacon if your light don't shine." Their Christmas-light collection of two-million-plus blinkers, twinklers, and strands was so bright that their neighbors complained. The flow of faithful spectators in cars caused mile-long backups. The neighbors, finally seeing the light, went to court. Disney came to the rescue and, in 1995, moved the whole thing to Orlando, adding a million or so bulbs to the display. You can see it all for the price of normal park admission ($48 adults, $38 kids 3 to 9).

Call ☎ 407-824-4321 for information; ☎ 407-934-7639 to ask about packages. Or, on the Internet, go to www.disneyworld.com.

Sailing the Seas with Disney

It took them a while to catch on, which is unusual for the Disney folks, but they finally discovered another place to expand their empire — the high seas. Despite delays, the **Disney Cruise Line** launched the *Disney Magic* and the *Disney Wonder* in 1998 and 1999, respectively.

The two ships have small differences. The *Magic* is Art Deco, with a giant Mickey in its three-level lobby and a *Beauty and the Beast* mural in its top restaurant, Lumiere's. The *Wonder* is art nouveau; Ariel commands its lobby, and its featured eatery, Triton's, sports a mural from *The Little Mermaid*.

The restaurants, nightlife, shows, and other onboard activities are very family oriented. One of the ships' unique features is a dine-around option that lets you move among main restaurants (each ship has four) from night to night while keeping the same servers. The line's three- and four-night voyages stop at Nassau and the WDW-owned **Castaway Cay** — a 1,000-acre playground for cruise guests. The *Magic* also has a seven-day itinerary that goes to St. Maarten, St. Thomas/St. John, and **Castaway Cay.**

Subtle differences aside, these two ships are nearly identical twins. Both are 83,000 tons with 12 decks, 875 cabins, and room for up to 2,400 guests. There are some adults-only areas but no casinos. Both ships have extensive kid and teen programs — broken into three age groups — that feature state-of-the-art computer equipment. There are also nurseries for 3-month- to 3-year-olds. Activities run from 9 a.m. to 1 a.m.

Three- to eight-year-olds can explore *The Oceaneer's Club.* It's designed to look like Captain Hook's ship, complete with cannons that have sound effects, crow's nests for lookouts, and ceilings painted with Disney-character constellations. There are also costume rooms for dress-up days, story times, and character appearances. When you first sign your kids up, you pick a password that only you know. Your kids also get an identification wristband. When you drop them off, they're logged in and you're the only one who can pick them up, via password. You're also given a pager that reaches the entire ship, Disney's out island, and parts of Nassau. That way, if the cast needs to reach you, they can just page you with a message.

Disney's *Oceaneer's Lab* is for 9- to 12-year-olds. It's themed with *Toy Story* characters and has a more high-tech atmosphere. There are planned activities and events throughout the day to ensure that your kids enjoy their vacation as much as you do. There are also projects with microscopes, lab experiments, and group explorations through-out the day.

Teen programs are centered on *Common Grounds,* a trendy coffee-house for their use only. It's not only a hangout, but a place for them to prepare for the comedy hour (the improv pros teach them funny-stuff basics), dances, and play games, including answering enough ques-tions correctly to win the ESPN Sports Challenge.

Beginning in May 2002, the *Disney Magic* will add a western Caribbean itinerary to its seven-day sailings. This one will go to Grand Cayman, Cozumel, and Castaway Cay. The ship will also continue its eastern Caribbean route (St. Thomas, St. Maarten, and Castaway Cay).

If you decide to book a Disney cruise, don't be shy. Always ask the magic question: Is that the best rate available? Disney reservationists seldom volunteer anything, but if you ask the right question you usually get the right answer.

Hwy. 528 at A1A, Cape Canaveral. ☎ *800-951-3532 or 800-939-2784. Internet:* www. disneycruise.com. *Seven-day land-sea packages include three or four days afloat with the rest of the week at a WDW resort. Prices range from $829–$4,299 for adults, $349–$749 for kids 3–17, and $99–$119 for kids under 3, depending on the resort you choose. Some packages include round-trip air, unlimited admission to Disney parks, Pleasure Island, the water parks, and Disney's Wide World of Sports. Cruise-only options for three nights are $439–$2,649 for adults, $229–$429 kids 3–17, and $99 for those under 3; four-night cruises are $539–$3,409 for adults, $329–$529 for kids 3–17, and $99 for kids under 3. Disney's seven-night cruises sell for $829–$4,299 for adults, $399–$799 for kids 3–17, and $99–$119 for kids under 3.*

Considering Another Cruise Option

Royal Caribbean offers week-long Orlando Experience packages that combine a Bahamas cruise on its *Sovereign of the Seas* with a two-day, two-park pass to **Universal Studios Florida** and **Islands of Adventure.** The package includes a three- or four-night cruise to Nassau and Coco Cay, with the remainder of the week spent at a Universal resort, such as the **Portofino Bay** hotel (see Chapter 8). You also get an additional day free at the theme parks, as well as a $20 meal voucher at the Hard Rock Café.

Rates for these cruise packages fluctuate wildly, depending on the season, the hotel you choose to stay in, and the number of days you sail. To get the best deal, we highly recommend calling **Royal Caribbean** and then talking to a travel agent to sort out your options.

Hwy. 528 at A1A, Cape Canaveral. ☎ 800-327-6700. Internet: www.rccl.com. *Seven-day, land-sea packages include three or four days aboard ship, the rest spent at a Universal Orlando resort. Prices for a three-night hotel/four-night cruise package start at $858 per person double. The price of a four-night hotel/three-night cruise package starts at $928 per person double. Children sharing a cabin with their parents pay $688 and up, depending on the cruise and hotel option selected.*

Chapter 22

Shopping at Walt Disney World

● ●

In This Chapter

▶ Shopping inside the parks

▶ Cruising the shopping districts

▶ Taking advantage of offbeat shopping options

● ●

*Y*our kids are begging for 14-carat mouse ears, your mother will have a cow if you don't buy her a pair of Donald Duck slippers, and you've always wanted a Winnie the Pooh cuckoo clock for the den. Then you see the price tags. *Gasp!* How can they get away with that?

You're an emotional and physical captive of a commercial enterprise sprinkled with feel-good pixie dust when you're at **Disney.** We don't know this for sure, but we think Disney's store managers use a simple formula for setting prices: Start with standard retail, then multiply by three.

But no matter how much we warn you, most of you probably won't escape without a contribution to the stockholders' fund, especially if it's your first trip to **Walt Disney World.** So before you start spending, here are a few things to think about:

✔ If there's a Disney Store near your city, much of what's sold in Disney's parks is available in their stores. Therefore, you don't need to rush into a purchase. (Notable exceptions are goods sold in the *World Showcase* pavilions at **Epcot.**)

✔ At the other end of the spectrum, many **WDW** shops sell products themed to their area of the park and it may be hard to find the identical item elsewhere. (But, you do get an eleventh-hour shot at the airport. See "Last Chance: Shopping for Disney Doodads at the Airport" at the end of this chapter.)

✔ Don't be fooled by someone offering you a "bargain." You usually can't find bargains or discounts in **WDW.** If someone offers you one (especially outside the parks), beware. The bargain or discount may be cheap, fake — or worse, a "hot" item.

✔ Theme park shops keep the same hours as the attractions: usually 9 a.m. to 7 p.m. and sometimes later.

✔ Don't forget to allow for 6-percent sales tax on purchases.

Loading Up Your Cart at Walt Disney World

In general, you will find three categories of merchandise in the Disney parks. Souvenirs that scream "Disney!" are the most common. (The number of choices will fog your brain.) Collectibles, including some not related to Disney, are another type. You find these in some of the *Main Street* shops in the **Magic Kingdom** as well as around the *World Showcase* in **Epcot.** The last category, merchandise from other countries, is a *World Showcase* specialty.

Don't lug around your loot. You can send your purchases from any store to designated areas near the entrance where you can pick them up as you leave the park. In the **Magic Kingdom,** you can pick up packages at *Guest Services* in the Plaza area. In **Epcot,** you can send your packages to *Guest Services* in the Entrance Plaza or the International Gateway in World Showcase for same-day pickup. **Disney–MGM Studios** shop clerks will send your goodies to *Guest Services* in front of the park. And, you can pick up your **Animal Kingdom** purchases at Garden Gate Gifts near the Entrance Plaza. (Allow at least three hours for delivery.) If you're a Disney resort guest, you can often have your packages delivered to your room for free — ask the shops about this service.

Magic Kingdom

The Emporium on *Main Street's* Town Square has a big selection of *Disneyana* (pricey collectibles, such as Minnie Mouse cookie jars). The *Main Street Gallery* inside *Cinderella's Castle* sells family crests, tapestries, suits of armor, and other medieval wares as well as miniature carousels.

House of Treasures in *Adventureland* peddles hats, Captain Hook T-shirts, ships in bottles, toy muskets, toy swords, and loads of other buccaneer stuff. It's outside the *Pirates of the Caribbean* ride.

The *Frontier Trading Post* in *Frontierland* hawks cowboy boots and hats, western shirts, coonskin caps, turquoise jewelry, belts, and toy rifles.

Liberty Square's *Yankee Trader* is a charming country store that sells Lion King and Pooh cookie jars, Disney cookie cutters, and fancy food items. *Ye Olde Christmas Shoppe* features holiday ideas.

Sir Mickey's in *Fantasyland* is supply central for a variety of Disney-motif trinkets. Wares at *Tinker Bell's Treasures* include Peter Pan merchandise, costumes (Tinker Bell, Snow White, Cinderella, Pocahontas, and others), and collector dolls.

Mickey's Toontown Hall of Fame in *Mickey's Toontown Fair* sells a large variety of cartoon-based souvenirs.

Mickey's Star Traders in *Tomorrowland* is another place to get a look at Disney collectibles.

Epcot

World Showcase pavilions carry items that represent their pavilion's country.

Heritage Manor Gifts in the *American Showcase,* for instance, sells autographed presidential photographs, needlepoint samplers, afghans and quilts, pottery, candles, Davy Crockett hats, books on American history, historically costumed dolls, classic political campaign buttons, and vintage newspapers with banner headlines such as "Nixon Resigns!" An artisan at the shop makes jewelry out of coins. You can also buy Disney art and character merchandise.

The *Canada* pavilion's *Northwest Mercantile* carries sandstone and soapstone carvings, fringed leather vests, duck decoys, moccasins, an array of stuffed animals, Native American dolls and spirit stones, rabbit-skin caps, knitted sweaters, and, of course, maple syrup.

China's Yong Feng Shangdian Shopping Department Store is a bustling marketplace filled with an array of merchandise including silk robes, lacquer and inlaid mother-of-pearl furniture, jade figures, cloisonné vases, tea sets, silk rugs and embroideries, dolls, fans, wind chimes, and clothing. Artisans demonstrate calligraphy here, too.

Emporia is a covered shopping arcade in *France.* Merchandise includes art, cookbooks, cookware, wines (there's a tasting counter), Madeline and Babar books and dolls, perfumes, and original letters of famous Frenchmen, such as Napoleon.

Germany's shops feature Hummel figurines, crystal, glassware, cookware, cuckoo clocks, cowbells, Alpine hats, German wines (there's a tasting counter) and foods, toys (German Disneyana, teddy bears, dolls, and puppets), and books. An artisan demonstrates molding and painting Hummel figures; another paints detailed scenes on eggs.

La Cucina Italiana and *Il Bel Cristallo* in *Italy* stock cameo and delicate filigree jewelry, Armani figurines, kitchenware, Italian wines and foods, Murano and other Venetian glass, alabaster figurines, and inlaid wooden music boxes.

The *Mitsukoshi Department Store* (Japan's answer to Macy's) stocks lacquerware, kimonos, kites, fans, dolls in traditional costumes, origami books, samurai swords, Japanese Disneyana, bonsai trees, Japanese foods, Netsuke carvings, pottery, and electronics. Artisans in the courtyard demonstrate the ancient arts of *anesaiku* (shaping brown rice candy into dragons, unicorns, and dolphins), *sumi-e* (calligraphy), and *origami* (paper folding).

Shops in and around the *Plaza de Los Amigos* (a moonlit Mexican *mercado* market with a tiered fountain and street lamps) display an array of leather goods, baskets, sombreros, piñatas, pottery, embroidered dresses and blouses, maracas, jewelry, serapes, paper flowers, colorful papier-mâché birds, and blown-glass objects (an artisan gives glass-blowing demonstrations).

Morocco's streets lead to the *souk,* a bustling marketplace where handcrafted pottery, brassware, hand-knotted Berber carpets, colorful Rabat carpets, ornate silver and camel-bone boxes, straw baskets, and prayer rugs are sold. You can also catch weaving demonstrations throughout the day.

Norway's shops sell hand-knitted wool hats and sweaters, toys (there's a Lego table where kids can play), wood carvings, Scandinavian foods, pewterware, and jewelry.

High Street and Tudor Lane shops in the *United Kingdom* display a broad sampling of British merchandise, including toy soldiers, Paddington bears, personalized coats of arms, Scottish clothing (cash-mere and Shetland sweaters, golf wear, tams, knits, and tartans), fine English china, Waterford crystal, and pub items such as tankards, dartboards, and so on. A tea shop occupies a replica of Anne Hatha-way's thatch-roofed 16th-century cottage in Stratford-upon-Avon. Other stores represent the Georgian, Victorian, Queen Anne, and Tudor periods.

Disney–MGM Studios

The *Animation Gallery* carries collectible cels, books about animation, arts-and-crafts kits for future animators, and collector figurines. *Sid Cahuenga's One-of-a-Kind* sells autographed photos of the stars, original movie posters, and star-touched jewelry and other items. Over at *The Darkroom/Cover Story,* you can have your photograph put on the cover of your favorite magazine, anything from *Forbes* to *Psychology Today* to *Golf Digest.* You can also buy costumes. *Celebrity 5 & 10,* modeled after a 1940s Woolworth's, has *Gone With the Wind* memorabilia, MGM Studio T-shirts, movie posters, and Elvis mugs.

Many of the park's major attractions also have merchandise outlets selling items such as *Indiana Jones* adventure clothing, *Little Mermaid* stuffed characters, *Star Wars* light sabers, and so on.

Few things are free at **WDW.** Their package delivery system, however, is an exception. Send your purchases to the front of the park, where you can collect them at the end of the day. (Allow three hours for delivery.) If you're staying at a Disney resort, you can have your packages delivered to your room, though sometimes things don't arrive until the next afternoon.

Animal Kingdom

The *Oasis's Outpost Shop* deals in T-shirts, sweatshirts, hats, and other souvenir items.

Beastly Bazaar in *Safari Village* has a wide selection of items related to the *Tree of Life* and the show, *It's Tough to Be a Bug! Creature Comforts* sells clothing, stuffed animals, and toys. *Wonders of the Wild* carries upscale, animal-theme apparel and home decorations. *Island Mercantile* offers theme merchandise that represents the park's lands.

Mombasa Marketplace/Ziwani Traders in *Africa* sells *Kilimanjaro Safaris* apparel and gifts as well as realistic animal items and authentic African gifts.

Chester & Hester's Dinosaur Treasures in *DinoLand U.S.A.* has wild and wacky dinosaur souvenirs, toys, and shirts.

Great things to buy at Epcot

Epcot's *World Showcase* shines in the shopping department. Although the suggestions here may not necessarily represent bargains — **Disney** never quits trying to lighten your wallet — they are the kind of unique and unusual items you may not find anywhere else.

✔ If you're into silver jewelry, don't miss the *Mexico* pavilion. You can find trinkets ranging from simple flowered hair clips to stone-and-silver bracelets.

✔ The shops in *Norway* have great sweaters, as well as Scandinavian trolls that are so ugly, you're likely to fall in love with them.

✔ In *China,* browse through jade teardrop earrings, Disney art, and more. Its merchandise is among the most expensive in **Epcot,** but also among the most fetching.

✔ *Italy's* 100-percent silk scarves and ties come in several patterns.

✔ Style-conscious teenagers may love a Taquia knit cap, something of a colorful fez-like chapeau, that's available in *Morocco.* You can also find celestial-patterned pottery.

✔ Wimbledon shirts, shorts, and skirts are among the hard-to-find items in the *United Kingdom,* which also has an assortment of tea accessories, sweaters, and Beatles memorabilia.

Disney Shopping outside the Theme Parks

Don't think the enticement to spend money magically disappears when you step outside the theme parks. **Walt Disney World** also encompasses some shopping districts that house a multitude of shops — many of which carry merchandise you can't get anywhere else — that offer you the chance to blow your budget.

Disney West Side

Disney West Side has many specialty stores where you can find unique gifts and souvenirs.

All Star Gear displays a wide array of apparel and accessories, including clothing in which Gretzky, Montana, and Shaq shed plenty of sweat. *Guitar Gallery* tempts string-strokers and wannabes with custom guitars and rare collectibles. *Hoypoloi Gallery* is a New Age store offering artsy glass, ceramics, sculptures, and other decorative doodads made from metal, stone, and wood. *Magnetron* is — well, wow! Can there be a market for this many refrigerator magnets? Smoking may be on the way to say-onara-ville, but *Sosa Family Cigars* beckons with sweet smells as well as a tradition reaching back to yesterday's Cuba. Over at *Starabilias,* the main events are jukeboxes, Coke machines, and other lost treasures of the last century. The *Virgin* (as in records) *Megastore* is a movie, music, and multimedia gold mine that also has a café and occasional live (rather than dead) performances.

Disney West Side (☎ **407-828-3800**; Internet: www.disneyworld.com) is on Buena Vista Dr. From I-4, exit on Hwy. 536 or Hwy. 535 and follow the signs. Some shop times vary, but the complex is open daily from 9:30 a.m. to 11:00 p.m.

Downtown Disney Marketplace

This *Size XXXL* shopping hub on Buena Vista Lagoon is a colorful place to browse, people-watch, have lunch, and maybe buy a trinket.

2R's Reading and Riting delivers shelves of bestsellers, bedtime favorites, Disney classics, and so on. *The Art of Disney* is a one-of-a-kind gallery that also includes sculpture, crystal, and more. *EUROSPAIN* comes calling with products that crystal and metal artists make before your eyes. *Harrington Bay Clothiers* has traditional men's clothing (but you can probably find Hilfiger, Nautica, and Polo a bit cheaper elsewhere).

The *Lego Imagination Center* is our shopping blue-light special — but not for its bargains. (Remember? There are no bargains in Disneyville.)

This is a great place for moms and dads to relax while your young whippersnappers unwind in a free Lego-building area beside the store. *Pooh Corner* duplicates the merchandise found at the **Magic Kingdom** ride. Speaking of Disney stuff, *World of Disney* comes with the (don't-hold-it-to-them) promise that if it exists and it's Disney, it's on their shelves.

Downtown Disney Marketplace (☎ **407-828-3800**; Internet: www.disneyworld.com) is on Buena Vista Dr. at Hotel Plaza Blvd. From I-4, exit on Hwy. 536 or Hwy. 535 and follow the signs. It's open daily from 9:30 a.m. to 11:00 p.m.

Sold! Bidding for Bargains at Disney Auctions

From pink Cadillacs to four-foot beer steins, *Walt Disney World's Property Control Department* regularly puts wacky treasures on the auction block. The president of the National Auctioneers Association calls these auctions the best-kept secret at **Disney.** In addition to cast-off goodies from the parks, hotels, and Mickey's other holdings, there are more common items, such as lawn mowers, flatware, and yesterday's props.

Items in Disney auctions fall into two categories: surplus and abused. Surplus means brand-spanking new (Disney bought too much when it launched its cruise line, for example), but how many people need flatware for 400 or a 750-gallon stainless cooking pot? As for the abused element, well, who needs a six-year-old van with enough miles to circle the planet six times? Auctions are held six or more times a year — always on a Thursday, when Disney employees get paid. Some of the more unusual items sold in the past include furniture from Miss Piggy's dressing room, a seven-foot Darth Vader replica, and a motorized surfboard. Call ☎ **407-824-6878** for the schedule, other details, and directions.

Disney also houses a store on premises that's normally open only to employees, but it welcomes the public on auction days. Discounts are said to reach 75 percent of park retail prices, but you know how inflated those prices are. However, the sticker prices easily beat anything you will find in the theme parks.

Dealing in Collectibles at Disneyana

Anything that's a true collectible or a signature Disney piece doesn't make it to Disney's public auctions (see "Sold! Bidding for Bargains at Disney Auctions," above). If such items don't wind up in one of the high-end shops within the theme parks, they're stashed away for *Disneyana* — a gathering of collectors and everyday folks who are obsessed with anything of value that bears a Disney character or logo.

Through the years, the Magic Mickey has earned something of a cult-like following, while his souvenirs have gone uptown. Fact is, collectibles are so popular there's an annual *Disneyana Convention* held each September. The convention draws more than 2,000 devotees, including one guy who wears 927 Walt Disney-related tattoos and a woman who has more than 500 Mickey Mouse watches and 10,000 buttons. There's even an auction where yesterday's ho-hum souvenirs sell for small fortunes. If you're a closet worshipper of all things Walt, call ☎ 407-824-4321 for more information on the *Disneyana Convention.*

Last Chance: Shopping for Disney Doodads at the Airport

Argh! You're already at the airport for the trip home and you forgot to buy a stuffed Goofy for Uncle Elmer. Well, you're in luck. **Walt Disney World** operates two stores at Orlando International Airport: *Flight of Fantastic* (☎ 407-825-6913) and *The Magic of Disney* (☎ 407-825-2301). They're located in Terminals A and B. These aren't like the Disney Stores in some of your hometowns. They only sell Walt Disney World trinkets — the kind you find in the theme park shops. (**Translation:** Forget discounts.) They also sell WDW multiday park tickets and can make your dinner-show reservations. These stores are open daily from 6 a.m. to 9 p.m.

Part VI
Exploring the Rest of Orlando

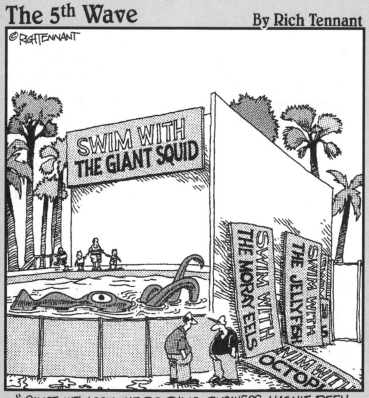

"SINCE WE LOST THE DOLPHINS, BUSINESS HASN'T BEEN QUITE THE SAME."

In this part . . .

Mickey is still the toughest mouse around, but he doesn't own Orlando anymore. Yes, this is still the town that Disney built. But the fact is, now that SeaWorld has opened its newest park, Discovery Cove, half of the eight big-league attractions in Orlando don't belong to Disney.

This part of the book explores the rest of Orlando, including the exciting attractions at Universal Orlando, as well as what you find at SeaWorld, the smaller attractions, and some of the best shopping venues outside the parks.

Chapter 23

Universal Studios Florida

• •

In This Chapter

▶ Discovering helpful Universal facts

▶ Seeing the best things at Universal Studios Florida

▶ Eating and souvenir shopping

▶ Following a suggested one-day itinerary

• •

*I*n Orlando, you soon get the picture, literally and figuratively, about which studio produces what films in the movie business. Both **Universal** and **Disney–MGM Studios** (see Chapter 19) spend plenty of money plugging their movies and characters. At **Universal,** that means you'll encounter *Twister, Hercules* (the live-action show, not the animated feature), *Terminator,* Barney, Yogi Bear, *Jaws, E.T.,* and many more. You'll also find plenty of grown-up, hurl-'em-and-twirl-'em rides such as *Back to the Future, Men in Black Alien Attack, Kongfrontation,* and *Earthquake.* But **Universal** is also a ton of fun for younger visitors, especially since *Woody Woodpecker's KidZone* came along with its pint-size rides, shows, and play areas.

As an added plus, **Universal** is a working television and movie studio where you might see a film being made. And there's always plenty of action at the Nickelodeon soundstages. That's where cable television's *The Swamp Thing, Clarissa Explains It All*, and the short-lived *SeaQuest DSV* were filmed. You can also see reel history displayed in the form of actual sets exhibited along Hollywood Boulevard and Rodeo Drive. Hanna-Barbera characters such as Yogi Bear, Scooby Doo, Fred Flint- stone, and more are on hand to greet you, as is a talented troupe of actors portraying Universal stars such as Harpo Marx and the Blues Brothers. And park shows such as *Terminator 2: 3D Battle Across Time* deliver heart-pumping excitement.

In this chapter, we give you helpful hints and basic knowledge about visiting **Universal Studios Florida** and experiencing its attractions.

Universal Studios Florida

PRODUCTION CENTRAL
Alfred Hitchcock: The Art of
  Making Movies **5**
The Bates Motel Gift Shop **6**
The Boneyard **7**
The Funtastic World of
  Hanna-Barbera **3**
Hanna-Barbera Store **4**
Nickelodeon Studios **2**

NEW YORK
Blues Brothers **11**
Kongfrontation **9**
Second Hand Rose **10**
Twister...Ride it Out **8**

THE FRONT LOT
Universal Studios Store **1**

HOLLYWOOD
The Gory, Gruesome
  & Grotesque Horror
  Make-Up Show **29**
Lucy, A Tribute **31**
Silver Screen Collectibles **32**
Terminator 2: 3-D Battle
  Across Time **30**

SAN FRANCISCO/AMITY

The Embarcadero

Amity Avenue

The Lagoon

CENTRAL PARK

Sunset Blvd.

Exposition Blvd.

WORLD EXPO

WOODY WOODPECKER'S KIDZONE

Film & TV Production Stage

$ Banking

G First Aid

Lockers

Restrooms

D Telephones

? Guest Services

Wheelchair & Stroller Rental

Exit to Vineland Rd. →

WORLD EXPO
Back to the Future: The Store **22**
Back to the Future...The Ride **19**
Men in Black Alien Attack **18**

WOODY WOODPECKER'S KID ZONE
Animal Actors Stage **23**
The Barney Store **21**
Curious George Goes to Town **28**

A Day in the Park with Barney **20**
E.T. Adventure **26**
E.T.'s Toy Closet **27**
Fievel's Playland **24**
Woody Woodpecker's
  Nuthouse Coaster **25**

SAN FRANCISCO/AMITY
Beetlejuice's Rock 'n Roll
  Graveyard Revue **12**

Earthquake—The Big One **13**
Jaws **16**
Lombard's Landing
  Restaurant **14**
Quint's Nautical Treasures **15**
The Wild, Wild, Wild West
  Stunt Show **17**

Finding out Important Park Information

In case you forgot to bring essential items or if you need special assistance while at the park, here's a list of services and facilities that may come in handy:

- **ATMs** accepting cards from banks using the Cirrus, Honor, and Plus systems are on the outside and just inside **Universal's** entrance and in San Francisco/Amity near Lombard's Landing restaurant.

- You can find **baby-changing tables** in all men's and women's rest rooms; **nursing facilities** are at *Family Services,* just inside the main entrance and to the right. (*Family Services* doesn't sell diapers, so make sure you bring enough of your own.)

- Disposable **cameras and film** are available at the On Location shop in the Front Lot, just inside the main entrance. One-hour photo developing is available, though we don't recommend paying park prices. You can find many cheaper one-hour places around town, including many near tourist-area motels.

- The park provides **car assistance** including battery jumps. If you need assistance with your car, raise the hood and tell any parking attendant your location. Use the call boxes located throughout the parking garage to call for security.

- **Universal Orlando** is located about half a mile north of I-4, Exit 30B, Kirkman Road or Hwy. 435. You may find construction in the area, so keep an eye out for the road signs directing you to **Universal Orlando.**

- Universal has its own version of Disney's FASTPASS, called **Universal Express**. Under the three-tiered system, guests of the **Portofino Bay** and **Hard Rock** hotels (see Chapter 8) only need to show their room keys to get at or near the front of the line for most rides. Multiday ticket buyers can go to any of 20 kiosks in the two parks and make reservations on up to three rides at a time, getting two windows in which to return for each. Waits usually are 15 minutes or less. Guests can make more reservations when those are used or expire. Single-day ticket holders can make one reservation at a time.

- You can find **first aid centers** between New York and San Francisco, next to Louie's Italian Restaurant, and just inside the main entrance next to *Guest Services.*

- **Park hours** are generally from 9 a.m. to 7 p.m., 365 days a year. Closing hours vary seasonally and depend on special activities within the park. For example, during Halloween Horror Nights, the park closes around 5 p.m., reopens at 7 p.m. (with a new admission fee), and remains open until at least midnight. The best bet is to call before you go so that you're not caught by surprise.

✔ **Information** is available at *Guest Services.* Before you arrive, call ☎ **800-711-0080,** 800-837-2273, or 407-363-8000 for information about new travel packages, as well as theme-park information. You can also write to *Guest Services* at **Universal Studios Florida,** 1000 Universal Studios Plaza, Orlando, FL 32819-7601, or visit its Web site, www.universalorlndo.com.

✔ **Rent lockers** for $5 a day including a $2 refundable deposit across from Guest Relations, near the main entrance.

✔ **Report lost children** to any staff member, then go to *Guest Services* near the main entrance or Security (behind Louie's Italian Restaurant, between *New York* and *San Francisco*). Make children under seven wear name tags in case they forget important information when they're upset.

✔ When **parking** in the multilevel garages, remember the theme and music in your area to help you find your car later. Or, do it the old-fashioned way: Write down your location. Parking costs $7 for cars and trucks. Valet parking is available for $12. Universal's garages are connected to its parks and have moving sidewalks, but reaching the gates is still a hoof.

✔ **Pet care** for your small animals is available at the shelter in the parking garages for $5 a day (no reptiles or overnight stays, please).

✔ **Rent strollers** in Amity and at *Guest Services,* just inside the entrance to the right. The cost is $7 for a single and $12 for a double.

✔ You can choose from several ticket options. A one-day ticket costs $48 (plus 6-percent sales tax) for adults, $38 for children 3 to 9. A two-day, two-park, unlimited-access pass is $89.95 for adults, $74.95 for kids; a three-day, two-park pass is $99.95 for adults, $79.95 for children 3 to 9. Multiday passes let you move between **Universal Studios Florida** and **Islands of Adventure** (see Chapter 24) during the course of a day. **Note:** Multiday passes also get you into the parks two hours before other guests and give you free access at night to the **CityWalk** clubs.

One other multiday, multipark option is the **FlexTicket.** This is the most economical way to see the various "other-than-Disney" parks. With the **FlexTicket**, you pay one price to visit any of the participating parks during a 14-day period. A four-park pass to **Universal Studios Florida, Islands of Adventure, Wet 'n Wild,** and **SeaWorld** is $160 for adults, $128 for kids 3 to 9. A five-park pass, which adds **Busch Gardens** in Tampa, is $197 for adults, $158 for kids. The **FlexTicket** can be ordered by calling ☎ **407-363-8000**, or online go to www.universalorlando.com.

✔ **Universal Studios Florida** and **Islands of Adventure** offer five-hour **VIP tours** for $120 per person, including the daily admission charge. These guided tours include line-cutting privileges and preferred seating at several attractions. For more information on the VIP tour, call ☎ **407-363-0045.**

 ✔ You can rent regular **wheelchairs** for $7 per day in Amity and at *Guest Services* just inside the main gate. Electric wheelchairs are $30 per day. Both require a $50 deposit.

 ✔ **Theme-park prices** often reflect the fact that you're a prisoner while inside. Expect to spend $5 for a rain poncho, $7 to $9 for sunscreen, $4.50 for a large beer, and $1.75 for a small bunch of grapes.

Exploring the Top Attractions

Universal matches **Disney** stride for stride, and in some cases is a half step ahead, when it comes to cutting-edge rides. Real, as well as virtual thrills, terrific special effects, mammoth screens, and 3D action are part of its successful mix.

The rides and shows at **Universal** are located in six zones: *Hollywood, New York, Production Central, San Francisco, Woody Woodpecker's KidZone,* and *World Expo.* The "Universal Studios Florida" map, found earlier in this chapter, can help you visualize the park's layout. You enter the park through the Front Lot. Once you're in line at an attraction, you're entertained by pre-shows that are better than the ones down the road at Disney.

Hollywood

Hollywood is to the right of the Front Lot, and its main streets include Rodeo Drive, Hollywood Boulevard, and Sunset Boulevard. Here's a list of the best that *Hollywood* has to offer:

 ✔ **Terminator 2: 3D Battle Across Time.** This attraction is billed as "the quintessential sight and sound experience for the 21st century!" and the park has little need to be modest about its claim. The director who made the movie, Jim Cameron, supervised this $60 million production. After a slow start, it builds to one of the best action shows in Orlando. Live actors and six giant Cyborgs interact with Arnie, who appears on screen (actually there are three huge screens). The crisp 3D effects are among the best in Orlando. (When liquid mercury falls from the screen, cold water really hits your legs.)

"That's my favorite!" The show could, however, be rated PG for violence and loud noises. Children under 6 may find the crashing and flying 3D effects too intense.

 ✔ **Gory, Gruesome & Grotesque Horror Make-up Show.** This show is a fantastic Hollywood presentation that gives you a behind-the-scenes look at how monster makeup is done, including the transformation scenes from such movies as *The Fly* and *The Exorcist.*

✔ **I Love Lucy, A Tribute.** This show is a remembrance of America's queen of comedy.

New York

New York is near the back of the park and includes rides and shows along 42nd and 57th streets, Park Avenue, and Delancy Street. The premiere attractions in this section are:

✔ **Kongfrontation.** King Kong has returned to the Big Apple. As you stand in line in a replica of a grungy, graffiti-scarred New York subway station, CBS newsman Roland Smith reports on Kong's terrifying rampage. Everyone must evacuate to Roosevelt Island, so it's all aboard the tram. Then, well, uh-oh. Cars collide and hydrants explode below, the tram malfunctions, and, of course, you encounter Mr. Banana Breath — all 40 feet and 12,000 pounds of him. He terrifies you and fellow passengers by dangling the tram over the East River. The big ape has 46 movements, including simulated noogies on top of the tram. Long-time New Yorkers will recognize the backdrop — it's Manhattan in 1976, the year Dino DiLaurentis made the second Kong movie, which starred Jessica Lange and Jeff Bridges.

"That ape was pretty stupid." It *was* a tad hokey, but the ride has a *40-inch height minimum,* and the big gorilla and the dark waiting area may frighten children under six.

✔ **Twister . . . Ride it Out.** The curtain rises in the movie town of Wakita, where Universal engineers have created a five-story funnel cloud by injecting two million cubic feet of air per minute (that's enough to fill four full-size blimps). The sensory elements are pretty incredible. Power lines spark and fall, an oak splits, and the storm rumbles at rock-concert level as cars, trucks, and a cow fly about while the audience watches from just 20 feet away. In the finale, the floor begins to buckle at your feet. Crowds have been known to applaud when it's all over.

"That was pretty scary, but I liked it." This attraction doesn't have a minimum height, but it carries Universal's *PG-13 rating,* meaning it may be a little too intense for younger children.

Production Central

Production Central is directly behind and to the left of the Front Lot. Its main thoroughfares are Nickelodeon Way, Plaza of the Stars, and 7th and 8th Avenues. Here are some of the area's highlights:

✔ **The Funtastic World of Hanna-Barbera.** Yogi Bear is the pilot of this motion-simulator/spaceship that travels through the galaxy in an effort to rescue Elroy Jetson from the evil Dick Dastardly. The ride includes lots of rock 'n' roll — dips, dives, and blasts of air when things explode. You hurtle through Bedrock, Scooby's Haunted Castle, and finally Jetsonville before — drat it! — Dick gets foiled again.

"That's awesome!" Although this is supposed to be a kiddie ride, riders *must be at least 40 inches tall*. Prior to the ride, you learn how cartoons are created in a pre-show area. After it's over, you can experiment in an interactive area with animation sound effects — boing! plop! splash! — and color your own cartoons. This is a great place for kids of all ages to take some time and play.

✔ **Nickelodeon Studios Tour.** Tour the soundstages where Nick shows such as *Kenan & Kel* and the *Mystery Files of Shelby Woo* are produced, view concept pilots, visit the kitchen where Gak and green slime are made, play game shows such as *Double Dare 2000,* and try new Sega video games. This 45-minute behind-the-scenes tour is a fun escape from the hustle of the midway, and there's a lot of audience participation. One child volunteer always gets slimed.

The studio doesn't open until 10:30 a.m.

"I didn't know slime tasted like applesauce." Fact is, it does. During the tour, guides explain that slime is made from leftover dessert. So if your slimed kid swallows some, green applesauce is probably as bad as the damage gets.

✔ **Other Production Central Shows.** *The Boneyard* displays props from some of the movies. *Alfred Hitchcock: The Art of Making Movies* is a tribute to the master of suspense, in which Tony Perkins narrates a reenactment of the famous shower scene from *Psycho*, and where *The Birds* — as if the movie weren't scary enough — becomes an in-your-face 3D movie. There's also an audience-participation segment in which some volunteers relive frightening scenes. Shows begin at noon.

San Francisco

This L-shaped zone faces the waterfront, and its attractions line The Embarcadero and Amity Avenue.

✔ **Beetlejuice's Rock 'n Roll Graveyard Revue.** Horrible creatures such as Dracula, Wolfman, the Phantom of the Opera, Franken-stein and his bride, and Beetlejuice show up to scare you silly. Their funky rock musical has pyrotechnic special effects and MTV-style choreography. It's loud and lively enough to scare some small children and aggravate many older adults. Young teens seem to like it the most.

✔ **Earthquake — The Big One.** Sparks fly shortly after you board a train. The whopper — 8.3 on the Richter scale! — hits as you pull into the Embarcadero Station, and you're left trapped as vast slabs of concrete collapse around you, a propane truck bursts into flames, a runaway train comes hurtling at you, and the station floods (65,000 gallons of water cascade down the steps). This is *Kongfrontation* (see "New York," earlier in the chapter) minus an ape. Prior to the ride you learn how *Earthquake,* the movie, was made, including a look at a $2.4 million set model. You then shuffle off to a soundstage where seven adult volunteers help re-create the big one.

"I liked that a lot." Children must be *at least 40 inches* tall. Loud noises, flames, and other special effects may frighten kids younger than six.

✔ **Jaws.** As your boat heads into a seven-acre, five million-gallon lagoon, an ominous dorsal fin appears on the horizon. What follows is a series of attacks from a three-ton, 32-foot-long, mechanical great white shark that tries to sink its urethane teeth into your hide — or at least into your boat's hide. A 30-foot wall of flame caused by burning fuel surrounds the boat, and you'll truly feel the heat in this $45-million attraction. We won't tell you how it ends, but let's just say that in spite of a captain who can't hit the broad side of a dock with his grenade launcher, some restaurant will be serving blackened shark later in the evening. (**Note:** The effects of this ride are more startling after dark.)

Well, it took J.J. a while to spit out his review for this attraction. This ride gave him a stiff neck (from tension) the first time he rode it. He was a little looser the second time around, but he kept hollering: "Gimme the gun! I'll shoot the shark."

✔ **The Wild, Wild, Wild West Stunt Show.** Stunt people demonstrate falls from three-story balconies, gun and whip fights, dynamite explosions, and other Wild West staples. This is a well-performed, lively show that's especially popular with foreign visitors who have celluloid visions of the American West.

Heed the splash zone or you will get very wet.

Woody Woodpecker's KidZone

This section of the park contains rides and attractions sure to please the littlest members of your party. If you're traveling with a number of youngsters, plan on spending a lot of time here. Some of the highlights include:

✔ **A Day in the Park with Barney.** This is **Universal**'s diabolical answer to **Disney**'s *It's a Small World,* one of those attractions that eats the brains and ignites the nerves of anyone but 2- to 6-year-olds and their loving parents. Set in a park-like theater-in-the-round, this 25-minute musical stars the Purple One, Baby Bop, and BJ. It uses song, dance, and interactive play to deliver an environmental message. This show can be the highlight of your youngster's day. The playground next door has chimes to ring, tree houses to explore, and lots of other things to intrigue little visitors.

✔ **E.T. Adventure.** You soar with E.T., who is on a mission to save his ailing planet, through the forest and into space aboard a star-bound bicycle. You also meet some new characters Steven Spielberg created for the ride, including Botanicus, Tickli Moot Moot, Horn Flowers, and Tympani Tremblies. A cool, wooded forest serves to create one of the most pleasant waits for any ride in central Florida, although you will have to endure two lines until you actually make it onto the ride.

✔ **Woody Woodpecker's Nuthouse Coaster.** This is the top attraction in the *KidZone,* an eight-acre concession **Universal Studios** made after being criticized for having too little for young visitors. Sure, it's a kiddie coaster, but the *Nuthouse Coaster* will thrill some moms and dads, too. Although it's only 30 feet at its peak, this ride offers quick, banked turns while you sit in a miniature steam train. It's very much like *The Barnstormer at Goofy's Wiseacres Farm* in the **Magic Kingdom** (see Chapter 17).

The ride lasts only 60 seconds, and you can wait as long as 40 minutes, but your children probably won't let you skip it.

". . . more, More, MORE!" We didn't think J.J. would ever run out of gas. Six trips on this ride and we had to drag him away. It has a *36-inch minimum height* and kids have to be 48 inches or above to ride without an adult.

✔ **More to Do in Woody Woodpecker's KidZone.** *Fievel's Playland* is a wet, western-themed playground with a house to climb and a small water slide. *Curious George Goes to Town* has water- and ball-shooting cannons, plus a huge water tower that empties (after an alarm), drenching anyone who doesn't run for cover. Nearby, *Animal Actors Stage* offers a 20-minute show featuring critters such as Mr. Ed, Beethoven, and Lassie.

World Expo

The smallest zone in **Universal Studios Florida** offers a lot of punch in its two rides. *World Expo* is on Exposition Boulevard, between San Francisco and KidZone. The top attractions here are:

✔ **Back to the Future . . . the Ride.** This ride has more warnings than a centipede has legs. Topping the list: If you have a problem with motion sickness, don't get on. If you don't have a problem with motion sickness, but have a problem with other people getting motion sick on you, you may want to invest $5 in one of those ponchos. (No sense ruining your new Mickey shirt, right?) There are also warnings for would-be riders who are pregnant or become dizzy, as well as those who are claustrophobic or have neck, heart, or back problems. These warnings are all justified.

Back to the Future offers you a chance at time travel in a simulator made to look like a DeLorean. Six to eight of you are packed into a car after a video briefing from Christopher Lloyd, also known as

Dr. Emmett Brown. Biff the Bully has stolen another DeLorean and you have to catch him. The fate of the universe is in your hands. The huge screen makes this ride very intense, but if you didn't heed the warnings and begin to feel some of the symptoms, just stick your neck out of your car — literally. You can see the other cars, lending the very true perspective that you're really only in a theater.

"WOW! Can we ride it again?" Maybe later. We forgot our ponchos. By the way, kids *must be 40 inches or more* to ride.

✔ **Men in Black Alien Attack.** You and your mates have to blast the bug-eyes or the end of New York and the rest of the world may be coming. You ride six-passenger cruisers, using your "zapper" to splatter up to 120 bug-eyed targets. You have to contend with return fire and distractions (noise, clouds of liquid nitrogen, and such), any of which can send you spinning out of control. Your laser tag-style gun fires infrared bullets. Earn a bonus by hitting Frank the Pug (to the right just past the alien shipwreck). The four-minute ride relies on 360-degree spins rather than speed for its thrill factor. Near the end, you're swallowed by a giant roach (it's 30 feet tall with 8-foot fangs and 20-foot claws) that explodes — dousing you with bug guts, also known as warm water — as you blast your way out. After you do, Will Smith rates you anywhere from a galaxy defender to bug bait. (There are 38 possible scores.)

Men in Black often has a *much* shorter line for single riders. If you're not alone but are willing to be split up, get on this line and hop right on a vehicle that has less than six passengers.

"That was double awesome! But those roach guts, yuck!" This ride-through video game has a *42-inch height minimum.*

Grabbing a Bite to Eat

There are more than a dozen places to eat at **Universal Studios Florida.** The main food attractions range from lobster to corn dogs. Quality-wise, things inside the park are on the same level as those found in the **Disney** parks (see Chapters 17 through 20). Here are our favorites by category:

✔ **Best sit-down meal.** Lombard's Landing, across from *Earthquake,* has a hearty fried clam basket, as well as lobster, steak, pasta, and burgers ($11–$30).

✔ **Best counter service.** Universal Studios' Classic Monsters Café is one of the newest eateries in the park and serves salads, pizza, pasta, and rotisserie chicken ($6–$11). You can find it off 7th Avenue near *The Boneyard.*

✔ **Best place for hungry families.** Similar to a mall food court, the International Food Bazaar offers a variety of ethnic food in one location. With options ranging from stir-fry to fajitas, this is a place where a family can split up and still eat under one roof. There are kids' meals for under $4 at most locations. The food is far from gourmet but a cut above regular fast food ($6–$11). It's located near the back of *Animal Actor's Studio* near the lagoon and the entrance to *Back to the Future*.

✔ **Best Snack.** The floats ($3–$5) at Brody's Ice Cream Shop are great refreshers on a summer afternoon. Brody's is located near the *Wild, Wild, Wild West Stunt Show* arena.

See Chapter 14, "Orlando's Restaurants from A to Z," for the best places to grab a bite at **Universal's CityWalk.**

Shopping at Universal Studios Florida

If **Disney** can do it, **Universal** can, too. Every major attraction at **Universal** has a theme store attached. Although the prices are high when you consider you're just buying a T-shirt, the Hard Rock Cafe in adjacent **CityWalk** is extremely popular and has a small but diverse selection of Hard Rock everything.

More than 25 other shops in the park sell souvenirs ranging from *I Love Lucy* collectibles to Bates Motel shower curtains. Be warned, however, that, unlike **WDW,** these shops are even more specific to individual attractions — if you see something you like, buy it. You probably won't see it in another store. Here's a sampling of the more unusual gifts available at some of the Universal stores:

✔ **Back to the Future — The Store.** Real fans of the movie series find lots of intriguing stuff here. One of the more interesting is a miniature version of the *Back to the Future* DeLorean.

✔ **The Bates Motel Gift Shop.** When house guests have stayed just a bit too long, you can send a not-so-subtle message by putting out these Bates Motel guest towels (next to your own butcher knife).

✔ **E.T.'s Toy Closet and Photo Spot.** This is the place for plush, stuffed animals including a replica of the alien namesake.

✔ **Hanna-Barbera Store.** Scooby Doo Slippers and Fred Flintstone T-shirts are great gifts for the young and young at heart.

✔ **Kongfrontation Store.** A video copy of the original movie that started it all is available, as well as several sizes of cuddly stuffed gorillas.

✔ **Quint's Nautical Treasures.** This is the place to go for a different kind of T-shirt. Tropical colors, with subtle Universal logos, are the hot items here.

✔ **Silver Screen Collectibles.** Fans of *I Love Lucy* will adore the small variety of collectible dolls. There's also a Betty Boop line. For an interesting, practical, and inexpensive little something to take home, check out the Woody Woodpecker back scratcher.

✔ **Universal Studios Store.** This store, near the entrance, sells just about everything when it comes to Universal apparel.

Using Our Suggested Itinerary

Spending one day at **Universal Studios** is sufficient if you arrive early and keep up a steady pace. The following one-day guide will help keep you on track to see the best of **Universal:**

✔ Skip the city sidewalks of the main gate and save *Terminator 2: 3D Battle Across Time* until later. Veer to the left and if the lines are relatively short, see *The Funtastic World of Hanna-Barbera.*

✔ If you're a late arrival, take the 45-minute *Nickelodeon Studios Tour* (4- to 14-year-olds will love it); otherwise, save it for the end of the day.

✔ Continue clockwise around the park, visiting *Twister, Kongfrontation, Jaws,* and *Earthquake.*

✔ Take a break for lunch, watch *The Wild, Wild, Wild West Stunt Show.* By now, the lines probably have thinned a bit at *Back to the Future, Men in Black,* and *E.T. Adventure.*

✔ If you haven't already, let your kids burn off some energy in *Woody Woodpecker's KidZone,* go to *Terminator 2,* and, if you didn't catch it earlier, the *Nickelodeon Studios Tour.*

✔ You may have time to revisit another attraction or beat the crowd to the parking lot.

A second day lets you revisit some of your favorite rides and shows or experience the ones you missed. With the pressure to hit all the major rides lessened, you can delay your *Nickelodeon Studios Tour* until day two (the first tour usually isn't until 10:30 a.m.), but in our opinion it's a must-visit if you have kids who watch this network. Visitors sometimes have a chance to participate in the taping of some of Nick's often-sloppy game shows. You can also visit the *Gory, Gruesome & Grotesque Horror Make-up Show* and *Beetlejuice's Rock 'n' Roll Graveyard Revue.*

Index of Top Attractions by Area

Hollywood
Terminator 2: 3D Battle Across Time
Gory, Gruesome, and Grotesque Horror
    Make-up Show
I Love Lucy: A Tribute

New York
Kongfrontation
Twister . . . Ride It Out

Production Central

The Funtastic World of Hanna-Barbera
Nickelodeon Studios

San Francisco

Beetlejuice's Rock 'n' Roll Graveyard
   Revue
Earthquake — The Big One
Jaws
The Wild, Wild, Wild West Stunt Show

Woody Woodpecker's KidZone

A Day in the Park with Barney
E.T. Adventure
Woody Woodpecker's Nuthouse Coaster

World Expo

Back to the Future the Ride
Men in Black Alien Attack

Chapter 24

Islands of Adventure

● ●

In This Chapter

▶ Knowing the details

▶ Hopping the Islands

▶ Finding take-home souvenirs

▶ Traveling around the Universe in a day

● ●

*U*niversal's second theme park opened in '99 with a vibrantly colored, cleverly themed collection of fast, fun rides wrapped into a 110-acre package. Roller coasters thunder above its pedestrian walkways, water rides careen through the center of the park, and theme restaurants are camouflaged to match their surroundings, adding to your overall immersion in the various "islands" in this adventure.

From the wobbly angles and day-glo colors of *Seuss Island* to the lush foliage of *Jurassic Park,* **Universal** has also done a good job of differentiating the various sections of **Islands of Adventure,** making it easier to navigate. (Unlike **Universal Studios Florida,** where it's sometimes hard to tell if you're in *San Francisco* or *New York.*)

This $1-billion park is divided into six areas: the *Port of Entry,* where you'll find a collection of shops and eateries, and the themed sections: *Seuss Landing, Toon Lagoon, Jurassic Park, Marvel Super Hero Island,* and *The Lost Continent.* **Islands of Adventure** has a large menu of thrill rides and coasters, plus a growing stable of play areas for younger guests. The trade-off is that there are few shows and stage productions.

Knowing Essential Park Information

Before you start on your journey through the park's rides and attractions, here are some mundane matters that you may need to know.

Islands of Adventure

PORT OF ENTRY
Island Skipper Tours **1**
Confisco Grille **2**
MARVEL SUPER HERO ISLAND
Incredible Hulk Coaster **3**
Cafe 4 **4**
Storm Force Acceletron **5**
Doctor Doom's Fearfall **6**
The Amazing Adventures of Spider-Man **7**
TOON LAGOON
Comic Strip Café **8**
Toon Trolley Character Meet and Greet **9**
Comic Strip Lane **10**
Popeye & Bluto's Bilge-Rat Barges **12**
Me Ship, The Olive **11**
Dudley Do-Right's Ripsaw Falls **13**
JURASSIC PARK
Jurassic Park River Adventure **14**
Camp Jurassic **15**

Pteranodon Flyers **16**
Triceratops Encounter **17**
Jurassic Park Discovery Center **18**
THE LOST CONTINENT
Dueling Dragons **19**
The Flying Unicorn **20**
The Enchanted Oak Tavern
  (and Alchemy Bar) **21**
The 8th Voyage of Sindbad **22**
The Mystic Fountain **23**
Poseidon's Fury:
  Escape from the Lost City **24**
Mythos Restaurant **25**
SEUSS LANDING
Green Eggs and Ham Cafe **26**
Caro-Seuss-el **27**
If I Ran the Zoo **28**
Circus McGurkus Cafe Stoo-pendous **29**
One Fish Two Fish Red Fish Blue Fish **30**
The Cat in the Hat **31**

✔ **AOL kiosks.** These compact stations allow Islands visitors to send and check e-mail. Look for them near the Confisco Grille in the *Port of Entry,* Mythos Restaurant in *The Lost Continent,* Captain America Diner in *Marvel Super Hero Island,* and in the Discovery Center in *Jurassic Park.* Using the kiosks is free, but there are notes asking you to spend no more than five minutes online. Attendants will shoo you away if you stay too long.

✔ **ATMs.** You can find machines accepting cards from banks using the Cirrus, Honor, and Plus systems outside and inside the park's main entrance and in *The Lost Continent* near the bridge leading to *Jurassic Park.*

✔ **Baby-changing and nursing facilities.** Parent-swap stations are located at all the major attractions, allowing one parent to wait with their under-age (or under-height) offspring while the other parent rides. Diaper-changing stations are also in all the rest rooms. You can find nursing facilities in the *Guest Services* building at the *Port of Entry.*

✔ **Cameras and film.** Purchase film and disposable cameras at De Foto's Expedition Photography, inside the main entrance to the right.

✔ **Car assistance.** If you need assistance with your car, raise the hood and tell any parking attendant your location, or use the call boxes located throughout the garage to call for security. The park provides battery jumps.

✔ **Directions to the park.** Universal Orlando's **Islands of Adventure** is about half a mile north of I-4, Exit 30B, Kirkman Road or Hwy. 435. You may find construction in the area, so keep an eye out for the road signs directing you to **Universal Studios.**

✔ Universal has its own version of Disney's FASTPASS, called **Universal Express.** The three-tiered system allows guests of the **Portofino Bay** and **Hard Rock** hotels to show their room keys to get at or near the front of the line for most rides. Multiday ticket buyers can go to any of 20 kiosks in the two parks and make reservations on up to three rides at a time, getting two windows in which to return for each. Waits usually are 15 minutes or less. Guests can make more reservations when those are used or expire. Single-day ticket holders can make one reservation at a time.

✔ **First aid centers.** You can find first aid centers just inside and to the right of the main entrance as well as in *The Lost Continent,* across from Oasis Coolers.

✔ **Hours. Islands of Adventure** is open 365 days a year, generally from 9 a.m. to 7 p.m. Closing hours vary seasonally and depend on special activities within the park.

✔ **Information** is available at *Guest Services.* Before you arrive, call
☎ **800-711-0080**, 800-837-2273, or 407-363-8000 for information
about new travel packages, as well as theme-park information. You
can also write to *Guest Relations* at **Universal Studios Florida,**
1000 Universal Studios Plaza, Orlando, FL 32819-7601, or visit its
Web site, www.universalorlando.com.

✔ **Rent lockers** for $5 a day, including a $2 refundable deposit, across
from *Guest Services,* near the main entrance. These are a smart
idea for any valuables, more so car keys and assorted other loose
valuables you might lose on the more active rides.

✔ **Lost children.** If you lose a child, grab the nearest staff member and
they will direct you to the "found children" area, probably *Guest
Services* or Security. Make children under 7 wear name tags for easy
identification in case they're too upset to talk when they're found.

✔ **Parking.** If you park in the multilevel garages, remember the
theme and music in your area to help you find your car later. Or,
do it the old-fashioned way and write it down. Parking costs
$7 for cars, vans, and trucks. Valet parking is available for $12.
Universal's garages are connected to its parks and have moving
sidewalks, but it's still a long walk to the gates.

✔ **Pet care.** You can leave your small animals at the shelter in the
parking garages for $5 a day (no overnight stays).

✔ **Strollers.** Look to the left as you enter the park through the turnstiles. Stroller rental costs $7 for a single, $12 for a double.

✔ You can choose from several **ticket options.** A one-day ticket costs
$48 (plus 6-percent sales tax) for adults, $38 for children 3 to 9. A
two-day, two-park, unlimited-access pass is $89.95 for adults,
$74.95 for kids; a three-day, two-park pass is $99.95 for adults,
$79.95 for children 3 to 9. Multiday passes let you move between
Universal Studios Florida (see Chapter 23) and **Islands of
Adventure** during the course of a day. **Note:** Multiday passes also
get you into the parks two hours before other guests and give you
free access at night to the **CityWalk** clubs.

One other multiday, multipark option is the **FlexTicket.** This is the
most economical way to see the various "other-than-Disney"
parks. With the **FlexTicket**, you pay one price to visit any of the
participating parks during a 14-day period. A four-park pass to
Universal Studios Florida, Islands of Adventure, Wet 'n Wild,
and **SeaWorld** is $160 for adults, $128 for kids 3-9. A five-park pass,
which adds **Busch Gardens** in Tampa, is $197 for adults, $158 for
kids. The **FlexTicket** can be ordered by calling ☎ **407-363-8000**,
or online go to www.universalorlando.com.

✔ **Universal Studios Florida** and **Islands of Adventure** offer five-
hour **VIP tours** for $120 per person, including the daily admission
charge. These guided tours include line-cutting privileges and preferred seating at several attractions. For more information on the
VIP tour, call ☎ **407-363-0045.**

✔ **Wheelchairs.** You can rent regular wheelchairs for $7 per day in the center concourse of the parking garage or to your left as you enter the turnstiles of the main entrance. Electric wheelchairs are $30 per day. Both require a $50 deposit.

Theme park prices often reflect the fact that you're a prisoner while inside. Expect to spend $5.00 for a poncho, $7.00 to $9.00 for sunscreen, $4.50 for a large beer, and $1.75 for a small bunch of grapes.

Practical Advice for Island Adventurers

In order to get the most out of your visit to the park, keep the following tips in mind when you're exploring the **Islands of Adventure:**

✔ **Short visitors.** Ten of the 14 major rides at **Islands of Adventure** have height restrictions (*from 40 to 54 inches*). You can find a parent-swap service at all major attractions, allowing you or your partner to ride while the other watches your tykes, but sitting in a waiting room isn't much fun for the little ones. Take your child's height into consideration before coming to the park, or at least some of its islands.

✔ **Jittery or health-restricted visitors.** See the note above about short visitors and add the warning that height isn't the only limiting factor. If you're pregnant, are prone to dizziness or motion sickness, or have heart, back, or other health problems, maybe you should head for a tamer park, such as Disney's **Magic Kingdom** (see Chapter 17), Disney's **Animal Kingdom** (see Chapter 20), **Universal Studios Florida** (see Chapter 23), or **SeaWorld** (see Chapter 25).

In July 2000, **Universal** added two notable attractions to its lineup to answer criticism that **Islands of Adventure** has too little for young guests. The *Flying Unicorn* is a small roller coaster that travels through a mythical forest and resides next to *Dueling Dragons* (this is a ride comparable to *The Barnstormer at Goofy's Wiseacres Farm* in Disney's **Magic Kingdom,** Chapter 17, and *Woody Woodpecker's NutHouse Coaster* at **Universal Studios Florida,** Chapter 23). *Storm Force* is a spinning attraction in which guests help Storm harness weather to fight her archenemy, Magneto.

✔ **Cruising the Islands.** If you hauled your stroller with you on your vacation, bring it with you to the park. It's a very long walk from your car, through the massive parking garage and the nighttime entertainment district **CityWalk,** before you get to the park. Carrying a young child and the accompanying paraphernalia, even with a series of moving sidewalks, can make the long trek seem even longer — especially at the end of the day.

✔ **Beat the heat.** Several rides require that you wait outside without any cover to protect you from the sizzling Florida sun. Bring some bottled water with you for the long waits (it costs $2.50 if you buy it in the park) or take a sip or two from the fountains placed in the waiting areas. Also, alcohol is more readily available at this park than at **Disney,** so remember that liquor, roller coasters, and sweltering heat can make for a messy mix.

✔ **Cash in on your AAA card.** You can save 10 percent on your purchases at any gift shop or on a meal in **Islands of Adventure** by showing your AAA (American Automobile Association) card. This discount isn't available at food or merchandise carts. Likewise, tobacco, candy, film, collectibles, and sundry items aren't included in discounts.

Exploring the Top Attractions at Islands of Adventure

Islands of Adventure's six sections, featuring more than 20 rides and attractions, plus numerous restaurants and shops are laid out in a circular pattern around a large lagoon. See the "Islands of Adventure" map at the beginning of this chapter to locate all of the attractions in the sections that follow.

Port of Entry

Think of the *Port* as the park's starting line. The entire race is before you, but the creators of **Islands of Adventure** want to juice you slowly. The aesthetics in *Port of Entry* resemble a faraway marketplace that you'd find in *Indiana Jones* — OOPS, that's *another* movie company. Anyway, this is the garden-variety "now-that-we-have-you-what-can-we-sell-you?" gate area where the park pushes stuff like junk food, souvenirs, and other completely unnecessary things while you're still suffering from ticket shock. From the *Port of Entry,* you can walk to the five other islands dotting the lagoon or, if you want a shortcut, go to *Island Skipper Tours* and catch one of the boats that chug you to the opposite side of the park.

Seuss Landing

The main attractions in *Seuss Landing,* a 10-acre island, are aimed at the younger set, though anyone who loved the good Doctor as a child will enjoy some nostalgic fun on the colorful rides. Universal had planned to add Sylvester McMonkey McBean's Unusual Driving Machines to Seuss Landing, but the idea appears to be in cold storage.

✔ **Caro-Seuss-El.** This not-so-ordinary carousel replaces the traditional wooden horses with seven whimsical Seussian characters (54 total mounts), including Cowfish, the elephant birds from *Horton Hatches an Egg*, and Mulligatawnies. They move up and down as well as in and out. Pull the reins to make their eyes blink or heads bob as you twirl through the riot of color surrounding the ride.

The ride also features a rocking-chariot platform and wheelchair-loading system that makes it a fun attraction for guests with disabilities.

✔ **The Cat in the Hat.** All aboard the couch! In this case, the couches are six-passenger futons that steer 1,800 people an hour through 18 show scenes. Any Seuss fan will recognize the giant candy-striped hat looming over the entrance and probably the chaotic journey. Comparable to, but a lot spunkier than, *It's A Small World* at **WDW**, *The Cat in the Hat* has become one of the signature "young" experiences of **Islands of Adventure,** though you may find it tame. Love it or hate it, you have to do it. The couches travel through scenes retelling *The Cat and the Hat* tale of a day gone terribly south. You'll also encounter old favorites like Thing 1 and Thing 2.

"That felt weird. My eyes are still spinning." The ride's highlight is a revolving 24-foot tunnel that alters your perceptions and leaves you feeling woozy. You must *be 48 inches or taller* to ride alone, and keep in mind that pop-up characters may scare younger children.

✔ **If I Ran the Zoo.** *If I Ran the Zoo* is an interactive playland for kids who enjoy everything from flying water snakes to a chance to tickle the toes of a Seussian animal. The 19 play stations include slides, wheels to spin, caves to explore, and other things to let your kids burn off some excited energy.

✔ **One Fish, Two Fish, Red Fish, Blue Fish.** On this attraction, your controls allow you to move your funky fish up or down 15 feet as you spin around on an arm attached to a hub. Watch out for squirt posts, which spray unsuspecting riders who don't follow the ride's rhyme scheme (and sometimes the ones who do follow it). Riders must be *48 inches or taller* to ride without an adult.

Marvel Super Hero Island

If you're a thrill junkie, you'll love the twisting, turning, stomach-churning rides on this island filled with building-tall murals of Marvel Super Heroes.

✔ **The Amazing Adventures of Spider-Man.** *The Amazing Adventures of Spider-Man* is a primo ride that combines moving vehicles, filmed 3D action, and special effects themed around the original web master. The script: While you're on a yawn-able tour of the *Daily Bugle* newspaper — *yikes!* — the boys in black hats filch the Statue of Liberty. Your mission is to help Spidey get it back. This ride is similar to *Back to the Future* at **Universal Studios Florida,** but it's not stationary. For example, cars twist and spin, plunge and soar through this comic book universe. Passengers wearing 3D glasses squeal as real and computer-generated objects alternately fly toward their 12-person cars. There's also a simulated 400-foot drop that feels an awful lot like the real thing.

Expectant mothers or those with heart, neck, or back problems shouldn't ride the *Amazing Adventures of Spider-Man.*

"I think I left my stomach back there." J.J. wasn't the only one. Dark scenes and some of the motion effects make this ride unsuitable for very young kids. The rest of you will probably want to give the ride another spin — a number of Universal employees rate it the best in the park. There's a *40-inch height minimum.*

✔ **Doctor Doom's Fearfall.** Look! Up in the sky! It's a bird, it's a plane. . . uh, it's you falling 200 feet if you're courageous enough to climb aboard. This towering metal skeleton provides screams that you can hear far into the day and night. The plot line: You're touring a lab when — are you sensing a theme here? — something goes horribly wrong as Doctor Doom tries to cure you of fear. You're fired to the top of the ride, with feet dangling, and dropped in intervals, leaving your stomach at several levels. The fall feels like the *Twilight Zone Tower of Terror* at **Disney–MGM Studios,** but with the additional sensation of hanging free.

If you're an expectant mother or you experience heart, neck, or back problems, you shouldn't ride *Doctor Doom's Fearfall. Minimum height is 52 inches*, and we recommend a minimum age of 10.

✔ **Incredible Hulk Coaster.** This ride may be for you if you think *Dueling Dragons* (see "The Lost Continent," later in this chapter) is for sissies. The *Incredible Hulk Coaster* is sure to knot your shorts and stomach as it literally rockets from a dark tunnel into the sunlight, while accelerating from 0 to 40 mph in two seconds. **Universal's** scriptwriters insist that it has the same thrust as an F-16. Although it's only two-thirds the speed of **Disney–MGM's** *Rock 'n' Roller Coaster,* this ride is in broad daylight, and you can *see* the asphalt! After you're launched, you spin upside down 128 feet from the ground, feel weightless, and careen through the center of the park over the heads of other visitors. If you're a coaster lover, you'll be pleased to know that this ride, which lasts 2 minutes and 15 seconds, includes seven rollovers and two deep drops. Sunglasses, assorted change, and an occasional set of car keys lie in a mesh net beneath the ride — proof of its motion and the fact that most folks don't heed our locker warning (see "Knowing

Essential Park Information," earlier in this chapter). As a nice touch, the 32-passenger metal coaster glows green at night.

Expectant mothers or those with heart, neck, or back problems shouldn't ride.

"No thanks. I'm too young to die." This is another ride that we think is best for riders 10 and older. Children must be _at least 54 inches tall_ to climb aboard.

✔ **Storm Force Accelatron.** This ride is little more than a 22nd-century version of the **Magic Kingdom's** _Mad Tea Party_ and its spinning teacups. While aboard, you and the _X-Men's_ Storm try to defeat the evil Magneto. To do that, you need to spin faster and faster. In addition to some upset stomachs, your motion creates a thunderstorm of sound and light, which gives Storm all the power she needs to blast Magneto into the ever-after (well, until the next riders arrive anyway).

Toon Lagoon

More than 150 life-size, sculpted cartoon images let you know you've entered **Toon Lagoon,** which is dedicated to your favorites from the Sunday funnies.

✔ **Dudley Do-Right's Ripsaw Falls.** Although this island is pretty Popeye-happy, the heroic Dudley stars on this splashy flume ride that drops 75 feet at 50 mph. (Apparently it was a bit too much for some riders who complained. **Universal** temporarily closed it in early 2000 to tame it a bit.) Your mission is to save the fair Nell from Snidely Whiplash. The boats take you around a 400,000-gallon lagoon and plunge you 15 feet below the water's surface, but this is mainly hype — the water is contained on either side of you. **Note:** You _will_ get very wet despite the contained water.

Expectant mothers or people with heart, neck, or back problems shouldn't ride this attraction, and children must be _at least 44 inches tall_. **Note:** We've received a few complaints from tall folks, who say that the boats on this ride offer legroom on par with that in an airline's coach section.

✔ **Me Ship, The Olive.** This three-story boat is a family-friendly playland with dozens of interactive activities from bow to stern. Kids can toot whistles, clang bells, or play the organ. _Sweet Pea's Playpen_ is a favorite of younger guests. Kids 6 and up love _Cargo Crane,_ where they can drench riders on _Popeye & Bluto's Bilge-Rat Barges_ (see the following bullet).

✔ **Popeye & Bluto's Bilge-Rat Barges.** Here's another water special — a churning, turning, twisting, listing raft ride with the same kind of vehicle as _Kali River Rapids_ at Disney's **Animal Kingdom** (see Chapter 20), but this one's faster and bouncier. You'll get wet from mechanical devices as well as the water cannons fired by guests at

Me Ship, The Olive (see the preceding bullet). The 12-passenger rafts bump and dip their way along a course lined with villains, most notably Bluto, Sea Hag, and a twirling octopus boat wash.

"I think they put ice water in there." He's right, the water is *c-c-cold,* which is a blessing on hot summer days but less so in January, and trust us — you can get completely soaked. Children must be *at least 48 inches tall* to ride.

✓ **Toon Trolley Character Meet and Greet**. Beetle Bailey, Hagar the Horrible, and Dagwood & Blondie are a few of the characters who show up several times daily in this comic-strip neighborhood. It's fun for visuals and passive moments, but it's one to skip if you're on a tight schedule.

Jurassic Park

All the basics from Steven Spielberg's wildly successful films, and some of the high-tech wizardry, are incorporated into this lushly landscaped tropical locale that includes a replica of the visitor's center from the movie. Expect long lines at the *River Adventure* and pleasant surprises at the *Discovery Center,* both described in the following section.

✓ **Camp Jurassic.** This play area, designed along the same lines as *The Boneyard* in Disney's **Animal Kingdom,** has everything from lava pits with dinosaur bones to a rain forest. Watch out for the spitters that lurk in dark caves. The multilevel play area offers plenty of places for kids to crawl, explore, and wear their batteries down. Keep a close eye on young children because it's easy to get turned around inside the caverns.

✓ **Jurassic Park Discovery Center.** The *Discovery Center* is an air-conditioned spot where you can relax while you learn something. The center has life-size dinosaur replicas and some interactive games, including a sequencer that lets you combine your DNA with a dinosaur's, as well as the *Beasaur* exhibit, where you can see and hear as the dinosaurs did. You can also play *You Bet Your Dinosaur* (a game show originally called *You Bet Jurassic*) and scan the walls for fossils. The highlight is watching a tiny velociraptor hatch in the lab. There are a limited number of interactive stations, so keep in mind that this attraction can consume a lot of time on busy days.

✓ **Jurassic Park River Adventure.** The adventure of this attraction begins slowly but soon throws you into a world of stormy skies and five-story dinosaurs, including a T-Rex, one of the most unrelenting, fearsome bullies to walk the planet. The ride lets you literally come face-to-face with five-story "breathing" inhabitants of Jurassic Park. At one point, a *Tyrannosaurus Rex* decides you look like a tasty morsel and at another spitters launch venom your way. To escape, you take a breathtaking 85-foot plunge in a flume that's steep and quick enough to lift your fanny from the seat. Did we mention that you'll get soaked?

I don't want to do that again — *ever!*" (At least he was brave enough to ride it through once. At test time, Spielberg made them stop the ride and let him out before the plunge.) Children must be *at least 42 inches tall.*

✔ **Pteranodon Flyers.** Maybe you remember that childish rhyme: "Birdie, birdie, in the sky; why'd you do that in my eye?" Well, *Pteranodon Flyers* will make you wonder if our cave-dwelling ancestors had to worry about such droppings from things with 12-foot wingspans.

The 10-foot metal frames and simple seats of this high-flying ride look flimsy. The landing is bumpy, and you'll swing side to side throughout. Unlike the traditional gondolas in sky rides, on *Pteranodon Flyers,* your feet hang free from the two-seat, skeletal flyer, and there's little but a restraining belt between you and the ground. Now that we've scared you, this is a kiddie ride — *single passengers must be between 36 and 56 inches;* adults can climb aboard *only* when accompanying someone that size.

This ride launches only two passengers every 30 to 40 seconds so the line can consume an hour even in the off-season.

✔ **Triceratops Encounter.** Meet a "living" dinosaur and learn from its "trainers" about the care and feeding of the 24-foot-long, 10-foot-high Triceratops. The creature's responses include realistic blinks, breathing, flinches, and leg movements. You can touch this heavyweight dino as it turns its head and groans.

The Lost Continent

Although they've mixed their millennia — ancient Greece with medieval forest — **Universal** has done a good job creating a foreboding mood in this section of the park, where the entrance is marked by menacing stone griffins.

✔ **Dueling Dragons.** This is the **Islands of Adventure** version of a dual-dueling roller coaster. The timer on this puppy is set for only 2½ minutes, but it comes with the usual health warnings and a scream factor of 11 on a 10-point scale. True coaster crazies love this intertwined set of leg-dangling racers that climb to 125 feet, invert five times, and on three occasions, come within 12 inches of each other as the two dragons battle, and you prove your bravery by tagging along. (Ride greeters ought to pass out diapers and a sedative.) The *Fire Dragon* can reach speeds of up to 60 mph, while the *Ice Dragon* makes it to only 55 mph.

For the best ride, try to get one of the two outside seats in each row. Also, pay attention, because the lines for both coasters split near the loading dock so that daredevils can claim the very first row. And, yes, that line is longer!

You shouldn't ride this ride if you're an expectant mother or if you have heart, neck, or back problems. (Why aren't you surprised?) Children must be *at least 54 inches tall.*

✔ **The Eighth Voyage of Sindbad.** The mythical sailor Sindbad is the star of a stunt demonstration that takes place in a 1,700-seat theater decorated with blue stalagmites and eerie, gloomy shipwrecks. The show includes six water explosions and 50 pyrotechnic effects including a 10-foot circle of flames. It doesn't, however, come close to the quality of the *Indiana Jones* stunt show at **Disney–MGM Studios.**

✔ **The Flying Unicorn.** This small roller coaster is similar to *Woody Woodpecker's Nuthouse Coaster* at **Universal Studios Florida** (see Chapter 23) and *The Barnstormer at Goofy's Wiseacre Farm* in the **Magic Kingdom** (see Chapter 17). That means a fast, corkscrew run sure to earn squeals, but probably not at the risk of someone losing their lunch. This one travels through a mythical forest next to *Dueling Dragons.* Riders must be *at least 36 inches tall.*

✔ **The Mystic Fountain.** This interactive smart fountain delights younger guests. It can "see" and "hear," leading to a lot of kibitzing with those who stand before the stone fountain, suitably named Rocky. It's a real treat for 3- to 8-year-olds.

✔ **Poseidon's Fury: Escape from the Lost City.** Clearly, *Poseidon's Fury* is the park's best show. That said, it's one of the park's only shows. It exposes you to fire and water in the same manner that *Earthquake* does at **Universal Studios Florida,** but it takes adventure to another level. The Keeper, a ghostly white character, leads you on a journey where you become trapped in a battle between the evil Poseidon, god of the sea, and Zeus, king of the gods. From a small room, you proceed through a 42-foot vortex — where 17,500 gallons of water swirl around you, barrel-style — and into the Temple of Poseidon. In the battle royale, the gods hurl 25-foot fireballs at each other. It's more interesting than frightening but still offers a thrill. It is not, however, worth the long lines that usually plague it, so if you're on a tight schedule, you can skip it.

Children younger than 7 may find the flaming fireballs, explosive sounds, and rushing water a little too intense.

Dining at Islands of Adventure

After all the action and angst of riding rides and visiting attractions, you're probably hungry. There are a number of stands in the park where you can get a quick bite to eat and a handful of full-service restaurants. The park's creators have taken some extra care to tie in restaurant offerings with the theme. For example, the Green Eggs and Ham Café may be one of the few places on earth where you're willing to eat tinted eggs. (They're sold in the form of an egg-and-ham sandwich for $5.95.) Thunder Falls Terrace Restaurant in *Jurassic Park* offers a rib-and-chicken combo as well as other options in the $8 to $12 range.

A mealtime adventure

At press time, the Confisco Grille in the Port of Entry was the only **Universal** restaurant where you can join characters for a bite. Yogi, BooBoo, Woody Woodpecker, Rocky and Bullwinkle, Scooby Doo, Fred, Barney, Fievel, and George Jetson are among the characters who may show up. (A rotating collection of characters comes to each lunch, so don't promise the kids a specific character.) The menu is basic — burgers, pork chops, shrimp, and such — but the meals are often less crowded than character meals at **WDW,** so the kids get more one-on-one time with each character. Character lunches at Confisco Grill are held from noon to 2 p.m. daily. You order meals off the menu ($9 to $16 adults, $4 kids 3 to 11). For more information, call ☎ **407-224-6339** or on the Internet go to www.universalorlando.com. You can make reservations 60 days in advance, and the venue periodically changes, so make sure that you call ahead.

Here are some of our park favorites:

- ✔ **Best sit-down restaurant.** At Mythos, selections include jerk grouper, lobster-stuffed potato, pepper-painted salmon with lemon couscous, or pan-fried crab cakes with lobster sauce and basil. This restaurant is best suited for older children and adults. Prices range from $10 to $19. Open daily 11:30 a.m. to 3:30 p.m.

- ✔ **Best atmosphere for adults.** The Enchanted Oak Tavern (and Alchemy Bar) has a cave-like interior, which from the outside looks like a mammoth tree, and is brightened by an azure blue skylight with a celestial theme. The tables and chairs are thick planks, and the servers are clad in wench wear. Try the chicken/rib combo with waffle fries for $13. You can also choose from 45 brands of beer.

- ✔ **Best atmosphere for kids.** The fun never stops under the big top at Circus McGurkus Café Stoo-pendous in *Seuss Landing,* where animated trapeze artists swing from the ceiling. Kids' meals, including a souvenir cup, are $6. The adult menu features fried chicken, lasagna, spaghetti, and pizza. Try the fried chicken platter for $7.50 or the lasagna for $6.79.

- ✔ **Best vegetarian fare.** Fire-Eater's Grill, located in *The Lost Continent,* is a fast food stand that offers a tasty veggie falafel for $5. You can also get a tossed salad for $3.

- ✔ **Best diversity.** Comic Strip Café, located in *Toon Lagoon,* is a four-in-one, counter service-style eatery offering fish and chips, Chinese food, Mexican food, and pizza and pasta ($5.59 to $7).

You can also find several restaurants (see Chapter 14) and clubs (see Chapter 28) just a short walk from **Islands of Adventure** at the new entertainment complex, **CityWalk.** If you get your hand stamped you can leave the park and return after eating.

Shopping at Islands of Adventure

The park's 20-something shops have plenty of theme merchandise. You may want to check out *Cats, Hats & Things* and *Dr. Seuss' All The Books You Can Read* for special Seussian material. *Jurassic Outfitters* offers an array of stuffed and plastic dinos, plus safari-style clothing. If you're a superhero fan, check out *The Marvel Alterniverse Store.*

You may find theme- or character-specific merchandise in only one store.

Here's a sample of some of the more unusual wares available:

- ✔ **Jurassic Outfitters.** You can find plenty of T-shirts with slogans like "I Survived (the fill-in-the-blank ride)" here.

- ✔ **WossaMotta U.** You can probably bet that no one at the office will have a Rocky or Bullwinkle ceramic mug, available at this store in *Toon Lagoon.*

- ✔ **Spider-Man Shop.** This shop specializes in its namesake's paraphernalia, including red Spidey caps covered with black webs and denim jackets with logos.

- ✔ **Picture This!** Mug for the camera and get Seussian-style, 5 × 7 or 8 × 10 souvenir photos.

- ✔ **Toon Extra.** Where else can you buy a miniature stuffed Mr. Peanut bean bag, an Olive Oyl and Popeye frame, or a stuffed Beetle Bailey?

- ✔ **Treasures of Poseidon.** This shop in *The Lost Continent* carries an array of blue glassware including tumblers, shot glasses, and oversized mugs, as well as brass sculptures.

Using Our Suggested Itinerary

You can see **Islands of Adventure,** like **Universal Studios Florida,** in one day if you keep up a steady pace. In this section, we provide sample itineraries that can help ensure that you see as much as possible while you're visiting **Islands of Adventure.**

If you have children under 10, try this itinerary to help you keep pace:

- ✔ As soon as you enter the park, go straight to *Seuss Landing,* an island where everything is geared to the young and young at heart. You'll easily spend the morning exploring real-life interpretations of the wacky, colorful world of Dr. Seuss. (The wild colors also make for good photographs.)

Make sure that you ride *The Cat in the Hat; One Fish, Two Fish, Red Fish, Blue Fish;* and *Caro-Seuss-El.* After all that waiting in line, let the little ones burn off some energy playing in *If I Ran the Zoo.*

✔ Grab some lunch at the Green Eggs and Ham Café.

✔ Head to *The Lost Continent* and enjoy the show at *Poseidon's Fury: Escape from the Lost City,* and then ride *The Flying Unicorn.*

✔ Spend some time at the *Camp Jurassic* play area. If you need a break, explore the *Jurassic Park Discovery Center.*

If your child is older, or you're a childless visitor:

✔ Go to *Dueling Dragons* and *Poseidon's Fury* in *The Lost Continent.*

✔ Amble over to *Jurassic Park* and visit the *Jurassic Park River Adventure* (the name masks a steep flume ride).

✔ Head to *Toon Lagoon* and grab some lunch at the Comic Strip Café before spinning down the river (and getting wet!) in *Popeye & Bluto's Bilge-Rat Barges* and taking the plunge down *Dudley Do-Right's Ripsaw Falls.*

✔ End your day at *Marvel Super Hero Island* where you can tackle the *Incredible Hulk Coaster, Doctor Doom's Fearfall,* and *The Amazing Adventures of Spider-Man.*

Index of Attractions by Area

Seuss Landing
Caro-Seuss-El
The Cat in the Hat
If I Ran the Zoo
One Fish, Two Fish, Red Fish,
   Blue Fish

Marvel Super Hero Island
The Amazing Adventures of
   Spider-Man
Doctor Doom's Fearfall
Incredible Hulk Coaster
Storm Force Accelatron

Toon Lagoon
Dudley Do-Right's Ripsaw Falls
Me Ship, The Olive
Popeye & Bluto's Bilge-Rat Barges
Toon Trolley Character Meet and
   Greet

Jurassic Park
Camp Jurassic
Jurassic Park Discovery Center
Jurassic Park River Adventure
Pteranodon Flyers
Triceratops Encounter

The Lost Continent
Dueling Dragons
The Eighth Voyage of Sindbad
The Flying Unicorn
The Mystic Fountain
Poseidon's Fury: Escape from the
   Lost City

Chapter 25

SeaWorld and Discovery Cove

● ●

In This Chapter

▶ Understanding the basics

▶ Checking out attractions

▶ Exploring Discovery Cove

▶ Deciding where to eat and shop

▶ Using an itinerary

● ●

*F*inishing seventh in an eight-horse attendance race is tough, but **SeaWorld** delivers something the other theme parks don't offer — a more relaxed pace with several animal encounters. It's enough to attract 5.2 million visitors a year. This modern marine park focuses more on discovery than on thrill rides, though it offers its share of excitement with *Journey to Atlantis,* a steep flume-like ride, and *Kraken,* a floor-less roller coaster. **SeaWorld's** more than 200 acres of educational fun feature stars such as Shamu and his family of performing killer whales, polar bears Klondike and Snow, and a supporting cast of seals, sea lions, manatees, penguins, dolphins, and so on. You can also feed some non-performing critters and feel the crushed-velvet texture of a gentle ray in various pools throughout the park.

SeaWorld's new sister, **Discovery Cove,** opened in summer 2000, and it allows guests to swim with a dolphin in an encounter that, at $199 per person, goes off the price chart. But **SeaWorld** is betting a fortune that as many as 1,000 people a day will bite the hook — and so far the gamble has been paying off.

SeaWorld

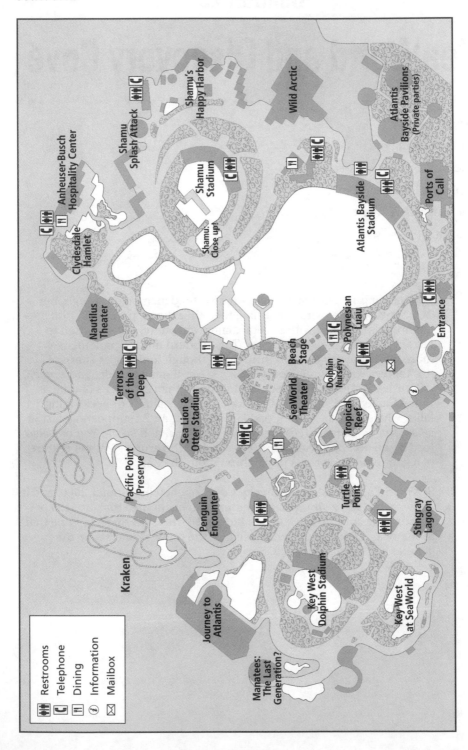

Gathering Important Information

Before we start wading through **SeaWorld's** attractions and shows, here's some practical information about the park:

- ✔ **ATMs.** You can find an ATM machine that accepts cards from banks using the Cirrus, Honor, and Plus systems at the front of the park.

- ✔ **Baby-changing and nursing stations.** Changing tables are in or near most women's rest rooms and at the men's rest room at the front entrance near Shamu's Emporium. You can buy diapers in machines located near all changing areas and at Shamu's Emporium. Likewise, there's a special area for nursing mothers near the women's rest room at *Friends of the Wild* gift shop, near the center of the park.

- ✔ **Cameras and film.** You can purchase film and disposable cameras at stores throughout **SeaWorld.**

- ✔ **Directions.** If you're driving south from Orlando, take exit 28 off I-4 and follow the signs. If you're heading north from Tampa, use exit 27A.

- ✔ **First Aid Center.** Registered nurses staff centers behind *Stingray Lagoon* and near *Shamu's Happy Harbor.*

- ✔ **Hours.** The park is open from 9 a.m. to 6 p.m., 365 days a year, and later during summer and holidays, when there are additional shows at night.

- ✔ **Information.** Write to **SeaWorld Guest Services** at 7007 SeaWorld Dr., Orlando, FL 32801, call ☎ **800-327-2424** or 407-351-3600, or visit www.seaworld.com to gather park information before you leave. Once inside the park, head for the Information Center, which is on your left as you enter the park.

- ✔ **Lockers.** You can rent them for $5 day (you will get a $2 refund if you return the key at the end of the day) next to Shamu's Emporium, just inside the park entrance.

- ✔ **Lost children.** Lost kids are taken to the Information Center, where a park-wide paging system helps reunite them with their families. Children under 7 should wear name tags.

- ✔ **Parking.** Parking costs $6 for cars, pickups, and vans. The parking lots aren't huge, so most people can easily walk to the park. Trams also run. Remember to note the location of your car, too. SeaWorld characters such as Wally Walrus mark sections, but it's easy to forget where you parked after you've spent the day barnstorming through attractions.

- ✔ **Pet care.** Board your pet for the day at the kennel between the parking lot and main gate. The cost is $4 a day (no overnight stays).

✔ **Strollers.** Rent dolphin-shaped strollers at the Information Center near the entrance. They cost $8 for a single, $14 for a double.

✔ **Tickets.** A one-day ticket costs $47.95 for adults, $38.95 for kids 3 to 9 (plus 6-percent sales tax). **SeaWorld** sometimes offers specials, such as a second day free.

If you're planning to see a number of non-Disney parks during your stay, consider the *FlexTicket*. This pass allows you to pay one price to visit any of the participating parks during a 14-day period. A four-park pass to **Universal Studios Florida, Islands of Adventure, Wet 'n Wild,** and **SeaWorld** is $160 for adults and $128 for children 3 to 9. A five-park pass, which also includes **Busch Gardens** in Tampa, is $197 for adults and $158 for kids. The *FlexTicket* can be ordered through **SeaWorld** at ☎ **407-351-3600;** Internet: www.seaworld.com.

✔ **Tours.** *SeaWorld's Adventure Express Tour* ($55 per person plus park admission) is a six-hour guided excursion that includes front-of-the-line access to *Kraken, Journey to Atlantis,* and *Wild Arctic;* reserved seating at two animal shows; and a chance to touch or feed penguins, dolphins, sting rays, and sea lions. It's the only way to dodge park lines, though they're not as long as those at the **Disney** and **Universal** parks.

Additionally, there are three one-hour options: **Polar Expedition Guided Tour** (touch a penguin), **Predators** (touch a shark), and **To The Rescue** (see manatees and sea turtles). All last about an hour and cost $7 for adults and $6 for children, plus park admission. Call ☎ **800-406-2244** or 407-351-3600 for information.

Visitors can also take 60-minute behind-the-scenes tours of the park's breeding, research and training facilities, or can attend a 45-minute presentation about **SeaWorld's** animal behavior and training techniques. Either option costs $7.95 for ages 10 and over, $6.95 for children 3 to 9, plus park admission. Although there are several tours given each day, you should make a reservation when you enter the park.

✔ **Wheelchairs.** Regular wheelchairs are available at the Information Center for $6; electric chairs are $30 plus a $25 deposit.

Exploring the Top Attractions

SeaWorld explores the mysteries of the deep in a format that combines wildlife-conservation awareness with laid-back fun. Close encounters with marine life are the major draw here, but you'll also find some excellent shows and thrill rides. To get a look at the park's layout, see the "SeaWorld" map at the beginning of this chapter.

Clyde & Seamore Take Pirate Island

A lovable sea lion-and-otter duet, with a supporting cast of walruses and harbor seals, stars in this fish-breathed comedy that comes with a swashbuckling conservation theme. The show is corny, but don't hold that against the animal actors. Besides, if you're going to spend much time at all at the high-tech rides and shows at the other theme parks, you'll be happy for the break.

Intensity Water Ski Show

It's hard to top this show, a crowd-pleaser for more than 15 years. The hyper-competition stars some of the most skilled athletes on water. The 20-person team includes world-class skiers, wake-boarders, and stunt men and women from across the United States performing non-stop aquabatics.

Journey to Atlantis

Taking a cue from **Disney's** Imagineers, **SeaWorld** has come up with a flume ride that carries the customary surgeon-general's warning about heart problems, neck or back ailments, pregnancy, seizures, dizziness, and claustrophobia. (Until the seat cushions were padded, there should've been a warning about hemorrhoids, too.) The story line of this attraction involves a battle of good versus evil, but what really matters is the drop — a wild plunge from 60 feet with luge-like curves and a shorter drop thrown in for good measure.

"That scared the heck out of me." The ride carries a *46-inch height minimum,* but the ride isn't quite as intense as *Splash Mountain* at **Magic Kingdom** (see Chapter 17) or *Jurassic Park River Adventure* in **Islands of Adventure** (see Chapter 24).

Key West at SeaWorld

It's not quite the way Hemingway saw it, but this five-acre sliver of paved paradise is a tree- and flower-lined Caribbean village that offers island food, street vendors, and entertainers. It has three animal habitats: *Stingray Lagoon,* where you get a hands-on encounter with harmless southern diamond and cownose rays; *Dolphin Cove,* a habitat for bottlenose dolphins set up for visitor interaction; and *Sea Turtle Point,* home to endangered and threatened species. Shortly after this area opened, the dolphins made a game of teasing visitors by swimming just out of arm's reach. But they soon discovered there are advantages to human interaction — namely smelt.

Speaking of smelt, you can get a half dozen of them (to feed the dolphins) for $3 or two trays for $5, and it's real easy to be melted by the dolphins' begging. We've spent half a park admission feeding the dolphins before coming to our senses.

Key West Dolphin Fest

At the partially covered, open-air Whale and Dolphin Stadium, Atlantic bottlenose dolphins perform flips and high jumps, swim at high speeds, twirl, do the back stroke, and give rides to trainers. Some false killer whales, or *Pseudocra crassidens,* also make an appearance to the accompaniment of calypso music. The tricks are impressive, but if you've seen a traditional tourist-park dolphin show, you already know the plot.

This show closed in the fall of 2000 for renovations but was expected to be open again about the time this book reaches your local bookstores.

Kraken

Launched in summer 2000, this coaster is **SeaWorld's** deepest venture into the world of thrill-ride battles. *Kraken* is named for a massive, mythological, underwater beast that Poseidon kept caged. This 21st-century version involves floor-less and open-sided 32-passenger trains that plant you on a pedestal high above the track. When the monster breaks loose, you climb 151 feet, fall 144 feet, hit speeds of 65 mph, go underground three times (spraying bystanders with water — or worse if you're weak of stomach), and make seven loops over a 4,177-foot course. This ride may be the longest 3 minutes, 39 seconds of your life. *Kraken* carries a *54-inch height minimum.*

Manatees: The Last Generation

This exhibit is as close as most people get to the endangered West Indian manatees. Underwater viewing stations, innovative cinema techniques, and interactive displays combine for a tribute to these gentle marine mammals. It's a nicer and roomier (for the manatees) exhibit than the tight quarters at *The Living Seas* in Epcot.

Penguin Encounter

The *Penguin Encounter* transports you via a moving sidewalk through Tuxedoville. The stars of the show are on the other side of a Plexiglas shield. You get a glimpse of them as they preen, socialize, and swim at bullet speed in a 22-degree habitat. You can also see puffins and murres (shorebirds) in a similar, but separate, area. Unfortunately, you get very superficial glimpses.

The Shamu Adventure

Everyone comes to **SeaWorld** to see the big guy, and he and his friends don't disappoint. This featured event is a well-choreographed show, planned and carried out by very good trainers and very smart Orcas. The whales really dive into their work! The fun builds until the video monitor flashes an urgent "Weather Watch" and one of the trainers utters the warning: "Uh-oh!" Hurricane Shamu is about to make landfall. At this point, many folks remember the splash-area warnings posted throughout the grandstand. Those who didn't pay attention when they arrived get one last chance to flee to higher and drier areas of the stadium. The Orcas then race around the edge of the pool, creating huge waves of icy water that profoundly soak everything in range. Veteran animal handler Jack Hanna also makes an appearance on the huge overhead monitors, compliments of ShamuVision.

"I'm f-f-freezing!" Don't say we didn't warn you about the splash area. Shamu's pool must be 40°F. So, if you want to stay dry, don't sit in the first 14 rows!

Shamu: Close Up! is an adjoining exhibit that lets you get close to killer whales and learn about breeding programs. Don't miss the underwater viewing area. You may get to see a mother with her big baby.

Shamu's Happy Harbor

This three-acre play area has a four-story net tower with a 35-foot crow's-nest lookout, water cannons, remote-controlled vehicles, and a water maze. It's one of the most extensive play areas at any park and a great place for kids to unwind. Bring extra clothes for the tots (or for yourself) because the *Harbor* isn't designed to keep you dry.

Terrors of the Deep

This attraction, formerly called *Shark Encounter,* was improved by the addition of some 220 species. Pools out front have small sharks and rays (feeding isn't allowed). The interior aquariums have big eels, beautiful lionfish, hauntingly still barracudas, and the fat, bug-eyed pufferfish, which are considered a delicacy in Japan. (They also pack the world's deadliest poison in their liver, kidneys, skin, ovaries, and eyes.)

This tour isn't for the claustrophobic: You walk through a Plexiglas tube beneath hundreds of millions of gallons of water. Also, small children may find the swimming sharks a little too much to handle.

Trainer for a Day

Expect to invest a sizable chunk of your day and budget in this eight-hour program. You get to work side by side with a trainer, preparing meals and feeding the animals, learning basic training techniques, and sharing lunch. It costs $349 and is limited to three people per day, so make reservations very early. You must be 13 or older, *at least 52 inches tall*, able to climb, and able to lift and carry 15 pounds of vittles. Call ☎ **407-370-1382** for more information.

Wild Arctic

Wild Arctic combines a high-definition adventure film with flight-simulator technology to evoke breathtaking Arctic panoramas. After a hazardous flight over the frozen north, visitors emerge at a remote research base, home to four polar bears (including star residents and polar twins Klondike and Snow), seals, walruses, and white beluga whales. Kids may find the bumpy ride a little much, but there's a separate line for those who want to skip the thrill-ride section.

More SeaWorld Fun

Other **SeaWorld** attractions include *Pacific Point Preserve,* a 2½- acre natural setting that duplicates the rocky northern Pacific Coast home of California sea lions and harbor seals (yes, there are more smelt opportunities here!), and *Tropical Rain Forest,* a bamboo and banyan-tree habitat that's home to cockatoos and other birds.

The 5½-acre *Anheuser-Busch Hospitality Center* offers free samples of Anheuser-Busch beers. Next door, stroll through the stables, and you may catch a glimpse of some of the famous Budweiser Clydesdale horses being groomed.

And, *Cirque de la Mer* (Circus of the Sea) incorporates talented and athletic performers in a spectacle similar to that of Disney's *Cirque du Soleil,* but on a much smaller scale. SeaWorld's version uses acrobats, musicians, and dancers in a production based on South American folklore that touches on everything from drama to side-splitting comedy. Staged in the Nautilus Theater, the show stars Peruvian comic Cesar Aedo.

Checking Out Discovery Cove

SeaWorld's second theme park opened in summer 2000. Its $100-million construction cost is one-tenth the sticker price of **Islands of Adventure,** but **Discovery Cove's** admission price is four times higher. You have two options: $199 per person plus 6-percent sales tax if you want to swim with a dolphin *(minimum age 6)*, or $119 if you can skip that luxury.

Almost everyone who does the dolphin encounter finds it exciting — just the kind of thing that makes for a most memorable vacation (although, if you have kids under 6 it's hard to imagine them getting $89 worth of fun out of their visit).

The park has 28 dolphins and each works from two to four hours a day. They're pretty incredible animals and, though their size may be a bit intimidating to some, they're very people-friendly. Most of them love their bellies, backs, and flukes rubbed. They also have an impressive bag of tricks. Given the proper hand signals, they can mimic the sound of a human passing gas, chatter in dolphin talk, and do seemingly effortless 1½ gainers in 12 feet of water. They also take guests for rides in the piggyback or missionary position.

The dolphin experience lasts 90 minutes, about 35 to 40 minutes of which is spent in the lagoon with one. Trainers use the rest of the time to teach visitors about these remarkable mammals. Encounters are limited to six guests per session.

Discovery Cove is an all-inclusive park, so in addition to the dolphin experience, you also get:

✔ Elbow room — there's a limit of 1,000 guests per day.

✔ Lunch (entrees include fajitas, salmon, stir fry, pesto chicken, and more), your towel and locker, and a mask, fin, and snorkel.

✔ Activities that include

   •Swimming near (but on the other side of Plexiglas from) black-tip sharks and barracudas

   •Snorkeling around a 1.3-million-gallon tank containing a coral reef with brightly colored tropical fish and another tank with gentle rays

   •Touching and feeding 300 exotic birds in the 100-foot-long aviary hidden under a waterfall

   •Cooling off under foaming waterfalls

   •Soaking up the sun on the beaches

   •Enjoying the soothing waters of the park's pools and rivers (freshwater and saltwater)

✔ Seven days of unlimited admission to **SeaWorld.**

We highly recommend reservations far in advance. But some of you live for spontaneity. There is a chance of getting in as a walk-up customer. The park reserves a small number of tickets daily for folks whose earlier dolphin sessions were canceled due to bad weather. The best chance for last-minute guests comes during any extended period of good weather.

To get to **Discovery Cove,** follow these directions to **SeaWorld:** If you're driving south from Orlando, take exit 28 off I-4 and follow the signs. If you're heading northeast from Tampa, use exit 27A.

For up-to-the-minute information on this new park, call ☎ **877-434-7268** or go to www.discoverycove.com.

Dining and Shopping at SeaWorld

The *Aloha! Polynesian Luau Dinner and Show,* a full-scale dinner show featuring South Seas food (mahi-mahi, chicken, and pork), song, and fire dancing, takes place nightly at 6:30 p.m. Park admission is required. The cost is $35.95 for adults, $25.95 for children 8 to 12, and $15.95 for children 3 to 7. Reservations are required (☎ **800-327-2424**).

There are also several counter-style or sit-down eateries at **SeaWorld.** Most meals cost less than $10 per person.

SeaWorld doesn't have nearly as many shops as the other major theme parks, but there are lots of surprisingly cuddly sea creatures. For example, you can buy a stuffed manatee at *Manatee Cove.* The *Friends of the Wild* gift shop near *Penguin Encounter* is also nice, as is the shop attached to *Wild Arctic.* Because of the Anheuser-Busch connection, the gift shop outside the entrance to the park offers a staggering array of Budweiser- and Busch-related items.

Using Our Suggested Itinerary

SeaWorld is a much slower-paced theme park than the other Orlando juggernauts, and there are only two rides where you'll have to fight the kind of crowds found at **Disney** and **Universal:** *Journey to Atlantis* and *Kraken.* If you arrive at park opening, we recommend hauling your keister to them straight off (go first to whichever appeals to you most, then suck it up and get in line for the other). Both are to the left of the entrance at the back of the park. If you arrive later or don't want to rush, experience those rides as your tour route allows.

The following itinerary will get you around the park in a convenient and timely fashion:

✔ Catch *The Shamu Adventure* at Shamu Stadium and visit *Wild Arctic.*

✔ Watch the *Intensity Water Ski Show* at Atlantis Bayside Stadium, and then visit *Clyde & Seamore Take Pirate Island* at the Sea Lion & Otter Stadium, followed by *Cirque de la Mer* at Nautilus Theater.

✔ If you've worked up a thirst, visit the *Anheuser-Busch Hospitality Center* and the *Clydesdale Hamlet* next door.

  ✔ After you're refreshed, see *Terrors of the Deep.*

  ✔ Feed the seals and sea lions at *Pacific Point Preserve* and say hi to the residents at *Penguin Encounter.*

  ✔ Tour *Manatees: The Last Generation, Key West at SeaWorld,* and *Stingray Lagoon.*

  ✔ Catch the *Key West Dolphin Fest* at Dolphin Stadium to end your day.

Index of SeaWorld Attractions

Clyde & Seamore Take Pirate
  Island
Dolphin Interaction Program
Intensity Games Water Ski Show
Journey to Atlantis
Key West at SeaWorld
Key West Dolphin Fest
Kraken

Manatees: The Last Generation?
Penguin Encounter
The Shamu Adventure
Shamu's Happy Harbor
Terrors of the Deep
Trainer for a Day
Wild Arctic

Chapter 26

Other Cool Attractions

● ●

In This Chapter

▶ Exploring smaller attractions

▶ Getting wet outside Walt's World

▶ Finding your way outside the city

● ●

*1*n Chapters 16 through 25, we familiarize you with the major theme-park players in and around Orlando. But, you're probably wondering if there's *anything* that's more relaxed, a little — and we mean a little — cheaper, or offers an out-of-this-world experience.

The answer to your question is yes.

In this chapter, we explore alternatives to the mega parks in town as well as some that are 30 to 90 minutes outside of Orlando.

In-Town Attractions

See Chapter 30 for a list of attractions that are cheaper than the ones we mention in this chapter. All the attractions in this section can be found on the "Orlando Area Attractions" map in this chapter.

China Town & Florida Splendid China

Ancient mysteries are the theme of this 76-acre attraction, which features more than 60 miniature replicas of China's most notable wonders. These include a half-mile copy of the 4,200-mile Great Wall, the Forbidden City's Imperial Palace, Tibet's Potala Palace, the Leshan Buddha originally carved into a mountainside, and the Mongolian mausoleum of Genghis Khan. The park also stages a 90-minute dance-and-acrobatic show, *The Mysterious Kingdom of the Orient,* nightly except Monday in the Golden Peacock Theater. It's included in your admission, or you can purchase a separate ticket for $15. Trams circle the park, stopping at major attractions.

3000 Splendid China Blvd. (off West Irlo Bronson Memorial Hwy./U.S. 192), Kissimmee. ☎ 800-244-6226 or 407-396-7111. Internet: www.floridasplendid china.com. *Hours: 9:30 a.m. daily, closing varies by season. Admission: $27.25 adults, $17.25 kids 5–12. Parking: free.*

Orlando Area Attractions

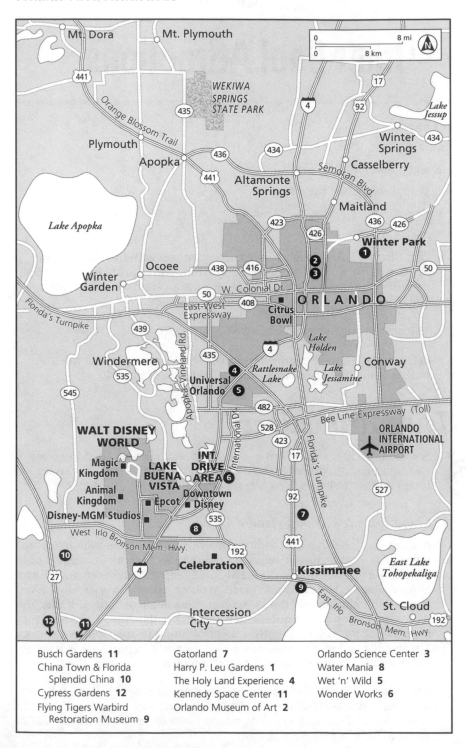

Busch Gardens **11**

China Town & Florida
  Splendid China **10**

Cypress Gardens **12**

Flying Tigers Warbird
  Restoration Museum **9**

Gatorland **7**

Harry P. Leu Gardens **1**

The Holy Land Experience **4**

Kennedy Space Center **11**

Orlando Museum of Art **2**

Orlando Science Center **3**

Water Mania **8**

Wet 'n' Wild **5**

Wonder Works **6**

Flying Tigers Warbird Restoration Museum

Tom Reilly, the founder and owner of this museum, restores vintage warplanes from World War II through Vietnam. His guided tours go through hands-on exhibits and a lab where his restorers perform magic before your eyes. The outdoor showroom includes a Corsair, B-17, P-38 Lightning, and three dozen others.

231 N. Hoagland Blvd. (south of U.S. 192), Kissimmee. ☎ *407-933-1942. Internet:* www.warbirdmuseum.com. *Hours: 9 a.m.–5 p.m. daily. Admission: $8 adults, $7 seniors 60 and older, $6 children 6–12. Parking: free.*

Gatorland

Founded in 1949 with a handful of alligators living in huts and pens, Gatorland today features thousands of alligators and crocodiles on 70 acres. Breeding pens, nurseries, and rearing ponds are scattered throughout the park, which also displays monkeys, snakes, birds, Florida turtles, and a Galápagos tortoise. There are three shows — *Gator Wrestlin'*, which is more of an environmental awareness program; the *Gator Jumparoo,* in which one of the big reptiles lunges 4 or 5 feet out of the water to snatch a long-dead chicken from a trainer's hand; and *Snakes of Florida.* The park has an open-air restaurant where you can try smoked gator ribs and nuggets, a shop where you can buy leather products (Gatorland operates a breeding farm for meat and hides), and a collection of rare snappers in its *Jungle Crocs of the World* exhibit. Younger guests enjoy the park's water play area and petting zoo.

South of Orlando. 14501 S. Orange Blossom Trail/U.S. 441 (between Osceola Parkway and Hunter's Creek Boulevard, Orlando). ☎ *800-393-5297 or 407-855-5496. Internet:* www.gatorland.com. *Hours: 9 a.m.–6 p.m. daily, sometimes later. Admission: $17.95 adults, $7.95 kids 3–12 including tax. Parking: free.*

Harry P. Leu Gardens

This delightful, 50-acre botanical garden on the shores of Lake Rowena offers a nice break from theme-park razzle-dazzle. Meandering paths lead through camphors, oaks, palms, and cicadas. The camellia collection is one of the world's largest, totalling some 2,000 plants in 50 species that bloom October through March. The exquisite formal rose gardens are the largest in Florida and contain 75 varieties. Italian fountains, statues, and a gazebo enhance the gardens. Other highlights include orchids, azaleas, desert plants, beds of colorful annuals and perennials, and a 50-foot floral clock. There are also 20-minute tours of the museum, which was built as a house in 1888. Inside you find Victorian, Chippendale, and Empire pieces.

1920 N. Forest Ave. (between Nebraska Street and Corrine Drive), Orlando. ☎ *407-246-2620. Internet:* www.leugardens.org. *Hours: 9 a.m.–5 p.m. daily except Christmas. Admission:$4 adults, $1 children grades K–12. Parking: free.*

The Holy Land Experience

Backers of this new attraction believe the Bible can compete with Mickey Mouse and Woody Woodpecker in the theme-park game. In February 2001, this $20-million park opened on 15 acres near **Universal Orlando.** The hope is to court folks interested in Bible heritage and the ever-after by transporting them to Jerusalem between the years of 1450 B.C. and A.D. 66 Instead of thrill rides, visitors explore models of Noah's Ark, the limestone caves where the Dead Sea Scrolls were discovered, 1st-century Jerusalem, and Jesus's tomb. The trimmings include a display of old Bibles and manuscripts, a Bedouin tent where biblical personalities tell Old and New Testament stories, and a café serving Middle Eastern food.

Marvin J. Rosenthal, a Christian convert and an ordained Baptist minister, caused a storm of controversy when he announced this attraction. Orlando-area rabbis, among others, protested its opening, saying they believe it's a ploy to convert Jews to Christianity. Less controversial, but still abrasive, was his refusal to hire certain Christians, including those who speak in tongues and believe in faith healing. The Holy Land has a 1,200-visitor capacity.

4655 Vineland Rd., Orlando. ☎ *866-872-4659 or 407-872-2272. Internet:* www.zionshope.org. *Hours: 10 a.m.–7 p.m. Mon–Thu, 10 a.m.–10 p.m. Fri–Sat, noon–7 p.m. Sun. Admission: $17 adults, $12 children 4–12. Parking is free.*

Orlando Museum of Art

A multimillion-dollar makeover a few years ago made this museum a local heavyweight capable of handling prestigious traveling exhibits. Even if you miss one, it's worth a visit for its rotating collection of 19th- and 20th-century American art, pre-Colombian artifacts dating from 1200 B.C., and African art.

2416 N. Mills Ave. (in Loch Haven Park), Orlando. ☎ *407-896-4231. Internet:* www.omart.org. *Hours: 10 a.m.–5 p.m. Tue–Sat, noon–5 p.m. Sun. Admission: $6 adults, $4 seniors and students, $2 children 4–11. Parking: free.*

Orlando Science Center

Dan Rather gave America a peek at the center after it was renovated in 1997. It drew his attention because it's the largest of its kind in the Southeast. (It didn't hurt that it meant a trip to Florida in February.) The new, four-story center has ten halls that allow visitors to explore everything from the swamps of Florida to the arid plains of Mars. One of the big attractions is the *Dr. Phillips CineDome,* a 310-seat theater that features films, planetarium shows, and laser-light presentations. In *KidsTown,* little folks wander in a miniature version of the world around them. One section has a pint-sized community that includes a construction site, park, and wellness center. *Science City,* located nearby, has a power plant, suspension bridge, and the *Inventor's Workshop,* a garage-like station for creative play. Children stopping by at *123 Math Avenue* work on puzzles and play with math-based toys that teach as they entertain.

777 E. Princeton St. (between Orange and Mills in Loch Haven Park), Orlando. ☎ *407-514-2000 or 888-672-4386. Internet:* www.osc.org. *Hours: 9 a.m.–5 p.m. Tue–Thu, 9 a.m.–9 p.m. Fri–Sat, noon–5 p.m. Sun. Admission:$9.50 adults, $8.50 seniors 55 and older, $6.75 kids 3–11; additional charges for the CineDome and planetarium. Parking: $3.50 in a garage across the street.*

Water Mania

This 36-acre water park offers a variety of aquatic thrill rides and attractions. You can boogie board or body surf in continuous-wave pools, float lazily along an 850-foot river, enjoy a white-water tubing adventure, and plummet down spiraling water slides and steep flumes. Ride the *Abyss,* an enclosed tube that corkscrews through 380 feet of darkness, exiting into a splash pool. There's a rainforest-themed water playground for children, a miniature golf course, and a wooded picnic area with arcade games, a beach, and volleyball. This park attracts fewer teens and young adults than the **Disney** water parks, which may make it a little more attractive to smaller children, parents, and grandparents.

6073 W. Irlo Bronson Memorial Hwy./U.S. 192, Kissimmee. ☎ *800-527-3092 or 407-396-2626. Internet:* www.watermania-florida.com. *Hours: 10 a.m.–5 p.m. daily Mar–Oct. Admission: $17 ages 3–adult. Parking: $5.*

Wet 'n Wild

Unlike Water Mania (see the preceding entry), this 25-acre Universal-owned water park is in the same league as **Disney's** *Typhoon Lagoon* and *Blizzard Beach.* It has several first-rate water rides, including *Fuji Flyer,* a six-story, four-passenger toboggan ride packing 450 feet of banked curves; *The Surge,* which offers 580 feet of greased curves and is billed as the fastest tube ride in the Southeast; and *Black Hole,* where two-person rafts shoot through 500 feet of twisting, sometimes dark passages. All three require that kids 36 to 48 inches have an adult with them. *Raging Rapids* is a simulated white-water run with a waterfall plunge; *Blue Niagra* has 300 feet of loops and dips *(48-inch height minimum)*; *Knee Ski* is a cable-operated knee-boarding course only open in warm weather *(56-inch height minimum)*; and *Mach 5* has a trio of twisting, turning flumes. The park also has a large kids' area with miniature versions of some of the grown-up rides.

If you're considering visiting several of the non-Disney theme parks, the most economical way to see **Wet 'n Wild, Universal,** and/or **SeaWorld** is with a *FlexTicket.* With it you pay one price to visit any of them in a 14-day period. A four-park pass to **Universal Studios Florida, Islands of Adventure, Wet 'n Wild,** and **SeaWorld** is $160 for adults and $128 for children 3–9. A five-park pass, which adds **Busch Gardens** in Tampa, is

$197 for adults and $158 for kids. The *FlexTicket* can be ordered through **Wet 'n Wild** at ☎ **800-992-9453 or**407-351-9453; Internet: www.wetnwild.com.

6200 International Dr. (at Universal Boulevard), Orlando. ☎ 800-992-9453 or 407-351-9453. Internet: www.wetnwild.com. Hours: vary seasonally but usually are at least 10 a.m.–5 p.m. Admission: $30 adults, $24 kids 3–9. You can rent tubes ($5), towels ($2), and lockers ($5, which includes a $2 deposit). Parking: $5.

Wonder Works

You're lost on an "uncharted island in the Bermuda Triangle" where scientists study weird science in an upside-down warehouse topped by a mysterious mansion. It's educational and fun, if you don't come expecting things to be as glitzy as they are in some of the major parks. You'll feel the tremble of an earthquake and the toupee-tossing winds of a hurricane. You'll learn dozens of fun facts. (Where are a cricket's ears? On its knees.) And you can challenge a tall dude to virtual hoops. There are more than 80 exhibits, but if you're not a good shot, steer clear of the laser tag game: it costs $6 above admission and can make for a frustrating few minutes.

9067 International Dr., Orlando ☎ 407-351-8800. Internet: www.WonderWorks Online.com. Hours: 9 a.m.–midnight daily. Admission: $14.95 adults, $11.95 kids 4–11 and seniors 55 and older; add $6 for laser tag. Parking: $2 an hour.

Fun Outside the City

After a few days in Orlando, you may think that this destination has everything anyone could want to do. So an attraction that's going to convince you to drive or hitch a ride to something one or two hours away probably has to be something special. That's a tall order, given all the stuff that's in this **World.** But we believe that three places are worth going out of your way to visit: Busch Gardens in Tampa, Cypress Gardens in Winter Haven, and the Kennedy Space Center at Cape Canaveral.

Busch Gardens

When this Tampa theme park grew out of a brewery in the '60s, the main (and only) attractions were a bird show and free beer. (You may be thinking, who could ask for anything more?) Well, both are alive and well, but the **Busch Gardens** of today is one of Florida's heavyweight attractions. Two things set it aside from its nearest rival (Disney's **Animal Kingdom**): its coasters and critters.

Busch Gardens has five — count 'em, *FIVE!!* — roller coasters to keep your adrenaline and stomach jumping. The newest one is *Gwazi,* a wooden wonder named for a fabled African lion with a tiger's head. This $10-million ride slowly climbs to 90 feet, before turning, twisting, diving, and *va-rrroommming* to speeds of 50 mph — enough to give you air time (also known as weightlessness). Fact is, these twin coasters, the *Lion* and the *Tiger,* provide 2 minutes and 20 seconds of thrills and chills, steep-banked curves, and bobsled maneuvers. There are six points on the ride where you're certain you're going to slam the other coaster as you hit 3.5 Gs. (That's science's way of saying that a 100-pound person would experience the same force of gravity as that on a 350-pound body.)

There's a *54-inch minimum height,* and the 15-inch seat is smaller than an airline seat, so it's a tight squeeze for thin folks and the next-best-thing to misery for larger models.

Busch's other four roller coasters are made of steel. *Kumba* is a 143-foot-high number that covers 4,000 feet of track at 60 mph. It jerks you with sudden turns and also has *a 54-inch height minimum. Montu* musses your hair at speeds exceeding 60 mph while the G-force keeps you plastered to your seat *(another 54-inch minimum). The Python* is a tad tamer, running through a double-spiraling corkscrew and a 70-foot plunge *(48-inch minimum). The Scorpion* offers a high-speed 60-foot drop and 360-degree loop *(42-inch minimum).*

Busch's critters have fewer places to hide and, therefore, are easier to see than those at **Animal Kingdom** (see Chapter 20). *Edge of Africa* and the *Serengeti Plain* allow views of lions, hippos, crocodiles, hyenas, and other animals that seem to roam free. (The *Serengeti,* by the way, recently got a facelift. Its 29 acres now have hills, 700 trees, 32 kinds of edible grass, and 300 animals that are encouraged to wander closer to the tourist-carrying trains by food, cool shade, and water misters.) For an extra $15 over the admission price, you can go on the 30-minute, guided *Serengeti Safari Tour,* which features an extra close look and a chance to feed giraffes, gazelles, and more. If you're eager for a hands-on wildlife experience, the safari is worth the extra money. By the time this guide hits bookstores, **Busch Gardens** plans to open *Rhino Rally,* an off-road ride that takes guests within 15 feet of white rhinos, elephants, cape buffaloes, antelopes, and other animals.

Nairobi's Myombe Reserve is home to gorillas; this area also has a baby animal nursery, petting zoo, turtle and reptile displays, and an elephant exhibit. *The Congo* features rare white Bengal tigers.

The park's three water rides are welcome relief from the summer heat. *Tanganyika Tidal Wave* and *Stanley Falls* flume ride are splashy fun. The *Congo River Rapids* ride is very similar to *Kali River Rapids* in **Animal Kingdom** (see Chapter 20).

In addition to the animals, your kids will love Dumphrey the Dragon in *Land of the Dragons,* as well as the sandy dig site at *King Tut's Tomb* and the friendly lorikeets of *Lory Landing.*

Buy your tickets in advance at the *Tampa Bay Visitor Information Center,* across Busch Boulevard from the park's entrance, to avoid long lines and save a couple of dollars.

Busch Gardens usually offers a special that lets you buy a second-day ticket for $12 per person.

Did we mention free beer if you're 21 or older? You can sample Anheuser-Busch products at the *Hospitality House.*

3000 E. Busch Blvd. (at McKinley Drive/N. 40th Street), Tampa. ☎ *800-423-8367 or 813-987-5283. Internet:* www.buschgardens.com. *Hours: 9:30 a.m.–6 p.m. daily, but the park sometimes opens at 9 a.m. and closes as late as 9 p.m. Admission: $47.95 for adults, $38.95 for kids 3–9. Parking: $6. Busch Gardens also sells the FlexTicket, which gives you 14 days of unlimited access to this park as well as* **Universal Studios Florida, Islands of Adventure, Wet 'n Wild,** *and* **SeaWorld** *in Orlando. The ticket costs $197 for adults and $158 for kids.*

Cypress Gardens

FDR was in his first term when this park opened in 1936. Water ski shows and flowers are still its bread and butter, but a lot has changed over the years.

The 200-acre attraction continues to showcase 8,000 kinds of plants, ancient cypress trees, ponds, lagoons, waterfalls, classic Italian fountains, bronze sculptures, and manicured lawns. In late winter and early spring, more than 20 kinds of bougainvilleas, 40 types of azaleas, and hundreds of varieties of roses burst into bloom. Crape myrtles, magnolias, and gardenias perfume the air, while hibiscuses and jasmines brighten the summer landscape. Festivals scheduled through the year honor mums, poinsettias, and others.

But years of transformation have turned **Cypress Gardens** into a less passive, more-than-just-visual park. Kids love *Carousel Cove,* where they can ride ponies and an ornate turn-of-the-20th century-style carousel. The adjoining *Cypress Junction* features an elaborately landscaped model railroad that travels 1,100 feet of track with up to 20 trains visiting miniature landmarks including New Orleans and Mount Rushmore. *Electric boats* navigate a maze of lushly landscaped canals in the original botanical gardens area. You can rise 153 feet in the *Island in the Sky* for a panoramic vista of the gardens and a beautiful chain of Central Florida lakes.

Cypress Roots, a museum of park memorabilia, displays photographs of famous visitors, including Elvis on water skis, and airs ongoing showings of *Easy to Love* starring Esther Williams, which was filmed here. *Calling All Animals* features a show-and-tell with a 6-foot savanna monitor lizard, an alligator, some colorful macaws, and a 15-foot albino py-thon that answers to the name of "Banana Boy."

On the water, **Cypress Gardens'** celebrated skiers (called the *Greatest American Ski Team*) keep a legendary tradition going with standards such as ramp jumping, the aqua-maid ballet line, a human pyramid, and a flag line — all with a little slapstick thrown in for good measure.

Fairy Tales on Ice visits a number of favorites including Sleeping Beauty, Snow White, the Hunchback of Notre Dame, and 1,001 Arabian Nights. On stage, *Variete Internationale* performs *"European Circus Magic,"* a show that features popular clowns Zaripov and Gratchik, who weave magic acts into their zany antics. A juggler, fire-eater, and gymnast also star in the show.

Wings of Wonder is a conservatory with more than 1,000 brilliant butterflies (50 species) in a Victorian-style, climate-controlled, free-flight aviary. This manmade rain forest features lush foliage, mini-waterfalls, and iguanas. There's also a hatching display that shows the various stages of butterfly metamorphosis.

The *Birdwalk Aviary* has 40 to 50 hand-raised lories and lorikeets that welcome visitors by landing on shoulders instead of their perches. The young Australian parrots are brilliantly colored and very inquisitive. They share the sanctuary with pheasants, ducks, and muntjacs (the smallest deer species in the world).

2641 S. Lake Summit Dr. (Highway 540 at Cypress Gardens Boulevard, 40 miles southwest of Disney World), Winter Haven. ☎ *800-282-2123. Internet:* www. cypressgardens.com. *Hours: 9:30 a.m.–5 p.m. daily, sometimes later. Admission: $33 for adults, $17 children 6–12. Parking: $6.*

Kennedy Space Center

Each time a space shuttle blasts into the heavens, someone you know wishes he or she could be an astronaut. Heck — maybe it's you. What a rush, eh? Riding a missile that's slightly more stable than a nuclear warhead, boldly going where no man or woman has gone before. But does your fantasy include these side effects?

- ✔ The shuttle's liftoff thrust is 7 ½ million pounds, which is equal to the giddy-up of 20 (that's not a typo) 747 jumbo jets. By the time you're in orbit 8 minutes later, you're lickety-splitting to the tune of 17,000 mph.

- ✔ Weightlessness makes your lower-body fluids rise like dead fish, bloating your face and causing your sinuses to feel like you've suddenly caught a wicked hangover.

Those are just two of the fun facts you may learn on a visit to the **Kennedy Space Center.** Highlights of the center include trips down memory lane and glances into the future of space exploration.

The center has three 5 ½-story, 3D Imax theaters that reverberate with special effects (the best are *L5,* a fictional look at the first space colony, and *The Dream Is Alive,* a rousing past-and-present focus on the Space Shuttle program).

The Visitor Complex has real NASA rockets and exhibits that look at space exploration well into this millennium. There are also hands-on activities for kids, a chance to meet a real astronaut, several dining venues, and a shop selling a variety of space memorabilia and souvenirs.

Bus tours (rent the audio tape for $5) run continuously. You can get off at the Vehicle Assembly Building, where shuttles are prepared for launch; the LC-39 Observation Gantry, which has a 360-degree view of shuttle launch pads; and the Apollo/Saturn V Center, which includes artifacts, photos, interactive exhibits, and the 363-foot-tall Saturn V rocket.

If you want to go out on the launch pads, take the *Then and Now* guided tour. This once daily, two-hour excursion focuses more on the history of the space program and stops at sites where the shuttle buses don't. You explore *Hangar S,* where the Mercury astronauts lived; launch pads for the Mercury, Gemini, and Apollo missions; the *U.S. Air Force Space and Missile Museum;* and historic *Cape Canaveral Lighthouse.*

On launch days, the Center is closed at least part of the day (it opens after early shuttle launches and six hours before the later ones). They aren't good days to see the center, but they're great days to observe history in the making. For $10 per person, you can go on a two-hour (longer if there's a launch delay) excursion to the *NASA Parkway* to see the liftoff. You must pick up tickets, available five days prior to the launch, on site. For information, call ☎ **321-449-4444.**

If you're staying in Orlando and don't have a car, you can arrange a trip to the center through Mears Transportation by calling ☎ **407-423-5566.** From **WDW,** it's $19 per person round trip (kids under 4 are free). Shuttles run only on Monday, Wednesday, and Friday. Mears does **not** run buses on launch days.

NASA Parkway/Fla. 405 (6 miles east of Titusville/ ½ mile west of Fla. 3), Cape Canaveral. ☎ 321-452-2121 for general information, 321-449-4444 for guided bus tours and launch reservations. Internet: www.kennedyspacecenter.com/. *Hours: 9 a.m.–dusk daily. A Maximum Access Badge (IMAX movies, bus tour, and additional exhibits) is $24 adults and $15 kids 3–11; add $20 to each for the Then and Now tour. Parking: free.*

Chapter 27

A Shopper's Guide to Orlando

· ·

In This Chapter

▶ Getting acquainted with Orlando's shopping districts

▶ Checking out malls, outlets, and more

▶ Exploring the antique district

· ·

*I*n this chapter, we provide you with a rundown of places outside the Mickey zone where you can blow your cash, assuming that you have the time — and that the theme parks haven't emptied your bank accounts yet. Because **Walt Disney World** is tops in Orlando at separating you from your money, discussing Disney-related shopping requires its own chapter — Chapter 22.

Checking Out the Shopping Scene

Orlando is not a shopper's paradise. Aside from certain Mickey souvenirs, you'll need a magnifying glass to find something available only in Orlando. The same goes for bargains on the more common items. Some of you may have been born with divining rods that can find a good buy in a blinding snowstorm, but Orlando is a destination that will test your rod's merit. You can find malls like the ones you have back home and a few factory outlets, and the city also has an antique district where it's fun to window shop (we guarantee the prices will cause sticker shock). But most of central Florida's tourist areas (Orlando, Kissimmee and the surrounding territory) are riddled with T-shirt shacks, jeans joints, and souvenir stands promising bargains that don't exist.

The same is true for the theme parks. If you line up at the registers at **Disney, Universal,** and the other parks, you pay more than what the merchandise is worth. But, if you must have those mouse ears, we've outlined Disney's shopping options in Chapter 22 and the other major theme parks' merchandise in Chapters 23, 24, and 25.

Here are three shopping heads-ups before you get started:

✔ **Sales tax.** In Orange County, which includes the International Drive area and most of the parks, sales tax is 6 percent. Kissimmee and the rest of Osceola County charge 7-percent sales tax.

✔ **Store hours.** Most of the stores we mention in this chapter are open seven days a week, from 9 or 10 a.m. until 9 p.m. (6 p.m. on Sundays). Small stores, including those in the antique district, usually close around 5 or 6 p.m. and often aren't open on Sunday.

✔ **Money.** Most stores accept major credit cards, traveler's checks, and, of course, cash. However, there may not be an ATM handy in some areas, and none of the stores accepts foreign currency or personal checks.

Exploring the Great Shopping Neighborhoods

Orlando doesn't have a central shopping district or districts. Instead, it has tourist areas that are best avoided unless you want cheap goods at high prices, as well as retail neighborhoods where locals shop, such as malls and so on. The following is a list of some of the more frequented shopping zones:

✔ **Celebration.** Think *Pleasantville* with a Mickey touch. This Disney-created town of 25,000 (and growing) is more a diversion than a good place to wear out a credit card. The downtown area has a half dozen shops, a couple of art galleries, four restaurants, and a trio of movie theaters. The shops peddle interesting — if overpriced — merchandise, but the real plus is the atmosphere. A lot of yuppies love it and, look, over there! Is that Ward and June Cleaver? From **WDW,** take U.S. 192 east five miles, past Interstate 4. The entrance to Celebration is on the right. Call ☎ 407-566-2200 for more information.

✔ **Kissimmee.** Southeast of the Disney parks, Kissimmee straddles U.S. 192/Irlo Bronson Memorial Highway — a sometimes tacky, too-often under construction stretch of highway lined with budget motels, smaller attractions, and every fast-food restaurant known to man. Kissimmee's shopping merit is negligible unless you're looking for a cheap T-shirt or a white elephant gift. (Rubber alligators, anyone?)

✔ **International Drive Area.** This tourist magnet is east of and extends seven to ten miles north of the Disney parks between Highway 535 and the Florida Turnpike. The southern end has a little elbow room, the mid-section is somewhat upscale, but the northern part is a tourist strip crowded with small-time attractions (there's bungee jumping for those who have a death wish), fast fooderies, and souvenir shacks. There most redeeming shopping draw: *Pointe Orlando* (see listing under "The Malls," later in this chapter).

Locally, International Drive is called *I-Drive*.

✔ **Downtown Orlando.** Orlando's downtown is actually northeast of the parks on I-4. The biggest draws here are the shops at **Antique Row** (see "Antiquing Downtown" later in this chapter).

✔ **Winter Park.** Just north of downtown Orlando, Winter Park began as a haven for Yankees escaping the cold Northeast. Today, Winter Park's centerpiece is Park Avenue, a collection of upscale shops and restaurants along a cobblestone street. Ann Taylor and Banana Republic are among the dozens of specialty shops. Park Avenue also has some art galleries. For more information on Winter Park, call ☎ **407-644-8281,** or head over to `www.winterpark.org` on the Web.

Finding the Big Names in Shopping

Orlando's reputation wasn't built on shopping. In fact, it's not even the number one shopping area in Florida, falling well short of Miami–Fort Lauderdale. But Orlando has attracted some big names, including a very small *Saks* and the promise of a *Bloomingdale's, Macy's,* and maybe a *Harrods.* It also has a growing stable of discount centers.

Factory Outlets

In the last decade, the tourist areas have bloomed with outlets where shoppers can find some name brand bargains — maybe. While many of the stores claim savings of 50 percent to 75 percent, well, to borrow advice from a popular rhyme, we suggest: "Things aren't always what they seem; skim milk masquerades as cream."

If you're a smart outlet shopper, you know the suggested retail prices for items before you hit the stores. Therefore, you know what is — and what *isn't* — a bargain. Here's a list of outlet stores and centers in and around Orlando:

✔ **Belz Factory Outlet World.** Belz (☎ **407-354-0126;** Internet: `www.belz.com`) is the granddaddy of all Orlando outlets. Located at 5401 W. Oak Ridge Road (at the north end of International Drive), it has 180 stores in two huge, enclosed malls and four annexes. (The only thing missing is a voting precinct.) The outlet offers 18 shoe stores (including Bass, Bally, and Capezio), 14 housewares stores (such as Corning, Oneida, and Mikasa), and more than 60 clothing shops (London Fog, Jonathan Logan, Guess Jeans, Aileen, Danskin, Jordache, Leslie Fay, Carole Little, Harvé Benard, Calvin Klein, and Anne Klein, for example). You can also buy books, toys, electronics, sporting goods, jewelry, and so on.

Don't kill yourself trying to get to every building. Many of the manufacturers have more than one location here, each with much of the same selection. And unless you're from out of the country, sportswear stores such as Nike and Reebok don't offer much of a deal, especially on shoes.

✔ **Lake Buena Vista Factory Stores.** The three dozen or so outlets here include Casuals (Calvin Klein, Ralph Lauren, and Tommy Hilfiger), Liz Claiborne, GAP, Jantzen, Osh Kosh, and Reebok. Savings are modest. This center has declined a little with the opening of the newer Orlando Premium Outlets (see the last bullet in this list). You can find these stores at 15591 S. Apopka-Vineland Road; ☎ 407-238-9301; Internet: www.LBVFactoryStores.com.

✔ **Quality Outlet Center.** On the smaller side, Quality Outlet Center has 20 stores, such as Arrow, American Tourister, Corning-Revere, Florsheim shoes, Magnavox, Laura Ashley, Adidas, Great Western Boots, Linens 'n' Things, Mikasa, Royal Doulton, and Villeroy & Boch. Savings here tend to be modest. You'll find the outlet at 5527 International Drive (one block east of Kirkman Road); ☎ 407-423-5885.

✔ **Orlando Premium Outlets.** Opened in July 2000, this 440,000-square-foot center is the newest kid on the block. It's being billed as Orlando's only upscale outlet, with 110 tenants such as Bottega Veneta, Coach, Cole-Haan, Donna Karan, Kenneth Cole, Nike, Polo/Ralph Lauren, Tahari, Theory, Timberland, and Tommy Hilfiger. Some of the best buys here are at Banana Republic, where jeans are usually half the price of those at other BR stores. It's at 8200 Vineland Avenue (just off the southern third of I-Drive); ☎ 407-238-7787; Internet: www.PremiumOutlets.com.

The Malls

The Orlando area contains several traditional shopping malls. Like tenants in malls everywhere, these merchants pay a hefty rent, so good buys are elusive. Arguably, a mall's best bargain is people-watching, which is free. Here's a list of Orlando's malls:

✔ **Florida Mall.** Fresh off a $70-million expansion, this mall's anchors include Dillard's, Saks, Burdines, JCPenney, Sears, an Adam's Mark Hotel, and more than 200 specialty stores, restaurants, and entertainment venues. You can find the Florida Mall at 8001 S. Orange Blossom Trail (at Sand Lake Road, four miles east of International Drive. For details, call ☎ 407-851-7234 or check out www.shopsimon.com.

✔ **Orlando Fashion Square Mall.** This city-side mall has marblelike walkways, indoor palm trees, and tenants that include Burdines,

Gayfers, JCPenney, Sears, 165 specialty shops, and an extensive food court. The mall is five miles from downtown Orlando at 3201 E. Colonial Drive; ☎ 407-896-1131.

✔ **Altamonte Mall.** Built in the early 1970s, this is the area's second largest mall, behind the newly expanded Florida Mall. Altamonte Mall big-league tenants include Gayfers, Burdines, and JCPenney, as well as 175 specialty shops. You can find it at 451 E. Altamonte Drive (about 15 miles north of downtown Orlando). For information call ☎ 407-830-4400, or surf over to www.mallibu.com.

✔ **Pointe Orlando.** Although it's set up like a mall, this complex's two levels of stores, restaurants, and a 21-screen IMAX theater aren't under one roof. Headliners among the 80 shops include Banana Republic, Foot Locker, and a 33,000-square-foot FAO Schwarz, whose exterior is adorned with a three-story Raggedy Ann. Inside FAO Schwartz, you can find a huge *Star Wars* area, including a seven-foot Darth Vader that retails for a cool $5,000, and a Barbie collection so large it makes some folks crazy — if they don't die of sticker shock first. Pointe Orlando (☎ 407-248-2838; Internet: www.pointeorlando.com.) is located at 9101 International Drive.

Antiquing Downtown

If you can think of nothing better than a relaxing afternoon of sifting through yesterday's treasures, check out **Antique Row** on Orange Avenue in downtown Orlando.

Flo's Attic (☎ 407-895-1800) sells traditional antiques. *Art's Cigars* (☎ 407-895-9772) is a two-story leather-and-tweed kind of place where you're encouraged to light up and enjoy the view of Lake Ivanhoe. *Wildlife Gallery* (☎ 407-898-4544) sells pricey, original works of art, including sculpture. And the *Fly Fisherman* (☎ 407-898-1989) sells — no surprise here — fly-fishing gear. You can sometimes watch people taking lessons in the park across the street.

All the stores we mention in this section are spread over three miles along Orange Avenue. The heaviest concentration is between Princeton Street and New Hampshire Avenue, although a few are scattered between New Hampshire and Virginia avenues. The more upscale shops extend a few blocks beyond Virginia. To get to **Antique Row** from the theme parks, take I-4 east to Princeton Street (Exit 43). Turn right on Orange Avenue. Parking is limited, so stop wherever you find a space along the street.

As for hours of operation, most of the stores on **Antique Row** are open from about 9 a.m. to 6 p.m., Monday through Saturday. (Storeowners usually run the stores, so hours can vary. A small number are open on Sunday, but it's not worth the trip from the resorts.)

Part VII
Living It Up After the Sun Goes Down: Orlando Nightlife

"Actually, they started out as just bickering pianos."

In this part . . .

Orlando's action used to literally rise and set with the sun, but that's hardly the case now. We tip our hats to those of you who still have the pizzazz for a nighttime adventure after a day in the parks. Whether you prefer rocking the night away, dancing until dawn, or dining while you watch knights rescue damsels in distress, you can liven up your evenings in Orlando, and this part of the book shows you how.

Chapter 28

Hitting the Clubs and Bars

- -

In This Chapter

▶ Rocking the night away at Walt Disney World

▶ Cruising the clubs at CityWalk

▶ Sampling Orlando's Old Guard nightlife

▶ Exploring hot spots inside Orlando's hotels

▶ Finding a few more places to boogie down

- -

Sure, you came for the sunrise-to-sunset rides, shows, and corn dogs. But you're still under

    A.   30

    B.   40

    C.   (write it in — we won't squeal)

Although Orlando has a reputation as a daylight destination, it's night-time menu continues growing as fun-seekers like you insist on a place to howl at the moon.

Clubs such as *Mannequins* and *House of Blues* at **Pleasure Island** and **Disney West Side** rock well into the wee hours. **Universal Orlando** entered the after-dark game in 1999 with its **CityWalk** entertainment district and such nightspots as *the groove* and *CityJazz*. Unfortunately, the grand dame of Orlando nightlife, **Church Street Station,** has been temporarily closed by new management, although *Cheyenne Saloon* remains open.

Many of the clubs that we list in the following section are open to anyone 18 or older, but remember: The *minimum drinking age* in Florida is 21, and the clubs will check your ID.

Enjoying the Pleasures of Pleasure Island

This six-acre, sometimes gated entertainment district is the home of several nightspots. Admission to the island is free from 10 a.m. to 7 p.m. Admission is $21, including tax, after 7 p.m., when the clubs open (admission is included if you have a Park Hopper Plus pass — see Chapter 16 for information on Disney admission passes). Self-parking is free. For information on **Pleasure Island,** call ☎ **407-934-7781,** or check out Disney's Web site at www.disneyworld.com.

Mannequins Dance Palace is the main event on **Pleasure Island,** and it's a high-energy club with a big, rotating dance floor. Being a local favorite makes it hard to get into, so arrive early, especially on weekends. Three levels of bars and mixing space are adorned with elaborately dressed mannequins. The DJ plays contemporary tunes loud enough to wake the dead.

You must be 21 to get into *Mannequins Dance Club,* and the staff is *very* serious about that.

The *Adventurers Club* is a multistory building that, according to WDW legend, was designed to be the library and archaeological trophy room for Pleasure Island founder and explorer, Merriweather Adam Pleasure, who was lost at sea in 1941. The club is decorated with early aviation photos, hunting trophies, and a mounted yakoose — a half yak, half moose that speaks, whether you're drinking or not. Also on hand are Pleasure's zany band of globetrotting friends and servants, played by skilled actors who interact with guests while staying in character. Improvisational comedy and cabaret shows are performed in the Library. You can easily hang out here all night, sipping potent tropical drinks in the library or the bar, where elephant-foot barstools rise and sink mysteriously.

If you're a fan of the BET Cable Network, you'll probably love *BET Soundstage* (☎ **407-934-7666**), which offers traditional R&B and the rhyme of hip-hop. You can dance on an expansive floor or kick back on an outdoor terrace. Cover charge for the *Soundstage* is included in the **Pleasure Island** pass, except for major concerts.

A very talented troupe — the Who, What and Warehouse Players — are the main event at the *Comedy Warehouse.* The group performs 45-minute improvisational shows based on audience suggestions. They do five shows a night.

Disco and polyester rule at *8Trax,* a 1970s-style club where 50 TV screens air diverse shows and videos over the dance floor. A DJ plays everything from "YMCA" to "The Hustle."

Downtown Disney

Adventurers Club **12**
AMC Theater Complex **7**
BET Soundstage **11**
Bongo's Cuban Café **8**
Cirque du Soleil **1**
Comedy Warehouse **13**
DisneyQuest **2**
8Trax **14**
Fulton's Crab House **20**
Ghirardelli Soda Fountain
& Chocolate Shop **23**
Guitar Gallery **5**
House of Blues **3**

Lego Imagination Center **22**
Mannequins Dance Palace **15**
McDonald's Fun House **21**
Planet Hollywood **9**
PI Jazz Company **16**
Portobello Yacht Club **19**
Rainforest Café **24**
Rock 'n' Roll Beach Club **17**
Virgin Megastore **4**
West End Plaza **10**
Wildhorse Saloon **18**
Wolfgang Puck Café **6**

The Wildhorse Saloon attracts country connoisseurs with some of the 20th and 21st centuries' best boot-scootin' music. If you don't know how to scoot, the Wildhorse Dancers can show you the moves before you hit the 1,500-square-foot dance floor. The cover charge is included in **Pleasure Island** admission except on nights of big concerts. Call ☎ **407-827-4947** or 407-828-8260 to find out if anyone is performing while you're in town.

Walt Disney World Nightlife

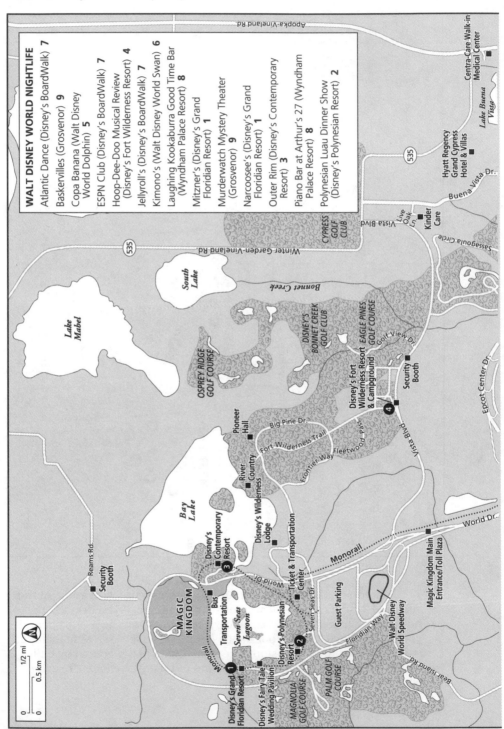

WALT DISNEY WORLD NIGHTLIFE

Atlantic Dance (Disney's BoardWalk) **7**
Baskervilles (Grosvenor) **9**
Copa Banana (Walt Disney World Dolphin) **5**
ESPN Club (Disney's BoardWalk) **7**
Hoop-Dee-Doo Musical Review (Disney's Fort Wilderness Resort) **4**
Jellyroll's (Disney's BoardWalk) **7**
Kimono's (Walt Disney World Swan) **6**
Laughing Kookaburra Good Time Bar (Wyndham Palace Resort) **8**
Mitzner's (Disney's Grand Floridian Resort) **1**
Murderwatch Mystery Theater (Grosvenor) **9**
Narcoosee's (Disney's Grand Floridian Resort) **1**
Outer Rim (Disney's Contemporary Resort) **3**
Piano Bar at Arthur's 27 (Wyndham Palace Resort) **8**
Polynesian Luau Dinner Show (Disney's Polynesian Resort) **2**

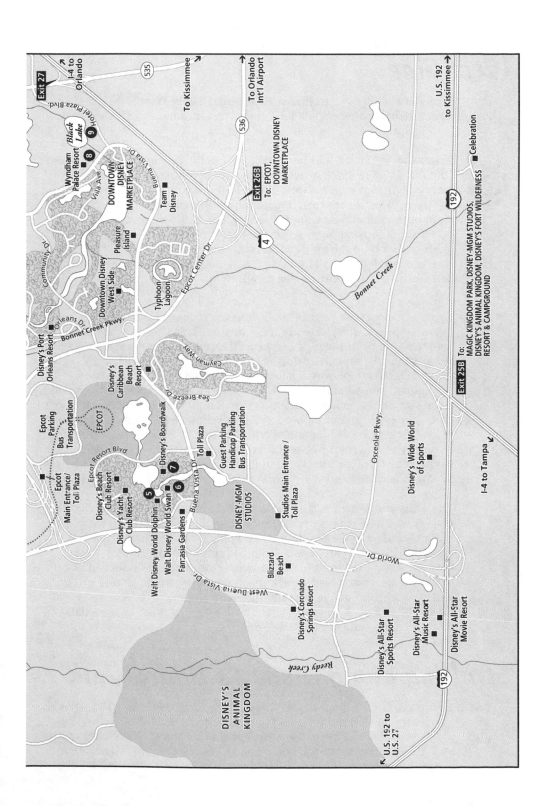

Exploring Downtown Disney West Side

Immediately adjacent to **Pleasure Island, Disney West Side** is a slightly newer district, where you'll find clubs, restaurants, and **DisneyQuest** (see Chapter 21).

Singer Gloria Estefan and her husband, Emilio, created *Bongo's Cuban Café* (☎ **407-828-0999;** Internet: www.bongoscubancafe.com), an eatery/nightspot where a Desi Arnaz look-alike may show up to croon a few tunes. The upbeat salsa music makes this place noisy, so flee to the patio or upstairs if you want privacy. All in all, this isn't one of Florida's better Cuban restaurants, so you're better off coming for the atmosphere rather than the food (which will run you about $10 to $26). The *Café* is open daily from 11 a.m. to 2 a.m. and doesn't take reservations. You can also find plenty of free self-parking.

Cirque du Soleil isn't your ordinary circus. It doesn't have any lions, tigers, or bears. But you won't feel cheated. This Circus of the Sun is nonstop energy. At times, it seems as if all 64 performers are on stage simultaneously, especially during the frenetic trampoline routine. Trapeze artists, high-wire walkers, an airborne gymnast, a posing strongman, mimes, and two clowns cement a show called *La Nouba* into a five-star performance. But if you're on a tight budget, this is gut-check time: Can you blow one or two day's entertainment budget on 90 minutes of fun? Tickets are $67 for adults and $39 for kids 3 to 9, yet there's rarely an empty seat in the 1,671-seat arena. Show times are at 6 and 9 p.m., Wednesday through Sunday, though times rotate. For information, call ☎ **407-939-7600,** or go visit their Web site at www.cirquedusoleil.com.

The walls and rafters in the *House of Blues* literally shake with rhythm and blues. The *House* is decorated with colorful folk art and the patio has a nice view of the bay. If you like spicy food, the jambalaya and gumbo ($15 to $20) are respectable. Sunday's Gospel Brunch ($28 for adults and $15 kids 4 to 12) has foot-stomping music served so-so food (omelets, roast beef, jalapeno smashed potatoes, cheese grits, and sausage). Brunch is the only time you can make reservations. Call ☎ **407-934-2583** or go to www.hob.com. *House of Blues* is open daily 11 a.m. to 2 a.m., and offers free self-parking.

Strolling along Disney's BoardWalk

This is part of the same-named resort (see Chapter 8). The **BoardWalk** is a great place for a quiet stroll or more. Street performers sing, dance, juggle, and make a little magic most evenings. *Atlantic Dance* offers retro-swing and contemporary Latin music ($5 cover charge). The rustic, saloon-style *Jellyrolls* offers dueling pianos ($5 cover charge). If you need a game fix, *ESPN Sports* has 71 TV screens, a full-service bar, food, and a small arcade, all without a cover charge. You can get information on all of these by calling ☎ **407-939-3463** or go to www.disneyworld.com on the Internet.

Dancing the Night away at CityWalk

Universal's answer to **Pleasure Island** is a two-level collection of clubs and restaurants located between its two theme parks. **CityWalk** (☎ **407-363-8000;** Internet: www.universalorlando.com) is open 11 a.m. to 2 a.m. daily. There's no admission, but several clubs have cover charges after 5 or 6 p.m., and some aren't open earlier than that. If you're planning to see only one or two clubs, it's cheaper to pay individually. CityWalk also now offers *party passes.* A pass to all clubs is $8; for $11 you get a movie at Universal Cineplex (☎ **407-354-5998**) and club access; combine dinner at one of eight restaurants with a movie or all-club access for $17 (tax and gratuity are included in this option; add a 6-percent sales tax for the first two). Universal also offers free club access to those who buy two- and three-day theme-park tickets (see Chapters 23 and 24).

Bob Marley — A Tribute to Freedom (☎ **407-224-2262**) has architecture said to replicate Marley's home in Kingston. Local and national reggae bands perform frequently. Light Jamaican fare is served under umbrellas. Hours are 4 p.m. to 2 a.m. Sunday through Friday and 2 a.m. to 2 a.m. Saturday. There's a cover of $4.25 after 8 p.m.; cover prices increase for concerts on special nights.

The collection of memorabilia at the *Downbeat Jazz Hall of Fame* ranges from Buddy Rich to Ella Fitzgerald. The adjoining *Thelonious Monk Institute of Jazz* is a performance venue that's also the site of workshops. You can browse through 500 pieces of memorabilia marching through Dixieland, swing, bebop, and modern jazz. Nationally acclaimed acts perform frequently. On the food side of the equation, look for tapas, sushi, and lamb chops. *The Institute of Jazz* is open 8:30 p.m. to 1:00 a.m. Cover charge is $3.25 (more for special events).

the groove (☎ **407-363-8000**) is **CityWalk's** answer to **Pleasure Island's** *Mannequins,* though it's not as crowded. The sound system is guaranteed to blow your hair back, and the dance floor is in a room gleaming with chrome. Music-wise, *the groove* features hip-hop, jazz fusion, techno, and alternative. A DJ plays tunes on nights when recording artists aren't booked. In addition to the main room, three alcoves have their own unique designs, bars, and specialty drinks to fit the mood. There are five entertainment areas with matching décor that ranges from vaudeville to the millennium. You must be at least 21 to enter, and it will cost you a cover charge of $5.25 for the privilege. The club is open from 9 p.m. to 2 a.m., sometimes later.

CityWalk

SPECIALTY SHOPS

All Star Collectibles **7**
Captain Crackers **4**
Cigarz at Citywalk **1**
Dapy **5**
Elegant Illusions **3**
Endangered Species **12**
Fossil **9**
Fresh Produce Sportswear **8**
Glow! **6**
Quiet Flight **10**
Silver **11**
Tabasco Country Store **2**
Universal Studios Store **13**

CityWalk's *Hard Rock Cafe* (☎ 407-351-7625) is the largest in the world, and the adjoining *Hard Rock Live* is the first concert hall bearing the name. There's also a free exhibit area in the cafe, where you can browse through displays of rock memorabilia, including the platform heels, leather jumpsuits, and tongue action of KISS. Concert charge varies by act. The cafe is open daily 11 a.m. to midnight.

Flip-flops and flowered shirts equal *Jimmy Buffett's Margaritaville* (☎ 407-224-2155). Canned music is piped through the building, with a Jimmy sound-alike strumming on the back porch. Bar-wise, you have three options. *The Volcano* erupts (we're not kidding) margaritas; the *Land Shark* has fins swimming around the ceiling; and the *12 Volt,* is, well, a little electrifying. The menu screams Key West. It includes cheeseburgers in paradise, mahi-mahi, and Key lime pie. See Chapter 14 for more on the vittles. *Margaritaville* is open from 11:30 a.m. to 2 a.m., and there's a $3.25 cover after 10 p.m.

Guessing the focus of a place that has a one-page food menu and a booklet filled with drinks doesn't take a genius. Just like the French Quarter's version, drinking is the highlight at *Pat O'Brien's* (☎ 407-224-2122). You can enjoy dueling pianos and a flame-throwing fountain while you suck down the signature drink — the Hurricane. No one under 21 is permitted after 7 p.m. *Pat O' Brien's* offers a limited menu of sandwiches, snacks, and treats like jambalaya and shrimp Creole. A meal will set you back $6 to $10. Hours are 4 p.m. to 2 a.m., and there's a $2 cover charge after 9 p.m.

Saying Goodbye to Church Street Station

The success of Orlando's first nightspot, **Church Street Station,** prompted **Disney** and **Universal** to enter the night games. Unfortunately, it may have worked too well as an inspiration. A downtown nightlife-and-dining cornerstone since 1974, the complex closed in spring 2001 following years of sagging attendance. Blame it on **Disney** and **Universal,** which have recently captured much of the nighttime entertainment market with the opening of **Pleasure Island, Downtown Disney West Side,** and CityWalk. Those new, multiclub venues left Church Street as a novelty act for those with the wheels and an inclination to drive 15 to 20 miles (or more) north of the parks and their resorts.

New owners have taken over Church Street, promising a rebirth, though there are few details available on future plans, and the first stage of that rebirth had the distinct sounds of a death rattle. Most of the major clubs were shut down permanently.

Downtown Orlando Nightlife

8 Seconds **2**

Cairo **6**

Cheyenne Saloon and Opera House **4**

Four Points By Sheraton
  Orlando Downtown **8**

Globe Café **7**

Harold & Maude's Espresso Bar **7**

Howl at the Moon Saloon **5**

Kit Kat Club **7**

Sak Comedy Lab **1**

Sapphire Supper Club **3**

Radisson Plaza Hotel Orlando **9**

Veranda Bed & Breakfast **10**

For now, the only headliner that remains open is the *Cheyenne Saloon and Opera House,* a tri-level, balconied saloon crowned by a lofty stained-glass skylight and constructed of golden oak lumber from a century-old Ohio barn. There's a Western theme throughout, including many oil paintings and 11 Remington sculptures. The Cheyenne's show features a country-western band, and well-known artists occasionally drop by to join in. If you know how to line dance or do the two-step, you'll love this place. If not, you can always take advantage of the slow songs. Balcony seating, in restored church pews, overlooks the stage — the setting for entertainment ranging from country bands to clogging exhibitions — and the dance floor.

The *Cheyenne Saloon and Opera House* is located at 129 W. Church St. (☎ **407-422-2434;** Internet: www.churchstreetstation.com). Admission is free. The club opens nightly at 5 p.m. and the first show is at 7:30 p.m. Metered parking is $1-an-hour, or you can use valet parking for $7. Take I-4 east to Exit 39/Anderson Street, stay in the left lane, and follow the signs. The saloon is located between Garland and Orange avenues in downtown Orlando.

Locating the Best Hotel Lounges

Some of Orlando's best nightlife is located in its hotels. Even the locals head to the resort areas for fun after dark. If you're staying at one of the places listed here, you can do an evening on the town without ever getting behind the wheel. None of the following charges a cover.

Mizner's at **Disney's Grand Floridian Resort & Spa** has an orchestra until 1 a.m. and an elegant library look; *Narcoossee's* in the same hotel offers Victorian décor and beer by the yard or half-yard. *Outer Rim* in the Contemporary Resort is trendy and close to the monorail. *Kimono's* in the **Walt Disney World Swan** becomes a karaoke bar after 8:30 p.m. *Copa Banana* in the **Walt Disney World Dolphin** has a DJ, dancing, and karaoke. Call ☎ **407-934-7639** for any of these.

The *Laughing Kookaburra Good Time Bar* in the **Wyndham Palace,** Lake Buena Vista (☎ **407-827-3722**), is open 7 p.m. to 2 a.m. with live music and a DJ most nights. The piano bar in the *Arthur's 27* in the Wyndham Palace (☎ **800-327-2990** or 407-827-2727) has a great view of Disney fireworks. *Baskerville's* in the **Grosvenor Resort Hotel,** Lake Buena Vista (☎ **407-827-6500**), has jazz nights Wednesday through Friday, 7 to 9 p.m., and a solve-it-yourself mystery show on Saturday, 6 and 9 p.m. The *Lobby Bar* at **The Peabody Orlando (☎ 407-352-4000)** is a popular gathering spot with piano music.

Exploring Orlando's Other Hot Spots

Orlando offers many other hot spots where you can enjoy the nightlife. Here's our list of favorites:

- ✔ **Cairo.** 22 S. Magnolia Ave. (One block off Orange Avenue.) One of the newer arrivals downtown, this popular club has bars on three levels. You can find lots of '70s retro clothes and kids trying to look older than their age. Reggae plays on the rooftop during the weekends. The club also offers ladies' and Latin nights. (☎ **407-422-3595;** Internet: www.cairo-nightclub.com. Open 10 p.m. to 3 a.m. Friday through Sunday, $6 and up cover charge. Street parking available.)

- ✔ **Cricketers Arms Pub.** 8445 International Drive (in the Mercado shopping plaza). Regardless of whether you're British or just a sympathizer, this pub is a fun place to party. The barkeep sells 17 import brands such as Boddingtons, Fullers ESB, and Old Speckled

Hen (☎ **407-354-0686**; Internet: www.cricketersarmspub.com. No cover for music; $10 when soccer's on the telly. Daily 11 a.m. to 2 a.m. Free parking.)

✔ **8 Seconds.** 100 W. Livingston Ave., Orlando. This honky-tonk has a cavernous interior and a huge dance floor where you can get free line-dancing lessons early in the evening. If you go, take the side trip to the parking lot on "Buckin' Bull Nights," when cowboys provide some extra entertainment in the ring. You can also find monster-truck pulls in the back lot. Country stars sometimes perform outside the ring. (Open 7 p.m. Friday to Saturday, $5 cover, 21 and older; $7 under 21. Parking in city lot $3. ☎ **407-839-4800**; Internet: www.8-seconds.com; $5 cover for 21 and older, $7 for 18 to 21; 8 p.m. to 2 a.m. Friday through Saturday; city lot parking $3.)

✔ **Howl at the Moon Saloon.** 55 W. Church Street. This is a fun bar that's open 6 p.m. to 2 a.m. daily. Your best bet: Go on a full moon — even if you're too shy to cock your head back and *howlllll* with the best. (☎ **407-841-9118**; Internet: www.howlatthemoon.com. $2 to $4 cover, Wednesday through Saturday)

✔ **Kit Kat Club/Globe Café/Harold & Maude's Espresso Bar.** 17-27 Wall Street Plaza (off Orange Avenue), Orlando. This three-for-one hotspot includes a billiards/cigar bar with live music (*Kit Kat,* ☎ **407-422-6990**); an Irish (and other) coffee and sandwich bar (*Harold & Maude's,* ☎ **407-422-3322**); and a small, urban eatery (*Globe Café,* ☎ **407-422-1669**).

✔ **Sak Comedy Lab.** 380 W. Amelia St., Orlando. Locals perform at this 200-seat club that has 8 to 10 performances weekly (usually Tuesday through Saturday). Favorites include Duel of Fools, where two teams face off in improvised scenes based on suggestions from the audience, and Lab Rats, where students play in improv formats. (☎ **407-648-0001**; Internet: www.sak.com. Admission is $8 to $12. Shows usually are at 8 and 10 p.m., plus midnight on Saturdays. Parking in metered lots usually runs about $1 an hour.)

✔ **Sapphire Supper Club.** 54 N. Orange Ave., Orlando. Some major-league acts perform at this downtown venue, including jazz legend and used-to-be-Orlando resident Sam Rivers. This joint is cool and jazzy, offering cigar and martini nights that young professionals and music lovers of every age dig. (☎ **407-246-1419**; Internet: www.sapphiresupperclub.com.) **Cover prices vary.**

Chapter 29

Dinner Shows and the Orlando Theater Scene

• •

In This Chapter

▶ Uncovering the truth about Orlando dinner shows

▶ Seeing the best shows

▶ Getting tickets

• •

*I*f a day at the theme parks isn't enough to satisfy your appetite for entertainment, Orlando's dinner-theater circuit serves up a diverse menu of amusements that will keep you entertained as you chow down. Solve a "murder," learn to hula, or cheer on a knight at a medieval joust. These other shows have been pretty popular over the last ten years or so, but, like everything else, there's a saturation point. During the last year, three entries have gone belly-up. The victims: *Blazing Pianos, Wild Bill's Wild West Dinner Extravaganza,* and (off with his head) *King Henry's Feast.*

Finding Out the Inside Scoop

Disney and Orlando have a reasonably busy dinner-show scene, but their offerings aren't like what you'll find in such high-flying cultural centers as Paris, New York, and London. Shows at Disney and in Orlando offer fun, not critically acclaimed drama. Most focus on entertaining the number one VIP: Kids. Therefore, in many instances, theater in Orlando is a little like eating in front of the television set.

Eating adds its own element of adventure to Orlando's dinner theater experience. Dinner-show fare, especially outside **Disney,** is right off the rubber-chicken circuit. Food at dinner-show theaters usually consists of a choice of two or three entrées (often overcooked) and school-lunch caliber side dishes. Your choice of food may explain why some theaters serve free wine and beer — to dull your palate — after you're seated, and before dinner is served.

The prices of the shows that we list in this chapter include food and pedestrian drinks, but not tax or tips.

Now Playing

In addition to the shows listed below, in 2001, Dolly Parton plans to open a **Dixie Stampede & Dinner Show** like those she already operates in Pigeon Forge, Tenn., Branson, Mo., and Myrtle Beach, S.C. That means 32 horses starring in a show that has plenty of riding, roping, wagon racing, and a friendly North–South rivalry that puts the audience on opposite sides of the Mason–Dixon line. The $20-million attraction will have 1,000 seats and won't serve alcohol. It will be located on Interstate 4, between **Walt Disney World** and **Universal Orlando.** An earlier location failed to get local approval, delaying construction.

Arabian Nights

If you're a horse fan, this show is a winner. It stars chiseled Arabians with a supporting cast of Belgians, Andalusians, and a Lipizzan. Many locals rate this the number one show in Orlando. On most nights the show opens with a ground trainer working one-on-one with a black stallion. The continuous action includes Wild West trick riders, the bareback daring of Ricky Suarez, and a thrilling chariot race. The meal, served during the two-hour show, includes salad, prime rib or vegetable lasagna, vegetables, rolls, dessert, sodas, and wine. You can meet and pet the stars after the show.

6225 W. Irlo Bronson Memorial Hwy. (U.S. 192, east of I-4 at Exit 25A). ☎ **800-553-6116** *or 407-239-9223. Internet:* www.arabian-nights.com. *Reservations recommended. Shows held daily, times vary. Admission: $37 adults, $24 kids 3–11. Free parking.*

Hoop-Dee-Doo Musical Revue

This is **Disney's** most popular show, so make your reservations early. Feast on a down-home, all-you-can-eat barbecue (country-fried chicken, smoked ribs, salad, corn on the cob, baked beans, baked bread, strawberry shortcake, and coffee, tea, beer, sangria, or soda). While you stuff yourself silly in Pioneer Hall, performers in 1890s garb lead you in a foot-stomping, hand-clapping, high-energy show that includes a lot of jokes you haven't heard since second grade. If you catch an early show, go to the *Electrical Water Pageant* at 9:45 p.m., which you can view from the Fort Wilderness Beach.

Be prepared to join in the fun, or the singers and the rest of the audience will humiliate you.

3520 N. Fort Wilderness Trail (at WDW's Fort Wilderness Resort and Campground).
☎ *407-939-3563. Internet:* www.disneyworld.com. *Reservations required. Shows:*
5:00, 7:15, and 9:30 p.m. Admission: Adults $46.33 kids 3–11 $23.78 including tax and
gratuity. Free self-parking.

Medieval Times

This is the Orlando branch of the restaurant that Jim Carrey visited in
the movie, *The Cable Guy*. Pig out on barbecued ribs, herb-roasted
chicken, soup, appetizers, potatoes, dessert, and a beverage. But
because this is the 11th century, you eat with your fingers from plates
while mounted knights run around the arena, jousting to please the fair
ladies. Arrive early and take a look at Medieval Village, a re-created
Middle Ages settlement.

4510 W. Irlo Bronson Memorial Hwy. (U.S. Hwy. 192, 11 miles east of the main
Disney entrance, next to Wal-Mart.) ☎ **800-229-8300** *or 407-396-1518. Internet:*
www.medievaltimes.com. *Reservations recommended. Performances nightly,*
times vary. Admission: $42 adults, $26 kids 3–12. Free parking.

MurderWatch Mystery Theatre.

Located in Baskervilles Restaurant, this all-you-can-eat buffet offers beef,
chicken, fish, and a children's buffet while diners try to solve the mystery. The restaurant, by the way, has a 19th-century décor and also
houses a Sherlock Holmes museum.

In the Grosvenor Resort at 1850 Hotel Plaza Blvd. (Turn west off Fla. 535 onto Hotel
Plaza Blvd.; it's close to Downtown Disney Marketplace.) ☎ **800-624-4109** *or*
407-827-6534, Internet: www.grosvenorresort.com. *Reservations recom-*
mended. Admission: $35 adults, $11 kids 3–11. Shows: Sat., 6 and 9 p.m. Free parking.

Pirates Dinner Adventure

The special effects at this show include a full-size ship in a 300,000-gallon
lagoon, circus-style aerial acts, music, and a little drama. Afterward,
you're invited to the Buccaneer Bash dance party. Dinner includes an
appetizer buffet with the pre-show, followed by chicken, beef, rice, vegetables, dessert, and coffee.

6400 Carrier Dr. (from Disney, take I-4 to Sand Lake Road, go east to International
Drive, then north to Carrier). ☎ **800-866-2469** *or 407-248-0590. Internet:*
www.orlandopirates.com. *Reservations recommended. Admission: $42 adults,*
$25.50 kids 3–11. Free parking. Shows: 7:45 p.m. nightly, doors open at 6:30.

Polynesian Luau Dinner Show

This delightful two-hour dinner show is a big favorite with kids, all of
whom are invited on the stage. It features a colorfully costumed cast of
hyperactive entertainers from New Zealand, Tahiti, Hawaii, and Samoa

performing hula, warrior, ceremonial, love, and fire dances on a flower-filled stage. The show takes place in an open-air theater (dress for night-time weather) with candlelit tables, red-flame lanterns meant to resemble torches, and tapa-bark paintings adorning the walls. Arrive early: There's a pre-show highlighting Polynesian crafts and culture (lei making, hula lessons, and more). The all-you-can-eat meal includes a big platter of fresh island fruits, roasted chicken and pork, corn, vegetables, red and sweet potatoes, pull-apart cinnamon bread, a tropical ice-cream sundae, and coffee, tea, beer, wine, or soda.

1600 Seven Seas Dr. (at Disney's Polynesian Resort). ☎ **407-939-3463**. *Internet:* www.disneyworld.com. *Reservations required. Shows: 5:15 and 8:00 p.m. daily. Admission: Adults $46.33, $23.782 kids 3–11 including tax and gratuity. Free parking.*

Getting Tickets

In some cases, you can make a reservation for dinner shows on the same day you want to attend. Sometimes, you can just walk up to the ticket window and buy a ticket (though we don't recommend it). However, in all but spur-of-the-moment cases, we recommend using the numbers in the listings in this chapter to book seats.

When it comes to **Walt Disney World** dinner shows, always make a Priority Seating reservation, ☎ **407-939-3463** (see Chapter 13). Disney's shows fill up fast, sometimes weeks in advance for weekend performances.

The Performing Arts Calendar and Getting Tickets

It may be known more for its theme parks and water rides, but Orlando is no Mickey Mouse town when it comes to high culture. The traditional arts don't stand much of a chance against Sleepy, Grumpy, and Dopey, but you can get a taste of high culture if you flee the parks and head to the city.

Concert halls and auditoriums

The city continues to dream of getting financing for a state-of-the-art performing arts center. Until that happens, there are two existing enter-tainment facilities, both of which fall under the umbrella of the *Orlando Centroplex.*

The *Florida Citrus Bowl* is a 70,000-seat venue used for concerts, which in the past have included such heavyweights as Elton John and the

Rolling Stones. It's at 1610 W. Church St. (☎ **407-849-2020** to get box office information, 407-839-3900 to charge tickets via TicketMaster; Internet: www.centroplex.com). Parking is $5.

TD Waterhouse Centre, formerly the Orlando Arena, has 17,500 seats and frequently hosts sporting events (the NBA's Orlando Magic and WNBA's Orlando Miracle play here) and big-name concert performers such as Garth Brooks, Elton John, and Bruce Springsteen. It also features family-oriented entertainment, including the Ringling Bros. Barnum & Bailey Circus every January and a slate of cultural offerings such as Broadway-style shows, ballets, plays, and symphony performances. It's located at 600 W. Amelia St. (☎ **407-849-2020** to get box office information, 407-839-3900 to charge tickets through TicketMaster; Internet: www.centroplex.com). Parking is $6.

Orlando's Official Visitors Center has a program called "OTIX!" that offers half-price tickets to 90 cultural activities, such as theater performances, the ballet, operas, and symphonies. But in most cases, tickets are for same-day performances. You can call ☎ **407-363-5872** for information, but you have to go to the center at 8723 International Drive (four blocks south of Lake Road) to get the tickets.

Theater

The *Orlando–UCF Shakespeare Festival's* spring shows herald Shakespeare at the **Walt Disney Amphitheatre** at Lake Eola Park in downtown Orlando. The festival's fall shows are staged indoors at the Marilyn and Sig Goldman Theater at 812 E. Rollins St. The company is known for placing traditional plays in contemporary settings and offers special programs throughout the year, such as *Shakespeare Unplugged,* a free reading series.

Tickets average $20 and sell pretty fast, so it's a good idea to call ahead for reservations. For more information, call ☎ **407-893-4600** or head online to www.shakespearefest.org. Parking is free during the outdoor season; there's metered parking in fall.

Opera

If you'd rather hear singing than see a play, the *Orlando Opera Company* is a local troupe with a repertoire of traditional fare that features guest artists from around the country. Standards include *Carmen, Macbeth,* and the *Marriage of Figaro.* Shows held during the October-to-May season are rarely sellouts. Tickets start at $15. Performances are staged at the Bob Carr Performing Arts Centre, 401 W. Livingston St. (☎ **800-336-7372** or 407-426-1700; Internet: www.orlandoopera.org). Parking is free.

Dance

The *Southern Ballet Theatre* stages traditional shows such as *The Nutcracker* with guest artists augmenting local talent. There has been a resurgence of interest in the ballet in recently, but performances rarely sell out. The season runs from October through May. Tickets start at around $15. Performances feature the Orlando Philharmonic Orchestra (see the "Classical Music" section that follows) and are at the Bob Carr Performing Arts Centre, 401 W. Livingston St. (☎ **407-426-1733** for information, 407-839-3900 to get tickets via TicketMaster; Internet: www.southernballet.org). Parking is free.

Classical Music

The *Orlando Philharmonic Orchestra* offers a varied schedule of classics and pop-influenced concerts throughout the year at the Bob Carr Performing Arts Centre. The musicians also accompany the Southern Ballet (see the preceding section on "Dance"). Tickets begin at $15. For more information, call ☎ **407-896-6700** or surf over to www.orlandophil.org. Parking is free.

Part VIII
The Part of Tens

The 5th Wave   By Rich Tennant

Tell them we work at one of the theme parks, and maybe they won't ask too many questions.

In this part . . .

Ah, tradition. The Part of Tens chapters are to Dummies books what hangovers are to New Year's Day — an integral part of the experience. In this part of the book, we feed you plenty of useful and fun information that we think is especially handy.

In the following chapters, we talk about some budget attractions that can stretch your dollars, tourist traps you should avoid (such as three-day-old seafood), and some fun ways to keep active when you're not at the theme parks.

Chapter 30

Top Ten Cheap Alternatives to the Parks

● ●

In This Chapter

▶ Spending some time at a museum

▶ Strolling through a "real" park

▶ Taking a leisurely boat tour

● ●

*I*n this chapter, we give you suggestions for great places to dodge crowds and save a few bucks while everyone else is emptying their wallets in the theme parks around Orlando.

Central Florida Zoological Park

The 400 critters that live in this 21-acre zoo include wreathed hornbills, kookaburras, bald eagles, mandrills, siamangs, black howler monkeys, Asian elephants, two-toed sloths, clouded leopards, cheetahs, caracals, and American crocodiles. The headliner is a lovable hippopotamus named Geraldine.

The park is located at 3755 N. U.S. 17/92 (in Sanford). Call ☎ **407-323-4450** for more information or visit www.centralfloridazoo.org on the Web. Admission is $7 for adults, $4 for seniors 60 and over, and $3 for kids 3 to 12. (Guests enter for half price every Thursday before 10 a.m., and seniors visit for half price every Tuesday.) The park is open daily 9 a.m. to 5 p.m.

Charles Hosmer Morse Museum of American Art

Although it's not a New York-quality house, this museum has a big collection of Louis Tiffany glass, created for the 1893 Colombian Expo in Chicago. The collection was expanded in 1999 when it moved to the

800-square-foot Tiffany Chapel in the Charles Hosmer Museum. A huge electrified chandelier and six stained-glass windows from that exposition are on display.

You can find the museum at 445 Park Avenue N., Winter Park. (Take the I-4 Fairbanks Avenue exit east to Park Avenue, go left and through four traffic lights.) Call ☎ 407-645-5311 or 407-645-5324 (a telephone recording) for more details, or check the museum's site on the Web at www.inusa.com/tour/fl/orlando/morse.htm. Admission is $3 for adults, $1 for students, and kids under 12 get in free. The museum is open Tuesday through Saturday 9:30 a.m. to 4:00 p.m. and Sunday 1 to 4 p.m.

Cornell Fine Arts Museum

This showplace has 6,000 works on display, making it one of Florida's most distinguished and comprehensive art collections. The museum also conducts lectures and gallery-talk walks.

The museum is located at the east end of Holt Avenue on the Rollins College campus in Winter Park. (Take I-4 Exit 45/Fairbanks Avenue east to Park, turn right, then left on Holt.) Call ☎ 407-646-2526 or visit www.rollins.edu/cfam for more information. Admission is free, and the museum is open Tuesday through Friday, 10 a.m. to 5 p.m., and Saturday and Sunday from 1 to 5 p.m.

Eatonville and the Zora Neale Hurston National Museum of Fine Arts

America's oldest black municipality is located just north of Orlando. Eatonville is the birthplace of Hurston — a too-little heralded, African-American author. The city hosts an annual festival in January honoring her and her work. A small gallery on the site displays periodically changing exhibits of art and other work, and you can grab a map for a walking tour of the community, established in 1887. *Make sure to call in advance to confirm the museum's business hours.*

The museum is at 227 E. Kennedy Boulevard, Eatonville. (Take I-4 to Exit 46 and make a quick left onto Lee Road, then left on Wymore, and then right on Kennedy. It's one-quarter mile down the road on the left.) Call ☎ 407-647-3307 or visit www.cs.ucf.edu/~zora for more information. The museum, which accepts donations as admission, is open Monday through Friday 9 a.m. to 4 p.m.

Farmers Market

Farmers Market is a fun Saturday-morning breakfast or lunch excursion. Peddlers sell fruit, vegetables, bagels, cheese, coffee, and more in a friendly setting.

The market is located at New York Street at New England Avenue, Winter Park. (Take I-4 exit 45/Fairbanks east to New York, then left two blocks to the market.) Call ☎ **407-623-3200** for more information. Admission is free, and the market is open Saturdays from 7 a.m. to noon.

Florida Audubon Center for Birds of Prey

This bird sanctuary — one of the biggest rehabilitation centers in the Southeast — flies under the radar of most tourists, making it a great place to get to know the winged wonders (owls and eagles) that earn their keep by entertaining the few visitors who do visit. The center is closed while a new, state-of-the-art rehab center and permanent residence are being built, but it's scheduled to reopen in fall 2001, so make sure that you call ahead before visiting.

The center is at 1101 Audubon Way, Maitland. (Take I-4 to Lee Road/ Exit 46, turn right, at first light/Wymore Road, go left, then right at the next light/Kennedy Boulevard Continue one-half mile to East Ave., turn left, and go to the stop sign at Audubon Way. Turn left, and the center is on the right.) Call ☎ **407-644-0190** or visit www.adoptabird.org/ for more information. The center accepts donations: $5 adults, $3 children 3 to 12. Visitor hours are Tuesday through Sunday, 10 a.m. to 5 p.m.

Holocaust Memorial Resource and Education Center

Exhibits at this center illustrate pre-war Jewish communities in Europe, Hitler's rise to power, the concentration camps, and the lives of camp survivors. There's also a memorial wall made from stone imported from Jerusalem.

The center is at 851 N. Maitland Avenue, Maitland. (Take I-4 to Exit 47, go east through merge with Maitland Boulevard, right at first light onto Maitland Avenue. It's in the Jewish Community Center at Maitland Blvd. and Maitland Avenue.) Call ☎ **407-628-0555** or visit www.holocaustedu. org for more information. The center accepts donations as admission Monday through Thursday, 9 a.m. to 4 p.m. and Friday, 9 a.m. to 1 p.m. The center is also occasionally open Sundays. Call ahead to confirm.

Kissimmee Sports Arena & Rodeo

The Kissimmee Sports Arena & Rodeo is a good way to fill a Friday night dance card, and it's only 20 minutes from the major theme parks. Events include saddle bronc and bull riding, calf roping, and barrel racing.

The arena is located at 958 South Hoagland Boulevard, Kissimmee. (Take I-4 Exit 25A/U.S. 192 east to Hoagland, and then go south one mile to the arena.) Call ☎ **407-933-0020** or visit www.ksarodeo.com for more details. Admission is $15 for adults, $7.50 for children 12 and under The fun begins every Friday at 8 p.m.

Lake Eola Park

This quiet hideaway in downtown Orlando offers the city's skyline as a backdrop. The lake has a cascading fountain that features a 12-minute evening light show. The park has a .9-mile walking and jogging path, a playground, and paddleboats for rent ($7 per half hour). FunnyEola features comedy acts the second Tuesday of each month at 7:30 p.m. There are also a variety of other performances, most of which are free (call ahead for more details). The Shakespeare Festival (April to early May) costs $5 to $30 nightly. Call ☎ **407-893-4600** for more information about the festival.

The park is located at Washington Street and Rosalind Avenue, Orlando. (Take I-4 to Anderson Street, exit right, turn left at the fourth light/ Rosalind. The amphitheater is on the right.) Call ☎ **407-246-2827** for more information about the park. Admission is free, and the park is open daylight hours daily, sometimes later. Call the park before you visit to confirm business hours.

Lakeridge Winery & Vineyards

This working vineyard produces some of Florida's more noteworthy vintages. Tours include a look behind the scenes and a video presentation. Tastings offer a sample of three or more wines.

The winery is at 19239 U.S. 27, Clermont. (Take U.S. 192 west of the **WDW** parks to U.S. 27, turn right and go 20 miles north.) Call ☎ **800-768-9463** or 352-394-8627 for more information. Tours and tastings are offered 10 a.m. to5 p.m. Monday through Saturday, 11 a.m. to 5 p.m. Sunday. Admission is free.

The Peabody Ducks

One of the best shows in town is short, but sweet and free. The Peabody Orlando hotel's five mallards march into the lobby each morning, accompanied by John Philip Sousa's "King Cotton March" and their own red-coated duck master. They get to spend the day splashing in a marble fountain. Then, in the afternoon, they march back to the elevator and up to their fourth-floor "penthouse."

The Peabody Orlando is located at 9801 International Dr. (between the Bee Line Expressway and Sand Lake Road). Call ☎ **800-732-2639** or 407-352-4000 for more information. Admission is free, and the ducks march daily at 11 a.m. and 5 p.m.

Winter Park Scenic Boat Tour

This peaceful water voyage has been operating since 1938. The narrated, one-hour cruises showcase the area's beautiful lakes and canals, Rollins College, Kraft Azalea Gardens, and a number of historic mansions.

The boat tour launches from 312 E. Morse Boulevard, Winter Park. Call ☎ **407–644-4056** for additional information about the tour. Admission is $7 for adults and $3 for children under 12. The daily tours run every hour from 10 a.m. to 4 p.m.

Chapter 31

Top Ten Fitness Activities (Other than Walking the Parks)

· ·

In This Chapter

▶ Enjoying water-related activities

▶ Getting land-based exercise

· ·

*W*ant some exercise other than walking the parks? **Walt Disney World** and the surrounding areas offer plenty of jaunts to keep you busy. The majority of these activities are most convenient for guests of Disney resorts and official hotels, but many other large resorts also offer comprehensive facilities (see Chapter 8 for more details). The **WDW** facilities described in this chapter are open to the public, no matter where you're staying. For further information, call ☎ **407-939-7529.**

Bicycling

Bike rentals (single- and multispeed bikes for adults, tandems, and children's bikes) are available from the Bike Barn (☎ **407-824-2742**) at **Fort Wilderness Resort and Campground.** Fort Wilderness has extensive and well-kept bike trails. Rates run $6.60 per hour, $18.87 per day plus tax. You can also rent bicycles with training wheels and baby seats. Helmets are available at no additional charge.

Boating

Along with a ton of man-made lakes and lagoons, **WDW** owns a navy of pleasure boats. **Capt. Jack's** at **Downtown Disney** rents Water Sprites, canopy boats, and 20-foot pontoon boats ($20–$32 per half hour). For information call ☎ **407-828-2204.**

The **Bike Barn** at **Fort Wilderness** (☎ **407-824-2742**) rents canoes and paddleboats ($6.13 per half hour, $10.38 per hour).

Fishing

Disney offers a variety of fishing excursions on the various Disney lakes, including Bay Lake and Seven Seas Lagoon. The lakes are stocked, so you may catch something, but true anglers probably won't find it much of a challenge. The excursions can be arranged 2 to 90 days in advance by calling ☎ **407-824-2621**. A license isn't required. The fee is $160–$185 for up to five people for two hours, including refreshments, gear, guide, and tax. Bait costs extra.

Here's a less-expensive alternative: Rent fishing poles at the **Bike Barn** (☎ **407-824-2742**) to fish in the **Fort Wilderness** canals. A license isn't necessary.

Golf

Walt Disney World operates five 18-hole, par-72 golf courses and one 9-hole, par-36 walking course. All are open to the public and offer pro shops, equipment rentals, and instruction. The rates are $100–$145 per 18-hole round for resort guests ($5 more if you're not staying at a **WDW** property). For tee times and information, call ☎ **407-824-2270** up to seven days in advance (up to 30 days for Disney-resort and official-property guests). Call ☎ **407-934-7639** for information about golf packages.

Beyond Mickey's shadow, **Golfpac** (☎ **800-327-0878** or 407-260-2288; Internet: www.golfpacinc.com) is an organization that packages golf vacations with accommodations and other features and prearranges tee times at more than 40 Orlando-area courses. The earlier you call (months, if possible), the better your options. **Tee Times USA** (☎ **800-465-3356**; Internet: www.teetimesusa.com) and **Florida Golfing** (☎ **866-833-2663**; Internet: www.floridagolfing.com) are two other companies that couple course and package information with a reservations service.

Hayrides

A wagon departs **Pioneer Hall** at Disney's **Fort Wilderness** nightly at 7 and 9:30 p.m. for 45-minute, old-fashioned hayrides featuring singing, jokes, and games. The cost is $6 for adults, $4 for children ages 3–10. An adult must accompany children under 12. No reservations; it's first-come, first-served. Call ☎ **407-824-2832** to get more information.

Horseback Riding

Disney's Fort Wilderness Resort and Campground offers 45-minute scenic guided-tour trail rides six times a day. The cost is $23 per person. Children must be at least 9 years old, and there's a maximum weight limit of 250 pounds. For information and reservations up to 30 days in advance, call ☎ **407-824-2832**.

The **Villas of Grand Cypress** opens its equestrian center to outsiders. You can go on a 45-minute, walk-trot trail ride (four times daily) for $45. A 30-minute private lesson is $55; an hour lesson is $100. Call ☎ **407-239-4700** and ask for the equestrian center.

Jogging

Many Disney resorts have scenic jogging trails. For instance, the **Yacht** and **Beach Club** resorts share a 2-mile trail; the **Caribbean Beach Resort's** 1.4-mile promenade circles a lake; **Dixie Landings** has a 1.7-mile riverfront trail, and **Fort Wilderness's** tree-shaded 2.3-mile jogging path has exercise stations about every quarter mile. Pick up a jogging trail map at any Disney property's *Guest Services Desk*.

Swimming

The **YMCA Aquatic Center** offers a full-fitness center, racquetball courts, and an indoor Olympic-size pool. Admission is $10 per person, $25 for families. For information call ☎ **407-363-1911**. The center is located at 8422 International Dr. (Take I-4 to Exit 29. Turn right at the end of the ramp. Turn right on International Drive. Turn right at second light.)

Tennis

Twenty-two lighted tennis courts are scattered throughout the Disney properties. Most are free and available on a first-come, first-served basis. If you're willing to pay, courts can be reserved up to several months in advance at two Disney resorts: the **Contemporary** and **Grand Floridian**. Both charge $15 per hour and also offer lesson times with the resident pros. Call ☎ **407-824-2270** to reserve court time at either resort. The **Contemporary** also offers a large pro shop, a ball machine, rebound walls, and equipment rentals.

Waterskiing

Call ☎ **407-824-2621** to arrange water-skiing trips (including boats, drivers, equipment, and instruction) at **Walt Disney World.** Make reservations up to 14 days in advance. The cost is $125 per hour for up to five people.

You can also get some time behind a boat at **Ski World** near downtown Orlando. Lessons are $35 per 20 minutes of water time. For information, call ☎ **407-894-5012**. To get there, take I-4 to downtown, then Exit 43, Princeton Street. Turn right at the bottom of the ramp. Turn right at the first light. It's about a mile on your left. The lake will be on your right.

Appendix

Quick Concierge

• •

*T*his handy section is where we've condensed the practical and
pertinent information — from airline phone numbers to mailbox
locations — you'll need to have a successful and stress-free Orlando
vacation. And, for those of you who believe in being really prepared,
we give you some additional resources to check out.

Orlando A to Z: Facts at Your Fingertips

AAA

American Automobile Association members
can contact their local offices for maps and
optimum driving directions or call ☎ 800-
222-4357 and ask to be transferred to the
office nearest you. Online, you can find information at www.aaa.com.

American Express

You can call ☎ 800-297-3429 or go to its Web
site at www.americanexpress.com/
travel to reach the card company's Travel
Service offices nationally. In Orlando, call
☎ 407-843-0004. American Express is the
official card of **Walt Disney World**; it has
windows at each of the four WDW theme
parks (see Chapters 17–20 for locations).

ATMs

Machines honoring Cirrus, Honor, Plus, and
other systems are common in all of Orlando's
theme parks (see Chapters 17–20 and 23–25
for locations). They're also at many banks,
shopping centers, and convenience stores
(see Chapter 3).

Babysitters

Many family-friendly accommodations have
some kind of sitting services, and several
have on-premise child-care facilities with
counselor-supervised activity programs.
Disney uses **KinderCare** sitters (see Chapter 4); ☎ 407-827-5444.

Camera Repair

Southern Photo (☎ 407-896-0322), in the
downtown area, is one of the best in central
Florida. Closer to the parks, try **Photo Time**
(☎ 407-352-1818) on International Drive.

Convention Center

The **Orange County Convention Center** (9800
International Drive; ☎ 407-345-5800) almost
always has something going on, and some
events are open to the public. The **Disney**
resorts, as well as some other hotels, provide
rides there for a fee. You can also use **Mears
Transportation** (☎ 407-422-4561). Once
there, you can ride around the neighborhood
on the **I-Ride Trolley** (☎ 407-354-5656;
Internet: www.iridetrolley.com). It

runs about every 15 minutes, 7 a.m. to midnight (75 cents for adults, 25 cents for seniors, and kids under 12 are free) on International Drive and is a good way to avoid the heavy traffic facing I-Drive motorists.

Credit Cards

Disney accepts American Express, Diners Club, Discover, MasterCard, VISA, and the Disney Card in all of its parks and most of the other venues. The list of cards accepted is larger in other places. (See Chapter 3 for general information.)

Customs

Every visitor 21 years of age or older may bring in to the United States, free of duty, the following: one liter of wine or liquor; 200 cigarettes or 100 cigars (but no cigars from Cuba) or 3 pounds of smoking tobacco, and $100 worth of gifts. These exemptions are offered to travelers who spend at least 72 hours in the United States and who haven't claimed the same exemptions within the preceding 6 months. You can't bring food (particularly cheese, fruit, cooked meats, and canned goods) and plants (vegetables, seeds, tropical plants, and so on) into the country. Foreign tourists may bring in or take out up to $10,000 in U.S. or foreign currency with no formalities; you must declare larger sums to Customs upon leaving.

Doctors and Dentists

There are basic first-aid centers in all of the major parks. If you need to see a doctor while you're in Orlando, you can get a reputable referral from **Ask-A-Nurse.** They'll ask whether you have insurance, but that's for information purposes only, so they can track who uses the system. It's a free service open to everyone. In Kissimmee call ☎ 407-870-1700; in Orlando call ☎ 407-897-1700. There's also a 24-hour, toll-free number for the **Poison Control Center,** ☎ 800-282-3171.

Disney offers in-room medical service 24 hours a day by calling ☎ 407-238-2000.

Doctors on Call Service, ☎ 407-399-3627, is a group that makes house and room calls in most of the Orlando area. **Centra-Care** has several walk-in clinics listed in the Yellow Pages, including ones on International Drive, ☎ 407-370-4881, and at Lake Buena Vista near Disney, ☎ 407-934-2273.

To find a dentist, call **Dental Referral Service,** ☎ 888-343-3440 (Internet: www.dentalreferral.com). Folks there can tell you the nearest dentist who meets your needs. Phones are staffed weekdays from 8 a.m. to 8 p.m. Check the Yellow Pages for 24-hour emergency services.

Emergencies

All of Florida uses ☎ **911** as the emergency number for police, fire departments, ambulances, and other critical needs. For less urgent requests, call ☎ 800-647-9284, a number sponsored by the **Florida Tourism Industry Marketing Corporation,** the state tourism promotion board. With operators speaking more than 100 languages, this service can provide general directions and help with lost travel papers and credit cards, medical emergencies, accidents, money transfers, airline confirmation, and much more.

Hospitals

Sand Lake Hospital, 9400 Turkey Lake Road (☎ 407-351-8550), is about 2 miles south of Sand Lake Road. From the WDW area, take I-4 east to Exit 29, turn left at the exit onto Sand Lake Road, and make a left on Turkey Lake Road. The hospital is 2 miles up on your right. **Celebration Health** (☎ 407-303-4000), located in the Disney-owned town of Celebration, is at 400 Celebration Place. From I-4, take Exit 25A. At the first traffic light, turn right onto Celebration Avenue. At the first stop sign, take another right.

Information

To receive local telephone information, call ☎ **411**. The other most common sources of information are **Walt Disney World,** Box 10000, Lake Buena Vista, FL 32830-1000 (☎ 407-934-7639; Internet: www.disney world.com, and the **Orlando/Orange County Convention & Visitors Bureau,** 8723 International Drive, Suite 101, Orlando, FL 32819 (☎ 407-363-5872; Internet: www.orlandoinfo.com).

Internet Access and Cyber Cafés

Have a laptop? To check your e-mail, all you need is a dataport, e-mail address, or free-mail account. You have to pay local and long-distance charges (expect up to 95 cents a minute, plus the $7 connection fee). Some places, such as the **Marriott Orlando World Center** and **Celebration Hotel** (see Chapter 8), offer a flat 24-hour fee (usually about $10). The **Peabody Hotel** has a slightly different rate to connect to your e-mail via dataport. The fee is 75 cents for the first minute and 10 cents for each additional minute. Some hotels without in-room connections have business centers where you can connect for an hourly fee. If you don't see a note about cost in Chapter 8, ask before booking your room.

If you already have a primary e-mail account, you can set your browser to forward mail to your free e-mail account while you're away.

Liquor Laws

Florida's liquor laws are pretty straightforward. You must be 21 to buy or consume alcohol. Some places that serve liquor allow you to enter if you're under 21, but most won't let you sit at the bar.

Mail

If you want to receive mail on your vacation and you aren't sure of your address, you can have your mail sent to you, in your name, in care of General Delivery at the main post office of the city or region where you expect to stay. **Orlando's main post office** (☎ 800-275-8777) is located at 1040 Post Office Boulevard. **Lake Buena Vista's main post office** (☎ 800-275-8777) is at 12133 S.

Apopka-Vineland Rd. You must pick up your mail in person and produce proof of identity (driver's license, passport, and so on).

Maps

AAA (see "AAA," earlier in this appendix) and other auto clubs usually provide maps for members. You can also find them in bookstores and libraries in your hometown and can buy them locally in most convenience stores.

Newspapers/Magazines

Check out the Sunday travel section in your hometown paper (or the one in the biggest city nearby) for bargains, ideas, and tips. After you land in O-Town, you can find a lot of bargains in the *Orlando Sentinel* (online, check out www.orlandosentinel.com) throughout the week. The paper's Friday **Calendar** section is a literal gold mine for current information on the area's accommodations, restaurant, nightclub, and attractions front.

Pharmacies

Walgreens drugstore, 1003 West Vine St. (Hwy. 192), just east of Bermuda Ave. (☎ 407-847-5252), operates a 24-hour pharmacy. There's also an **Eckerd** drugstore at 7324 International Dr. (☎ 407-345-0491) and 1205 West Vine (☎ 407-847-5174) that's open 24 hours a day.

Police

In any emergency, call ☎ **911.** If you have a cellular phone and need help, dial ☎ ***FHP** for the **Florida Highway Patrol.** Otherwise, call the Orlando police nonemergency line at ☎ 407-246-2414 or the **Orange County Sheriff's Office** at ☎ 407-532-5298 or 737-2400.

Rest Rooms

Foreign visitors often complain that public toilets are hard to find, but Orlando isn't any worse than most U.S. cities. True, there aren't any public rest rooms on the streets, but you can usually find one in a bar, restaurant, hotel, museum, department store, convenience store, attraction, fast food barn, or service station — and it'll probably be clean. In particular, Mobil service stations have made a public pledge to provide spic-and-span bathrooms, most decorated with homey touches. Note, however, that restaurants and bars in resorts or heavily visited areas may reserve their rest rooms for the use of their patrons. To qualify as a patron, pay for a cup of coffee or a soft drink, and you'll avoid arguments. Within the theme parks, rest rooms are clearly marked on the park maps. Don't panic if you see that the flushing handle is missing. Many new toilets are installed with lasers that trigger the flush automatically when you leave the stall.

Safety

Don't let the aura of Mickey Mouse allow you to lower your guard. Orlando has a crime rate that's comparable to other major U.S. cities. Stay alert and remain aware of your immediate surroundings. Keeping your valuables in a safe-deposit box (inquire at your hotel's front desk) is a good idea, although nowadays many hotels are equipped with in-room safes. Keep a close eye on your valuables when you're in a public place, such as a restaurant, theater, or even an airport terminal. Renting a locker is always preferable to leaving your valuables in the trunk of your car, even in the theme park lots. Be cautious and avoid carrying large amounts of cash in a backpack or fanny pack, which thieves can easily access while you're standing in line for a ride or show. If you're renting a car, carefully read the safety instructions that the rental company provides. Never stop in a dark area, and remember that children should never ride in the front seat of a car equipped with air bags.

Smoking

If you smoke, you most likely know to expect a diminishing playground. Restaurant space and hotel rooms for smokers are evaporating. The Wizard of Diz not only cut space and stopped selling tobacco years ago, but it has also started establishing precious few "you can smoke here" areas in the outside world. Light 'em while and where you can.

Special Diets

Some local restaurants will arrange for special meals, including kosher, if you call in advance. **Disney** (☎ 407-939-3463) does a good job at this.

Taxes

Expect to add 11 or 12 percent to room rates and 6 to 7 percent on most everything else — except groceries and health supplies or medical services.

Taxis

Yellow Cab (☎ 407-699-9999) and **Ace Metro** (☎ 407-855-0564) are among those cabs serving the area. But for day-to-day travel, cabs are expensive unless your group has five or more people. Rates are $2.50 for the first mile, $1.50 per mile thereafter.

Telephone

Local calls within the 407 area code require **10-digit dialing**, even if you're trying to get the store right across the street. You must dial 407 plus the local number. If you're making a long-distance call, it's just like anywhere else in the United States: dial 1 (or 0 for an operator-assisted call), followed by the area code and seven-digit number.

Time Zone

Orlando is on eastern standard time from late fall until mid-spring, and on eastern daylight time (one hour later) the rest of the year. That means, when both of Mickey's gloved hands are on 12 noon in Orlando, it's 7 a.m. in Honolulu, 8 a.m. in Anchorage, 9 a.m. in Vancouver and Los Angeles, 11 a.m. in Winnipeg and New Orleans, and 6 p.m. in London.

Transit Info

Lynx (☎ 407-841-2279; Internet: www. golynx.com) bus stops are marked with a paw print. The buses serve **Disney, Universal,** and **International Drive** ($1 for adults, 25 cents for kids and seniors; $10 for an unlimited weekly pass), but they're not very tourist-oriented.

Weather

Call ☎ 321-255-0212 to get forecasts from the **National Weather Service.** When the phone picks up, punch in **412** from a touch-tone phone, and you'll get the Orlando forecast. Also check with **The Weather Channel** if you have cable television or go to its Web site, www.weather.com.

Toll-Free Numbers & Web Sites

Airlines

Aer Lingus
☎ 800-474-7424 in the U.S.
☎ 01-886-8888 in Ireland
www.aerlingus.com

Air Canada
☎ 888-247-2262
www.aircanada.ca

Air New Zealand
☎ 800-262-2468 in the U.S.
☎ 800-663-5494 in Canada
☎ 0800-737-767 in New Zealand
www.airnewzealand.co.com

Alaska Airlines
☎ 800-426-0333
www.alaskaair.com

America West Airlines
☎ 800-235-9292
www.americawest.com

American Airlines
☎ 800-433-7300
www.im.aa.com

British Airways
☎ 800-247-9297
☎ 0345-222-111 in Britain
www.british-airways.com

Canadian Airlines International
☎ 800-426-7000
www.cdair.ca

Continental Airlines
☎ 800-525-0280
www.continental.com

Delta Air Lines
☎ 800-221-1212
www.delta.com

Hawaiian Airlines
☎ 800-367-5320
www.hawaiianair.com

Midway Airlines
☎ 800-446-4392
www.midwayair.com

Northwest Airlines
☎ 800-225-2525
www.nwa.com

Qantas
☎ 800-474-7424 in the U.S.
☎ 612-9691-3636 in Australia
www.qantas.com

Southwest Airlines
☎ 800-435-9792
www.southwest.com

Spirit Air
☎ 800-772-7117
www.spiritair.com

Trans World Airlines (TWA)
☎ 800-221-2000
www.twa.com

United Airlines
☎ 800-241-6522
www.ual.com

USAirways
☎ 800-428-4322
www.usairways.com

Virgin Atlantic Airways
☎ 800-862-8621 in the Continental U.S.
☎ 0293-747-747 in Britain
www.virgin-atlantic.com

Car-van-truck-rental agencies

Advantage
☎ 800-777-5500
www.arac.com

Alamo
☎ 800-327-9633
www.goalamo.com

Avis
☎ 800-331-1212 in the Continental U.S.
☎ 800-879-3847 in Canada
www.avis.com

Budget
☎ 800-527-0700
www.budgetrentacar.com

Dollar
☎ 800-800-4000
www.dollar.com

Enterprise
☎ 800-325-8007
www.enterprise.com

Hertz
☎ 800-654-3131
www.hertz.com

National
☎ 800-227-7368
www.nationalcar.com

Payless
☎ 800-729-5377
www.paylesscarrental.com

Rent-A-Wreck
☎ 800-535-1391
www.rentawreck.com

Thrifty
☎ 800-367-2277
www.thrifty.com

Major hotel and motel chains

Best Western International
☎ 800-528-1234
www.bestwestern.com

Clarion Hotels
☎ 800-252-7466
www.hotelchoice.com

Comfort Inns
☎ 800-228-5150
www.hotelchoice.com

Courtyard by Marriott
☎ 800-321-2211
www.courtyard.com

Days Inn
☎ 800-325-2525
www.daysinn.com

Doubletree Hotels
☎ 800-222-8733
www.doubletree.com

Econo Lodges
☎ 800-553-2666
www.hotelchoice.com

Fairfield Inn by Marriott
☎ 800-228-2800
www.fairfieldinn.com

Hampton Inn
☎ 800-426-7866
www.hampton-inn.com

Hilton Hotels
☎ 800-445-8667
www.hilton.com

Holiday Inn
☎ 800-465-4329
www.basshotels.com

Howard Johnson
☎ 800-654-2000
www.hojo.com/hojo.html

Hyatt Hotels & Resorts
☎ 800-228-9000
www.hyatt.com

ITT Sheraton
☎ 800-325-3535
www.sheraton.com

Knights Inn
☎ 800-843-5644
www.knightsinn.com

La Quinta Motor Inns
☎ 800-531-5900
www.laquinta.com

Marriott Hotels
☎ 800-228-9290
www.marriott.com

Motel 6
☎ 800-466-8536
www.motel6.com

Quality Inns
☎ 800-228-5151
www.hotelchoice.com

Radisson Hotels International
☎ 800-333-3333
www.radisson.com

Ramada Inns
☎ 800-272-6232
www.ramada.com

Red Carpet Inns
☎ 800-251-1962
www.reservahost.com

Red Lion Hotels & Inns
☎ 800-547-8010
www.redlion.com

Red Roof Inns
☎ 800-843-7663
www.redroof.com

Residence Inn by Marriott
☎ 800-331-3131
www.residenceinn.com

Rodeway Inns
☎ 800-228-2000
www.hotelchoice.com

Sleep Inn
☎ 800-753-3746
www.sleepinn.com

Super 8 Motels
☎ 800-800-8000
www.super8.com

Travelodge
☎ 800-255-3050
www.travelodge.com

Vagabond Inns
☎ 800-522-1555
www.vagabondinn.com

Wyndham Hotels and Resorts
☎ 800-822-4200
www.wyndham.com

Orlando Tourist Offices Abroad

Country/Continent	*Telephone Number*	*Web Site*
Argentina	☎ 0800-888-6752	www.orlandoinfo.com/argentina
Asia	☎ 81-3-3501-7245	www.orlandoinfo.com
Belgium	☎ 32-2-705-7897	www.orlandoinfo.com
Brazil	☎ 0800556652	www.orlandoinfo.com/brasil
Germany	☎ 0800-100-7352	www.orlandoinfo.com/de
Japan	☎ 3-3501-7245	www.orlandoinfo.com
Latin America	☎ 407363-5872	www.orlandoinfo.com/latinoamerica
Mexico	☎ 01-800-800-4636	www.orlandoinfo.com/mexico
Spain	☎ 407-363-5872	www.orlandoinfo.com/espana
U.K.	☎ 0800-092-2352	www.orlandoinfo.com/uk

Finding More Information

If you want more detailed information on attractions, accommodations, or just about anything else that's in Orlando, you won't find getting it difficult.

Some excellent sources for tourist information, maps, and brochures include:

✔ The **Orlando/Orange County Convention and Visitors Bureau** can answer tourist questions and send you maps and brochures. You should receive a packet in about three weeks, and it will include the *Magicard,* which is good for up to $500 in discounts on accommodations, car rentals, attractions, and more. It's located at 8723 International Dr., Suite 101, Orlando, FL 32819. For information, call ☎ **407-363-5872** (voice — you can talk to a real person!), ☎**800-643-9492** or 800-551-0181 (automated). Or, head on the Internet to www.orlandoinfo.com.

✔ Get your info straight from the Mouse's mouth. Contact **Walt Disney World,** Box 10000, Lake Buena Vista, FL 32830-1000 (☎ **407-934-7639;** Internet: www.disneyworld.com), to order vacation brochures and information on all the theme parks, attractions, dining, accommodations, and more.

✔ For information on **Universal Studios Florida** (see Chapter 23), **Islands of Adventure** (see Chapter 24), and **CityWalk** (see Chapter 28), contact **Universal Orlando,** 1000 Universal Studios Plaza, Orlando, FL 32819 (☎ **800-837-2273;** Internet: www.universal orlando.com). The company will also send you vacation brochures, including information on restaurants and accommodations.

✔ **SeaWorld** offers vacation brochures with information about its main park, its restaurants, its hotel partners, and on Shamu's new kingdom, **Discovery Cove,** where you can swim with dolphins. Write to 7007 SeaWorld Dr., Orlando, FL 32801 or call ☎ **800-327-2424** or 407-351-3600. Online, surf over to www.seaworld. com. For information on **Discovery Cove,** call ☎ 877-434-7268 or head over to www.discoverycove.com.

✔ Get in touch with the **Kissimmee – St. Cloud Convention and Visitors Bureau,** 1925 E. Irlo Bronson Hwy./U.S. 192, Kissimmee, FL 34744 (☎ 800-327-9159; Internet: www.floridakiss.com), for a package of maps, brochures, coupon books, and a guide to local accommodations and attractions.

✔ The city's daily newspaper, the **Orlando Sentinel,** operates a Web site at www.orlandosentinel.com. It offers entertainment information ranging from restaurants and hotels to theme parks and the performing arts.

Fare Game: Choosing an Airline

Travel Agency:_____ Phone:_____

Agent's Name:_____ Quoted Fare:_____

Departure Schedule & Flight Information

Airline:_____ Airport:_____

Flight #:_____ Date:_____ Time:_____ a.m./p.m.

Arrives in:_____ Time:_____ a.m./p.m.

Connecting Flight (if any)

Amount of time between flights:_____ hours/mins

Airline:_____ Airport:_____

Flight #:_____ Date:_____ Time:_____ a.m./p.m.

Arrives in:_____ Time:_____ a.m./p.m.

Return Trip Schedule & Flight Information

Airline:_____ Airport:_____

Flight #:_____ Date:_____ Time:_____ a.m./p.m.

Arrives in:_____ Time:_____ a.m./p.m.

Connecting Flight (if any)

Amount of time between flights:_____ hours/mins

Airline:_____ Airport:_____

Flight #:_____ Date:_____ Time:_____ a.m./p.m.

Arrives in:_____ Time:_____ a.m./p.m.

Notes

Making Dollars and Sense of It

Expense	Amount
Airfare	
Car Rental	
Lodging	
Parking	
Breakfast	
Lunch	
Dinner	
Babysitting	
Attractions	
Transportation	
Souvenirs	
Tips	
Grand Total	

Notes

Sweet Dreams: Choosing Your Hotel

Enter the hotels where you'd prefer to stay based on location and price. Then use the worksheet below to plan your itinerary.

Hotel	Location	Price per night

Places to Go, People to See, Things to Do

Enter the attractions you would most like to see. Then use the worksheet below to plan your itinerary.

Attractions	Amount of time you expect to spend there	Best day and time to go

Going "My" Way

Itinerary #1

- ☐ _____
- ☐ _____
- ☐ _____
- ☐ _____

Itinerary #2

- ☐ _____
- ☐ _____
- ☐ _____
- ☐ _____

Itinerary #3

- ☐ _____
- ☐ _____
- ☐ _____
- ☐ _____

Itinerary #4

- ☐ _____
- ☐ _____
- ☐ _____
- ☐ _____

Itinerary #5

- ☐ _____
- ☐ _____
- ☐ _____
- ☐ _____

Itinerary #6

- ☐ _____
- ☐ _____
- ☐ _____
- ☐ _____

Itinerary #7

- ☐ _____
- ☐ _____
- ☐ _____
- ☐ _____

Itinerary #8

- ☐ _____
- ☐ _____
- ☐ _____
- ☐ _____

Itinerary #9

- ☐ _____
- ☐ _____
- ☐ _____
- ☐ _____

Itinerary #10

- ☐ _____
- ☐ _____
- ☐ _____
- ☐ _____

Menus & Venues

Enter the restaurants where you'd most like to dine. Then use the worksheet below to plan your itinerary.

Name	Address/Phone	Cuisine/Price

Notes

Index

● *F* ●

• *Accommodations Index* •

• *Restaurant Index* •

Discover Dummies Online!

The Dummies Web Site is your fun and friendly online resource for the latest information about *For Dummies* books and your favorite topics. The Web site is the place to communicate with us, exchange ideas with other *For Dummies* readers, chat with authors, and have fun!

Ten Fun and Useful Things You Can Do at www.dummies.com

1. Win free *For Dummies* books and more!
2. Register your book and be entered in a prize drawing.
3. Meet your favorite authors through the Hungry Minds Author Chat Series.
4. Exchange helpful information with other *For Dummies* readers.
5. Discover other great *For Dummies* books you must have!
6. Purchase Dummieswear exclusively from our Web site.
7. Buy *For Dummies* books online.
8. Talk to us. Make comments, ask questions, get answers!
9. Download free software.
10. Find additional useful resources from authors.

Link directly to these ten fun and useful things at **www.dummies.com/10useful**

For other titles from Hungry Minds, go to **www.hungryminds.com**

Not on the Web yet? It's easy to get started with *Dummies 101: The Internet For Windows 98* or *The Internet For Dummies* at local retailers everywhere.

Hungry Minds™

Find other *For Dummies* books on these topics:
Business • Career • Databases • Food & Beverage • Games • Gardening
Graphics • Hardware • Health & Fitness • Internet and the World Wide Web
Networking • Office Suites • Operating Systems • Personal Finance • Pets
Programming • Recreation • Sports • Spreadsheets • Teacher Resources
Test Prep • Word Processing

FOR DUMMIES
BOOK REGISTRATION

Register This Book and Win!

We want to hear from you!

Visit **dummies.com** to register this book and tell us how you liked it!

- ✔ Get entered in our monthly prize giveaway.

- ✔ Give us feedback about this book — tell us what you like best, what you like least, or maybe what you'd like to ask the author and us to change!

- ✔ Let us know any other *For Dummies* topics that interest you.

Your feedback helps us determine what books to publish, tells us what coverage to add as we revise our books, and lets us know whether we're meeting your needs as a *For Dummies* reader. You're our most valuable resource, and what you have to say is important to us!

Not on the Web yet? It's easy to get started with *Dummies 101: The Internet For Windows 98* or *The Internet For Dummies* at local retailers everywhere.

Or let us know what you think by sending us a letter at the following address:

For Dummies Book Registration
Dummies Press
10475 Crosspoint Blvd.
Indianapolis, IN 46256

BESTSELLING
BOOK SERIES